Unveiling the Whale

Studies in Environmental Anthropology and Ethnobiology

General Editor: **Roy Ellen**, FBA
Professor of Anthropology, University of Kent at Canterbury

Interest in environmental anthropology has grown steadily in recent years, reflecting national and international concern about the environment and developing research priorities. This major new international series, which continues a series first published by Harwood and Routledge, is a vehicle for publishing up-to-date monographs and edited works on particular issues, themes, places or peoples which focus on the interrelationship between society, culture and environment. Relevant areas include human ecology, the perception and representation of the environment, ethno-ecological knowledge, the human dimension of biodiversity conservation and the ethnography of environmental problems. While the underlying ethos of the series will be anthropological, the approach is interdisciplinary.

Unveiling the Whale

Discourses on Whales and Whaling

Arne Kalland

Berghahn Books
New York • Oxford

First edition published in 2009 by

Berghahn Books
www.berghahnbooks.com

©2009 Arne Kalland

Library of Congress Cataloging-in-Publication Data
Unveiling the whale : discourses on whales and whaling / edited by Arne Kalland.
    p. cm.—(Studies in environmental anthropology and ethnobiology)
Includes bibliographical references and index.
ISBN 978-1-84545-581-1 (alk. paper)
    1. Whales—Public opinion.   2. Whaling—Public opion.   3. Whaling—
Environmental aspects.   4. Communication and culture.   5. Communication
in nature conservation.   6. Maritime anthropology.   I. Kalland, Arne.
QL737.C4U58 2009
333.95'95—dc22   2009012811

British Library Cataloguing in Publication Data
A catalogue record for this book is available from the British Library

Printed in the United States on acid-free paper

ISBN: 978-1-84545-581-1   hardback

Contents

List of Tables and Figures

Tables

Figures

Preface

My interest in whaling dates from the early 1980s, when I did research on the history of fishing villages in Northern Kyushu, Japan. I quickly realized from historical documents that commercial whaling was an important activity from the seventeenth century onwards. After publishing a paper on premodern Japanese whaling (Kalland 1986) I was invited to an international workshop in 1988 to study the role of whaling culture in Japanese coastal communities today (Akimichi et al. 1988). The background for the study was the moratorium on 'commercial whaling' that was imposed by the International Whaling Commission (IWC) in 1982. We were twelve scholars—mostly anthropologists—from six different countries (Japan, Canada, the U.K., the U.S., Australia and Norway) attending the workshop. Most of us had several years of research experience in Japan, and in the following years these and other scholars wrote more than thirty papers on aspects of small-type coastal whaling in Japan. In 1991 I led a similar study on the culture of minke whaling in Norway (ISG 1992).

My research interest soon turned from the topic of whaling culture to the whaling issue. I began to ask myself a number of questions, which to a large extent echoed questions asked by whalers. These were both 'why' and 'how' questions. Among the former was why Japanese and Norwegian whalers were not allowed to exploit comparatively healthy stocks of minke whales when the Alaskan Inuit were allowed to hunt what was then believed to be a highly endangered stock of bowhead whales. Another puzzle to me—having eaten whale meat since childhood—was why it was considered morally more suspect to eat whale meat than to eat pork and beef. I could understand why vegetarians were against whaling, but many supporters of the anti-whaling campaign, I soon discovered, ate their steaks with great appetite. What, then, is the crucial difference between a whale and a cow? In short, why have whales become important environmental icons in much of the Western world? If ecology could not provide a fully satisfactory answer to the important 'why' questions, how was it possible to turn the IWC from the position of promoting whaling to that of preservation in the span of a decade?

To me, the position of the whalers was self-evident and hardly needed any explanation. But foreigners have repeatedly asked me why a few whalers do not find something else to do in affluent countries troubled by labour shortages. It is even more difficult for them to understand why the governments in Japan and Norway stubbornly support an economically insignificant industry despite all the international condemnation they receive.

At least two parties are needed to pitch a fight, and we have to look at both sides of the divide to understand how the situation has become polarized and deadlocked. I do not pretend to be 'objective' and neutral, although I hope I do not romanticize any of the positions. Whether we like it or not, as researchers we are coloured by our own values, and I do not see whales as persons but as a natural resource that can be exploited, like fish and deer, if this can be done sustainably. My main sympathy lies with the whalers. But there are other reasons to look more critically at the anti-whaling discourse. Today this discourse is hegemonic in much of the Western world. This means that it is taken for granted by a large segment of the population that whales are endangered and have unique qualities that make them deserving of special treatment. To me one of the main tasks of anthropology is to ask critical questions about what is regarded as common sense or politically correct.

This book is the result of a multi-sited study. Since 1988 I have visited most of the whaling communities in Japan and Norway, attended meetings of the IWC (both as delegate and as observer) and other whaling-related organizations, discussed the issues with activists and delegates on both sides and scrutinized what they have said and written. During these twenty years I have received assistance and encouragement from many people and institutions. My gratitude goes first and foremost to Japanese and Norwegian whalers who opened their homes to me and took me into their confidence. Scholars from a number of disciplines have also shared their insight with me over the years. They are too many to name, and here I will mention only four fellow anthropologists to whom I am particularly indebted: Prof. Milton M.R. Freeman (University of Alberta, Edmonton) who invited me to the workshop in 1988 and has encouraged me ever since, Prof. Brian Moeran (at that time at the School of Oriental and Asian Studies, London), Ass. Prof. Frank Sejersen (at the Institute of Eskimology, Copenhagen University) and Prof. Harald Beyer Broch (from my own department in Oslo). The latter three and I have co-authored works from which I have taken some of the paragraphs used in chapters 5 and 6 of this book. Many other colleagues have made important comments on drafts, conference papers and articles published during these years. I am especially grateful to two reviewers whose thoughtful comments and suggestions were highly appropriate and appreciated. It is not their fault that I have not been able to follow all their suggestions fully. Among institutions that have assisted me in this study I will foremost express my gratitude to the staff at the IWC, the Institute of Cetacean Research, the North Atlantic Marine Mammal Commission and the High North Alliance.

It has been a great pleasure to work with Berghahn Books and I have received valuable guidance and encouragement during the final preparation of the manuscript from Marion Berghahn, Ann Przyzycki and not least from my copy editor Jaime Taber. Finally, I will thank copyright holders for their permission to use their illustrations here.

Arne Kalland
Nesøya, January 2009

Abbreviations

ACS	American Cetacean Society
ASCOBANS	Agreement on the Conservation of Small Cetaceans of the Baltic and the North Seas
AEWC	Alaska Eskimo Whaling Commission
ASW	aboriginal subsistence whaling
AWI	Animal Welfare Institute
BWU	blue whale unit
CHH	common heritage of humankind
CERF	Coastal Ecosystems Research Foundation
CITES	Convention on International Trade in Endangered Species
CSI	Cetacean Society International
EAAM	European Association for Aquatic Mammals
ECCO	Eastern Caribbean Cetacean Commission
ECS	European Cetacean Society
EIA	Environmental Investigation Agency
EII	Earth Island Institute
FoE	Friends of the Earth
GATT	General Agreement on Tariffs and Trade
HNA	High North Alliance
HSUS	Humane Society of the United States
ICC	Inuit Circumpolar Conference
ICESCR	International Covenant on Economic, Social and Cultural Rights
ICR	Institute of Cetacean Research (Tokyo)
ICRW	International Convention for the Regulation of Whaling
IFAW	International Fund for Animal Welfare
IRCS	Inuit Regional Conservation Strategy
ISI	Indigenous Survival International
IUCN	World Conservation Union
IWC	International Whaling Commission

JCCMNB	Joint Commission on Conservation and Management of Narwhal and Beluga
LTCW	large-type coastal whaling
MMPA	Marine Mammal Protection Act
MSY	maximum sustainable yield
NAFTA	North American Free Trade Agreement
NAMMCO	North Atlantic Marine Mammal Commission
NGO	nongovernmental organization
NMP	New Management Procedure
NOAA	[U.S.] National Oceanic and Atmospheric Administration
POD	People-Ocean-Dolphin
RMP	Revised Management Procedure
RMS	Revised Management Scheme
RSPCA	Royal Society for the Prevention of Cruelty to Animals
SMM	Society for Marine Mammalogy
SPCA	Society for the Prevention of Cruelty to Animals
SWTD	swim-with-the-dolphins
STCW	small-type coastal whaling
TAC	total allowable catch
TTD	time to death
UNCED	United Nations Conference on Environment and Development
UNCLOS	United Nations Convention on the Law of the Sea
UNEP	United Nations Environmental Programme
WCED	World Commission on Environment and Development
WCW	World Council of Whalers
WDCS	Whale and Dolphin Conservation Society
WWF	Worldwide Fund for Nature (aka World Wildlife Fund)

Introduction

Environmentalism is rooted in perceived ecological problems caused by human activities. Many people are genuinely concerned that nature, which is basically seen as inherently good and in harmony with itself, is being threatened by two human-induced processes: contamination of habitats and depletion of natural resources. Modernity is seen as the cause of both processes. Industries and modern agriculture discharge dangerous chemicals into the soil, air and sea; factories and motored traffic emit gases that cause global warming, depletion of the ozone layer and acid rain; and mass consumption creates enormous waste problems. At the same time natural resources are depleted: land is stripped of its forests; plants and animals are brought close to extinction. We are told that the problems are escalating and that we have no time to waste if we are to secure sustainable living also for coming generations. Many of the environmental problems are seen as transnational in scope, and species and habitats in far away places are increasingly perceived as common heritage of humankind. Global solutions are called for.

Whaling is among the environmental issues that have attracted most international attention since the early 1970s. When the International Whaling Commission (IWC) in 1982 voted for a moratorium on all whaling for commercial purposes, the justification was ecological. It was obvious to most observers that industrial whaling had severely depleted many whale stocks, some of which had been brought close to extinction. The majority of the IWC's member nations argued therefore that whaling had to cease until better whale stock estimates were available and a new 'revised management procedure' (RMP) had been designed to safeguard exploitation in the future. The RMP was unanimously adapted by the IWC's scientific committee in 1992, and our knowledge on whale stocks has improved markedly. Several observers—even among those opposed to whaling—now believe that some stocks might sustain controlled hunting. The world's minke whale population is probably even larger today than in the past.[1] Nonetheless, the moratorium has been retained and the IWC has failed to undertake a comprehensive assessment of the effects as called for in the 1982 decision.[2] Moreover, most of the large international environmental organizations have continued their campaigns against minke whaling unabated. Whaling therefore continues to be a highly controversial issue on the global arena and sours national relations particularly between Japan and countries like Australia, New Zealand and the United States.

The whaling issue has become highly polarized, but in contrast to many other environmental issues, the polarization does not run between environmental nongovernmental organizations (NGOs) on one side and government agencies on the other. On the contrary, we find that NGOs and authorities work closely together on both sides of the divide. At the annual IWC meetings, for example, representatives from international NGOs may not only participate as official delegates from anti-whaling nations; they may even have prepared some of the official papers. On the other side, the major Norwegian environmental NGOs, including the largest (Naturvernforbundet) which is affiliated with the international Friends of the Earth (FoE), as well as the Norwegian chapter of the Worldwide Fund for Nature (WWF), regard the current level of minke whaling in the Northeast Atlantic as sustainable and therefore unproblematic. Some activists—including Nature and Youth, allegedly the only environmental youth organization in Norway—openly support Norwegian whaling (Aasjord 1991, 1993; Sørensen 1993). Unless one is prepared to dismiss the integrity of Norwegian environmental NGOs, their position should be taken as an indication that there is more to the anti-whaling movement than ecology and sustainability.

The whaling controversy cannot be understood without considering the larger context within which the whaling issue is situated. In this book I will argue that what has turned whaling into one of the most controversial environmental issues today is not that all whales are at the brink of extinction—which they are not—but that whales in much contemporary Western thought stand in a metonymic relationship to nature (i.e. whales represent nature at large) and, at the same time, in a metaphoric relationship to society (i.e. whales symbolize human relations). Metonymically whaling has come to represent people's domination and destruction of nature—'saving whales is for millions of people the crucial test of their political ability to halt environmental destruction', writes one of the leading figures within the anti-whaling movement (Holt 1985: 192). As metaphors whales have come to epitomize values and qualities that we like to see in our own species but that many of us feel we have lost. Both the destruction of nature and the loss of human values are widely attributed to the process of modernization, and campaigns against whaling can therefore be interpreted in terms of cultural critique.

This book, then, is not about whales and whaling per se but about their representations. My point is not to dis(prove) the intelligence and feats of whales and whalers, but to analyse how people construct knowledge—or communicate, in the widest sense of the term—about whales and whaling. A discursive analysis will be offered not only to understand the flow of messages traded between pro- and anti-whaling camps, but to locate the messages socially and historically. A statement is formulated both on the background of earlier statements and with an addressee in mind, with the intent to make an impact on future events (Ricoeur 1981; Bakhtin 1986). One purpose of the book is to explore how two opposing discourses on whales and whaling—a hegemonic anti-whaling discourse versus an alternative pro-whaling discourse—have evolved over time through a process of schismogenesis (Bateson 1958). One important reason for this polarization is a shift in the anti-whaling representation of whales from 'the whale as natural resource' to 'the whale as person'; i.e. ethical and moral arguments have greatly replaced ecological ones. Although the two positions are not entirely incompatible, the dialogue between the two sides has broken down.[3]

A discursive analysis will furthermore help us to take the wider approach of political ecology—here defined as the study of political struggles for control over natural resources—to locate the various positions and actors in the conflict. This may help us to understand why saving whales has been important for 'millions of people' and has become a 'crucial test', and why U.S. laws offer marine mammals better protection than that accorded to other species (Manning 1989: 220). It will also show that the whaling issue provides an arena where NGOs and authorities can unite on each side, thereby swapping political legitimacy and building personal relations that can be useful in areas where relations are less harmonious. The large whales are unique in that they are the only species under the management of a global body, the IWC, which is open to all independent nations in the world. Whales, more than any other species, can therefore be viewed as a common heritage of humankind.

Political ecology will also help us understand why the anti-whaling movement has not achieved its goal despite thirty years of intensive campaigning. If anything, whaling is on a slow increase after a nadir around 1990. An important question is why the tide seems to be changing. Why do some whaling nations (i.e. Iceland, Japan and Norway) put so much effort into protecting this marginal business employing a few hundred people in each country, despite all the international condemnation and negative public relation they receive? And why have some indigenous peoples (the Inuit in Canada and the Makah in Washington State) resumed hunting of large whales? And why did the Maori, who have no intention of hunting whales, become a member of the World Council of Whalers (WCW) and invite its third general assembly to New Zealand? Perhaps whaling has become an important rallying point to people who feel their lifestyles are challenged by outsiders? In order to answer such questions we have to consider both the whalers' points of view and how whaling has emerged as an important symbol of rational resource management to peoples and nations that still rely to a considerable degree on the extraction of renewable natural resources.

Discourses on the Environment
and Human-Animal Relations

The concept 'discourse' will here be used to denote s a set of statements that provides a way for communicating about a particular topic at a particular historical moment (Hall 1997: 44). It forms a systematically-organized set of statements (Fowler 1991: 42). Each statement—a claim, an argument, a story or a practice—comes in packages and is with a high grade of probability accompanied by other statements from the same package. Discourse is central to the production of knowledge and defines both *what* can meaningfully be said about a subject and *how* the subject can be meaningfully talked about. A discourse can therefore be considered an institutionalized way of thinking, one that helps people make sense of the world and provide guides for their conduct. In that sense it is closely resembles a cultural model.

It can be difficult to delimit discourses and set borders where one discourse ends and another begins. They are not static but are continuously changing. Unlike cultures, discourses are not associated with bounded social entities (Milton 1993: 9). Lacking fixed borders, discourses can best be perceived as fields of gravitation where some of the statements in the package are more central than others. Discourses may also be embedded in each other and can therefore work at several levels. Very often, statements in one discourse will be appropriated from other discourses. In the case of whaling we will see that competing anti- and pro-whaling discourses try to appropriate the same statements from external discourses.

In this book I will argue that whales and whaling can be talked about in different ways, and at times one may wonder whether people are talking about the same animals and the same activities. In a sense they are not. They are talking about different cultural representations of reality. We are exposed to conflicting representations of the world. What we at any moment in history believe to be true— i.e. what we think of as our knowledge, which is not necessarily consistent with objective reality—is a product of discourses. Where several discourses compete in their representations of the world, one discourse will often be in the position to define the agenda and formulate the major questions (and give the answers) that alternative discourses must relate to. In this case we can talk about a hegemonic or dominant discourse that defines the 'natural order of things'. The whaling debate is a typical case. Chapter 6 will explore how pro-whaling discourses are responses to, and have been framed by, the anti-whaling discourses analysed in Chapters 1–4. Power is therefore an indispensable aspect of discourse.

For a long time the two sides did not have the same access to power. Anti-whalers defined the agenda and the anti-whaling discourse produced an anti-whaling world, 'a global anti-whaling society spreading from the West, where being "against whaling" is the universalising norm, and whaling the marginalised exception' (Epstein 2005: 26). Many people today take it for granted (i.e. they know as true) that whales are intelligent but endangered and that whaling is cruel and unnecessary. The pro-whalers have in vain spent considerable time, money and energy to refute these claims. However, they have in recent years become more powerful as they have managed to appropriate their adversaries' rhetoric to their own benefit, and thus been able to define some of the premises themselves.

The arguments against whaling take many different forms, but are mainly taken from four external discourses on the environment and human-animal relations, which conveniently can be arranged in a [2, 2] matrix. One dimension is the use versus no-use axis; the other separates ecosystem approaches from a focus on individual animals. Each reflects major ideological differences (Table I.1).

Conservation

Conservation is commonly defined as 'the management of *human use* of organisms or ecosystems to ensure that it is sustainable' (IUCN, UNEP and WWF 1991: 210, emphasis added).[4] A crucial notion here is that what is usually termed 'resource management' says more about people than about natural resources, although science may give important premises for management decisions. Management defines restrictions and opportunities on human extraction of natural resources and implies having the power to exclude people from access to certain natural resources. Another important point to make is that conservation and sustainability should not be taken as synonyms. Sustainability may be taken to mean an extraction of natural resources at a level that does not lead to overharvesting of species or to habitat degradation; a situation that for various reasons can prevail regardless of people's knowledge or intentions. Conservation, on the other hand, implies a degree of design. To Smith and Wishnie (2000: 501) conservation must not only prevent or mitigate resource depletion, species extermination or habitat degradation, but must be designed to do so. Otherwise sustainability might be a mere side effect of external factors. A society can be sustainable without conserving or conserve without achieving sustainability. When people do not do more harm to their environments, it might be because of low population density, relative isolation with no external pressure, few market outlets, limited technologies or unattractive resources or habitats. Conservation, on the other hand, is designed to regulate people's relations with their physical environment to optimize

Table I.1 Discourses on the Environment and Human-Animal Relations

	Ecosystem Approach (environmentalism)	Individual Animals (animal welfare/rights)
use	conservation (anthropocentric)	animal welfare (anthropocentric)
no-use	preservation (anthropo- or ecocentric)	animal rights (zoocentric)

resource use while at the same time safeguarding species, habitats and biodiversity. This is the view expressed in reports like *Our Common Future* (WCED 1987), *Caring for the Earth* (IUCN et al. 1991), and *Agenda 21* (UNCED 1992). In this sense, most whalers today present themselves as conservationists.

There are, however, considerable disagreements as to what nature can tolerate in terms of exploitation. Thompson, Ellis and Wildavsky (1990) and Douglas (1996) have—although using slightly different terms—suggested four representations, or myths, of nature's resilience. The first suggests that nature is benign or robust. Natural resources are seen as practically inexhaustible and there to be taken, so what one individual catches does not seriously affect others. This view thus goes with an individualistic mode of behaviour. This representation has informed much marine resource management since the publication of Hugo Grotius' seminal *Mare Liberum* in 1609, although most bureaucrats and professional resource managers today tend to subscribe to a second view (variously termed perverse or tolerant) which also depicts nature as robust but only within certain limits. Restrictions are necessary and the individual is therefore placed under control, with management seen as a careful balance of privileges and obligations (Sejersen 1998: 223). The institutional arrangements tend to be hierarchical. The third view outlines nature as unpredictable or capricious. This is a somewhat fatalistic way to perceive nature and only luck—or luck combined with skill—can give success. Management might be meaningless from an ecological point of view, as natural fluctuations are beyond our influence and control. Finally, a fourth view marks nature as a fragile or ephemeral place that can easily be ruined by pollution and overexploitation. Hence great care must be taken and the precautionary principle is mandatory to avoid a total global collapse. This is the favoured myth among many of the environmentalists.

Preservation

When nature is seen as fragile, severe restrictions on resource use, if not total bans on all extraction, are called for. If such prohibitions are meant to be temporary arrangements—as was the original intention of the moratorium on commercial whaling—they fall under the heading of conservation. But when a prohibition for one reason or another is meant to be more or less permanent—as has become the case with the whaling moratorium—we can talk about preservation (sometimes the term 'protection' is used in the literature). IUCN et al. (1991: 211) defines preservation as 'keeping something in its present state'; ideally it means to keep nature in its pristine state. In other words, preservationists seek to close parts of nature from all 'consumptive' human exploitation. Parts of nature—an area or certain species—are set aside not necessarily to prevent depletion of resources but for aesthetic, moral, recreational, educational or scientific uses. When nature is preserved because of its value to human beings, such preservation can be labelled 'reformist' and 'anthropocentric'. In its most radical expression, however, preservationists are against any human engagement, including management, of what they perceive as wild animals or habitats (i.e. wilderness). These advocates claim that nature has intrinsic value in and of itself (Regan 1984; Nash 1989). They take an ecocentric approach.[5]

Thus, conservationists and preservationists are guided by very different ideologies in their approaches to management, and conflicts between them have escalated globally. The conflicts over human use of rainforests and charismatic megafauna such as African wildlife and marine mammals have been particularly bitter. Preservation implies that local resource users have been excluded from the natural resources they used to harvest. The preservation of the spotted owl and 'ancient forests' have turned thousands of loggers out of work along the northwest coast of North America (Satterfield 2003), people in Africa and elsewhere have been driven from their homes when their land was converted to national parks (West and Brechin 1991; Brockington 2002; Igoe 2003), protected elephants have ruined agricultural land in southern Africa (Bonner 1993) and activists effectively closed markets for pelts in their attempt to save seals in the Arctic (Herscovici 1985; Wenzel 1991; Lynge 1992). Local resource users who are excluded from their natural resources see preservation as a direct threat to their well-being imposed by external people with very different values from their own. People who are denied access to natural resources not only become less flexible in their adaptation to the environment, and thus more vulnerable to seasonal and annual fluctuations; they also suffer consequences for their feelings of belonging and identity (Chapter 5).

Animal Welfare

A number of NGOs work for the welfare of animals, although there is hardly any consensus as to what the term 'animal welfare' actually means. At a minimum, the position advocates an anti-cruelty attitude towards animals, i.e. animals should not suffer unnecessarily. The approach presumes that animals are sentient beings able to feel pain and that all animals that can feel pain have an equal interest in avoiding it. This is the essence of morality (Tester 1991: 3). There has been a long philosophical debate over whether animals can feel pain (e.g. Singer 1990), but it seems now to be widely accepted that at least higher vertebrates (including cetaceans) can do so, although this does not necessarily mean that pain evokes responses in animals in the same way that it does in humans.

But our own perceptions of pain are changing. Whereas pain by humans is *felt* physically or biologically, it is *experienced* and *perceived* culturally (Czordas 1994). Tolerance to pain seems to have declined in modern society, and painkillers have become important merchandise. Modern society has become a pain-denying society, where the absence of pain has become a mark of civilization. It seems that we also have become less tolerant to animal pain. When we cannot avoid inflicting pain on animals that we for some reason want to use, or whose habitat we want to exploit, we face a problem. To solve this dilemma, cruelty is often limited to mean unnecessary or unjustified pain (Regan 1992: 50). In other words, inflicting pain and killing animals may be morally acceptable, provided it is for a higher good and done as 'humanely' as the circumstances make possible. The concept of need is important here and much used in the rhetoric about whaling. One philosopher who has taken this utilitarian view is Peter Singer, who argues that 'nonhuman animals should not be killed or made to suffer significant pain except when there is no other way to satisfy important human needs, it follows that whaling should stop' (Singer 1978: 8). The problem with such a position is, of course, how to define 'important human needs'. People have diverse opinions as to what needs are: humans have basic needs such as food, shelter and clothing but also need social and cultural security and a 'meaningful' life. Subsequent chapters will explore why cultural needs of Inuit whalers legitimize whaling within the IWC regime, whereas the cultural needs of their Japanese and Norwegian colleagues do not.

A position within the animal welfare movement that brings it closer to the position of the conservationists goes beyond mere protection against animal suffering at the hands of humans. To minimize suffering is only one side of utilitarianism; to maximize pleasure is the other side. In either case, as pointed out by Tom Regan (1992: 54), the welfare advocates argue both that it is important to secure that *individual* animals have a good life and that the suffering and even death of some animals can be justified to improve animal (including human) welfare *in general*. Pleasure for some can compensate for the pain of others. People are morally obliged to pursue actions that cause more pleasure than pain.

One of the main critiques of the animal welfare position is its problematic association with key concepts like pain, cruelty and needs, which all are open to interpretation and manipulation. By extending inviolable *rights* to all animals there is, in theory at least, no room for negotiation.

Animal Rights

Peter Singer's *Animal Liberation*, first published in 1975, has had tremendous impact on the animal rights movement.[6] But to Singer animal suffering is acceptable if it is unavoidable in order to meet important human needs. Tom Regan, another prominent animal rights philosopher, finds this position faulty because neither anti-cruelty legislation nor animal welfare is sufficient in order to protect animals. Both are compatible with exploitation. Whereas hunting in theory may be compatible with animal welfare—whalers have sometimes called themselves animal welfare advocates because they kill the whales as swiftly and painlessly as possible—animal rights are incompatible with hunting. Nor can a utilitarian emphasis on aggregates provide a foundation for the claims of an individual over the group (Tester 1991: 5). Calling himself an abolitionist, not a reformist, Regan (1992: 55) defends the individual rights of animals because they have an intrinsic value in and of themselves. They have rights to live and to not feel pain. Stephen Clark, in *The Moral Status of Animals*, also argues against utilitarianism because it is 'notoriously ill-suited to a defence of *rights* which are precisely the individual's defence against factitious calculations of the greater good' (Clark 1977: 22). To him all creatures have a right to self-realization and a right to live according to their genetic potential without interference from human beings. A corollary to this view is therefore vegetarianism.

Not all animals are given rights, however. As pointed out by Tester (1991: 14), it has never been the intention of most animal rights advocates to extend rights to all animals. An exception, perhaps, is Earth First! founder Dave Foreman, who claims that 'all life forms, from virus to the great whales, have inherent and equal rights to existence' (Foreman 1980). Such an uncompromising view brings us into an impossible position, since all food production, including agriculture and foraging, implies the taking of animal lives in some form or other. And most of us try to recover from illnesses, which implies fighting bacteria and viruses. Several criteria have therefore been suggested to limit rights to certain animals. Most animal rights advocates would today argue, along with Jeremy Bentham, that animals should acquire rights if they are sentient beings able to suffer (Bentham 1960: 412, quoted in Tester 1991: 96). In practice, rights are mostly limited to an inner circle of mammals or animals most like us. Whale rights advocates take their rhetoric from the animal rights philosophers and explicitly limit its application to cetaceans (e.g. D'Amato and Chopra 1991).

Unity in Diversity

Several writers have noticed the seeming incompatibility between the system orientation of conservation and preservation and the focus on the wellbeing of individual animals taken by animal welfare and rights groups (Manes 1990; Eckerley 1992; Regan 1992; Ryder 1992; Milton 1996, 2002). Central to the former discourses is the concern for biodiversity and sustainable use of natural resources. What is at stake is the future of particular ecological systems, and those with a system orientation might at times be willing to sacrifice the interest of individual animals for a higher good. I will therefore call these environmental or ecological discourses. The animal welfare and animal rights advocates, on the other hand, are concerned with our treatment of individual animals. But whereas spokespersons for animal welfare are preoccupied with how animals are treated and slaughtered, the animal rights advocates are against any use of animals whatsoever (Regan 1984). Animals should not be sacrificed for a higher good. These will be called animal welfare/rights discourses.[7] Whereas natural sciences have important roles to play in the environmental discourses, moral and ethics inform the animal welfare and rights positions.

The difference between the environmental and animal welfare/rights positions is not least seen in the relationship between ecocentric preservationists and animal rights advocates. Whereas animal rights activists want to include 'all sentient beings as inside the moral community' (Midgley 1983: 89), deep ecologists, as argued by Arne Naess and not least Aldo Leopold, also include the land: 'The land ethics simply enlarges the boundaries of the community to include soils, waters, plants, and animals, or collectively the land' (Leopold 1949: 204). Deep ecology subjugates the individual to land ethics. Whereas the animal rights advocate is compassionate, the deep ecologist may be ready to sacrifice the individual for the sake of the ecosystem.[8] Regan therefore depicts deep ecology as a main adversary of animal rights (Regan 1992: 58–60). The difference is one of atomistic versus holistic approaches. The animal rights orientation is atomistic in that it treats each individual animal in isolation. As Eckersley observes, to animal rights advocates it would not matter whether one kills the last twenty members of a sentient endangered species or twenty individuals of another equally sentient species that might be abundant (Eckersley 1992: 47). To the ecosystem approach, however, this difference is crucial.

Despite their different ideologies and orientations there is not always a sharp line between environmental and animal welfare/rights groups in practical politics (Wenzel 1991: 36). Animal rights groups have become increasingly concerned with ecological systems in order to protect the habitats of animals, and environmental groups have taken many of their most important symbols from the animal world and thus engage themselves in the protection of non-endangered species (Dalton 1994: 46). This is, as we shall see, not least the case in the whaling debate, where anti-whaling activists have found a fertile field of collaboration despite working from different philosophical platforms.[9] The four discourses on the environment and human-animal relations presented here should therefore be taken as ideal types only.

Unpacking the arguments on both sides of the divide will disclose that to a considerable degree they are composed of statements taken from the four discourses introduced above. Both sides phrase much of their rhetoric in terms of biological diversity and sustainability. A priori one should therefore expect that such statements could create a common ground for understanding, but on the contrary, there exists a competition between anti- and pro-whalers about the ownership of these statements. A case in point is the term 'environmentalist' itself. It has become an important rhetorical device amongst whalers and anti-whaling advocates alike, and both groups try to appropriate the term for themselves and deny that the term may characterize their opponents. Both sides undercommunicate—and even deny—agreements that may exist between them. At the same time, internal disagreements within camps are largely ignored. What we can witness is an example of progressive differentiation that Gregory Bateson has called *symmetric schismogenesis* (1958: 175), a kind of vicious circle where two rivals or competitors engage in an escalating conflict much like in an arms race. Analysing conflicts about large predators in Norway, Ottar Brox (2000) has reformulated Bateson's model in a way that will be useful also for my purpose. Brox is interested in political polarization, but whereas Bateson looked at the competition *between* groups, Brox looks at *intragroup* rivalry. He suggests that when two groups with opposite or conflicting values are confronting each other, members within each group will try to 'outdo each other in the *expression of commitment to the common shared values*' in what he calls an 'expressive competition' (Brox 2000: 389, original emphasis). Much of the rhetoric about whales and whaling can be understood in this light. To distance themselves from the other camp, and to express their commitment to the protection of whales at least as strongly as their co-activists, many opponents to whaling have taken a position that is very close to that of animal rights, the only position that is totally incompatible with whaling. The whaling issue has thus provided environmental and animal welfare/rights groups a common ground that clearly sets them off from the whalers. A similar process among whalers has reduced whales to pests. Those who take the middle ground have become muted.

The following chapters will explore how these discourses have been employed by both sides in the whaling controversy. I will try to identify the main actors behind the discourses, analyse their representations of reality and isolate the central statements. The last part of this introductory chapter will present the historical context for the conflict. Chapter 1 outlines how whales have been represented in anti-whaling discourses to form an image of a 'superwhale', which brings together characteristics from a number of different species of whales. It serves as a strong icon for the anti-whaling movement and is a powerful metaphor for a utopian world humans have lost. Chapter 2 introduces some of the main anti-whaling organizations and how they have switched from environmental to animal welfare and rights discourses in their representation of whaling and whalers. It will be argued that their rhetoric—using war metaphors that divide humankind into good environmentalists and bad whalers—has done much to create a totemic polarization of the world. In Chapter 3 I will analyse how the anti-whaling campaigns have changed the whale products' commodity path, i.e. the route a commodity travels from production through consumption (Appadurai 1986). The markets for meat and oil products have to a large extent given way to a global market for symbolic representations.

Chapter 4 will explore the work of the International Whaling Commission (IWC), focusing on the issues being discussed at its annual meetings. Special attention will be directed to how this global forum is being polarized into a group of 'like-minded' countries opposed to whaling and a group of pro-whaling nations. The next two chapters move the focus from the anti-whalers and their campaigns to the whalers. Chapter 5 takes a closer look at the economic, social and cultural importance of whales and whaling in whaling communities, whereas Chapter 6 will concentrate on their responses to the global anti-whaling campaigns. The final chapter will, besides summarizing the argument, focus more narrowly on the polarization of the issue, the symbolic power of whales and whaling, and to what extent whales can be considered the 'common heritage of humankind'.

The Context

The anti-whaling campaigns can only be understood in terms of changing hu-man-animal relations, the development of the environmental movement and the development of the whaling industry itself. Each of these developments has been detailed elsewhere and will only be summarized here.

The Rise of the Green Movement

Environmental disasters are not a modern phenomenon but can be traced back to the early civilizations in the Middle East, Greece and China, if not even to pre-agrarian societies. However, the development of an environmental *movement* is much more recent and can be dated to the mid 1800s, when the impact of industrialization and urbanization on the physical environment had become ap-parent to many people. Industrial pollution, poor urban living conditions and destruction of wildlife gave reasons for concern and could no longer be ignored (Dalton 1994).

The early movement in England was unmistakably coloured by an Arcadian view of nature. Because there was little 'wild' nature left to preserve, much at-tention was given to the preservation of the aesthetic qualities of the English landscape with its rural villages and endless hedges and pastures, long idealized in paintings and poetry. Thus the National Trust was established in 1893 as a holding company for people who wanted to donate historical or natural sites to preservation. Other European countries embarked on similar programmes to preserve what were perceived as national heritages (Dalton 1994). But the envi-ronmental movement in Europe was not confined to the preservation of rural landscapes. The scientific revolution sparked considerable interest in natural his-tory among the upper and middle classes, and a number of works on natural his-tory were published from the eighteenth century onwards—at this time cetology (the study of cetaceans or whales) was established as a branch of biology (e.g. Hunter 1787; Lacépède 1804; Melchior 1834). Conservation of wildlife, first of all of birds, gained popularity towards the end of the nineteenth century. England was in the lead when the first campaign was formed in 1867 to protect seabirds slaughtered at Yorkshire. And in the 1870s and 1880s groups were formed to end the widespread use of plumage in women's fashions. On the continent farmers were concerned about the killing of migratory birds beneficial to agriculture, and a German petition eventually led to the Convention for the Protection of Birds Useful to Agriculture, signed in 1902. By then national associations for bird pro-tection had been formed in countries like Germany and the Netherlands.[10]

Birds were important in the formation of the early environmental movement in the United States as well, but the movement took a different path than in Eu-rope. Large stretches of land were perceived as wilderness by the white settlers—although not by the Native Indians—and this wilderness received the same attention that cultured landscape received in England. The idea to set aside some of the wilderness as national parks gained popularity. The focus on protecting nature within national parks soon sparked a controversy between preservationists and conservationists: between those who prioritized recreational and educational uses of nature and those who opted for sustainable use of the natural resources, particularly forests (Satterfield 2003).

This first wave of environmental groups and movements on both sides of the Atlantic were reformist in character, whether they had conservationist or preservationist goals. Nature should be protected for people to enjoy; many of the sanctuaries (particularly in the colonies) were meant to facilitate hunting. Much had been achieved by the early twentieth century. People had taken a keen interest in wildlife and landscapes, and powerful mass organizations were formed (McCormack 1989; Dalton 1994). Sanctuaries and national parks were established and wildlife protected. The highly successful Treaty for the Preservation and Protection of Fur Seals was signed by Great Britain (for Canada), Japan, Russia and the United States in 1911; the treaty 'represented a major victory for the concept of international cooperation' (Gay 1987: 128). The International Congress for the Protection of Nature, established in 1913, had plans to discuss whaling the following year, but the outbreak of World War I put an end to this (Stoett 1997: 22).

The war and the economic difficulties in the interwar years halted much environmental work, and few achievements were made. Nonetheless, it was during the 1930s that the first serious international efforts were made to regulate whaling.[11] The first convention to regulate whaling was signed in 1931, more out of concern over a saturated market for whale oil than out of an inclination to conserve of whale stocks, however. The International Agreement for the Regulation of Whaling was formed in 1937 and amended the next year.

World War II marked a watershed in international cooperation in many ways, including the field of resource management. Whaling was high on the agenda, and the International Convention for the Regulation of Whaling (ICRW) was signed in 1946; the International Whaling Commission became active three years later. Various environmental initiatives were taken by the United Nations, for example the establishment in 1948 of the IUCN (World Conservation Union),[12] which is an umbrella organization for a mixed bag of government agencies and NGOs.

By that time the environmental movement was at a threshold. The 1960s and 1970s saw a marked radicalization of the movement, giving birth to what has been termed New Environmentalism (Nicholson 1987) or Radical Ecology (Merchant 1992). Whereas environmentalism previously had been reformist, the many new NGOs that were now formed called for nothing less than a social revolution. The environmental problems facing the world—pollution, depletion of natural resources and the threat of nuclear holocaust—were seen as consequences of people's lifestyles: a reaction against global overpopulation and capitalist society with its excessive consumption and social injustices. A new awareness of a *global* environmental crisis emerged. People were told that urgent measures were required to avoid an imminent environmental apocalypse.

New Environmentalism comes in several, often mutually exclusive, wrappings, and at least three basic forms can be observed (e.g. Merchant 1992). Deep ecology, a term coined by the Norwegian philosopher Arne Naess (1972), claims that the traditional reform environmentalism is shallow in that it only tries to cure symptoms rather than to address the fundamental contradiction that exists in the human relationship with nature nowadays. Deep ecology, on the other hand, calls for a new environmental ethics, a bioethics based on the principle of 'biospheric egalitarianism' between all living organisms and a feeling of unity with planet Earth. It recognizes the intrinsic value of nature and thus takes a biocentric or ecocentric position rather that the anthropocentric position of the old movement. It represents a kind of primitivism (Lovejoy and Boas 1935), a return to a Golden Age when humans lived in harmony with nature and within the limits of the land's carrying capacity. Many, including Naess himself (1989: 29), have argued that a drastic reduction in the human population is needed. An extreme view is expressed by some Earth First!ers who have hailed AIDS and African famines as Gaia's own 'solution' to the population problem (Scarce 1990: 91–92; Lee 1995: 102–10). Much of deep ecology thinking is fundamentally misanthropic.

Being heavily inspired by Eastern philosophy and Native American thought (Snyder 1980; Devall and Sessions 1985; Anker 2007), deep ecology shares many features with spiritual ecology. But spiritual ecology takes this a step further by developing a highly ritualistic relationship with a nature infused with spiritual powers. In its eclectic approach to religion and rituals—seeking truth from ancient animism and paganism as well as from contemporary world religions—spiritual ecology constitutes an important undercurrent of the New Age movement. Through communication with nature, not least with cetaceans, and at times even with extraterrestrial beings, an ultimate unity with the planet Earth—epitomized by the Greek earth goddess Gaia—can be achieved.

The third main line of thought within New Environmentalism includes a variety of positions that try to bridge the gap between greens and reds: from anarchistic social ecology (Bookchin 1982) and ecologism (Dobson 1990) to neo-Marxian eco-socialism (Benton 1993; Pepper 1993). They attempt to integrate social justice with sustainable living, seeing both social and environmental problems as consequences of industrialization and the capitalist mode of production. They all want to bring the human back into green politics and warn against the anti-humanist sentiment in much ecocentric writings, not least among the deep ecology activists. According to Pepper, anti-humanism has blinded the green movement to the most important environmental issues of today: 'street violence, alienating labour, poor and overcrowded housing, inner-city decay and pollution, unemployment, loss of community and access to services, and dangerous roads', all seen as products of the capitalist mode of production (Pepper 1993: 148–49).

Perhaps for this reason—or more likely because they find the whaling issue trivial compared to social injustices befalling billions of people—they have been largely mute on the whaling issue.

Changing Human-Animal Relations

Animals have always been important to human societies, not so much because they are 'good to eat' but because they are 'good to think' (Levi-Strauss 1962: 89). Animals are good to think first of all because they—being both like us and different from us—constitute the 'other' that allows people to reflect over what it means to be human. Ted Benton (1993: 229) therefore concludes that 'all thinking about animals is covert thinking about humans'. Animals, then, are a means to define what it is to be human, and as human society changes, so do our relations and perceptions of animals.

A number of social scientists and historians of ideas have tried to trace how human-animal relations have changed in Western societies over the last few centuries (e.g. Menninger 1951; Elias 1978, 1982; Thomas 1983; Löfgren 1985; Ritvo 1987; Tester 1991; Franklin 1999). Several trajectories have been suggested, most of them focused on a greater physical separation of humans and beasts caused by modernization. Keith Thomas (1983) sees early cruelty towards animals as a means to mark the border between humans and animals and locates humans at the apex, just when close physical contiguity blurred this border. Later industrialization and urbanization made room for a more sentimental approach to animals, as there was no longer a need to mark the distinction between humans and animals by brutal force. At the same time, some selected species of animals were brought into the human realm as pets. As this was typically an urban phenomenon, a dichotomy was created between rural beasts, which were increasingly excluded from human contact, and urban pets, which were increasingly included.

People's treatment of animals became linked to class, and anti-cruelty legislation was an attempt to civilize the labour class (Franklin 1999: 22). Kindness to animals became a yardstick for being civilized and not animal-like (Elias 1978, 1982). Also Peter Singer (1990: 9) views our treatment of animals in terms of a civilizing process, a process begun with the emancipation of slaves and women and to be completed by the emancipation of animals. In this rhetoric a connection has been made between violence against animals and violence against humans (Ritvo 1987). In other words, one ought to be kind to animals not only because they have any moral relevance per se but because such kindness signals one's worth as a human being. 'Our duties towards animals . . . are indirect duties towards humanity' (Kant, quoted in Tester 1991: 65). Animals thus come to play an important role in the symbolic construction of human identity.

There can be little doubt that human-animal relations have changed dramatically. However, a historical analysis does not bring us far in answering why some animals—say, whales—receive more attention than others. If we want to

understand why the whaling issue became one of the most high-profile campaigns ever launched by the environmental movement, it is not sufficient to analyse the history of whaling—although this is an important factor. We also have to
consider the symbolic meaning of whales and whaling.

Some animals are apparently 'better to think with' than others, and many
social scientists have tried to answer the question why this is so. Bronislaw Malinowski (1954: 44) suggested that 'the road from wilderness to the savage's belly
and consequently to his mind is very short', implying that it is the animals with
the largest nutritious or economic value that also become the most powerful symbols. However, this is not only a simplistic view but empirically wrong. Analyzing
totem animals among the Tallensi in Africa, for example, Lévi-Strauss (1962:
72–75) found that they did not constitute a zoological, economic or magic class
of natural objects. Only a few were important resources. Raymond Firth (1930–
31) has even suggested that it is not the edible but the inedible elements that are
associated with the supernatural. We should not expect to find the reason for
selecting certain animals in utilitarian factors.

Malinowski wrote about 'savages'; the psychoanalyst Karl Menninger (1951)
about modern society. He argued that there is a growing tendency in modern
society to treat certain animals as totems because the modern human needs to
compensate for being alienated from nature or for her/his inability to satisfy social
and emotional, including sexual, cravings in company with fellow human beings.
No doubt, many people keep pets for such reasons, but such psychological reduc-
tionism has not much to offer in answering the question why some wild animals
(e.g. whales, seals, elephants, pandas) are more powerful symbols than others.

Another psychological perspective is offered by some ethologists who claim
that people are naturally attracted by certain features found in both our own species and others. According to Konrad Lorenz (1981), one of the leading ethologists of his time, positive responses are triggered by infantile features—e.g. large
and round heads, big eyes, short and thick limbs, general softness and clumsy
movements. These features trigger in the adult an innate urge to nurture and thus
secure the survival of a helpless infant. The anthropologist Elizabeth Lawrence
(1989) finds a strong tendency in North American culture, and we can probably
add in contemporary cultures generally, towards neoteny, i.e. retention of youth-
ful traits into adulthood. Infantile features are obvious in comic strip figures like
Mickey Mouse, Bambi and Snoopy, but Lawrence also points out the neoteny
in many of the popular breeds of dogs.[13] This perception can help explain the
popularity of seal pups and giant pandas, but its relevance for the popularity
of whales is less obvious, although 'smiling', playful dolphins might qualify, as
may the killer whale, which, with its round snout and black-and-white pattern,
resembles the giant panda. Perhaps more relevant is the social ecologist Stephen
Kellert's extensive research on U.S. attitudes to animals and wildlife. He found
that people are far more aware of emotional issues involving large and 'higher'
animals, but that the most important factors influencing their willingness to

protect endangered wildlife were aesthetics, phylogenetic closeness to humans and the reason for endangerment—direct causes, such as exploitation, were more important than indirect causes like habitat loss (Kellert 1988: 160). Although the preferential attitudes that are said to exist towards large and juvenile-looking animals in modern society may help turn cetaceans into powerful symbols, this alone cannot account for their popularity. There are undoubtedly other factors that work in the same direction.

A different line of thought is provided by structuralists like Claude Lévi-Strauss, Mary Douglas and Edmund Leach. These anthropologists see the world as a continuum that, by the use of language (taxonomies, i.e. systems of classification), is broken into separate categories. Douglas's main interest is in phenomena that do not easily fit into such categories, e.g. bats (mammals with wings like birds) and snakes (terrestrial animals without legs). Such 'nonfits' challenge our systems of classification, and as anomalies they become unclean and potentially dangerous. She argues that society only accepts the consumption of clean animals, which implies that meat from a dangerous or anomalous animal is either excluded through taboos or accepted only in rituals (Douglas 1966). She illustrates the first option through an analysis of biblical food taboos regarding sea creatures without scales and fins, terrestrial animals without four legs and birds that cannot fly: 'Any class of creatures which is not equipped for the right kind of locomotion in its element is contrary to holiness' (Douglas 1966: 55).

Lévi-Strauss too is occupied with systems of classification. But unlike Douglas he is first of all interested in discontinuities between humans and animals (rather than between animals). Animals create problems because they are both like us and different from us. Animals can also be included in our social universe, but their place is always ambiguous. Animals very different from us, such as birds, can be given human names, writes Lévi-Strauss (1966: 204), because 'they can be permitted to resemble men for the very reason that they are so different'. For the same reason birds are allowed to 'form a community which is independent of our own but, precisely because of this independence, appears like another society'. Through such anthropomorphism animal society is modelled *on* human society, but frequently being idealized it in turn becomes a model *for* our society. Hence birds (and whales, as we will see in subsequent chapters) acquire a didactic mission in a social critique. Animals are therefore not only good to think with, they are also good to teach and learn with (Tapper 1988: 51).

It is the simultaneous 'Demand for Difference' and 'Demand for Similitude' (Tester 1991) or the 'opposed but complementary principles of separation and continuity' (Willis 1990: 7) that make some animals more likely candidates for totemic attention than others. Totemism is taxonomy where nature is used to classify people. And it is not primarily a relationship between man and his totem, as often has been claimed, but a similarity in differences. In the words of Lévi-Strauss (1966: 115), '[t]he homology [that the totemic institutions] evoke is not between social groups and natural objects but between the differences which

manifest themselves on the level of groups on the one hand and that of species on the other', where 'the resemblances and differences of animal species are
translated into terms of friendship and conflict, solidarity and opposition' (Lévi-
Strauss 1962: 87). In other words, perceived natural differences are translated
into cultural ones. Not only have whales figured as totems in some preindustrial
societies, but totemism, as I will argue in Chapter 2, is an important part of the
anti-whaling rhetoric.

Edmund Leach (1964) tries to go beyond simple binary oppositions when
he constructs a homology between human and animal worlds. He argues that
the way the British categorize their social universe is reflected in the way they
categorize animals. People are classified as close kin (with a strong incest taboo),
not very close kin (intercourse accepted but not marriage), neighbours (friends,
potential affines) and distant strangers (no relations). Animals are put in the following categories: pets (close, inedible), farm animals (tame but not so close;
edible if immature or castrated), field animals (game, edible if in sexually intact
form) and remote wild animals (inedible); vermin (inedible) makes a fifth category cutting across the others. From this Leach stresses the association between
sexual intercourse and eating. The English, he claims, do not have sex with sib-
lings and strangers, nor do they eat pets and wildlife. He further suggests that
animals closest to self are the most tabooed and insulting, because these animals
are particularly ambiguous and therefore need to be separated from us.

Leach's thesis has been soundly demolished by John Halverson (1967), for
both theoretical and empirical reasons. Nonetheless, it may have some heuristic
value, helping us understand how animals can be reclassified for historical reasons. Whales are a case in point. Whaling is no longer an economically viable industry in former whaling nations like Australia, New Zealand, the Netherlands,
the UK and the U.S., and whales have ceased to be considered a natural resource.
Reclassification is therefore possible. To refrain from catching whales can now
be seen as a civilization process, and in much of the Western world whales are
increasingly seen as metaphorical pets (see Chapter 3). However, to Icelandic and
Norwegian whalers who have been denied access to what to them are still an important natural resource, whales have rhetorically turned into a competitor and
pest (rats or cockroaches of the seas; see Chapter 6).

Reclassification of animals opens up new metaphors, or as the mentalists may
prefer to claim, new metaphors bring about a reclassification. 'Through metaphors
we understand the abstract [or unknown] in terms of the concrete [or known]'
(Lakoff and Johnson 1980: 112), and nature in its material form provides human beings with a rich reservoir of possible metaphors and symbols. People are
keen observers of natural phenomena and use these observations creatively to say
something about human behaviour by giving attention to resemblances between
the social and natural worlds. But it is important to note, as Douglas (1990) so
clearly has stressed, that these resemblances or similarities are culturally constructed: we select certain features and ignore others. Successful new metaphors create

previously unrecognized resemblances, creating new knowledge that might later become shared. As will be argued in Chapter 1, whales in many Western cultures fall taxonomically between mammals and fish, which according to Douglas predisposes us towards these animals. As long as whales were an economic resource, however, this predisposition was overridden by pragmatism. During the heyday of modernity, whales were simply seen as mountains of meat or huge oil containers. When whaling ceased to be of economic importance, the focus placed upon whales could become solely cognitive. New and widely shared metaphors, which to a large extent have anthropomorphized whales in Western societies, have been created. Human society is used metaphorically to understand whales. They have become 'the humans of the ocean', our marine cousins or brethren.

But this is only half the story. Perhaps more important for turning whales into a powerful *environmental* symbol, is the tendency to let whales stand metonymically for nature and whaling for human destruction of natural resources. Whales are therefore not only used metaphorically to tell us what it means to be human, but used metonymically to tell us what human beings are doing to nature. In combination these two processes have, as I hope will be clear from Chapters 1 and 2, produced an image of a misanthropic human whose nature it is to destroy her/his natural environment. But first, some words must be said about what the issue allegedly is all about: whaling.

Whaling, Past and Present

It is beyond the scope of this book on global discourses on whales and whaling to offer a detailed account of contemporary whaling activities or a comprehensive history of whaling. But because history is invoked by all parties in the whaling debate, it is necessary to outline briefly some of the main features of whaling in the past if we are to understand how this debate is constituted. It will also be necessary to outline whaling operations found in the world today in order to help readers to appreciate some of the differences that exist between past and present whaling operations, as well as between contemporary whaling regimes. Important questions to ask are what 'whale' and 'whaling' actually mean. Perhaps surprisingly for some readers, these are in fact two of the most hotly debated issues.

The term 'whaling' easily calls forth memories of when large whales were caught by a fleet of modern catcher boats and rendered into oil on huge factory ships. The environmental and animal welfare advocates have played on this image. The typical Greenpeace image shows small inflatable boats fronting large catcher boats or blocking the slipway to the deck of a factory ship.[14] And indeed, the history of industrial whaling has its ugly features. But this picture is largely of bygone days.

Whaling has been conducted in many parts of the world for more than a millennium, but industrial whaling probably first emerged among the Basques along the Bay of Biscay about one thousand years ago. In Japan whales have been hunted for commercial purposes at least since the late sixteenth century, but this expanded greatly after the net-hunting method was invented in the 1670s. The Dutch, British, Germans and French began industrial whaling in the early seventeenth century, and the Yankees towards the end of that century. The technologies used were simple and the hunt dangerous. Large whales were attacked from small oared boats carrying whalers who threw harpoons or spears into the whales. Despite their rudimentary methods, these early whalers were able to bring some whale populations close to extinction, forcing the whalers to find new catching grounds. As of the 1530s Basque whalers crossed to Labrador after the stock of right whales had declined in the Bay of Biscay. Fleets of Basque, Dutch, British, German and French whalers quickly exhausted the bowhead stocks around Svalbard (Spitsbergen), whereupon whalers moved to Davis Strait in the early eighteenth century to repeat the work there. The Atlantic bowhead whale was close to extinction by the time North American whalers had worked the Hudson Bay catching ground. Industrial whalers also decimated the stocks of gray whale along the Pacific coast and reduced the stocks of bowheads in the North Pacific. Only the old industrial whaling in Japan seems to have been sustainable, probably because the net-whaling method was conducted close to shore, where catches were relatively modest.

In the 1860s whaling underwent a technological revolution when the Norwegian Svend Foyn invented modern whaling. With a harpoon gun mounted at the bow of a steam ship, it became possible to hunt the fast-swimming rorquals (blue, fin, sei and Bryde's whales) efficiently. Foyn's first catching ground was Finnmark County in Northern Norway. By 1885 there were thirty-five catcher boats operating from nineteen shore stations in Finnmark, and by 1910 Norwegian entrepreneurs had expanded their operations throughout most of the world. Everywhere the result was depletion of stocks. The right and bowhead whales were protected in 1937 under the 1931 Convention for the Regulation of Whaling, the Pacific gray whales were protected in 1946,[15] and the humpback and blue whales were protected by the IWC in 1963 and 1965,[16] respectively. By the early 1970s only Japan and the Soviet Union continued whaling in the Antarctic; other whaling nations had ceased operations because low quotas could not justify the expenses.[17]

The history of industrial whaling strongly informs the images people have of whaling even today. But most contemporary whaling has little in common with industrial whaling of the past. The management regime developed by the IWC is much more robust, and control is strict. With few exceptions whaling is small-scale, conducted by owner-operated boats carrying crews of a handful people living in small rural communities, and the whales are processed into meat and largely consumed domestically.

The IWC today operates with several categories of whaling. A crucial distinction is the one between 'aboriginal subsistence whaling' (ASW) and 'whaling for commercial purposes'. The moratorium is imposed only on the latter.

Whereas ASW is defined by the IWC as 'whaling for purposes of local aboriginal consumption carried out by or on behalf of aboriginal, indigenous or native peoples who share strong community, familial, social and cultural ties related to a continuing traditional dependence on whaling and the use of whales' (Donovan 1982: 83), commercial whaling is nowhere defined. The management regimes for these two categories of whaling are very different. In commercial whaling quotas are decided according to stock abundance estimates, but in ASW they are largely calculated on the basis of people's perceived needs.

Aboriginal Subsistence Whaling (ASW)

This category was defined by the IWC in 1981 in order to allow the Alaskan Inuit (Eskimos) to continue hunting of bowhead whales at a time when stocks were estimated to be less than 2,000 animals, making bowhead one of the most endangered of all whale species at the time. Fortunately, the scientists were wrong and the estimate has since been increased to between 8,200 and 13,500.[18] The Alaskan Inuit have been given a quota of 280 landed bowhead whales for the 5-year period from 2008 to 2012, with no more than sixty-seven whales struck in any year, and this quota included bowheads caught by the native peoples of Chukotka. An addition fifteen unused strikes can be carried over from previous years (Schedule 13[b]1 to the ICRW). Small skiffs are used in the hunt, and the main weapon is the hand-held darting gun. Floats attached to harpoon lines slow the whale down and prevent it from sinking. Recently radio transmitters have been attached to the floats, so that a harpooned whale can more easily be traced and retrieved. Occasionally whalers have received assistance from aircrafts or vessels engaged in the petroleum industry (Stoker and Krupnik 1993).

The Chukotka whalers have been given a quota of 620 gray whales for the same 5-year period, with a maximum of 140 animals (of an estimated population of 21,900–32,400) killed in any one year (Schedule 13[b]2). Until the beginning of the 1990s these whales where caught by large Russian catcher boats crewed by ethnic Russians on behalf of the indigenous population, but now they are taken with much simpler technologies by the people themselves. In return for receiving a few of the bowhead whales of the Alaskan quota, the Chukotkans have handed over a few of the gray whale quota to the Makah tribe in the state of Washington. After several years of preparation—and amidst much noise from anti-whaling activists—in 1999 the Makah killed their first gray whale in more than seventy years, using a 36-foot Chinook canoe with a crew of eight people. A .50 calibre rifle was used to put the whale to death. A second whale was shot in September 2007.

Inuit whaling in Greenland is also defined as ASW, and for the 2008–2012 period the IWC has set West Greenland's annual quotas of struck animals at nineteen fin whales from a population of 3,200 (between 1,400 and 7,200 with a 95 per cent confidence interval), 200 minke whales from a population of 10,800 (range 3,600–32,400) and, for the first time, two bowhead whales from a population of 1,230 (range 490–2,940). East Greenland has been given an annual quota of twelve minke whales from a population of more than 60,000 animals. Unused parts of the quotas can be carried forwards according to specified rules (Schedule 13[b]3). Some of the minke whales are chased by a number of skiffs and shot with rifles, but most of the minke and all the fin whales are caught by fishing vessels using modern, efficient penthrite grenade harpoons. Finally, the current humpback whale hunt in St. Vincent and the Grenadines has also been endorsed under the ASW clause, although it is of recent origin. The quota for the 2008–2012 period is twenty whales taken (Schedule 13[b]4) from a population of about 11,600 animals (range10,100–13,200).

Commercial Whaling

When the moratorium on commercial waling was adopted in 1982, Japan, Norway, Peru and Russia (then the Soviet Union) objected to the decision. Peru and Japan have since withdrawn their objections. However, Norway and Russia have retained their objections and are therefore not legally bound by that decision. Nevertheless, Russia has curtailed commercial whaling, and Norway halted such whaling in 1987 until better abundance estimates were available. Norway resumed commercial whaling in 1993 under strong international condemnation. Only minke whales are hunted, and in 2005 about thirty-five Norwegian fishing vessels caught 639 whales in the North Atlantic from an estimated population of 174,000 animals (range 125,000–245,000). Norway has chosen to use the Revised Management Procedure—which the IWC has accepted but failed to implement—to calculate catch quotas. Iceland resumed commercial hunting of minke and fin whales in 2006.

Japan also wants to resume its coastal minke whaling, which shares most features with minke whaling in Greenland, Iceland and Norway and fits IWC's 'small-type whaling' category defined as 'catching operations using powered vessels with mounted harpoon guns hunting exclusively for minke, bottlenose, beaked, pilot or killer whales' (Schedule I.1.C). Japan's proposal for a new category termed 'small-type coastal whaling', which shares features both with ASW (in having strong cultural values) and commercial whaling (in producing commodities for the market), has been turned down by the IWC. Japan also wants to resume commercial minke whaling in the Antarctic.[19]

Scientific Whaling (Special Permit Whaling)

The ICRW also grants any contracting government the right to issue special permits authorizing its nationals 'to kill, take and treat whales for purposes of scientific research' (Article VIII.1). The contracting government sets the quotas and is only obliged to inform the IWC about its intention and to provide the scientific results to the IWC's Scientific Committee. The United States was the first country to use this clause, and by 1982 more than a hundred such permits had been issued by governments in, e.g., the United States, the Soviet Union, South Africa, Canada and Japan.[20]

Iceland, Japan, Norway and South Korea issued special permits to themselves upon the imposition of the moratorium in 1986–88. South Korea ended its research whaling by 1987, but the other three countries—particularly Japan—have run lethal research programmes over a number of years and have been severely criticized for this. Scientific whaling is today highly controversial, and in many anti-whaling discourses it is represented as 'commercial whaling in disguise'.

In 2005 IWC members reported catches of 2,313 whales altogether, the highest number since the implementation of the moratorium, including forty-two whales struck and lost.[21] Of these, the IWC had given quotas for only the 388 whales struck under the ASW clause. Japan and Iceland had given themselves quotas under the scientific whaling clause, and Norway had given itself a quota under the objection clause. All these catches were legal according to the ICRW. Four whales were reported to have been caught illegally, three minke whales by Korea and one Bryde's whale by St. Vincent and the Grenadines (IWC 2007a).

These figures tell only part of the story. First, they do not say anything about whaling conducted by countries that are not members of the IWC. From 1991 to 2005 nine bowhead whales were caught by Canadian Inuit, under strong international protests and U.S. threats of sanctions. However, no protests are levied on Indonesian traditional whaling. In 1998 there were nineteen whaling boats in Lamalera, and twenty-six sperm whales were taken. Some whales are also caught by villagers from Lamakera. Little is known about current whaling activities in the Philippines, where whales are hunted off Palawan and the central Visayan Islands. The main target is the Bryde's whale (Tan 1997).

Second, and more important, IWC figures do not cover catches of small whales. The term 'whale' is ambiguous. In common parlance species of the order *Cetacea* are often divided into the categories whales, dolphins and porpoises. The majority of the IWC member states take the term whale to mean only baleen whales (*Mysticeti*) plus the sperm whale, the largest of the toothed whales (*Odontoceti*).[22] This has caused considerable controversy within the IWC as to its competence to address catches of toothed whales other than the sperm whale— the so called 'small cetaceans'.[23] In fact, the IWC's operational definition of whale locates the vast majority of catches outside its sphere of competence.

The largest number of whales killed comprises small cetaceans taken by IWC members. The most controversial operations are pilot whale drives in the Faroe Islands and dolphin drives in Japan. The former is the best-documented whaling regime in the world, with law texts going back to 1298 and almost unbroken catch records from 1584. About 1,200–1,400 animals are taken annually—from an abundant population of about 780,000 animals—in drives during which a number of skiffs and other small boats chase whales towards a beach where they are slaughtered. Meat and blubber are distributed for free throughout the local communities, with very little reaching the market. Pilot whaling in the Faroe Islands is perhaps the whaling regime that best fits the IWC's definition of ASW, yet as will be shown later, it receives some of the most vehement attacks from the protectionists. Inuit catches of the allegedly endangered narwhal and beluga have received scant notice, however. Dolphins are hunted in many countries both inside and outside the IWC, but a 'dolphin drive' search of the world wide web (4 April 2008) overwhelmingly returned protests against Japanese drives.

Meanwhile, cetaceans accidentally killed in fishing operations far outnumber all these figures. Many minke whales reportedly die in South Korean fishing nets every year, and in Denmark an estimated 4–5,000 harbour porpoises are drowned in cod nets annually. Yet these deaths receive hardly any international condemnation. Even more porpoises and dolphins may die in Italian gill nets. The number of small cetaceans killed in purse seines and driftnet fisheries has in the past been staggering. In 1960, an estimated 853,000 dolphins were killed by purse seiners catching tuna in the Pacific, 85 per cent of this total was accounted for by U.S. seiners (Bonanno and Constance 1996: 126). It is a misnomer to call these catches 'incidental' as the fishermen deliberately took advantage of the fact that yellowfin tuna for some unknown reason follow the spotted, spinner and common dolphins. The purse seine that was developed by the tuna fishermen in San Diego 'uses speedboats, helicopters, and small explosives . . . to herd the dolphins into a net of nearly a mile in circumference' (Bonanno and Constance 1996: 124–25) in order to catch the tuna (see also Orbach 1977).

In 1972, the year when the United States first proposed a moratorium on commercial whaling and the year when the U.S. Marine Mammal Protection Act (MMPA) prohibited all catches and harassment of marine mammals, the tuna fleet was given a grace period of two years, during which an additional half a million dolphins—mostly spotted and spinner dolphins—died in U.S. tuna nets (Bonanno and Constance 1996: 127–28). The goal was to reduce incidental catches 'to an insignificant level approaching a zero mortality', which in 1980 was set at 20,500 indefinitely (Bonanno and Constance 1996: 131). Worldwide by-catches of cetaceans may still account for more than 300,000 mortalities a year (WWF 2004: 1). The IWC, then, at present manages less than 1 per cent of cetaceans killed.

The heyday of the anti-whaling campaigns lasted from 1987, when the moratorium was first implemented, until the establishment of the Southern Sanctuary in 1994. This was a time when twenty or more interventions could appear daily at an online discussion group;[24] now several days may pass between each posting. This was also the period when the IWC's scientists developed the Revised Management Procedure and concluded that some whale stocks could be harvested. When these conclusions did not have any impact on IWC policy, it became obvious to many that the IWC had turned from conservation to preservation. Iceland therefore left the organization in 1992, and Norway resumed commercial whaling the following year. The organization became polarized and entered a deadlock from which it has been unable to escape. In the pro-whaling rhetoric, the IWC ceased to function as intended by the ICRW , and observers have predicted its rapid disintegration. Yet not only do old members continue to attend (Iceland rejoined in 2002)—although often grumblingly—but new countries continue to seek membership, bringing the total number of members to eighty-two (as of 27 November 2008). The reasons for this seeming paradox will, it is hoped, become clearer from the following chapters.

Notes

1. Referring to an Australian source (*A Universal Metaphor: Australia's Opposition to Commercial Whaling*, Report of the National Task Force on Whaling, Environment Australia, May 1997), Greenpeace gives the current world population of minke whales at 880,000 against an original pre-hunting population of 490,000 animals (retrieved 10 March 2008 from archive. greenpeace.org/~oceans/whaling/whalepopulations.html). In other words, the minke whale population is today almost twice the original level according to anti-whalers' own figures. A reason for this expansion despite whaling activities is, according to Japanese scientists, probably that minke whales have taken over the niches previously exploited by the larger baleen whales (see Chapter 7). Still, Greenpeace has repeatedly claimed that the minke whale stocks are severely depleted.

2. The text of Article 10(e) calling for the moratorium reads: '[C]atch limits for the killing for commercial purposes of whales from all stocks for the 1986 coastal and the 1985/86 pelagic seasons and thereafter shall be zero. This provision will be kept under review, based upon the best scientific advice, and by 1990 at the latest the Commission will undertake a comprehensive assessment of the effects of this decision on whale stocks and consider modification of this provision and the establishment of other catch limits.'

3. The perspectives of both sides of the debate will be considered but more emphasis will be given the anti-whaling discourse because this is hegemonic and has laid the premises also for the alternative discourse. I have tried to be fair in my treatment but I am fully aware that nonetheless my presentation inevitably may be coloured by my personal views and values, as outlined in the Preface.

4. What is managed, then, is strictly speaking whaling, not whales. However, I will occasionally use 'management of whales' for the sake of variation.

5. For a discussion of terms like anthropocentrism, ecocentrism and biocentrism, see e.g. O'Riordan 1981; Pepper 1993.

6. This does not mean that animal rights advocacy is new. Jeremy Bentham wrote on animal rights in 1789 (Bentham 1960 [1789]) and Henry Salt in 1892 (Salt 1980 [1892]).

7. Other definitions and taxonomies have been suggested. Kay Milton (1996: 218) suggests that environmentalism is best seen as a discourse about protection of the environment, with environment 'loosely identified as the complex of natural phenomena with which we share the universe and on which we depend' (Milton 1993: 2). Hence animal welfare and rights are subsumed under environmentalism. Robyn Eckersley (1992) in her discussion of major streams of environmentalism suggests a continuum from anthropocentric to ecocentric orientations—from resource management, through human welfare, ecology, preservation, and animal liberation to true ecocentrism.

8. Deep ecology has for the same reason been accused of not paying proper respect to the rights of individual human beings (e.g. Guha 1989; Ferry 1995).

9. Although animal welfare/rights advocates and environmental organizations collaborate closely on many issues—including that of whaling—the distinction should be maintained if we are

to understand the whaling nations' responses not only to their international critiques, but to the organizations themselves. To many organizations it is important to be identified as an environmental organization rather than as an animal welfare/rights organization. Whereas the environmental movement has emerged as a powerful political force at a global scale, animal rights advocates are only recently escaping the image of being a small group of fanatic freaks (Franklin 1999).

10. The motives behind the bird preservation groups were both altruistic (e.g. stop harvesting plumage of exotic birds) and humanistic (protect agriculture). But it is also important to keep in mind the new popularity of birdwatching, which was made possible by better means of transportation, binoculars and publication of books on the natural history of birds. Moreover, since the mid 1800s representation of birds had changed, and selected species came to serve didactic purposes among the bourgeoisie (Löfgren 1985). Good birds became models for the moral life: their life was 'characterized by values like domesticity, matrimonial fidelity and thrift' (Löfgren 1985: 201). But not all birds were good. The sparrow was typically a bad bird: 'Its voice was shrill, its plumage dirty grey, it moved around in noisy mobs, behaved aggressively and lived on grain [i.e. was a thief] and horse manure . . . They often came to symbolize the bad city life' (Löfgren 1985: 201–2).

11. Some countries had already imposed restrictions at the national level. In 1895 Norway banned whaling in the southernmost part of the country between 16 December and 15 March (Tønnessen 1969: 165) and imposed a total ban on catches of large baleen whales outside Northern Norway in 1903. Iceland banned whaling in 1915.

12. The original name was International Union for the Protection of Nature, which in 1956 changed to International Union for Conservation of Nature and Natural Resources (IUCN).

13. The Chihuahua, for example, 'has been bred by humans as a neotenized form that often serves as a child surrogate', and Pekinese and Boston terriers are 'in adult form approximately the body size of a human newborn' (Lawrence 1989: 63).

14. Even the well reputed *Times* (London) makes such distortions: 'The modern whaling vessel . . . is a self-sufficient factory ship able to flense, butcher and pressure-cook an ocean leviathan in less than an hour. Inspectors awaiting the vessels in port may find it extremely difficult to determine the number and species of the cetaceans slaughtered' ('Sleep of the Deep', 18 June 1996). The fact is that the only factory ship in operation today—used in Japanese scientific whaling—does not pressure-cook anything but produces food for the Japanese table, and inspectors have been on board these vessels for many years. The ship furthermore now carries a number of scientists.

15. The population of eastern North Pacific gray whales has fully recovered and the species has been removed from the endangered list. The population might even have exceeded the carrying capacity of its habitat in the late 1990s. The number of gray whales found dead along the Northwest Coast of the U.S. increased sharply in 1997 and reached a peak in 1999 and 2000, when several hundreds were found dead. Many of them were emaciated (www.cascadiaresearch.org/gray/Strand-19April05.htm), and one likely reason for the deaths is that they were running short of food. Besides poor health and death, shortage of food leads to decreasing growth and fertility rates.

16. The humpback whale is recovering rapidly and is approaching 60 per cent of its original level. The blue whale, on the other hand, is still severely depleted.

17. Soviet whalers operated outside the logic of the free market, whereas the Japanese had a home market for whale meat, which fetched higher prices than the whale oil produced by the other whaling nations.

18. This and subsequent estimates as well as quotas can be retrieved from www.iwcoffice.org. The figures are based on 95 per cent confidence interval.

19. This population was in the late 1980s estimated at 761,000 (510,000–1,140,00 with 95 per cent confidence interval), but this has recently been contested.

20. Retrieved 29 November 2008 from http://www.iwcoffice.org/conservation/permits.htm

21. Norway caught 639 minke whales for commercial purposes. Japan, under its scientific pro-gramme, captured 1,078 minke whales, a hundred sei whales, fifty Bryde's whales, ten fin whales and five sperm whales, whereas Iceland took thirty-nine minke whales. Authorized as ASW, Greenland's catch was 180 minke whales and thirteen fin whales; the U.S. caught sixty-eight bowheads, Russia two bowheads and 124 gray whales. St. Vincent and the Grenadines caught one humpback and one Bryde's whale; the latter was caught illegally. These figures include forty-two whales struck and lost. South Korea reported three minke whales caught in nets (IWC 2007a).

22. The baleen whales are the blue whale (including pygmy blue), fin whale, sei whale, Bryde's whale, minke whale, gray whale, humpback whale, bowhead whale, pygmy right whale and southern and northern right whales (the latter probably divided between North Pacific and North Atlantic species).

23. These are often classified as 'porpoises and dolphins'. However, whereas the term porpoise is commonly used for any of the six species of the family *Phocoenidae*, 'dolphin' is used in several ways. It may mean any of the small cetaceans (including porpoises) or only the bottlenose dolphin. Most commonly the term covers species of the families *Delphinidae* (about thirty-five species, but not including killer and pilot whales) and *Platanistoidea* (four or five species of river dolphins). However, such a categorization leaves important species of the families *Momodontidae* (narwhal and beluga) and *Ziphidae* (about twenty species of beaked whales) unaccounted for. In this book 'whale' will therefore be used to mean all cetacean species, whereas 'dolphin' will mostly be limited to species of the *Delphinidae* (but not to killer and pilot whales) and *Platanistoidea*.

24. marmam@lists.uvic.ca

Chapter 1

The Creation of a 'Superwhale'

In her book *Loving Nature: Towards an Ecology of Emotion*, Kay Milton takes issue with social constructionists on several accounts. To her, meaning is neither the property of knowledge in the mind, nor the property of representations used in communications. Rather, meaning is 'generated in the relationship between that knowledge and those representations' (Milton 2002: 32). In other words, the meaning of a representation depends on the extent to which it resonates with existing knowledge. She also objects to the way constructionists tend to deal with knowledge as a process limited to social learning, which she thinks misses one important point: that we learn not only from our social environment but also directly from our natural environment. 'Throughout our lives we learn from our whole environment . . . What we learn about the world depends on how we, as individual organisms, engage with it' (2002: 32).

Maybe so, but very few people have experienced direct engagements with cetaceans. Most people meet whales only through representations, and our knowledge about these animals is mostly built on representations presented through books, photos and movies. Even engagements like whale watching and swim-with-dolphin programmes are carefully staged, and the human participants are expected (and often instructed) to behave and feel in a particular way. Few people in the past had any knowledge about whales, and the representations that emerged in the 1970s resonated in all likelihood with knowledge external to whales (e.g. political, religious and ecological knowledge). A new narrative on whales and whaling was taking form based on images of Moby-Dick and whaling of bygone days. Whaling nations were slow to grasp this challenge. When they finally responded and tried to present alternative representations, many people had already created their images, or cultural models, of whales and whaling. These alternative representations were therefore dismissed as distorted or false, or as propaganda fabricated by the whaling industry. This might be one reason why it has been so difficult for whaling nations to change what has been termed the world opinion on whales.

In this chapter, I will first explore how a body of knowledge about whales has been created by the circulation of carefully selected representations of cetaceans. By lumping together traits found in a number of different species, an image of a 'superwhale' has emerged. Secondly, I will address why so many people today subscribe to this image, by arguing that cetaceans are animals that easily can be ascribed symbolic significance. Finally, I will argue that the superwhale is located at the centre of a whale-as-person narrative, a narrative that not only produces a powerful metaphor for a world that modern human beings allegedly have lost on our road to modernity, but also is seen as a prerequisite to the anti-whaling discourse taken up in Chapter 2.

Uniquely Special

A new line of arguments against whaling came to the forefront around 1990. We are now told that whales are unique and therefore it is immoral to kill them. Usually no nuances are being made between the close to eighty cetacean species. Features from different species have been lumped together to create an image of a superwhale (Kalland 1992a, 1993). We are told that the whale is the largest animal on earth (this applies to the blue whale), has the largest brain on earth (the sperm whale), has a large brain-to-body-weight ratio (i.e. is intelligent, the bottlenose dolphin), has a pleasant and varied song (the humpback whale), is friendly (the gray whale), is endangered (the bowhead and blue whales) and so on.[1]

A number of sources contribute to this whale narrative: scholarly papers on cetacean behaviour written by scientists, doomsday prophesies by environmental activists and testimonials made by people participating in what can best be termed a cetacean cult. Few agree with all the elements in the narrative. The ideas that whales are endangered and deserve better than being killed to satisfy human desires are probably subscribed to by the largest number of people. The idea that whales are extraterrestrial beings sent to Earth as a kind of Messiah to save the planet, is on the other hand less widely held. But these elements are connected; they inspire and support each other, and it is therefore necessary to consider also claims that most people undoubtedly will find ridiculous. Together the elements form what may be called the contemporary whale narrative. The product—the superwhale—has, as we shall see in Chapter 3, found a large and expanding market among those who need a green conscience and credibility.

Whales are, according to Robbins Barstow (1991), the president of the Cetacean Society International (CSI), special in five different ways: biologically, ecologically, culturally, politically and symbolically.

Biologically Special

First, says Barstow, the whales are biologically special. The blue whale is the largest animal on earth—David Day (1991: 68) writes that '[w]hales are the Grand

Canyon and Mount Everest of the animal world'—but the cetacean family also includes small porpoises measuring hardly more than one and a half metres.[2] Yet it is their intelligence that has received most attention, and it is this factor more than anything else that forms the basis for the claim that whales are in the ocean what human beings are on land.

Dolphins are in particular believed to be intelligent. In his well-known science-fiction novel *The Hitchhiker's Guide to the Galaxy*, Douglas Adams writes (1986: 113): 'On planet Earth, man has always assumed that he was more intelligent than dolphins because he had achieved so much—the wheel, New York, wars and so on—whilst all the dolphins had ever done was muck about in the water having a good time. But conversely, the dolphins had always believed that they were far more intelligent than man—for precisely the same reason.' What was probably a joke for Adams has been taken very seriously by others. Dolphin intelligence has become the strongest key element in the dolphin narrative. Some would place dolphins even above human beings. One of them is John Lilly, neurophysiologist, the unchallenged dolphin guru and, according to Cochrane and Callen (1992: 77), a father of the New Age. Quoting Lilly's (1967) pioneering work on human-dolphin communication, the lawyers Anthony D'Amato and Sudhir K. Chopra have argued in the *American Journal for International Law* (1991) for whale-rights based on the unique intelligence of whales.

The evidence for this intelligence is found partly in the size and architecture of the brain and partly in the animals' behaviour. Barstow claims that the sperm whale has 'by far the largest brain of any creature ever to have lived on our planet' (1991: 6), and Lilly therefore believed that the sperm whale probably is the most intelligent creature on earth (quoted in Darby 2008:116). But in fact the sperm whale brain is only slightly bigger than that of an elephant (7.8 and 7.5 kg, respectively). On the other hand, the sperm whale's brain constitutes only 0.021 per cent of the animal's body weight, as compared to 0.08 per cent for a cow, 0.15 per cent for the elephant, and 2.1 per cent for human beings (Freeman 1990: 112). There are also great differences between cetacean species, and the brain of a bottlenose dolphin is relatively speaking more than hundred times the size of the blue whale's brain. This fact alone should caution us not to make sweeping generalizations about cetacean intelligence.

Several species of dolphins do have large brains compared to body weight—the bottlenose dolphin, with a brain size slightly larger than ours, has a ratio of 0.94 per cent. Not only its size, but also its structure has been compared to the human brain. A former leader of Greenpeace's anti-whaling campaign claimed in an article entitled *The Humans of the Oceans* ('Havets mennesker') that 'it is generally accepted that the structures of the dolphin and human brains, both regarding size, the number and area of convolutions of the brain and cellular organization are identical' (Gylling-Nielsen 1987: 11, my translation from Danish). Others speculate that the dolphin brain even surpasses the human brain in complexity (e.g. Cochrane and Callen 1992: 78–81; McKenna 1992: 53).

However, it is by no means generally accepted that the dolphin and human brains are identical. On the contrary, some authors have argued that dolphin brains are more similar to those of hoofed animals (e.g. Bryden and Cockeron 1989: 161). Margaret Klinowska (1988: 46), professor at Cambridge University and a special advisor to the World Conservation Union (IUCN), concludes that the dolphin's brain has not evolved significantly since the cetacean ancestors left land for a life in water some twenty-five million years ago, and may in fact be more similar to the brains of hedgehogs, anteaters and bats (Klinowska 1988: 46; see also Bryden and Cockeron 1989: 161; Howard 1995: 262–63).

Another argument used to highlight the intelligence of dolphins is their behaviour. Some species of dolphins can be trained, and apparently they can learn tricks from each other. Their playfulness is taken as proof of their intelligence—teasing being a recurring theme in dolphin stories (Hatt 1990: 249). 'Play is a hallmark of intelligence and is indispensable for creativity and flexibility', writes Lilly (1967: 58), and Virginia McKenna, perhaps best known as an actor in the movie *Born Free* (1964), writes: 'Of all the animals in the world, dolphins seem most whole-heartedly to enjoy life, to leap and play just for the fun of it' (1992: 44). Besides indicating childish innocence, their play is taken to imply intentional behaviour. Amanda Cochrane and Karena Callen—both with a background from health and beauty sections of women magazines—have claimed that the dolphins 'analyze situations, not just react to them, and make decisions on the basis of its findings much in the same way as we do' (Cochrane and Callen 1992: 82).

Closely connected with the debate about cetacean intelligence is the claim that whales can communicate and even may have developed a language. Whereas some are impressed by the sperm whale which, with a recorded 223 dB, produces the loudest sound made by any animal (Darby 2008: 88), many more have been intrigued by the clicks of the dolphins. Like bats, dolphins use these clicks (or ultrasound) for navigation and to locate and perhaps to stun their prey (Norris 1974). However, in the dolphin cult ultrasound is given a much more prominent role. Dolphins are allegedly able to scan friends and foes alike. Dolphins may pay special attention to pregnant women and they may even be able 'to scan the lining of the womb in order to determine the stages of the menstrual cycle' (Cochrane and Callen 1992: 14). Their clicks, together with their whistles, are seen as a means of communication. Computing mathematically the number of possible combinations of clicks and whistles, it has been calculated that dolphins can emit and receive ten times or more information through their senses than humans can (Fichtelius and Sjölander 1973; Odent 1990: 80).

The question of cetacean intelligence is highly controversial (e.g. Prescott 1981; Pryor 1981), and Gregory Bateson, who in the 1960s was invited by Lilly to study his dolphins, addressed this question early on. His premise was that mammal communication is largely about relationships, and socially active mammals tend to have larger brains than solitary animals in order to interpret the intentions of the others (Bateson 1973: 337). This may explain why dolphins that cooperate tightly during hunts need relatively larger brains than baleen whales feeding on krill. Moreover, whereas terrestrial mammals, including humans, communicate through a combination of vocalization and kinesics, the marine environment has imposed restrictions on the repertoire available to whales. They have lost the ability to use facial and most bodily expressions to convey information, and Bateson suggests that there has been an evolutionary shift from kinesics to vocalization (1973: 341). The evolutionary shift may have made it more difficult to understand cetaceans because we are used to communicating about relationships mainly by means of kinesics and paralinguistic signals, which is an analogic mode of communication, whereas cetacean vocalization is a digital mode (1973: 342–43). However, this vocalization should not be taken as something resembling a human language. To Bateson the uniqueness of human language lies not in its ability to handle abstractions but in its ability to communicate about things other than relationships (1973: 337).

Ability to communicate does not necessarily imply high intelligence, as the rich repertoire of signals among the honeybees testifies. The more modest among the whale protectionists have argued that it is impossible to compare whale and human intelligence because they have been developed to meet very different challenges. To Richard O'Barry, who trained Flipper before he turned against dolphinariums and started to break into them in order to release dolphins into the wild, the question about intelligence 'boils down to the simple fact that they are as intelligent in their world as we are in ours' (O'Barry 1991: 14). When proof is hard to find, Roger Payne (1991: 21), who has a PhD in biology and pioneered whale song research and once served as the IWC commissioner for Antigua, concludes in the absence of evidence to the contrary that 'whales are aware of their lives and of their interests, simply because that seems to be the most parsimonious conclusion'.

Ecologically Special

Barstow is also of the opinion that whales are ecologically special. Many whale protectionists point out that whales have a much longer history than *Homo sapiens* does. They may have evolved at a time 'when men were insignificant nocturnal insectivores', to use the words of Lyall Watson (1985: 48), a writer of parapsychology and once a member of the Seychelles's delegation to the IWC. Although Klinowska (1988: 46) claims that the cetacean brain has not evolved significantly since their ancestors returned to the sea, others are of the opinion that the whales have had more time than humans to develop into intelligent, rational beings. It seems that the longer cetaceans have lived on Earth, the better. Some authors claim a 25–30 million-year history for whales, whereas others suggest 50 (Williams 1988: 17) or even 70 million years (WWF-Denmark 1990). The long history of whales seems to give them some unique rights to the oceans, where they lived long before humans 'intruded into the marine ecosystem' (Gylling-Nielsen

1987: 11). The whales thus emerge as the 'aborigines' of the sea, a premise leading ultimately to closing the oceans to many human activities in the same way
that aboriginal lands are being closed to certain activities of white people.

The antiquity of cetaceans seems to place whales above humans. Their ancient
history implies that cetaceans have existed far longer than we have but without
playing havoc with Earth: 'the Cetacea have demonstrated a capacity to survive
far longer than we have on this planet . . . man in his present form has only
existed 1/150th of the time that the dolphins have existed and survived' (Lilly
1978: 92–93). In this view they are more advanced than human beings, and they
may have more to teach us than we have to teach them, not least when it comes
to the question of sustainable living (see below).

Furthermore, Barstow points out that the whales are at the top of the food
chain. The baleen whales are the largest eaters of zooplankton, and the killer
whale is the largest predator. This is hardly controversial, nor is the claim that
we all depend on oxygen in the atmosphere. But his assertion that 'the proper
balance in the amount of oxygen in the earth's atmosphere produced from the
plankton . . . is kept in check most critically by whale consumption' (Barstow
1989: 13) is not substantiated in any way. The leap from this kind of ecological
argument to the following letter written by a UK woman to the Faroese government is not that great (quoted in full in Sanderson 1990: 199): 'The Slaughter
in the Faroes of the dolphins and whales is causing untold damage to the ozone
layer. The special sound the dolphins and whales emit holds the ozone layer
together. It is the utmost importance to stop this terrible slaughtering of these
wonderful creatures, so many of which are far more evolved than man . . . PS:
The dolphins are the guardians of this planet.'

It is difficult to talk about a uniform ecological adaptation for all cetacean
species. There are considerable differences in ecological adaptation between
plankton-eating baleen whales and toothed carnivores; between those living most
of the year in polar waters with a low degree of biodiversity and those living in
rich tropic waters; between those that feed on large depths and those feeding in
shallow rivers; and between those that annually migrate thousands of miles and
those that stay within a narrow region. Pro-whalers, i.e. people who support sustainable whaling, have voiced the opinion that it is difficult—and dangerous—to
claim that certain mammals are ecologically more important than others. They
ask on what criteria we shall base such a ranking among living species. To them
every species has a special role to play in the ecosystem, *Homo sapiens* included.
We are all unique in a way.

Finally, it is widely believed that whales are endangered.[3] But only a few of
the more than seventy-five species of cetaceans were endangered at the time the
moratorium was imposed on commercial whaling (Aron 1988). That the minke
whale—which Greenland, Iceland, Japan and Norway want to harvest—was not
endangered and might have been more abundant in the Antarctic than ever (Gulland 1988: 44) was not mentioned. Nor was the fact that there were—according

to U.S. estimates (Aron 1988: 104)—about two million sperm whales, even though they were on the list of endangered species. That a few species, such as the blue and bowhead whales, are endangered does not, in the whalers' view, justify a total moratorium on the killing of all whales. Barstow confesses that scientific data show that 'at least some species of whales could easily sustain a resumed, strictly regulated harvest, without threatening species survival' (Barstow 1989: 10). It is this fact that forces him to take up moral and ethical issues involved in the commercial harvesting of whales.

Culturally, Politically and Symbolically Special

To Barstow whales are culturally unique, not only because whales—like the 'friendly' gray whales—allegedly have a greater capacity than any other animal to enrich our lives through peaceful contact,[4] but also because they have a universal appeal to the human spirit and are unmatched invokers of awe. Moreover, they have special aesthetic qualities, are supremely photogenic, and play an important role in education in that they for 'persons of all ages and background . . . become breakthrough educational motivators'. Furthermore, whales appear to carry no grudges against people despite being victimized by human predation for centuries (Barstow 1991: 6). This is taken as a proof that 'whales in the wild [are] uniquely tolerant of the peaceful proximity of human beings' and that they even may initiate such interaction (Barstow 1989: 13). They love us and enjoy entertaining us; thus we mutually enrich each other's lives (Barstow 1991: 7).

Undoubtedly, cetaceans have fascinated people all over the world and figure prominently in myths and legends (e.g. Alpers 1960; Cochrane and Callen 1992; McKenna 1992). In many cultures whales are seen as embodied deities. In Greek mythology, Apollo turned himself into a dolphin to rescue people lost in a gale; in Japan whales might be regarded as the embodiment of Ebisu, the patron deity of fishing. In Vietnam, cetaceans receive humanlike funerals to become 'Angels of the Sea'. Both in the Amazon and in Micronesia dolphins are believed to take human form to attend village celebrations, but the metamorphosis may also go the other way, as in Greek mythology. People in some Oceanic societies may turn into dolphins when they die, and among the Haida in British Columbia it is believed that humans may take the form of a killer whale if they drown.

Plutarch remarked about 1,900 years ago that the dolphin 'is the only creature who loves man for his own sake . . . [seeking] friendship for no advantage' (cited in Cochrane and Callen 1992: 57). A common theme in several of the stories from ancient Greece is the friendship between boys and dolphins. Moreover, stories about people saved or assisted by dolphins are widely cherished and shared, although hard to document properly.[5] According to Cochrane and Callen (1992: 11), dolphins 'seem to direct their attention towards those people who are weak and ailing, or, in other words, to those who are in distress.' Robert Stenuit (1968: 159) suggests that sailors should be equipped with recordings of dolphin distress signals to be turned on automatically in case of shipwreck, so that 'all the dolphins within range would come to the rescue, as in Aesop's fable'.

Dolphins are known to have assisted men in less dramatic ways. From a number of locations there are reports about collaboration between fishers and dolphins in catching fish, past and present (Lamb 1954; Alpers 1960: 33–35; Stenuit 1968: 155–57; Slater 1994: 79–80). It is also claimed that dolphins can have a positive effect on the physical as well as the mental well-being of human beings, and psychologists, psychiatrists and others have turned to dolphin therapy. Swimming with dolphins is said to have a positive effect on people suffering from a number of illnesses and handicaps, not least on autistic children and people with Down's syndrome or depressions (Smith 1987; Cochrane and Callen 1992; Dobbs 1992). But as Cochrane and Callen admit (1992: 22), there is 'little scientific proof that the dolphin's ultrasound is powerful enough either to scan our bodies in any detail or induce a physiotherapeutic effect' (see also e.g. Brensing 2006.)

Whales are depicted as lovely, gentle, peaceful, graceful, magnificent, beautiful, playful, innocent and so on. The list of positively valued characteristics can be extended almost endlessly. 'Whales and dolphins are one-dimensional beings. They are only *positive!*' writes Paul Spong (1992: 25), who brought the anti-whaling issue into Greenpeace (Brown and May 1991: 32). Everything the whales do is interpreted in a positive way.[6] Even the killer whale, one of the fiercest predators on earth, has a tendency to be depicted as good in this narrative. Its scientific name, *orca*, is often preferred to the term killer whale. When killer whales attack other cetaceans they are pictured as gentle killers (e.g. Jalakas 1993). And when killer whales at Sealand in Vancouver pulled a 20-year-old trainee into the pool and maltreated her for ten minutes before she died, the manager of the establishment suggested that '[t]hey were just playing. It was a tragic accident' (*Daily Telegraph*, 22 February 1991). But those who have seen Sir David Attonbourgh's footage of killer whales playing with, and killing, sea lions, may have difficulty accepting that the incident in Vancouver was a mere tragic accident.[7]

Whales have made a great impact in popular culture around the world, and the value of nonconsumptive use of cetaceans today far exceeds the value of whaling. A number of books, magazines, TV and radio broadcasts, motion pictures, records, paintings and other art objects, whale-watching tours, dolphinariums and computer games cater to the consumers. Dolphins, in particular, stir people's imagination, and have become popular in science fiction as well as in New Age literature.

Politically the whales are regarded as special because they do not know national borders, which is one reason why it is claimed that whales must be managed by international bodies. But this is not unique to whales: it is equally valid for some fish and birds, which may travel much longer distances than toothed whales, which, with the exception of adult sperm whales, usually do not migrate widely (Watson 1985: 51). What has turned cetaceans into a global resource or into a common heritage of humankind is not least the existence of a global management body (IWC) that gives substance to the image of a global village.

If whales are culturally and politically unique, this is so not due to some unique qualities in whales per se, but because of how whales are represented and perceived. In other words, the perceived cultural and political uniqueness of whales is an effect of human activities and thus a cultural product—according to pro-whalers, created mainly by urban people in the Western world under certain economic and political conditions. What is culturally and politically unique about whales is no more than an invention of the human—or certain humans'—mind. The same can be said about the symbolic uniqueness of whales. Barstow points out that whales have come to symbolize concern for all life on this watery planet (1991: 7), but this tells us more about human society and culture than about whales.

Some have gone a step further and constructed a cultured whale, an individual spending much of its time engaged in cultural creativity. With their claimed capacity for storytelling, for example, it is no surprise to find that dolphins are supposed to have a rich and ancient culture, and that they 'represent the closest approach to civilization, not as defined in terms of machine or technology, but as realized among all intelligent beings, cetacean or human, where communication and social bonds transcended the mere exigencies of life' (Abbey 1990: 80).[8] The humpback whale's rich repertoire of sounds inspired Heathcote Williams to write the following poem about whale songs and oral traditions allegedly going fifty million years back (1988: 17):

> Webs of elegant cetacean music stretch around the globe;
> Lyrical litanies on the bio-radio
> That draw on an oral tradition of submarine songs
> From a living memory bank, founded fifty million years ago.

Nobody has satisfactorily explained how new humpback songs spread like pop music over large areas. There is little reason to doubt that whales can learn from each other, just as fox pups learn to hunt from their mother. The crucial question is whether this learning process is limited to some aspects of innate behaviour or also includes abstract reasoning, i.e. to what extent they have cultures.

Let us summarize why whales are held to be unique. We have seen that the narrative constructs a whale that is the largest animal on earth, has the largest brain, might be as intelligent as human beings or more so, sings pleasant songs, is friendly, is endangered and so on. By talking about *the* whale, an image of a single whale possessing all these traits emerges. But such a creature does not exist outside the human mind. It is a mythic creation—a superwhale that has come to represent all species of cetaceans. They are our pseudo-ancestors and counterparts in the oceans.

Why Cetaceans? Symbolic Significance

Why this fascination for cetaceans? Why do so many people and organizations spend so much time and energy on creating this image, and why does the super-whale have such an appeal and apparently sell so well (see Chapter 3)? Why are marine mammals offered better protection by U.S. laws than any other species (Manning 1989: 220)? There are a number of answers to these questions, ranging from economy and politics to information management and psychology.

The most obvious answer is that cetaceans are indeed endangered, but as I have already indicated and will further substantiate throughout this book, this is empirically inaccurate. Some stocks can sustain a controlled harvest. When there are no longer ecological reasons to prohibit a limited and controlled harvest of some whale stocks, why do so many organizations that claim to fight for the en-vironment and not for animal rights continue their campaigns against whaling? Why have international environmental organizations not followed the example set by the largest Norwegian groups, including Naturvernforbundet and Nature and Youth, which both are associated with the Friends of the Earth? They left the anti-whaling bandwagon in the early 1990s when scientific data convinced them that a carefully monitored exploitation of certain whale stocks did not put these at risk.

In the first place, there are, as whalers are quick to point out, pragmatic rea-sons to jump on the anti-whaling bandwagon. In Chapter 3 I will argue that environmentalists as well as animal rights activists have learned that whales open people's purses. Furthermore it will be argued that whaling is an ideal issue for national governments and polluting industries to support. The question remains, however, why ordinary people attach so much importance to whales and there-fore more readily donate money in order to save them rather than endangered bats, for example. The grim history of industrial whaling is certainly one reason, and I will return to this below. But this is not the whole story. People might be concerned about the well-being of individual whales or think they have a right to be left alone. Although it might well be an invention of the mind, the unique-ness of cetaceans appears unquestionably real to many people who may feel awe seeing a large whale breaching or a dolphin performing its antics. According to E.O. Wilson's biophilia hypothesis, we are genetically programmed to respond emotionally to other life forms (Wilson 1984), and Véronique Servais (2005: 225) suggests that people's emotional involvement with dolphins is based on basic ethological signals that human beings perceive as attentive love. Although preferential attitudes toward large (Kellert 1988) and juvenile looking animals (Lorenz 1981; Lawrence 1989) may help turn large whales and 'smiling' dolphins into likely candidates for attention, there are undoubtedly other factors that work in the same direction. In the Introduction it was argued that some animals are better to 'think with' than others. In other to understand this we have to turn to an analysis of the potential symbolic significance of cetaceans and the medium through which they move.

The Symbolic Power of Whales and Water

First, cetaceans are animals that easily can be ascribed symbolic significance. In the way in which we categorize the world around us, mammals usually have four legs and walk on land. But the cetaceans live in the sea and not on land, and they have fins and not legs. Unlike fish, their tails are horizontal rather than vertical, and they have no scales. And unlike fish, they breathe the air and suckle their infants like terrestrial mammals. Whales live on the boundaries between water and air (Bryld and Lykke 2000: 184), and may form an anomalous category of animals since they do not easily fit into our simple categories of mammal and fish (Kalland and Moeran 1992: 5–6), something Aristotle observed when he tried to classify all animals breathing air as terrestrial and those taking in water as aquatic. He found that the dolphin did both (Alpers 1960: 85). In medieval Scandinavia, before the Reformation, people could eat whale meat on Fridays and during Lent because whales were classified as fish and not meat. In Norway whale meat is still sold in fish shops. The same is true for Japan, where *kujira* (whale) is written by integrating the characters for 'fish' and 'capitol' (i.e. the main or biggest fish). In much folk taxonomy whales are neither 100 per cent fish nor 100 per cent mammal. Nor do they fit easily into clear categories of the wild and the tame. Some whale species are among the few wild animals that voluntarily seek human companionship, thus creating disorder between nature and culture. Whales are betwixt and between, and it is, according to Mary Douglas (1966), exactly those animals that are difficult to fit into our cognitive maps that become the object of myths and taboos. Among other such betwixt-and-between animals are seals (marine mammals like whales), bats (mammals with wings like birds) and snakes (terrestrial animals crawling without legs).

Second, whales move in salt water. We know very little about what is going on in the oceans, which opens the sea to manipulation and myth creation (Pálsson 1991: 95; Kalland and Moeran 1992: 7–8). The ocean has always been the abode of monsters and fabulous animals (see Bright 1989). Moreover, the ocean—consisting largely of salt and water, which are both important purifying agents used in religious rites throughout the world—becomes *the* symbol of purity,[9] or of untouched nature or wilderness, and thus stands in sharp contrast to the polluted soil on which we land mammals tread. It is we who move on land who pollute the pure sea. When the Danish chemical company Brøste 'bought' a sperm whale from the WWF in order to improve its green image, the whale was given the long name 'Brøste's pioneer whale loves pure salt water' (*Brøstes pionerhval elsker rent saltvand*).

But salt water has other qualities. We all started our lives in the uterus submerged in this kind of fluid, and salty water is thus indispensable for our own existence. It has been suggested that people's attitudes to marine mammals are reflections of an unconscious memory of, and yearning for, life in the mother's womb (Lynge 1990: 60; Bryld and Lykke 2000: 166–67). 'Water not only links back with our evolutionary aquatic past, but also offers a comforting reminder of our first nine months of life, spent bobbing around in the soothing environment of the amniotic fluid', write Cochrane and Callen (1992: 27). Heathcote Williams plays on the same theme in one of his poems (Williams 1988: 12):

> Whales play, in an amniotic paradise.
> Their light minds shaped by buoyancy, unrestricted by gravity,
> Somersaulting,
> Like angels, or birds;
> Like our own lives, in the womb.

Yet despite having lived our first nine months in water, we are unable to swim like a whale. Without technological aids such as diving gear and submarines we are confined to life on land. Human beings may harbour a feeling of envy towards whales, just as there is a feeling of envy towards birds for being able to move freely in the skies. Physically we are tied to the Earth and socially we are tied by conventions. Wild animals moving in elements from which human beings usually are excluded easily become symbols of the freedom many of us are longing for. 'Whales are a symbol of this freedom, and that is why people have grown to love them', writes a reader to *Fish International* (Neubacher 1992: 3). The humpback whales, and to a certain extent some of the dolphins, bridge the realms of sea and air, which makes them doubly fascinating. The humpback is able to jump out of water, waving its long flippers like wings, and Greenpeace's inflatable humpback has been flown in anti-whaling demonstrations around the world. This longing for freedom comes also to the fore when humpback whales fly through the air in Japanese advertisements, often carrying children on their backs.

This point is further enhanced when whales are presented as extraterrestrial beings, thus conflating the depth of the oceans with outer space. To Lilly dolphins are extraterrestrial beings, and he is not alone in harbouring such ideas. The Danish feminists Mette Bryld and Nina Lykke, who have called their book about the dolphin cult *Cosmodolphins*, provide a fascinating analysis of this dolphin-in-space narrative that encapsulates NASA, LSD, the New Age and world politics (Bryld and Lykke 2000).

Measured against the freedom of the seas and air, land becomes a prison; hence water symbols escape (Jung, cited in Odent 1990: 66). It is gravity more than anything else that confines us to a life in a two-dimensional world. According to the late Jacques-Yves Cousteau—one of the most respected cetacean advocates—'gravity is the original sin. Redemption will come only when we return to the water' (Odent 1990: 57), and some people see water birth as a step in that direction. Ecofeminist Estelle Myers (1997) views this kind of delivery as negation of birth, at least in its Christian form. Believed to be gentler and less painful and traumatic for both mother and child, water birth breaks the biblical curse 'in pain shalt thou bring forth children' (Genesis 3:16) and thereby also the established social order. Water birth, then, can be seen as a protest against Christianity and male dominance. Water offers a feminine world, a world without gravitation and sin, a blissful world before the Fall from Grace; a world in sharp contrast to the male terrestrial world dominated by gravitation. Hence, whale society offers a critique of modern male-dominated human society (Frøvik 1995: 68–72).

A Social Critique

Although whales might be animals that easily can be ascribed symbolic significance, it is a historical fact that most people in Western societies paid little attention to marine mammals for nearly 2,000 years. We therefore need to explain why whales are accredited with so much significance at this particular juncture in history. The rise of the anti-whaling campaigns can hardly be perceived as separate from the rise of the alternative movement of the 1960s (see Introduction, this volume), which was a reaction against wars, nuclear holocaust, racial and sexual oppression and increasingly against pollution and depletion of natural resources.

The history of industrial whaling has come to symbolize humans' reckless exploitation of natural resources. The large cetacean species have been depleted one after another. Overexploitation may have started with the right whale stocks in the Bay of Biscay in the sixteenth century, although the reason for their disappearance is still somewhat controversial. However, there is no doubt that British, Dutch and North American whalers in the eighteenth and nineteenth centuries brought the stocks of right and bowhead whales close to extinction in the North Atlantic. Moreover, with the invention of modern whaling in the 1860s, fast-swimming rorquals came within reach of the whalers. Within a century most of the stocks of large whales were severely depleted, and the blue whale was brought close to extinction. In the 1980s only the smallest of the baleen whales—the minke—was still hunted. The International Whaling Commission (IWC) had been unable to prevent this ecological disaster, and it is not difficult to understand why many people developed a deep distrust for the IWC and the whaling industry. Whaling came to epitomize growing environmental problems.

In their search for alternatives, and with the whales' symbolic potential as a starting point, whale society is portrayed as a world we, the human beings, have lost on our road to modernity. Whereas the whales have lived in peaceful coexistence with their surroundings for twenty-five million years or more, human beings have played havoc on the earth and lost their Paradise after only a fraction of that time. Rapid urbanization has been seen as leading to alienation and loss of purpose in life, to collapse of social networks, to soaring crime and divorce rates, and to the young increasingly turning to drugs. Our social skills have been undermined. In much of the argument about the peculiarities of whales we are presented precisely with the qualities that urban men and women seem to have lost, if we ever had them in the first place. According to Lyall Watson (1985: 48), 'our best-developed areas [of the brain] are those which deal with the elaboration of motor skills made possible by our hands, while cetaceans seem to concentrate on areas of social perception. Dolphins show marked development of those parts of the brain responsible for orientation, social skill, emotional self-control and perhaps even humour'.

With this perspective, their inability to manipulate nature through technology is no longer seen as a disadvantage but has become a virtue (Bryld and Lykke 2000: 202). Dobbs is among those who see the lack of hands as beneficial: '[Dolphins] have neither the stimulation nor the distraction of mechanical objects. This allows their higher thought processes greater freedom to develop what I call, for want of a better word, the spiritual aspects of their lives' (Dobbs 1992: 137–38). The dolphin cult then offers a powerful critique of technology—and materialism—made possible by human hands.

Closely related to this is the question of caring for each other. The superwhale is endowed with all the qualities we would like to see in our fellow humans: kindness, caring, playfulness. Whereas commercialization has penetrated most human relations, whales are depicted as the guardians of old values. They allegedly care for the sick and dying, while people in the urbanized Western world pay hospitals and old people's homes to take care of ageing relatives, thus removing the sick and dying from sight. Ours is a death-denying society (Lawrence 1989: 73). Moreover, the superwhales take care of each other's calves, babysit and run nurseries (Watson 1985: 41), without charging anything for these services. Not only do they care for their own kind, they allegedly come to rescue human beings. Men and women might also have behaved nobly, but that was in the past. Today money rules, and many people carry with them a nagging bad conscience; bad conscience for not taking care of ageing parents and for not giving children the attention they need.

Whether we have lost our social skills through rapid social change, or whether we have never been very clever in handling social relations, as implied by Watson (1985: 48), the message is the same; we are in these respects inferior to whales. We have something to learn, and whales are therefore used for didactic purposes, just as 'good' birds have been used to educate the children in bourgeois values (Löfgren 1985). The whales, and 'nice' birds, have become models for us to emulate. In Lévi-Strauss's terms, whale society has become a metaphor for the lost human paradise or utopian world, and caring for whales has become a metaphor for kindness, for being good. Encountering whales may generate private reflection on the quality of everyday life

We may have something to learn from the cetaceans. In order to communicate with these 'minds in water' (McIntyre 1974) and partake in their wisdom, Lilly, in the 1960s, started research on 'dolphinese' with grants from NASA. He envisioned a future in which dolphinariums have gone from being prisons to becoming 'interspecies schools, educating both dolphins and humans about one another' (Lilly 1978: 3). One direction this cooperation may take is joint scientific research (Lilly 1978: 121–28), where dolphins may conduct research on us.

Both Larry Niven's science fiction novel *World of Ptavvs* and David Brin's *Startide Rising* feature dolphin anthropologists.

For many whale enthusiasts, however, the main lesson we can learn from whales does not lie in the direction of science but in their profound wisdom about the meaning of life. In the words of Joan Ocean:[10] 'Our latest research involves merging our individual energy fields and our atomic structure with the harmonic frequencies of dolphin and whale sounds and sonar. Learning to make this simple shift, we meet many new aspects of our consciousness and our soul or life force. As the dolphins have taught us, it is by activating our golden, spiralling sphere of energy to create a field that aligns with the Universal rhythms that allows us to traverse many realms and interact with places and people outside of our present, known reality.'

The whale is not only a guide; to some people it is a messenger and saviour. The messages are sometimes rooted in the profound cetacean wisdom, but at times there seems to be a cosmic or divine mind outside both whales and human beings, if we are to believe the more spiritual aspects of the narrative. Dolphins may serve as instruments or mediums for a higher power. The dolphin takes on the character of a Messiah, a belief that perhaps has its origin in Douglas Adams's *The Hitchhiker's Guide to the Galaxy*, where the dolphins leave Earth after giving up on warning people about its impending destruction.

Personhood

Studying North American attitudes to animals, Stephen Kellert (1988: 160) found that the second most important factor in determining people's willingness to save endangered animals (the aesthetic being the most important) was phylogenetic relatedness to humans, i.e. 'the closer the biological relation of the endangered animal to human beings, the greater the likelihood for public support for the species'. Closeness and familiarity facilitate identification, but Milton finds whales unlikely candidates for human identification, as 'they are more like huge fish than mammals, they live in environment which many people fear, and, even today, relatively few westerners have seen a whale' (Milton 2002: 119). However, biological relations can be imagined, or constructed, as the Greenpeace advertisement 'Are whales "almost human"?', prepared to recruit more Australian sponsors, clearly shows.

In this plea for donations, an image of a superwhale is first drawn: the whale is intelligent, monogamous, lives in family groups, is gentle, sings and cries. Then this superwhale is anthropomorphized in several ways. First, terms normally used to describe human activities or situations are used for whales; e.g. *pregnancy* rather than *gestation*. Secondly, the fact that some whales may have a lifespan similar to humans', i.e. sixty-seventy years, has inspired Greenpeace to construct parallel life cycles for whales and humans, dividing whales into age-sets—such as the teens, puberty, maturity and old age–that are not even recognized in all human societies:

After 10 months of pregnancy, a whale is born. Mum cares for her calf closely until
its [sic] "teen-age".
  Puberty. The young whale plays with other young whales in rehearsal for choos-
ing a mate.
  Maturity. The whale finally chooses a partner for life.
  Old age. At around 50 or 70 years . . . the whale dies after a full and active life.

Meanwhile, in the quest to turn whales into humans biological facts are tampered
with. Most cetaceans do not live in stable partnerships; rather, they are promiscuous. Few live in 'family' groups, at least not as family is usually defined. The
intelligence of some of the species is also highly questionable. The conservative
Danish newspaper *Berlingske Tidende* refocuses the comparison between people
and cetaceans by stressing what makes humans dolphin-like (Uhrskov and Færch
1993: 6). Under the heading *Mennesket delfinens kusine* (The Human Being—The
Dolphin's Cousin), body parts are systematically compared to give credence to
Elaine Morgan's (1990) claim that humans are descended from an aquatic ape.
  The process of anthropomorphism goes on longer with whales than with most
other animals. They mate belly to belly, breastfeed their young and are depicted as
living in societies similar to our own, i.e. they live in families rather than in pods
(e.g. Myers 1997; Cousteau and Paccalet 1988: 191). What *Homo sapiens* is on
land, cetaceans are in the sea (Barstow 1991: 7). They are our brethren; they have
become the humans of the sea (Gylling-Nielsen 1987). In short, they think and
feel like humans (e.g. Nollman 1990). They are depicted as sentient individuals
with personhood. Milton points out that the criteria most often used in Western
discourse to represent personhood seems to be 'the capacity to act autonomously
and intentionally, the capacity for emotional experience, and moral worth' (Milton 2002: 27). Much of the focus has indeed been on the intelligence of whales,
their capacity to communicate abstract ideas, and their social behaviour. Milton
continues (2002: 119): 'What turned whales from relatively unknown animals
into persons were revelations about their complex family relationship, their intelligence and their system of communication.' As I have tried to indicate, however,
this image of an intelligent, family-oriented and communicative whale is contested and rests on a highly selective reading of evidence.
  I have so far focused on the superwhale as a conflation of traits found in a
number of different cetacean species. There is also a tendency in the opposite
direction. In order to bestow cetaceans with the capacity of autonomy and intentionality, they are also individualized in various ways. Some whales are given
names. The most famous is undoubtedly Moby-Dick, the white whale in Herman Melville's classic novel of 1851. Another famous cetacean is Flipper, who
actually is a composite of several dolphins performing different stunts. Originally
the name of a killer whale, Shamu has become a role model played by a number
of killer whales at SeaWorld in San Diego (California). By giving a succession of
whales the same name, an impression of continuity is created; any hints of illness

and death are thus suppressed and a long-lasting relationship between people and whales can be established. However, the most famous killer whale is probably Keiko, the star of the movie *Free Willy* and the target of the most extensive release operation ever undertaken.

Some wild whales are also individualized. Solitary dolphins that have accepted human company have been given names such as Jojo, Fungie, Donald, Opo, Percy, Simo, Horace, Dorah and Jean Louis. Most of the cetaceans offered in adoption programmes have also been given personal names, and genealogies are created to map their 'kinship' relations. Species in which individuals easily can be recognized by the shape of their fluke (humpback and sperm whales) or by their colour patterning (killer whales) are most popular in adoption and nonlethal research programmes because this makes it possible to follow these individual whales over time.

In a recent paper, anthropologist Adrian Peace (2005) has described how whales are individualized by whale watching organizers and guides, who interpret the behaviour of whales encountered in strongly anthropomorphized terms to the spectators. Moreover, they give individual whales characteristics such as especially good, smart, caring and playful, by which 'the whale assumes the status of a fully sentient, even socially complex, being . . . [and] assumes a range of human attributes, from having direction, motivation and purpose' (Peace 2005: 200). This enables whales and humans to respond in mutually and emotionally meaningful ways to each other (Peace 2005: 201). Identification with a particular whale, and not merely with a species, is thereby made possible—witness the tremendous interest in the fate of Keiko.

Milton argues that 'representations of personhood in terms of moral worth are particularly important in nature protection' (Milton 2002: 28). She further suggests that environmentalists (what she calls 'nature protectionists') relate to nature in two different ways: one assumes that nature is composed of personal agents [i.e. intentional beings] worthy of moral concern or respect, the other that it is composed of impersonal objects and mechanisms, i.e. resources for human use (Milton 2002: 23, 148). Whereas the latter implies a pragmatic or scientific approach to nature, the former is open to the full participation of emotions. The legitimacy of emotions in questions of resource management is, as we shall see in chapters to follow, highly contested by pro-whalers.

In this chapter we have seen that whales are animals that easily can be ascribed symbolic significance. Building on what seems to be an almost inborn susceptibility towards whales—at least partly caused by classificatory ambiguities, ideas about pure and salty water, and a feeling of awe or identification—an image of a superwhale has been created by combining features taken from a number of different cetacean species. The superwhale narrative has become a powerful social critique. By the circulation of carefully selected representations, this creature has been given high intelligence, great social skills and moral integrity. We shall see in Chapter 3 how the superwhale has been turned into a commodity of considerable value. Before we do so, however, we need to know more about the anti-whalers and locate their rhetoric according to discourses defined in the Introduction.

Notes

1. This does not mean that whales cannot be discriminated and individualized. Often they are, a theme I will return to towards the end of the chapter.

2. When I bring in additional and sometimes contradictory information, it is not necessarily to correct information but to indicate how important a role selectivity plays in representations.

3. In an international survey, between 65 and 70 per cent of the respondents in Australia, England, Germany and the United States believed wrongly that all large species of whales were endangered, as did 41 per cent in Norway and 50 per cent in Japan (Freeman and Kellert 1992).

4. In fact, the gray whale can be dangerous, and mature whales were therefore avoided by many indigenous hunters. It was known as a 'devil fish' (Dumond 1995: 58). Other whales have also been regarded as dangerous. By the late medieval period, fabulous tales of sea monsters had become dominant in much of Europe. For example, Erik Hansen Schönneböl had this to say about whales off his North-Norwegian domain Lofoten in 1575: 'About mid-summer, many large and terrifying kinds of whales . . . cause great damage in this part of the country; overturn and toss many large boats about, and swallow many people . . . It also happens often that [fishermen] manage to escape and reach the shore before the whale, only to die shortly because . . . their blood, gushing up their throats, chokes them to death in fear' (quoted in Lindbekk 1978: 322, my translation).

5. Alpers, whose book provides 'all the materials . . . for a new cult of dolphinolatry' (M.R. in a review in *The Observer*, 13 November 1960), does not believe that dolphins deliberately save people from drowning. Commenting that dolphins have been seen frenetically pushing a waterlogged mattress ashore, he seems to imply that it is part of dolphin's playfulness or, perhaps, an inborn instinct made necessary to push their own infants up for air (Alpers 1960: 72). His doubts are usually ignored by other dolphin lovers, and to Cochrane and Callen, who otherwise borrow liberally from his book, Alpers becomes a cynic (1992: 66). Carol J. Howard, on the other hand, shares the doubts about dolphins' intentionality: 'Nobody talks about how many people the dolphins push back out to sea' (1995: 270). There are, however, some reported cases of unhelpful dolphins (Klinowska 1992: 33; see below).

6. That actual whale behaviour may fall far short of this idealized picture is generally ignored. Both male and female dolphins might be highly promiscuous, and they 'have incredible active sex lives. They masturbate from an early age and pursue promiscuous homosexual and heterosexual contacts that seem to be purely social' (Odent 1990: 63). Gangs of males may rape females and harass them into submission (Booth 1989; Winton 1992: 18). They may sexually assault human beings, showing a preference for women. Facing such charges, 'dolphin enthusiasts insist that there is little sensuality in its [penis] use; they point out that because the dolphin has no hands, its penis acts as a useful instrument and as a sensory device' (Hatt 1990: 252).

7. Whales held in captivity are sometimes pictured as dangerous by whale protectionists, implying that they are dangerous because they are not allowed to live naturally (e. g. Williams 2001). Similarly, when stories are told about dolphins killing their young or smaller species (Ross and Wilson 1996), human destruction of their habitat might be blamed.

8. Former Vice President of the United States Hubert Humphrey partook in such speculations when he quoted the Russian dolphinologist Yabalkov at the 1970 U.S. Senate hearings on the Marine Mammal Protection Act: 'Dolphin society are extraordinarily complex, and up to ten generations coexist at one time. If that was the case with man, Leonardo da Vinci, Faraday, and Einstein would still be alive . . . Could not the dolphin's brain contain an amount of

information comparable in volume to the thousands of tons of books in our libraries?' (quoted in Williams 1988: 179).

9. That water is widely used for purification hardly needs documentation, but it is less widely known that salt is used in rituals throughout the world. Salt removes pollution inflicted by death in Buddhist traditions and is seen as an important purifying agent in Shinto. In India a gift of salt symbolizes good luck, whereas to spill a bowl of salt is a bad omen in Christian societies. Jesus called his disciples 'the Salt of the Earth', and salt was widely used in Greek and Jewish rituals (http: //www.saltworks.us/salt_info/si _HistoryOfSalt.asp, retrieved 15 February 2008). Salt figures also in neopaganism, witchcraft and New Age beliefs (www.luckymojo.com /salt.html, retrieved 15 February 2008).

10. Retrieved 12 April 2008 from www.joanocean.com/Human-do.html.

Chapter 2

The Whale Protectionists

In the previous chapter we saw that cetaceans have great potential as symbols to people in widely dispersed cultures, both ancient and contemporary. Whale protectionists and media have skilfully played on our susceptibility towards cetaceans and created an image of a superwhale by lumping together traits found in a number of species, thereby masking the great variety that exists in size, behaviour and abundance between the almost eighty species of cetaceans.

The superwhale, with all its cetacean and human qualities, has proved to have enormous economic and political potential. In the anti-whaling discourse whales have come to play the role of a metonym for nature, and the image of the 'whale has become the emblematic animal for the entire ecological movement' (Day 1991: 68). The whaling issue has become a symbol to the environmental and animal welfare/rights movements. 'Saving whales is for millions of people a crucial test of their political ability to halt environmental destruction', writes Holt (1985: 192). If we cannot save whales, then what else can we save? In this chapter we shall take a closer look at organizations working for the protection of cetaceans and analyse their interests and rhetoric before we move on to the next chapter to analyse the strategies they pursue in order to bring an end to 'consumptive utilization' of these animals.

Who They Are

The environmental and animal welfare/rights movements saw explosive growth after 1960 and particularly during the 1980s, and the whaling issue was a major contribution to this expansion. Greenpeace was among the most successful organizations, and its income in the UK alone climbed from £175,000 in 1980 to £ 4.5 million nine years later (Anderson 1993: 56). Other NGOs had similar growth, and a dedication to 'saving the whale' was a common feature to many of them. Today there are hundreds of national and international NGOs campaigning against whaling, and close to one hundred attend the annual IWC meetings as observers. This figure includes a great variety of NGOs. Organizations like Project Jonah, the American Cetacean Society (ACS), the Cetacean Society International (CSI), the Whale and Dolphin Conservation Society (WDCS) and the Whale Fund are single-purpose groups that aim specifically to protect cetaceans, while others—e.g. Greenpeace, the World Wide Fund for Nature (aka the World Wildlife Fund, WWF) and the International Fund for Animal Welfare (IFAW)—are more general in coverage but nevertheless have earned substantial parts of their incomes from sea mammal campaigns.

People are attracted to the save-the-whale cause for a number of reasons, and this is clearly reflected in the great differences in focus, ideology and policy of the many anti-whaling organizations. Judging from their own rhetoric they seem to fall within three main groups. Environmental organizations are genuinely concerned with biodiversity and see themselves fighting against depletion of whale stocks. Animal welfare and rights organizations are more concerned with the well-being and rights of individual animals, whereas a third group of organizations are mostly concerned with interspecies communication and our relationship with spiritual beings. There are also considerable differences in their strategies, which run from violence to political lobbying, letter writing and seminars. It is impossible to introduce all the organizations that work in one way or another to save whales, and only some of the most active and influential organizations will be presented here.

With its royal patronage and close ties with the World Conservation Union (IUCN) and the United Nations Environmental Programme (UNEP), the WWF has acquired considerable international standing with millions of supporters. In 2006 the WWF-Network had an income of 704.5 million Swiss francs (about US$ 550 million) with a surplus close to 100 million francs (US$ 77 million) (WWF 2007: 16). It runs a number of conservation projects around the world and in many ways continues the approach of the first-generation conservationists (e.g. Sierra Club, Audubon Society and Royal Society for the Protection of Birds). The WWF can be considered a typical reformist organization aiming at ecosystem conservation without seriously challenging the political system. Controlled trophy hunting as well as tourism may be seen to foster its objective, but the WWF has also been one of the strongest proponents of national parks, sanctuaries and wildlife protection throughout the world, often against the interests of local peoples (e.g. Bonner 1994; Igoe 2003). It has usually concerned itself not with people's quality of life but with the protection of biodiversity and habitats. However, during the 1980s, when sustainable development became a new buzzword, particularly within reformist environmentalism, some mainstream conservation groups like the WWF became more attentive to human needs (Princen 1994: 46). The report *Caring for the Earth: A Strategy for Sustainable Living* (IUCN et al. 1991), co-authored by the WWF, thus argues forcefully for local participation in resource management. However, in its position paper on whaling the WWF makes an exception for cetaceans (WWF 1992), and the organization has taken a high profile in the anti-whaling campaign. Whales are perceived as 'flagship species',[1] and according to WWF President Kathryn Fuller (1995), 'whales are for watching. We oppose commercial whaling because whales have an intrinsic value as mammals of great intelligence, whose behaviour and language set them apart'.

With the perhaps naïve assumption that there is a simple relationship between people's perceptions and their actions, the WWF has put much effort into educating people about what the organization sees as right values. As early as the 1960s, the WWF sponsored recordings of whale songs, and it has organized programmes for whale watching as well as whale adoption—all activities that the WWF sees as strategies to educate people to a more anti-whaling position. The WWF has for the same reason taken an interest in religion. To celebrate its twenty-fifth anniversary, for example, the WWF invited representatives from Buddhism, Christianity, Hinduism, Islam and Judaism to a meeting in Assisi to discuss their possible contribution to sustainable development (WWF 1986). With this the WWF embraced the 'religious environmentalist paradigm'—postulating a close relationship between religious beliefs and environmental behaviour (Pedersen 1995; Kalland 2005)—and has thereby partly legitimized spiritual ecology.

The NGO that has been most closely associated with the anti-whaling campaign is Greenpeace. It has taken a radical approach to environmental problems and stages dramatic actions against pollution and degradation of the human environment, but unlike the WWF it has not run any development projects. It started in 1970 as a small Canadian group of activists protesting U.S. nuclear tests at the Aleutian island of Amchitka, but soon turned to the protection of marine mammals. It did not itself initiate the campaigns against sealing and whaling, but it was innovative in its strategies for bringing these issues to the masses. Established by journalists like Robert Hunter of the Vancouver *Sun* and Ben Metcalfe of CBC, Greenpeace has always been clever at getting media attention. By way of the media Greenpeace has become an important source of information and is to some extent able to define the problem and frame the debate (Anderson 1993; Hansen 1993).

Greenpeace has always claimed that it is fighting commercial sealing and whaling for ecological reasons, but since its early years Greenpeace leaders have been inclined towards spiritual ecology and animal welfare/rights. One of the founders wrote that 'we must seriously begin to inquire into the rights of rabbits and turnips, the rights of soil and swamp, the rights of the atmosphere, and ultimately, the rights of the planet' (Hunter 1979: x). Several of the early leaders had a very special relationship with whales. Paul Spong and Robert Hunter organized a call-in for whales, where hundreds of people gathered on a beach in California to telepathically call whales from all corners of the world (Pearce 1991: 22). They brought musical instruments with which to serenade the whales during their interception of Soviet whaling in the Pacific (Yearley 1991: 69). Another early Greenpeace leader, Patrick Moore, who had a PhD in ecology, did not want to reduce the whaling issue to a question of sustainability: 'The general public is not going to understand the science of ecology, so to get them to save the whale you have to get them to believe that whales are good' (quoted in Pearce 1991: 27).

Greenpeace is eclectic in its arguments and has been termed both an animal welfare (Davies in Mowat 1990: 157) and animal rights (Herscovici 1985: 22) organization. Whalers—and most sealers—view Greenpeace as one of the most fanatic animal rights organizations. If we are to place Greenpeace within the framework proposed in the Introduction to this volume, however, it comes closer to Dobson's ecologism, trying to integrate social justice with sustainable living, seeing both social and environmental problems as consequences of industrialization and the capitalist mode of production. But the organization shows strong tendencies towards an animal rights position when it comes to especially charismatic fauna like whales, seals and kangaroos.

Greenpeace is among the world's leading environmental groups. In 1994 it had more than six million supporters, employed more than 1,000 full-time and hundreds of part-time staff, and operated a fleet of eight ships (Wapner 1996: 47). However, since then the organization has lost more than half its supporters and much of its financial strength, though it still had an income of about € 170 million in 2005 (Greenpeace-International 2006). About 25 per cent was spent on fundraising, down from 39 per cent in 1995. There was some very critical press coverage by the early 1990s (Fox 1991; Schwarz 1991; Spencer, Bollwerk and Morais 1991), and loss of credibility related to the oil rig *Brent Spar* in 1995 had a further negative impact on the organization. But although Greenpeace has experienced setbacks, it is still among the biggest of the environmental NGOs and has an issue ownership (Ansolabehere and Iyengar 1994) of whaling, a position that has given it easy access to the media and considerable authority and legitimacy.

Paul Watson, a Canadian and one of the cofounders of Greenpeace, embarked on a crusade against whalers and sealers in what he envisioned as the Third World War (Gabriel 1991: 56). In 1975 he fought sealers on the ice floes off the coasts of Newfoundland as well as Russian whalers in the North Pacific. In 1977 he was expelled from Greenpeace because of his militancy, but he has continued his fight through his Sea Shepherd Conservation Society, based in Seattle. Sea Shepherd was to become 'the navy of Mother Earth'—with Earth First! serving as Mother Earth's army (Manes 1990: 111). Watson has made 'ecotage' his trademark. He openly brags about the sinking of whaling and fishing vessels, and has promised to pay a US$ 10,000 reward to anybody who sinks a whaling ship (Sea Shepherd n.d.). Countries have asked for his extradition, but U.S. authorities have taken what many people perceive as an international terrorist under their protective wing. His behaviour has nevertheless reduced his credibility, and both he and his organization have been ousted from the IWC. Despite this fact, Sea Shepherd claims that '[t]he Society has official observer status at IWC meetings' and that it is 'operating as an unofficial policing arm of the Commission' (Sea Shepherd n.d.).

Figure 2.1   *Sea Shepherd intercepting Japanese research whaling.*
(courtesy by Institute of Cetacean Research, Tokyo)

Among the NGOs that focus more narrowly on cetaceans is the U.K.-based Whale and Dolphin Conservation Society (WDCS). The WDCS claims to be 'the world's most active charity dedicated to the conservation and welfare of all whales, dolphins and porpoises'.[2] Although it is a one-issue organization in that it is solely dedicated to saving cetaceans, it is broad in its approach. The WDCS runs campaigns against all kinds of whale and dolphin killing—'Dress it up how you like—whaling is murder and murder is wrong'.[3] The organization is also against keeping cetaceans in captivity, swim-with-whales programmes, habitat loss and other perceived environmental changes harmful to the whales (e.g. depletion of the ozone layer, emission of greenhouse gases, pollution of the oceans by chemicals and noise). The WDCS lobbies politicians, 'educates' the public through glossy journals and other publications, and runs whale watching tours, whale adoption programmes and whale rescue operations. Among the WDCS's claimed successes are the development of whale watching as a viable economic alternative to whaling, the exposure of 'gangs of whale meat smugglers', the creation of a whale sanctuary in Mexico, saving 'the life of thousands of trapped and stranded whales, dolphins and porpoises' and ending the hunt of killer whales around Iceland for sale to aquariums.[4] Its credibility with the media and the public is largely confined to the U.K., although it now has offices in several countries.

In its campaigns to put an end to Faroese pilot whaling, the WDCS has collaborated closely with the more radical International Fund for Animal Welfare

(IFAW) and Environmental Investigation Agency (EIA). IFAW was founded by Brian Davies, a Canadian who first became involved in animal welfare when he had to bring a badly injured dog hit by a car to hospital, an experience that brought him into the New Brunswick Society for the Prevention of Cruelty to Animals (SPCA). In 1965 he became captivated by seals, 'one of the loveliest creatures God ever created' (Davies 1990: 9), and he made the New Brunswick SPCA one of the main organizations involved in the anti-sealing campaign. However, when the SPCA decided to drop the campaign upon concluding that the hunt was conducted humanely, Davies left to establish IFAW in 1969 (Herscovici 1985: 22).

Today IFAW claims to be among the world's biggest animal welfare organizations with some two million contributors.[5] IFAW runs a number of campaigns, of which the one against sealing remains important. 'We are totally committed to protection of seals. Other than that, we are opportunistic' (Davies in Mowat 1990: 164).[6] However, of expenses close to US$ 90 million in 2006, IFAW spent 22.3 per cent on the whaling issue, with sealing coming in second place with 21.5 per cent (IFAW 2006). It was in 1979 that IFAW went into the anti-whaling business by sending 'a survey team to the Indian Ocean and later placed the IFAW plane at the disposal of whale conservationists' (Davies 1990: 144). Davies has taken a special interest in the Faroe pilot whaling, and the organization has gained a certain ownership of this issue in addition to the one on sealing.

Davies' original strategy was to bring people—foremost the media and celebrities like Brigitte Bardot—to the ice in order to attract maximum media coverage. The seal hunt was 'a media event that was particularly attractive to television. The blood on ice, the dark-clothed men swinging clubs. It had all the elements of a continuing allegory of man against nature, of good and evil' (quoted in Mowat 1990: 150). This strategy met with mixed success until Davies took the issue directly to Brussels in 1983 in a successful attempt to close the EU market for seal pelts. Davies proved to be an efficient lobbyist, attracting several politicians to his course. In 1996 the press could disclose that the British Labour Party had received one million pounds from IFAW, the largest single donation the party has received from an external source (Wintour and Calvert 1996). At least one EU parliamentarian has served as a special adviser to IFAW, and several scientists have been on IFAW's payroll. Another important strategy employed by IFAW is consumer boycotts. First used together with Greenpeace against Canadian fish products during the anti-sealing campaigns, IFAW has launched several boycott campaigns against the Faroe Islands to protest that country's pilot whaling, an activity that has particularly infuriated Davies.

The Environmental Investigation Agency (EIA) is another NGO that has run a series of high-profile boycott campaigns against the Faroe Islands (Day 1992: 25). The EIA—founded by Allan Thornton, a Canadian and former Greenpeacer—sees itself as 'the animal detective' and 'undercover investigator' who 'at great personal risk . . . has won many victories on behalf of endangered species'.[7] Apart from its work on behalf of the African elephant, the EIA has taken a special interest in small cetaceans—or 'the forgotten whales'—and focuses particularly on what it perceives as a 'global war against small cetaceans'.

A number of North American organizations work for the welfare of animals in general and the protection of whales in particular, operating on a spectrum between reformist animal welfare organizations that are concerned with pain and the more radical animal rights advocates. Established in 1951, the Animal Welfare Institute (AWI) was one of the first organizations to launch a 'Save the Whales' campaign back in 1971. It still has a certain grip on the anti-whaling campaign. AWI is in many ways similar to the Humane Society of the United States (HSUS). Besides being active against whaling, both organizations are opposed to swim-with-whales programmes (even as a therapeutic means) and to keeping cetaceans in captivity. They have also been active in the campaigns for 'dolphin-safe' tuna and bringing the killer whale Keiko 'home' to Iceland. The Cetacean Society International (CSI) has been engaged in the same campaigns. Focusing more narrowly on cetaceans, the CSI has a position in the United States that the WDCS has in the United Kingdom. The aim of the CSI is to eliminate all activities harmful to whales.[8] In 1983 its director, Robbins Barstow, took the initiative to 'Whale Alive', a global conference on nonconsumptive utilization of whales (Day 1992: 189).

The Earth Island Institute (EII) is both broader and more radical in its approach. Based in San Francisco, it was established in 1982 by the late David Brower, one of the leading radicals within the New Environmentalism. In 1969 he was expelled from the Sierra Club because of this radicalism, and later he was also ousted from Friends of the Earth (FoE), an organization he himself had founded. The EII mostly depends on grants from private foundations and public funds. Like the WWF, the EII runs a number of conservation projects around the world but has also run projects built on the ideology of environmental justice. The objective of its International Marine Mammal Project dovetails with those of AWI, HSUS and CSI. The EII expresses pride in having initiated the 'successful' rehabilitation of Keiko, whereas the HSUS claims to have been among the project's architects. The EII, together with some other North American NGOs, has recently campaigned against the U.S. Navy testing powerful low-frequency active sonar systems, believed to have killed many whales off Greece and the Bahamas.[9] Despite the concern of the IWC, in October 2004 the navy's permission to emit the noise was extended for another two-year period.

The more moderate American Cetacean Society (ACS) seems to avoid direct actions. The ACS claims to be the oldest organization directed solely towards the protection of whales, and since its establishment in 1967 it has used whale tourism, public lectures and educational materials to get people turn their backs on whaling and dolphin shows. The ACS values scientific research highly and looks upon itself as a mediator between researchers and the public; the organization sponsors research and organizes international conferences. The aim, however, is not science per se but protection of cetaceans. The ACS selects and interprets research findings to suit its own purpose, which is clearly mirrored in the themes of the conferences.[10]

Finally, some words should be said about the many more or less loosely structured organizations—many are little more than private websites—devoted to cetacean spirituality and inspired by the New Age.[11] Some of these organizations claim to conduct research and to be fighting for the rights of marine mammals, but the majority maintain a low profile in campaigns against consumptive utilization of whales. The aim of several of these groups is personal development, and many of their meetings resemble religious ceremonies (Servais 2005). What they share is a spiritual orientation towards cetaceans, and together they are important actors in fostering a new human-cetacean relationship.

A Multifaceted Movement

The anti-whaling organizations vary considerably in their structure, ideologies, focuses and strategies. The WWF and Greenpeace illustrate this clearly. Both can be said to have acquired issue ownership (Ansolabehere and Iyengar 1994) of the whaling issue, a position that gives them a considerable degree of authority and legitimacy with easy access to the media. They are to a great extent able to define the agenda and lay the premises for how the issue is to be interpreted and pursued, and they are invited to appear as experts and commentators in the media. Issue ownership is important symbolic capital to bring to other issues and arenas; such a position enables them to put forward issues 'almost irrespective of how real the threat is' (Yearley 1991: 73). Whereas Greenpeace and the WWF hold issue ownerships of whaling in general (see Hansen 1993 for the case of Greenpeace), other organizations may have ownership of certain, more limited issues related to whales and whaling, enjoy a more local or regional ownership or have become associated with particular strategies. The WDCS, for example, has such a position within the U.K., whereas the EIA's ownership is more limited to small cetaceans. The EII has obtained an ownership position for the issue of dolphin-safe tuna and the HSUS has done the same for the issue of dolphin therapy.

Both the WWF and Greenpeace can, according to their general ideology, be classified as environmental organizations. Despite their ecological orientation, however, when it comes to whaling both organizations have, as we will see below, in fact switched to a more animal welfare/rights position while still trying to argue from an ecological position. But there are also important differences between the two NGOs. The WWF represents the mainstream conservation orientation: it is reformist and does not question central cultural values. It aims to save threatened wildlife, working for the perpetuation of species and preservation of natural landscapes. It is an insider (Cracknell 1993: 15) that has close and regular contact with bureaucracy, receives considerable public funds and may undertake some commissioned work for government departments. Its main strategies are lobbying, education and conservation/preservation projects.

Greenpeace, on the other hand, is a typical representative of the New Environmental movement: it is more orientated towards ecologism and is in general more concerned with pollution and life quality in modern society. Greenpeace has long been associated with daring stunts, direct mail and consumer boycotts. It is an outsider that tends to resist being coopted by bureaucracy; the ability to see the other point of view is perceived as a threat to one's commitment to the cause (Hunter 1979, in Milton 1993: 7). It is therefore more dependent on membership dues, gifts and sales of merchandise.

It is not easy to locate anti-whaling NGOs according to the four discourses defined in the Introduction. In their arguments against commercial whaling they all use statements from both environmental and animal welfare/rights discourses. However, on other issues they are more divided. Greenpeace and the WWF are not engaged in campaigns against dolphinariums or swim-with-dolphin programmes, but leave these issues to NGOs that are motivated first and foremost by animal welfare and rights concerns, such as AWI, CSI, HSUS and WDCS. These organizations are also against the Makah gray whale hunt and strong supporters of the 'dolphin-safe' tuna label. In the latter case Greenpeace deserted the no-tolerance position and accepted that the U.S. tuna fleet annually can take a few thousand dolphins as by-catch and still sell the tuna as dolphin-safe. Other NGOs are more difficult to define. The EII has many environmental projects but must be classified as an animal rights organization when it comes to cetaceans. IFAW has tried to promote itself both as a leading animal welfare organization and as an environmental NGO, but the IUCN, a kind of umbrella organization to government agencies and environmental NGOs, has on several occasions denied IFAW membership because it does not consider IFAW to be an environmental organization. Sea Shepherd is in a similar position. Of the NGOs introduced here, Greenpeace and the WWF are those most clearly motivated by environmental concerns. Nonetheless, whalers see these two organizations as their main adversaries. One reason for this is obviously their power and influence. However, there is also frustration over what looks like lost opportunities. The potential field of common interest between people making a living from the sea and particularly Greenpeace is extensive, but tapping it is impossible in the present situation.

Leadership and Membership

There are considerable differences in leadership style between the groups. In general they have a reputation for secrecy, and it is often difficult to get reliable information from the groups themselves (Herscovici 1985: 110–11; Dunlop and Mertig 1992). They also tend to be heavily top-down structured, with significant grassroots influence in only a minority of the NGOs (Dalton 1994: 105). Small NGOs are often run by their founders, who may single-handedly determine their goals and policies while volunteers mostly 'perform maintenance functions'

(Dalton 1994: 97). But large organizations too may lack democratic decision-making processes. In his study of environmental NGOs in Western Europe, Russell J. Dalton found that over time NGOs tend to develop highly centralized oligarchies (Dalton 1994: 100).

Greenpeace is a case in point. It soon developed into an organization with what the Danish daily *Politiken* called a 'Leninist' leadership structure (Vilstrup 1991: 8). Of 700,000 German members around 1990, only thirty were entitled to elect the seven board members (Schwarz 1991: 88–89), while in Sweden only eleven of the 150,000 paying members had the right to vote (Eyerman and Jamison 1989: 106). The organization's hierarchical structure is also visible in how it handles media: unlike the more open Friends of the Earth, Greenpeace has a centralized press office, and only authorized representatives are allowed to answer questions from the media (Anderson 1993: 56; Hansen 1993: 168) Greenpeace, like many of the anti-whaling groups, is centrally controlled, and members are mere financial sponsors without any other role to play (Dalton 1994: 107).

Few environmental and animal welfare/rights organizations give democratic decision-making processes high priority. On the contrary, Brian Davies of IFAW, for example, argues that there is no use for grassroots decision-making because there is no time to waste on democracy (Herscovici 1985: 77). This view is not surprising, given the anti-humanist and misanthropic inclination of much environmentalist and animal rights writing. When humans are seen as a destructive species out of control (Franklin 1999: 3), authoritarian measures are easily called for. This is most clearly seen in militant groups like Sea Shepherd, Earth First! and the Animal Liberation Front, all of which act as self-proclaimed representatives for nature. Scholars (e.g. Hardin 1972; Heilbroner 1991) have also contributed to legitimizing authoritarian regimes, and several philosophers have pointed out the totalitarian tendency of deep ecology (e.g. Ferry 1995; Anker 2002).

On the other hand, the lack of democratic decision-making processes may look surprising because of the social background of leaders and supporters of the environment and animal welfare/rights movements: they tend to be recruited from the same social strata as political liberals. A study from Western Europe, for example, showed that the environmental movement attracted better-than-average educated people from the middle class, and that there were particularly many 'from professions that specialize in the creation and application of information and symbols: scientists, teachers, journalists, and public administrators' (Dalton 1994: 118). This background gives them both potential organizational skills and familiarity with the manipulation of political symbols (1994: 132). Adrian Franklin, following the work of Savage et al. (1992), suggests that two lifestyle groups make up much of the support for animal rights: the 'trend-setting ascetic aesthetes' and the 'postmoderns'. Both are well educated, but whereas the ascetic aesthetes are relatively low-paid workers in the public sector (in government, health and education, in particular), the postmoderns are characteristically 'affluent professionals working particular in media, design and creative areas'

(Franklin 1999: 190). Their different lifestyles correlate with how they relate to nature. The ascetic aesthetes dominate as birdwatchers, wildlife photographers, members of vegetarian organizations and hunt saboteurs, while the postmoderns are more inclined to go whale watching and visit theme parks (1999: 90). Susan Davis substantiates this observation in her study of SeaWorld in San Diego. The visitors are mostly white, upper-middle-class college graduates; only 11 per cent were classified as 'non-Anglo ' in 1992 (Davis 1997:36). As a group they differ from the customers of other theme parks in California (e.g. Disneyland and Six Flags-Magic Mountain), which attract many more people of colour, but they are similar to the social background of visitors to national parks (Davis 1997: 36–38). Dalton interprets the lack of grassroots democracy to mean that supporters accept professionalization and centralization in the name of efficiency (Dalton 1994: 100). Another reason, as suggested by Franklin (1999: 189), can be that the supporters of the movements are motivated by sentiments and emotions rather than by ethical arguments and idealism.

Linkages between Groups

Environmentalists and animal welfare/rights groups compete in many ways for media attention, access to politicians, funds and support. Success for one group may imply a loss for a competitor. Greenpeace and Sea Shepherd have quarrelled over who should be credited with boarding a whaling vessel in Norway (press releases from the organizations, 2 June 1993), for ecotage in Iki, Japan, in 1982 (Scarce 1990: 105) and for daring protests against Soviet whaling on the Chukchi Peninsula (Scarce 1990: 103; Day 1992). The EIA has accused Sea Shepherd of destroying a boycott campaign against the Faroe Islands (Pearce 1991: 31), and there have been quarrels on the beaches of Australia over who should receive credit for rescuing stranded whales. There are disagreements among NGOs over the status of indigenous whaling and over the tuna fishery. Organizations have broken up over ideological as well as strategic disagreements.

But the NGOs also collaborate closely on many issues and support each other's campaigns financially and in other ways. NGOs have established a number of international forums: rather than competing for market shares, they have realized that the situation is a win-win one. They can—at least to a certain point—benefit from collaborating by enlarging the pie. Dalton (1994: 246–47) points out that the most effective movements are those composed of a diverse array of groups with a variety of styles that enable different groups to develop alliances with a wide network of other interest groups and public institutions. Hence, there might be tactical advantages in having a movement apparently fragmented into a large number of groups with different structural set-ups, focuses, ideologies and strategies. This does not mean that all the groups endorse everything said and done; rather, they all have their separate agendas and generally agree to under-communicate where they happen to disagree.

Anti-whaling NGOs cooperate in a number of ways, particularly during the annual IWC meetings when they lobby together, stage joint press conferences and jointly publish the newssheet *ECO*. In 1990 more than sixty national and international organizations formed the Global Cetacean Coalition, which committed itself to making the moratorium permanent and to extending the IWC's competence to cover the management of all cetacean species (Iwasaki-Goodman 1994: 218–19). Moreover, there are often close linkages between the militant organizations and the more moderate ones in terms of both funds and personnel. The moderate organizations may even pay others to do the dirty work. The WWF, with its non-militant approach, has supported militant groups, for example in the late 1970s when it helped Greenpeace set up offices in European countries, provided capital for the organization's first ship and funded its mission to protest against whaling in Iceland (Brown and May 1991: 54; Pearce 1991: 22–24; Dalton 1994: 169). Greenpeace also got financial support from Friends of the Earth to establish its London and Paris offices (Dalton 1994: 40). Thus the WWF has funded other NGOs to do what its own sponsors within the UN and royal families would have considered too militant for the WWF to take upon itself. Moreover, the WWF has, together with other anti-whaling NGOs, funded payments of national commissioners and delegations to the IWC in order to bring about the moratorium on commercial whaling (Chapter 4). Greenpeace in turn has given financial support to the even more militant Earth First! in the United States (Taylor 1991). In a similar vein, the Royal Society for the Prevention of Cruelty to Animals (RSPCA) sponsored the outfitting of the *Sea Shepherd*, the ship used by Paul Watson to ram the whaling ship *Sierra* in 1979 (Manes 1990: 109).

Kay Milton (1996: 210) has observed that '[militant activities] make the more moderate environmental groups seem all the more reasonable, and create a better chance of negotiating some kind of advance for environmental protection'. According to its founder, Dave Foreman, Earth First! was established exactly because 'there was a need for a radical wing that makes the Sierra Club look moderate' (quoted in Manes 1990: 70; see also Cracknell 1993: 18). In fact, the militant organizations enable less militant ones to take a *stronger* position than before (Tokar 1988: 33) while still looking moderate. One should therefore not be too rash to claim that ecotage always is counterproductive, as Rothenberg has done (1995).

There is also a flow of personnel within the anti-whaling movement. Some have created their own organizations after a career in older ones. Some were forced out, like Paul Watson, who established Sea Shepherd when he was expelled from Greenpeace, and David Brower, who formed the Friends of the Earth (FoE) when he was ousted from the Sierra Club and then the Earth Island Institute when he was forced to leave FoE. Stephen Best established the more uncompromising International Wildlife Coalition when he fell out with IFAW's Brian Davies, and Allan Thornton had a past in Greenpeace before he established the

EIA. Whereas these entrepreneurs left to establish more radical groups, movement from radical to more conservative organizations seems to be more common in European NGOs, according to Dalton (1994: 121).

What They Say: The Hegemonic Discourse on Whaling

I suggested in the Introduction that the arguments against whaling could be placed within four main discourses according to whether they are based on environmental or animal welfare/rights arguments. In 1972, when the proposal for a moratorium on whaling was first suggested at the United Nations Conference on the Human Environment in Stockholm, the justification was phrased in ecological terms. The right and bowhead whales had been endangered since the nineteenth century, and the humpback and blue whales met the same fate in the following century. Some other species had been reduced dramatically despite the IWC's attempts to manage them in a sustainable way. Perhaps even more disturbing, several of the species did not show any sign of recovery even after they were protected. Environmental considerations and the precautionary principle therefore won the day when in 1982 the IWC voted for a moratorium—or 'zero catch limits' as the official term has it—on whaling for commercial purposes. The majority argued that the moratorium, which was to be reconsidered in 1990 at the latest, was necessary until better population estimates and a new management model (the Revised Management Procedure, RMP) were available.

Since the moratorium went into effect in 1987, the IWC's Scientific Committee has concluded that several whale stocks can be exploited sustainably. The northeastern Pacific gray whale has fully recovered and has been removed from the endangered list, and the Antarctic stocks of minke whale that Japan wants to exploit have been estimated at 761,000 animals, a tally assumed to be well above the original level.[12] This assumption is, as we later will see, of paramount importance to the Japanese perspective. The two stocks of minke whales exploited by Norway—the northeastern Atlantic and central North Atlantic stocks with a combined estimated abundance of 174,000 animals—are both regarded as healthy. The North Atlantic stock of fin whales, estimated at 30,000, is also able to sustain a regulated annual catch. At the same time scientists developed the RMP, which became the most sophisticated management tool ever devised for any marine exploitation. The Scientific Committee adopted the RMP in 1992. The conditions for reevaluating the moratorium were therefore met, but so far (as of January 2009) the IWC has failed to follow its own decision from 1982.

From Ecology to Whale Rights

Whale protectionists have reacted to these developments since the early 1990s in various ways. It seems to be easier for the animal and whale rights advocates than for environmentalists to accept the new estimates of whale populations, since the arguments of the animal welfare and rights groups are not based on ecological considerations but on the ethics of killing. Their arguments are not endangered by higher whale population figures or better management tools. Thus the president of the Cetacean Society International (CSI) could write that 'the science is now on [the whalers'] side. We can't even talk about extinction. Our arguments now focus on ethical, aesthetic, and moral reasons for the protection of the individual whale, not the population or the species' (Shields 1992: 2).

The moral/ethical arguments against whaling follow mainly two lines, based on animal welfare and animal rights, respectively. According to the former, the hunt should be made illegal if pain is inflicted upon the animal; according to the latter, whaling should be stopped because the animals have intrinsic value. We saw in the Introduction that an important premise in the welfare discourse is the animal's ability to feel pain, something cetaceans undoubtedly possess. It is furthermore claimed that whales can suffer indirectly when individual animals are killed and close social relations are interrupted. These experiences are believed to be particularly traumatic if close ties—as between cow and calf or between mates in monogamous relations—are broken (Frøvik 1995: 60–61). Moreover, whalers may shoot 'key individuals in the maintenance and transmission of cultural traditions . . . [which] could therefore affect the cultural integrity of the community' (Wilson and Jordan n.d.: 14). Also considered morally perverse is hunting 'animals that do not flee, and killing animals who approach to play' (n.d.: 6). Having no natural enemies, whales are said to be poorly equipped physiologically and mentally to cope with such dangers, making the hunt unfair (n.d.: 6).[13]

The IWC has established the Humane Killing Working Group to review killing methods and to discuss to what extent suffering is inflicted upon animals during the chase and subsequent killing in an attempt to make the hunt more humane. It is impossible to achieve instant death in all cases, and, as is true of all kinds of hunting activities, pain will inevitably be inflicted on some of the animals (Barzdo 1981; Gillespie 1997). But how do we quantify animal suffering, and how much pain is acceptable before the hunt is deemed inhumane? Many people will answer that any form of suffering is unacceptable, at least insofar as the whaling activities are deemed unnecessary from a perspective of physical survival (see Singer 1978). This is the view of the Australian IWC commissioner and former IWC chairman P. Bridgewater, who in an interview said that there was no need to catch 'extremely large and beautiful animals' when meat can be obtained in simpler and cheaper ways (Denmark Radio 1991). This comment fell at a time when Australia was launching a major drive to bolster beef exports; by the mid 1990s Japan had emerged as the main market for Australian beef (Epstein 2005: 223).

Neither is there much need for other whale products, as good substitutes have been developed. Some environmental and animal welfare organizations nonetheless accept that some indigenous peoples have nourishing, cultural and social needs to hunt whales, whereas these same NGOs use the general wealth as an argument against whaling in the Faroe Islands, Iceland, Japan and Norway.

Animal rights advocates argue that it is wrong to use the pain argument because only rights can secure total protection in the future (Gillespie 1997). Whales shall not be utilized in any way: 'Just as whales are not here for us to kill for our purposes, so they are not here for us "to study", or "to watch", or "to play with"' (Jamieson and Regan 1985). Many have voiced the opinion that whales have rights because they are special. During a preparatory meeting for the 1992 UNCED conference in Rio de Janeiro, New Zealand suggested total protection of whales because 'they include the largest animals ever seen on this planet, with brains larger than and almost as complex as our own, making them in a sense the equivalent in the marine environment of human beings in the land environment . . . to approach these awe-inspiring intelligent and unique creatures from the viewpoint of their intrinsic worth, as fellow citizens of planet Earth, with perhaps much to teach us' (New Zealand 1991).

Victor Scheffer, former member of the U.S. Marine Mammal Commission, writes: 'I see no need to extend this protective ethics [rights] to rabbits, or chickens, or fish. Whales are *different*' (quoted in Gilliespie 1997: 369). To David K. Wills (1992: 3) of the HSUS, 'in fact, whales, clearly in and of themselves, are valuable far beyond any instrumental purpose we as people may have for them. The true value of whales is in their complexity as sentient and intelligent life. The true value of whales is in their position in the hierarchy of creation'. These rights are unconditional. To D'Amato and Chopra (1991), indigenous peoples have rights only as long as these do not infringe on the rights of whales. They do realize, however, that an abrupt interruption of whaling might impose considerable hardship on some indigenous populations, and therefore suggest that they temporarily be given some assistance by countries that earlier were engaged in commercial whaling (D'Amato and Chopra 1991: 60). Several NGOs (e.g. the WDCS, EII, HSUS and Sea Shepherd) have taken this position and campaign also against whaling conducted by indigenous peoples.

Alexander Gillespie (1997) finds that the arguments for whale rights are based on anthropomorphism and the superwhale myth, and suggests that this position is an attempt by nonvegetarians to avoid bestowing rights on animals from which their own food comes. In order to avoid extending rights to domesticated animals Wilson and Jordan (n.d.: 20) have suggested in a paper on whale ethics that 'human use of any animal species is permissible only if the diversity, integrity and stability of the biotic community are upheld. Any individual animals taken should be thoughtfully selected, skilfully and humanely killed.' These requirements are well designed to meet the needs of the meat industry, as animals on industrial farms are never allowed to form any biotic community in the first place. Gillespie implies that only by bestowing rights on all animals are we able to avoid such inconsistencies.

To groups that are concerned with ecological issues, however, the logical consequence of higher population estimates ought to be a feeling of relief accompanied by a switch to other issues. Yet by and large this has not happened except in Norway, where all the major environmental NGOs have left the anti-whaling bandwagon and found other things to do. The Norwegian Society for the Conservation of Nature (Naturvernforbundet, Friends of the Earth-Norway) justified its position in the following terms, after first stressing that the prerequisite for any catches must be that such activities do not pose a threat to the stock:

> The national council [of Naturvernforbundet] has, however, observed that the IWC on several occasions has made decisions that are not in accordance with recommendations from the commission's own Scientific Committee. Moreover, the IWC has decided against scientific whaling in 1988, 1989, and 1990, where these decisions are contrary to Article 8 of the Convention. The whaling issue has an important principle character as an environmental issue. The national council therefore finds it necessary to warn that an unclear practice from the IWC can contribute to the loss of respect and confidence in international environmental treaties in general. (Naturvernforbundet 1991, my translation from Norwegian)

Some anti-whaling advocates have changed their arguments from ecology to ethics, thus crossing the line between environmentalism and animal welfare.[14] Michael Sutton of WWF-USA admits that the organization will 'have a hard time continuing' to argue ecologically (Bright 1992: 69). Thus the WWF, which prides itself on being committed to the principle of sustainable utilization of natural resources, took the opposite view in its *Position Statement on Whaling and the IWC*: 'Even if the IWC . . . could guarantee that whaling was only carried out on a truly sustainable basis, WWF would remain opposed to the resumption of whaling' (WWF 1992: 1). To bring this new position into harmony with the International Convention on the Regulation of Whaling, the WWF has voiced the opinion that it is time to change the convention from one regulating whaling to one protecting whales (Sutton 1992: 2).

Greenpeace has taken a similar position. In the publication *The Whale Killers*, Greenpeace-UK's wildlife campaigner Andy Ottaway asked: 'Even if it was possible to have an economically-viable commercial whaling industry which did not deplete whale stocks, would it be desirable, or even morally right, to have one? There are strong arguments for opposing whaling on purely ethical ground.' (Ottaway 1992: 3). In 1994, Executive Director of Greenpeace-UK Peter Melchett (1994) stated, 'Greenpeace is opposed to all commercial whaling and would never support any system which would authorize quotas to kill whales.'

Both Greenpeace and the WWF—and many other NGOs—argue that whales cannot be hunted humanely, that whales are uniquely special creatures, and that they have intrinsic value. This change in rhetoric can also be observed at the governmental level. The U.S. Marine Mammal Commission, for example, expressed the need to rewrite the convention so that it can take account of 'non-consumptive values' of whales (Twiss 1992), whereas the U.S.'s former IWC commissioner, John Knauss, wanted to continue the fight against whaling for ethical reasons because it was no longer possible to do so based on science (*Marine Mammal News*, 17(5), May 1991, p.4).

Anti-whaling countries have on various occasions justified their position with references to prevailing sentiments. New Zealand claimed to be talking on behalf of the world opinion when, in its opening statement to the IWC meeting in 1994, it stated that 'we will work to maintain the moratorium on commercial whaling because it reflects the current reality of world opinion' (New Zealand 1994). Tony Baldry, Britain's fisheries minister, said on 8 May 1996 in a statement to Parliament that '[c]ommercial whaling is opposed by the vast majority of our citizens and by Parliament . . . Accordingly, the U.K. will oppose any move to end the current moratorium on commercial whaling'. Finally, in May 1993 in a note to Iceland, the United States wrote that '[s]ince . . . scientific analyses now show that some populations of minke whales are likely to be able to sustain a limited harvest, it was time to review U.S. policy . . . [T]here is presently no support in the U.S. Congress or among the American public for commercial whaling. Therefore, the United States has decided not to support resumption of commercial whaling'.[15]

But appropriating the animal welfare/rights discourses has a cost. The WWF's position was opposed by its Danish chapter. A letter of 21 January 1992 from WWF-Denmark to WWF's international headquarter echoes arguments long used by whalers and may explain why some NGOs are reluctant to abandon the ecological arguments for ethical and moral ones:

> We find it extremely dangerous for WWF and our overall messages if we begin to use non-scientific, purely ethical arguments for regulating or even prohibiting the life styles and cultural values of other people or cultural groups. What real basis do we have for claiming, for instance, that the ethics of middle-class Americans or Britons is better than the ethics of the Icelandic, the Faroese, the Norwegian and even the Japanese? Seen in a historical perspective it is a very hard case to argue . . . We also fear that the tendency to value ethic arguments more highly than scientifically based arguments runs counter to some of the basic principles stated in the WWF's Mission, e.g. that WWF will be a multicultural organization and that we will listen carefully to local communities and respect their position.

The switch to a moral/ethical discourse does, as claimed by WWF-Denmark, imply a cultural imperialistic position. To organizations that openly want to convert all people to their particular worldview, this may not be a problem. But the situation is different for organizations that claim to base their operations on purely ecological considerations. Knowing that ecological arguments against whaling are more palatable than ethical and moral ones to a number of people, firms and government agencies, and realizing that the 'terms of the [whaling] convention have required that this debate be conducted in a scientific guise' (Butterworth 1992: 532), many activists are reluctant to ignore the legitimacy scientific arguments can give. Organizations that like to be considered ecologically oriented, the WWF and Greenpeace included, are more than reluctant to change from an ecological discourse to one based on animal welfare or rights. According to Brian Davies of IFAW, who regards Greenpeace as an animal welfare organization (Mowat 1990: 157), it was only for strategic reasons that an animal rights position was not directly presented during the seal protest (Wenzel 1991: 4). Organizations that are openly animal welfare/rights oriented (e.g. IFAW, WDCS, HSUS) often use ecological rhetoric for such reasons. They realize that to base their campaigns on only moral and ethical arguments will deprive them of the legitimacy science can give. But their ecological arguments have partly changed in character.

Staying with the Ecological Discourse

One strategy is to refute new population estimates and accuse the scientists behind the RMP and the new estimates of being incompetent, biased and 'bought' by governments of whaling nations—forgetting that the majority of the IWC's Scientific Committee comes from anti-whaling countries and that some are affiliated with anti-whaling organizations. The models of the scientists are carefully scrutinized and tested in order to cast doubt on the reliability of the latest population estimates. Given the nature of science there will always be uncertainties, and as Yearley (1991: 73) points out, where the public has no independent access to truth but the claims made by the two sides, it is likely to accept the claims of the NGOs. By casting doubt on research, it is possible to continue claiming that whales are at the brink of extinction.

In the early 1990s, both the WWF and Greenpeace continued to argue as if minke whales were close to extinction when they launched their 'Save the last whale' campaigns. The WWF continued to use the IWC's outdated stock estimates from 1985 in its arguments against Norwegian catches of minke whales (Kemf, Phillips and Baragona 2001: 15). Terms like depleted, threatened and endangered are often used in a very imprecise way, and there is a tendency to exaggerate the potential scope of commercial whaling. People's lack of detailed knowledge about various species of whales is exploited not least by the media. The British *The Mail on Sunday* claimed that '[o]nce again the blue whale . . . will be ruthlessly hunted, although there are probably less than 1,000 remaining from 250,000 that used to roam the oceans' (Revill and Smith 1992: 8). Besides offering a low figure for the remaining blue whale population, the newspaper failed to mention that blue whales have been protected since 1965 and that there is still unanimity as to upholding this protection. The newspaper deliberately exploited people's ignorance as to the status of the many different species of whales, enabling protectionists to generalize from the situation for one species to the others.

Another strategy is to misrepresent scientific reports. This is quite common within the world of politics. Too often scientists' assumptions and reservations are lost on the politicians who are eager to find arguments for their position. But scientists themselves also deliberately misrepresent data. South African mathematician and member of the IWC's Scientific Committee D.S. Butterworth takes issue with scientists pursuing this strategy and, with special reference to the Antarctic minke whale population, thinks the time is overdue 'to speak out against the near-farcical pronouncements of some international organizations regarding endangered species' (1992: 533). As an example he presents the concept 'protected status', which is imposed on any whale stock below the 0.54K level (54 per cent of original abundance). The 0.54K value was originally 'related to catch-maximization considerations and had nothing to do with any likelihood of extinction'. Anti-whalers—including scientists—both within and outside the IWC have deliberately confused the terms protected and endangered 'to give the public the impression that a stock placed in this category would be in danger of extinction' (Butterworth 1992: 532).

Even if whale protectionists accept new population estimates, they often bring new arguments into the ecological discourse (Butterworth 1992), a strategy whaling nations perceive as foot-dragging. They might argue that we do not know enough about the natural fertility and mortality rates, and that each stock must be managed separately to safeguard genetic diversity. Another argument is that whales today are exposed to a number of new environmental threats, and that we do not yet know their impact on whales and their habitats. It is feared that emissions of toxic substances like heavy metals and PCB can damage reproduction, and in some cases contamination of blubber and meat has been found to exceed the acceptable limits for human food. Other dangers to cetacean health are collusions with ships, entrapments in fishing gear, loss of habitats and noise, not least from the U.S. Navy testing powerful sonar systems. The possible impact of climatic change has also been used in arguments against whaling. After pointing out that the effects of global warming 'are largely unpredictable', an EIA report goes on to say that they are 'potentially devastating for cetaceans' (Perry, Clark and von Post 2001: 2). In short, by claiming that we have insufficient scientific knowledge they can paint a bleak future for the whale populations. In the end, in lack of scientific evidence to support their case, they may resort to the precautionary principle, as they did when the moratorium was adapted in 1982 (Heazle 2006:155).[16]

Finally, it is also claimed, particularly by Greenpeace, that the whale population is irrelevant because commercial whaling will—by a law of nature, it seems—lead to overexploitation and extinction. They tend to take the history of pelagic, industrial whaling as evidence (Greenpeace International 1992: 1) and point to economic theories postulating that it is economic rationally to bring resources to extinction if the monetary discount rate is higher than the natural growth rate of the resource (Clark 1973). This might be the case with some whale species, but the argument is only valid if profit maximization is the sole motive, which is seldom the case. Using the argument, the protectionists can feed on the memory of bygone days when large pelagic fleets hunted some species close to extinction in search of whale oil. There is no doubt that large-scale industrial operations have a bad history and several species have been seriously depleted as a result. But this empirical fact, which is disputed by no one, is extended to all types of commercial whaling. Such an argument not only ignores the progress in the IWC's management procedures since the 1970s (Chapter 4), but it also further denies humankind the ability to learn from past mistakes.[17]

Finally, the argument overlooks important differences in whaling regimes. There is a tremendous difference between Antarctic whaling during the Whaling Olympics of the 1950s and 60s and coastal minke whaling of today. That coastal minke whaling in Iceland, Japan and Norway has very little in common with the old pelagic whaling but, on the contrary, shares many of the characteristics found in aboriginal subsistence whaling (ISGSTW 1992), does not seem to affect their rhetoric in the least. To equate these forms of whaling distorts the issue because: (1) whereas the main product of the old industrial whaling was oil, which was in high demand at the time, the most important product from minke whaling has always been meat, for which there is a limited market; and (2) the coastal whaling boats are small and family-operated under an economic rationality different from that of the large pelagic expeditions (see ISGSTW 1992; Kalland and Sejersen 2005). There is thus little continuity between the two forms of whaling, except in Japan, where there has been a certain flow of personnel and capital between the two (Kalland and Moeran 1992). Again we see how differences—this time between whaling regimes and not between species—are deliberately ignored to create stereotypes with little empirical foundation.

A Totemic Worldview

Environmental issues are complex and beyond the comprehension of most of us. To mentally organize a bewildering array of conflicting messages, simplifications are called for, and this is to a great extent done through symbols. It is, particularly in technologically simple societies, common to use symbols from nature. One such symbolic system is totemism; an understanding of society where social relations are expressed through mostly natural symbols. A totem is usually a natural phenomenon that stands in a special ritualistic and symbolic relationship to a group of people and gives legitimacy and identity to the group. Totemism is a kind of taxonomy where nature is used to classify people. People's relationship to their totem can take on a religious aura, and in most totemic societies people are obliged to protect their own totem.

It can be argued that parts of the environmental and animal welfare/rights movements make use of totemic systems of thought, through which sociocultural differences are expressed through perceived natural differences. Often animals serve as a group's totem, and Lévi-Strauss (1966: 37) has pointed out that '[t]he beings which native thought endows with significance are seen as exhibiting a certain affinity with man'. As we saw in the previous chapter, the superwhale has this affinity with humans. Unlike most animals, they mate 'face to face, like man' (Williams 1988: 41), and whale songs are carried together with those of humans on Voyager I and II through space. We are told that whales are at least as intelligent as we are, are more skilled in handling social relations and deserve whale rights, and there is talk of whalekind as a counterpart to humankind. But the whale—or rather the superwhale—has taken on other characteristics of the totem as well.

Often, but not always, a group of people regards their totem as their ancestor. Few people claim that the whales are our ancestors, but by stressing the antiquity of whales and claiming that whales might be placed on a higher level than *Homo sapiens* on the evolutionary pyramid it can be argued that they have come to play the role of pseudo-ancestors. Moreover, a totem is frequently regarded as 'the guardian spirit and helper' (Freud 1960: 2), and the many stories of whales—particularly dolphins—rescuing people at sea clearly testify to this ability among cetaceans.

In return for their services, people come 'under a sacred obligation . . . not to kill or destroy their totem and avoid eating its flesh' (Freud 1960: 2). Although this prohibition is not absolute or universal in totemism (Durkheim 1976), protecting the whales has become the foremost duty of many people, as became clear to the world when three gray whales were trapped in the ice off Barrow, Alaska, in 1988 (Rose 1989). But unlike in traditional totemic societies, as found among the Aborigines in Australia and Indians in North America, where prohibitions extend only to the group with that particular totem, and unlike the Hindus, who do not try to impose the prohibitions of killing and eating cows on the rest of humankind, whale protectionists try to make the prohibition universal. They thus continue a form of Western cultural imperialism known from Christianity. It is the merger of totemism and cultural imperialism that has turned whaling into a national symbol in some of the protectionists' target societies (see Chapter 6).

Finally, the totem plays a leading role in giving people a common identity. Events of many different kinds serve to unite whales and whale-savers: attacks on whalers at sea and in harbours, demonstrations in front of embassies and dolphinariums, whale watching tours, swim-with-whale encounters, series of seminars and conferences, rescues of stranded whales and release of captive dolphins (see next chapter). The most important event of all is the annual meeting of the IWC, where the world is divided into the so-called like-minded group and the whaling nations. Here whale protectionists can display their whale art objects and emblems on badges, T-shirts, posters and so on. Although the outcome of the meetings in recent years has been more or less known beforehand, the meetings themselves give attendees the opportunity to meet like-minded politicians, activists and journalists.

Through these events like-minded people are brought together, and solidarity and group identity are maintained and strengthened. But totemism is more than a means to integrate groups of people. Totemism is a taxonomy where nature is used to classify people. In this discourse whales serve as the totem for 'nature-loving' people—but what about the whalers' totem? Since whales for the protectionists function metonymically for nature as a whole, it follows that the totem of the whalers ought to be some man-made object. Money serves this function ideally for radical ecologists and animal rights advocates who, with their often anti-capitalist orientation, see money as a morally corrupting agent reducing everything to the question of profit (Bloch and Parry 1989). Money can thus be used metaphorically for commercialism and the values we have lost. By claiming money as the totem for whalers, the protectionists signal that whalers are people hardly worthy of inclusion in the moral community. In this totemic scheme humankind then is divided into two opposing categories: good people who care for the earth and the future, versus bad people who seek short-term profit. The rhetoric of the protectionists is cast in the metaphor of war.

The War Metaphor

A Greenpeace consultant held two factors to be important for raising money: a sense of urgency and an easily identifiable enemy (Spencer et al. 1991: 179). Whether the whale protectionists claim that the whales are at the brink of extinction or that they are suffering unbelievable cruelty, people are receptive to the message that there is no time to waste. 'URGENT. We must hear from *all* whale lovers within the NEXT 14 DAYS', proclaimed the WDCS (Whyte 1994, original emphases) when asking for funds for its boycott campaign against the Faroe Islands. Many activists have openly stated that the situation is so critical that time cannot be spent on democratic procedures. In times of war, democracy seems to be a luxury.

The war metaphor is a favourite one among 'Green Warriors'. The report *The Global War against Small Cetaceans*, published by the EIA, is but one telling example; David Day's book *The Whale War* is another. In the latter publication whale activists employ 'warships' in 'invasions' (Day 1992). IFAW founder and president Brian Davies, who has a background as a career soldier in the Canadian army, is also among those who think in terms of warfare: 'There's a sense of glory about war' (quoted in Hollander 1984: 246). Most of these people employ warfare at the rhetorical level, although Paul Watson and his Sea Shepherd actually are engaged in what they perceive as the Third World War.

At one level the metaphor is used to convey an image of an uneven fight between defenceless whales and greedy whalers, often ending in massacres. We have seen in Chapter 1 how whales are depicted in positive terms. The whalers are portrayed as the whales' opposite. Accused of using inhumane killing methods, they are typically portrayed as cruel, brutal, reckless, barbaric, savage, sadistic and greedy. They are poachers and pirates engaged in evil and criminal activities, defying international law and 'willing to wipe out the world's last whales for profit' (Moore 1991). Norwegian whaling policy has been likened to apartheid (hy 1992: 7) and the Nazi extermination of Jews (Watson 1993).

The moral integrity of the whalers is thus questioned. Anti-whalers paint a dim picture of whalers. In addition to killing whales, they are potentially violent towards fellow people, if we are to believe Gert Sørensen, a Danish Greenpeace activist. On the pretext of being a scientist he was welcomed onboard a Norwegian minke whaler, but he went ashore after a couple of days because he was afraid that the whalers might stab him if his identity was revealed (Claudi 1988: 91). The World Society for the Protection of Animals (WSPA 1988) suggests that children exposed to hunting activities are more likely to show violent, criminal behaviour towards others. Even scholarly journals may portray whalers as evil. In *The American Journal of International Law* the lawyers D'Amato and Chopra (1991: 27) write that 'the mind set that exults in the killing of whales . . . overlaps with the mind set that accepts genocide of "inferior" human beings'. Sean Whyte, chief executive of the WDCS, takes great pain in juxtaposing the friendly whales and the barbarous whalers:

Figure 2.2 *'Molly the minke' harpooned by 'Ocean Assasin'. Greenpeace demonstration at IWC meeting, Dublin 1995. (courtesy by Laila Jusnes)*

'The victims of the relentless bloodlust are pilot whales . . . living peacefully in close-knit family groups, nurturing their young and caring for each other. The family ties are so close, many scientists believe that they beach themselves in an effect to help a relative who is too old or sick to keep on its journey through the deep. These features of pilot whale society also make them easily prey for the Faroese people who, **whenever the mood takes them, embark on a frenzied orgy of savage slaughter**' (emphasis as in original; Whyte 1994: 1).

The above quote brings to light yet another aspect of the narrative, namely how the animals are put to death. Some of the more moderate organizations claim, without going into detail, that whaling methods are inhumane and not worthy of civilized nations. But others—and the mass media seem to take the lead—think that the crueller the slaughter appears, the better. Faroese whalers 'smash gaffs into the flesh' of the pilot whales while a minke whale is left 'to thrash around for hours in its death throes' (Swain 1992: 30). AWI (2007: 3) claims that even in modern whaling 'the probability of obtaining a clean strike with a swift death is extremely low and animals can take hours to die'.[18] Through such rhetoric NGOs and media compete in expressing their commitment to the anti-whaling cause, and in the process beasts are turned into gentle humans while hunters are turned into beasts.

Whalers make excellent enemies. The task of portraying whalers in this way has been made easier by the memory of bygone days, when large pelagic fleets hunted some large whales almost to extinction in the search for oil. Furthermore, because only a few nations engage in whaling, the cost of the moratorium is borne by the few and makes whalers easily identifiable and thus ideal scapegoats for environmental disasters and human cruelty to animals. Significantly, whalers tend to live in remote areas with only limited possibilities of influencing central governments. Sealers make good enemies for the same reason.

If whalers are portrayed in negative terms, the activists are given a positive image. In the narrative of the whale protectionists, the positive qualities ascribed to whales are extended to people who 'defend' them and 'fight' against the 'bad' whalers and their supporters. In a number of money-raising pleas good people are asked to open their hearts, and wallets, for the noble cause of saving animals. In a Christmas message pleading for contributions, Brian Davies appealed to donors in the following terms: '[W]e're pressing for peace . . . not pain. For care and compassion . . . not clubbing and killing. For kindness . . . instead of cruelty' (December 1991). The annual IWC meetings, demonstrations, whale watching and swim-with-whales séances have all a ritualistic imprint that underpins the feeling of community and mission.

The war metaphor divides humankind into good guys and bad guys, the good guys being the like-minded people who fight to save their peaceful whale friends from the bad guys who want to kill out of greed. This has made it possible to reduce complicated ecological and ethical questions to one simple dichotomy.

Table 2.1 A Totemic View of the World

Caring for the Earth	Seeking short-term profit
Totem: whale	Totem: money
nature	man-made objects (commodities)
subsistence	commercialism
indigenous people	industrial world
traditional	modern
protectionist	whaler
pure	polluted
good	bad
civilized	barbaric
spirituality	materialism
sharing	profit maximization
feminine	masculine

Through this process a set of binary oppositions emerges in the narrative of many whale protectionists, which is strongly resented by the whalers.

The Primitive and Barbaric vs. the Civilized

Some further examples of the rhetoric used in creating the above scheme—which also seems to fit the sealing issue (Wright 1984; Herscovici 1985; Wenzel 1991)—are in order here. As we have already seen, whalers are frequently accused of using cruel and inhumane killing methods, and their moral integrity is questioned. Whalers, and their supporters, are often portrayed as less civilized than the like-minded group. Some whale protectionists perceive a linear evolution from primitive societies where people, due to poverty and lack of alternatives, are impelled to catch whales in order to survive, to civilized societies where people can afford to let the whales live. To animal rights advocates there is an ethical progression through which people are first liberated from the yokes of racism, then of sexism, and finally of speciesism, e.g. discrimination on the basis of species (Singer 1990: 9). In Barstow's (1989: 11) evolutionary scheme, mankind has progressed from cannibalism, to emancipation of slaves, to liberation of whales. The protectionists invariably find themselves at the top of this evolution. At the same time, animal rights—no interference with other species—implies distance from the animals, and the process of civilization is therefore measured against our distance from animals (Tester 1991: 163). Attitudes to whales and whaling are frequently used to measure this progress.

When Australia, the Netherlands, Great Britain and the United States ended their own whaling operations because they were no longer profitable, whales could be moved from the category 'edible' to that of 'inedible'. To say yes to whaling became, for many people, synonymous with being uncivilized. To a former leader of Greenpeace-Norway, whaling was incompatible with having an opera, and to Sir Peter Scott, who held the post of WWF chair for more than twenty years, 'no civilised person can contemplate the whaling industry without revulsion and shame at the insensitivity of our own species' (quoted in Davies et al. 1991: 2). For d'Amato and Chopra (1991: 49) caring for whales signals a progression from self-interest to altruism or from individualism to communalism. The British newspaper, *The Times*, wrote in an editorial—after first pointing out that minke whales are plentiful—that a 'return to the cruelty of existing methods of whaling by Norway, Japan and Iceland will damage their reputation as civilized societies' ('Beaching the Whalers', 29 May 1991). A few days later, British Minister of Agriculture John Gummer promised before the Parliament to do his utmost to prevent Iceland from leaving the IWC. 'I want to keep Iceland within the fold of civilized nations' (3 June 1991). When Norway decided to resume minke whaling, House Merchant Marine Committee Chairman Gerry Studds called this 'a large step backwards for mankind' showing 'flagrant disregard for the international moratorium on commercial whaling [that] severs [Norway's] tie to every other nation on this planet' (quoted in Caron 1995: 168). Victor Scheffer (1991: 19) sums it up by claiming that caring about whales is a mark of personal and societal maturity.

Another important opposition in this totemic scheme is the one between subsistence and commerce, as marine mammal hunting seems to be particularly revolting if it is done for commercial purposes. The protectionists stress that the products from whales reach a commercial market for luxury items, i.e. meat at expensive Japanese restaurants. Apparently, commercial activities are not compatible with the wilderness. Only people 'living in nature', i.e. aboriginal peoples, can therefore exploit these animals without distorting the binary scheme, and they can only do so by being 'authentic' and behaving 'traditionally', which means that aboriginal peoples can hunt whales as long as the products do not enter the commercial marketplace.[19] Greenpeace's Gylling-Nielsen was crystal clear when he said 'that the only reasonable argument on which we can support the indigenous peoples' claims to harvest the resources of nature, is if it necessary to sustain life' (IWGIA 1991: 28). The need argument was introduced by animal welfare advocates in order to solve the contraction between life and death (see Introduction). Subsistence and cultural needs were taken into account when the IWC authorized aboriginal subsistence whaling (Donovan 1982), and most of the anti-whaling groups have endorsed this kind of whaling even though its simpler technologies inflict far more pain on the whales than modern commercial whaling does.

Whereas aboriginal peoples have been given a concession to catch whales to satisfy cultural needs, this has been denied commercial whalers. Here needs are seen strictly in material terms, and the whalers have no need to catch whales because they share the general prosperity of the capitalist societies in which they live and work. They can afford to buy pork, beef and turkey. The argument, of course, raises the question of how to decide what people need without being ethnocentric or cultural imperialist: why is there a need to hunt foxes and big game for sport, or to eat turkey at Thanksgiving?

Whalers argue that whaling is more than making a living. Whaling is a way of life and must be seen 'as a process whereby hunters mutually create and recreate *one another*, through the medium of their encounter with prey' (Ingold 1986: 111). To deny whalers' cultural needs, the protectionists take an extreme materialistic position, which may surprise many people who have taken the movement's general anti-capitalist rhetoric at face value. By arguing that there is no need to kill whales, they turn whaling into a senseless activity that can only be understood in terms of 'greed' and 'short-term profit'.

There is a form of imperialism underlying this reasoning, where one perceives a linear evolution from primitive societies of whalers to civilized societies where people can afford to let the whales live. Indigenous peoples who still lack operas can go on catching whales, as long as this is done for subsistence. But if some whale products are sold at the market, this simple binary scheme becomes disordered. The conclusion is that indigenous peoples can continue whaling only as long as they remain 'primitive nature peoples' properly protected against the market. In this way, the 'civilized world' also gets a living museum enabling people to measure their own progress along the path to civilization, meanwhile also acquiring a means to control indigenous populations politically.

The world has known many sacred animals, but there are two aspects that separate the totemic view of the whale protectionists from more traditional totemic systems. First, activists have a missionary inclination. A Hindu tolerates that an American eats beef, but an activist does not accept that the Japanese eat whale meat. Hence, a Western tradition of cultural imperialism is continued. Second, the totem is for sale and bestows a green image on those who jump on the bandwagon and pay for a seat among the 'good' people. In the next chapter I will argue that many people have taken this opportunity.

Notes

1. These are species that appeal to the public and have other features that make them suitable for communicating conservation concerns. Other WWF flagship species—or charismatic megafauna—are elephants, giant pandas, the great apes, marine turtles, rhinos and tigers (retrieved 15 February 2008 from http://www.worldwildlife.org/endangered/index.cfm).
2. Retrieved 15 February 2008 from www.wdcs.org.
3. From a full-page advertisement in the *The Times*, 1 May 1996.
4. Retrieved 17 September 1999 from www.wdcs.org.
5. Retrieved 15 February 2008 from www.ifaw.org/ifaw/general/ default.aspx?oid=18005.
6. For the devastating impact the anti-sealing campaign had on Inuit society, see e.g. Herscovici 1985 and Wenzel 1991.
7. Retrieved 4 July 2007 from www.eia-international.org.

8. Retrieved 15 February 2008 from http://csiwhalesalive.org.
9. Retrieved 15 February 2008 from www.awionline.org/oceans/Noise/.
10. In 2002 the topic for the conference was 'The Culture of Whales' and in 2004 it was 'Learning from Whales: Education, Inspiration, and Action'.
11. A number of these web pages are organized in a mutually enhancing way, making it easy to surf from one website to the next.
12. Some Japanese scientists are of the opinion that the population has increased dramatically because more krill became available after the stocks of the large whales (blue, fin and right whales) were depleted. I will return to this question in Chapter 5.
13. Whales do in fact have enemies. Both killer whales and sharks may attack whales, and whales may also fight each other, some times with fatal results.
14. This caused an editorial in *The Times* ('How Not to Save Whales', 30 June 1992) to observe that 'the moratorium was flawed. It was introduced originally in the name of conservation, at a time when the extinction of virtually all whales seemed imminent. Its continuation is demanded now in the name of animal welfare. Iceland and Norway are entitled to accuse the anti-whaling majority of nations in the International Whaling Commission of changing the rules half way through the game'.
15. Retrieved 25 March 2008 from www.highnorth.no/Library/Policies/National/we-th-ri.htm
16. The precautionary principle is meant to deal with situations of scientific uncertainty: 'When an activity raises threats of harm to human health or the environment, precautionary measures should be taken even if some cause and effect relationships are not fully established scientifically. In this context the proponent of an activity, rather than the public, should bear the burden of proof' (Wingspread Statement, http://www.sehn.org/wing.html, retrieved 27 December 2008). As there always will be an element of scientific uncertainty, an extreme interpretation of the precautionary principle can lead to inaction. Tore Schweder (2001) and Michael Heazle (2006) have aptly shown how the scientific uncertainty card has crippled the IWC in two periods: first before 1962, when the Netherlands repeatedly referred to scientific uncertainty as a justification for opposing reductions in quotas, and then since the 1980s, when scientific uncertainty (and the precautionary principle) has been used to oppose resumption of commercial whaling.
17. With reference to the significant underreporting of Soviet catches between 1948 and 1973, it has been argued that whaling cannot be controlled. But much of the illegal Russian activities occurred before an international inspection scheme was introduced in the pelagic hunt in 1972 (Aron, Burke and Freeman 2000: 180; Berzin 2008).
18. When Norway reports that the majority of the animals is killed instantly and that the average time to death is about two minutes, AWI claims that such data are self-collected by the whalers. But they are in fact reported by trained vets.
19. These attitudes are nowhere better expressed than in the 1931 whaling convention, which stated that the convention did not apply to aborigines provided that: (1) they use canoes, pirogues or other exclusively native craft propelled by oars or sails; (2) they do not carry firearms; (3) they are not in the employment of persons other than aborigines; (4) they are not under contract to deliver the products of their whaling to any third person (Birnie 1985: 681–82).

Chapter 3

Diverting the Commodity Path

In 1976, at an international conference on marine mammals held in Norway, some people got together and tried to estimate the low-consumptive—i.e. non-lethal consumption—value of cetaceans. They arrived at an estimate of about US$ 100 million, which was about the same value as for commercial whaling at that time (Scheffer 1991: 17–18). Since then commercial whaling has almost ceased, while the low-consumptive value has increased manifold. What we have witnessed during the last three decades is, to use a phrase taken from Appadurai (1986), a diversion of a preordained commodity path, i.e. the route a commodity—loosely defined as goods and services of exchange value—travels from production through consumption has been altered.

One kind of diversion is theft, and many whalers see the sales and adoptions of whales—and here they include the sale of whale images, which have contributed so importantly to the finances of environmental and animal rights groups—as theft, not only of the whales, which they feel belong to them through several generations' involvement in whaling, but of their livelihood, pride and culture. The moratorium imposed on commercial whaling by the International Whaling Commission (IWC), has made whale protectionists the main economic beneficiaries of cetaceans, which, together with seals and elephants, have turned out to be one of the most important sources of income for environmental as well as for animal welfare/rights groups.

One objective of this chapter is to explore the strategies protectionists have used to turn meat, oil and other whale products into products of no exchange value and thereby eliminate their status as commodities (Appadurai 1986: 13). In Chapter 2 we saw that whale protectionists have used rhetoric taken from both environmental and animal welfare/rights discourses. Some NGO spokespeople still claim that whales are close to extinction or that whaling is by nature unsustainable, whereas others have switched from an environmental discourse to one on animal welfare or rights. In this chapter we will take a wider perspective and also include nonverbal arguments employed to decommoditize whale products.

A second objective is to show how anti-whaling groups have responded to a growing demand among individuals, companies and governments to appear green by turning the superwhale into a commodity. Using environmental and animal protection discourses as the cultural framework for exchangeability (Appadurai 1986: 13), companies have acquired green legitimacy (and partial immunity) by economically supporting anti-whaling organizations and the superwhale myth. Government agencies have obtained the same in return for political legitimacy. Decommoditization of meat and oil and commoditization of the superwhale are simultaneous processes in the diversion of the commodity path, and both find legitimacy through the annual IWC meetings and other 'tournaments of value', where 'central tokens of value in the society' are contested (Appadurai 1986: 21).

Why Cetaceans? *Strategische Opportunisten*

People are attracted to the 'save the whale' cause for a number of reasons, not only environmental ones. In Chapter 1 we saw that whales are animals that can be as-cribed great symbolic significance in many cultures. They are good to think with. They are apparently also good to feel with. There are pragmatic reasons why some NGOs continue their campaigns against whaling as well. Conflicts over natural resources are often explained as a conflict between traditional harvesters who are motivated by short-sighted economic interests and protectionists who altruisti-cally fight for values generally held in high esteem (Selle and Strømsnes 1996: 285). This is a gross oversimplification of the situation, and it is naïve to believe that environmental and animal welfare/rights organizations are influenced only by ethical values and not by economic self-interests. Despite their self-proclaimed lack of self-interest, anti-whaling campaigns provide protectionists with poten-tial for profit making as well as influence and fame. Of course, it is easy to level such accusations against the anti-whaling movement, and the whalers and their friends have done so repeatedly. But there is evidence to support such an accusa-tion, although not necessarily against all the organizations and activists involved. These campaigns have proved extremely efficient fundraisers for many of these organizations, some of which have been labelled money-making machines (see Schwarz 1991; Spencer et al. 1991).

Dalton found in his study of environmental groups in Western Europe in general 'that staff members selected campaigns that they thought would gen-erate more popular support' (1994: 106). Greenpeace-Germany legitimized its engagement in the campaign against seal hunting by citing the need to increase membership: 'It was surely important to Greenpeace at that time to get bigger . . . I found it completely legitimate to use a cute animal with large eyes.'[1] David McTaggart, a long time leader of Greenpeace, has stated that 'I'm not really an animal person, but I was starting to see the value of a warm and fuzzy issue that appeals to people emotionally . . . The whales are a real people magnet, and in democratic societies if you've got the people behind you, you've got the power' (quoted in Darby 2008: 105). Harald Zindler, a Greenpeace leader in Germany, called themselves 'strategische Opportunisten' (Schwarz 1991: 105), while Steve Sawyer, international director of Greenpeace, has stated that 'our philosophy on issues is extraordinary pragmatic. We choose the ones we feel we might be able to win' (quoted in Pearce 1991: 40). Therefore it is not surprising that Greenpeace readily joins issues proven popular by others. The whaling and sealing campaigns are cases in point. Both issues were developed by others. According to Andreas Hansen (1993: 171), 'Greenpeace's claim-making activity is . . . at its most effective . . . in term of framing and elaborating environmental dimensions which are already in the public domain as issues and problems'. The novelty Greenpeace brought to these campaigns was the mass media. Established by journalists, Greenpeace has always been clever at getting media attention for its protests.

Access to the media is of paramount importance to the NGOs for at least four reasons. (1) The media serve as channels of communication between the NGOs and their present and potential members (Dalton 1994: 186). Such channels are particularly important when the supporters are widely dispersed geographically and have little firsthand knowledge of whales and whaling. (2) The NGOs see the media as important tools in educating people and changing public opinion in the desired direction. (3) Media help to create and reinforce an identity for the anti-whaling movement and serve to mobilize human and financial resources for NGOs and the movements as a whole. (4) The media, by helping the movements to gain credibility and legitimacy, may thus improve their position to influence other arenas, including the political one.

The desire for media coverage is key to understanding strategies used by the environmental entrepreneurs competing to find markets for their ideas. A campaign must meet three goals to be successful in the media: it must command attention, claim legitimacy and evoke action (Solesbury 1976). Issues are carefully selected and timed with these goals in mind. An exposition on television requires a different format from a lengthy article in the serious press. Writing about the campaign against harp seal hunting on the ice floes off Newfoundland, Alan Herscovici (1985: 197) points out that 'a ten-second shot of a bloody white-coat seal on the North Atlantic ice fields is television. Lengthy expositions on game management and complex mathematical population models are not'. Audiences seem more receptive to environmental arguments than to animal rights, to traditional conservation than to radical ecology, and to animal welfare than to animal rights. Hence, there is a tendency, as we saw in Chapter 2, to frame their messages in the language of the environment rather than in the language of animal rights.

Campaign leaders are well aware of the importance of of media appeal, and sealing has, as we have seen, been particularly attractive to television. The juxtapositions of red blood and white ice, of dark-clothes men and white seal pups, and of athletic adult men and practically immobile newborn animals underscore the unfairness of the match.[2] With the arrival of Brigitte Bardot, the seal hunt story became 'blood and death and sex. No more potent combination could be put together' (Hunter 1979: 380). It was easy to create an enemy, one of the require-ments the consultant to Greenpeace identified as crucial in order to raise money, the other being the ability to give an impression of urgency (Spencer 1991: 179). The seal hunt was also attractive because it involved a highly mediagenic ani-mal laden with symbolism (Kalland 1994) and allowed a focus on a predictable hunt confined to a small geographical area during a few short weeks. The hunt gave the campaign a spectacular focus and direction, and made it unnecessary to mobilize supporters and organize large-scale protests over an extended period of time, which may have exhausted the energy of the movement and its supporters (Dalton 1994: 197) as well as emptied it of newsworthiness.

The whaling issue has not been less attractive. Whales are among the most popular and charismatic animals, and they feature prominently in nature pro-grammes as well as in environmental campaigns. Confrontations can narrowly be focused on the annual meetings at the IWC and a few hunts. Moreover, its history easily turns whaling into a potent symbol of anthropogenic destruction of the environment, an image further underlined by footage of activists in inflatable boats lined up against Russian and Japanese factory ships. Dolphins trapped in tuna purse seines also make spectacular footage, and the campaign against tuna seining in the East Tropical Pacific (ETP) was propelled into the limelight by a video shot by a biologist in collaboration with Earth Island Institute (Bonanno and Constance 1996: 185).

Several NGOs have become adept at creating news, knowing very well that the media have a preference for dramatic, visible actions (Hansen 1993).[3] Chas-ing whaling ships in high seas has made it easy for such groups to monopolize news reporting, and camera crews are indispensable parts of these voyages. In this way activists can provide television channels with dramatic footage of mediagenic whales, saving work for the reporters (Yearley 1991: 74), or NGOs may invite sympathetic media people to cover their activities.[4] People appreciate stunts as well, 'because those doing it are risking arrest, injury, and even death—and all for a cause that transcends narrow self-interest' (Princen 1994: 35). Hence, organiza-tions tend to exaggerate crises and the strength of their adversaries.

Commanding attention is only a first step: the attention must be interpreted and used to build up credibility and legitimacy. Such credibility is not only need-ed to build confidence with the public—an important precondition for fundrais-ing—but to open the doors to governmental and other decision-making offices, from where they can engage directly in the formation and reform of international institutions (Princen 1994: 36). In the next chapter we shall see how NGOs have formed alliances with governments and become important players in the IWC.

Sometimes credibility follows directly from media exposure, but sometimes a spectacular but illegal action can turn the great majority of the public away in dismay and even invite counterclaims about irresponsibility and irrationality (Cracknell 1993). This has been a problem to, for example, the Sea Shepherd Conservation Society, whose violent actions have never gained legitimacy outside a small group of animal rights followers—some of whom are Hollywood celebrities, however. Credibility is more than anything a question of information management. Whether reporting from street demonstrations, asking for boycotts of products from whaling nations or simply requesting donation through ads, the groups have to frame their message according to the perceived target audience in order to build up legitimacy.

The image of the superwhale is ideally suited for information management. The general audience is hardly able to discriminate between the many different species, so a variety of characteristics can be conflated into one endangered, intelligent superwhale. The same process is to some extent at work regarding whaling. There are several different whaling regimes, but there is a tendency to conflate them. Hence, no distinction is made between the old pelagic whaling fleet with its mother ship and a number of catcher boats—mostly a thing of the past—and the small fishing boat catching minke whales during a short summer season.[5]

The main sources of information have often been governments and scientists, but these sources have been seriously challenged when it comes to environmental issues. For understandable reasons, governments and scientists are often seen as part of the problem. Some activists have turned their backs on science, an attitude that to some extent has undermined their credibility among decision-makers and with the press, if not with the public. But some have turned to science in order to improve their credibility. Dalton (1994: 81) suggests that linkages to research institutes and educational foundations are one reason for the growing strength of the environmental movement. But this is not science for its own sake. As scientists may differ in opinion in terms of both what the reality looks like and how to interpret this reality, science can be used selectively to produce strategic information. Knowledge is transformed into an organizational weapon (Eyerman and Jamison 1989: 113–14). The objective truth of a statement may not be important, but what people believe to be true is. Hence, according to Yearley, 'the correctness of social problem claims was comparatively *un*important in determining their public impact' (1991: 115, italics as in original). NGOs might get little media coverage if they stick to facts and are less economical with the truth (North 1987, cited in Yearley 1991: 139).

Although NGOs may use science selectively, the media seek their knowledge. Tending to be unaware, or deliberately ignoring, that environmentalism is a multi-billion-dollar industry where NGOs may have an economic self-interest in exaggerating crises, the media often regard the NGOs' knowledge as less tainted than that of governmentally employed scientists. As already pointed out, Yearley (1991: 73) has suggested that when people have no independent access to the truth, they are likely to accept the actvists' version of the case.[6] Moreover, by running single-issue campaigns the NGOs are often in a better position than scientists to give the simple and uncompromising answers the public wants. The 1988 seal pest in the North Sea is a case in point. Greenpeace immediately defined it as pollution-related. This enabled the organization to take ownership—a crucial

gatekeeping role (Anderson 1993: 62)—of this issue and thereby lay the premises for its discourse. When virologists later identified a phocine distemper virus
(PDV)—similar to measles in humans—as the cause of the epidemic (Anderson
1993: 62), this did not make headlines.

When information for various reasons cannot be monopolized or manipu-
lated, the credibility of certain NGOs may be seriously undermined. This has
happened to Greenpeace on several occasions. Olga Linné (1993), for example,
found that Danish broadcasters were much more sceptical towards the organization than their British colleagues, a fact she attributes to the damage the anti-
sealing movement had done to the Inuit and Greenland's economy, a situation
that has gone largely unnoticed in the U.K. For the same reason, anti-whaling
organizations have had difficulties in establishing themselves in whaling countries like Norway and Japan, where the public has access to alternative knowledge. Greenpeace's lack of credibility on this issue in whaling countries has had
an impact on its image in general, and the organization has failed to acquire the
position of ownership of any environmental issue in Norway (Aanes 2001). Loss
of credibility related to the *Brent Spar* episode further impacted negatively on the
organization in Europe.[7]

Finally, media exposition should evoke action. It must suggest a better future
and give the impression that something can be achieved. To win—or at least to
give the impression of winning though dramatic exposition in the media—is
important in order to attract supporters. Successes attract people to the cause and
'a large membership provides legitimacy for organizations that claim to speak
for the public interest . . . members provide this group with an entrée to government offices and positions on policy advisory committees' (Dalton 1994: 86). As
already stated, NGOs have a tendency to select issues that seemingly are easy to
win, preferably against great odds.

Before a campaign is launched, the chances of winning must therefore be considered good: the issue must be 'in', and the campaign activities must be able to
reach a wide audience through mass media (Eyerman and Jamison 1989). Brian
Davies of the International Fund for Animal Welfare (IFAW) seeks 'areas where
it is possible to achieve something in the moderately near future' (in Mowat
1990: 164). Such support comes, perhaps not surprisingly, primarily in campaigns where companies, unions and nations do not feel that their own positions
are threatened. For most multinationals and governments, saving a wild animal
in a remote corner of the globe is a safe campaign. Whaling is a marginal industry
in marginal regions, which implies that the social, cultural and economic costs
in terms of lost livelihood and negative image are externalized; i.e. they are not
borne by those who organize the campaigns and their supporters. That whaling is of no economic importance in anti-whaling countries implies that few
people will rise up to support its cause (Holt 1985: 192–93). Whale protectors
are therefore allowed to dominate the arena. The rewards to governments and
corporations, in terms of their green image, are substantial (see Rose 1989). The

anti-whaling campaigns, therefore, offer governments and industries opportunities to show their consideration for the environment, while the campaigns have proved excellent fundraisers for the environmental and animal protection movements. As early as 1988 Gulland (1988: 45), an advisor to the IWC, pointed out that '[t]here may no longer be urgent reasons of conservation for continued pressure to strengthen the control of whaling, but there are sound financial reasons for groups that depend on public subscription to be seen to be active in "saving the whale"'.

The whaling issue seems to be easily won, at least in the mass media. Whales are not only animals of great symbolic significance; many people also consider them extremely photogenic and among the most charismatic animals on Earth. Sidney Holt—one of the most uncompromising advocates against whaling, a member of the IWC Scientific Committee and an advisor to IFAW—believes it should be easy to save whales because 'they are extremely attractive forms of wildlife: some of them sing, and many people have become familiar with their underwater performances on film and video' (Holt 1985: 192–93).

The Anti-whaling Campaigns

The strategies employed to bring whaling to an end have been varied. In order for a campaign to be successful, a number of strategies or activities must be employed simultaneously. Many activities are expressive and aimed at influencing policy makers, educating or changing public opinion, and mobilizing resources and support for the organizations. NGOs that rely on individual membership dues and donations—as do most of the anti-whaling organizations—are likely to place a high priority on expressive tactics and symbolic actions, primarily to present the movement's goals to the public and to mobilize their support (Dalton 1994). The construction of the superwhale myth has been an important prerequisite, as has the rhetoric that dichotomizes people into good and bad. Words have not been enough, however, and more tangible strategies have been pursued as well. NGOs campaigning against whaling probably number in the hundreds, and they differ in ideological outlook as well as in campaign design. Some activists have opted for coercion by means of ecotage, harassment and intimidation.

Direct Actions to Interrupt Whaling

Among the early activities that attracted international coverage was an attempt to stop dolphin drives in Japan, first brought to international attention through an article in *National Geographic*. In 1980, a foreign activist cut the nets that held a school of dolphins captive at Katsumoto, Iki. (I will return to the situation in Katsumoto in Chapter 6.) More recently, activists have attempted to interrupt Japan's scientific whaling in the Antarctic. Activists in inflatable boats have on several occasions managed to position themselves between catcher

boats and whales, and they have furthermore tried to prevent minke whales
being winched up the slipway of the mother ship. Both Greenpeace and Sea
Shepherd ships have tried to interrupt Japanese whalers in the Antarctic, leading to collisions and other dangerous situations. Recalling the Convention for
the Suppression of Unlawful Acts against the Safety of Navigation, the IWC has
condemned 'any actions that are a risk to human life and property in relation
to the activities of vessels at sea' and urged 'Contracting Governments to take
actions, in accordance with relevant rules of international law and respective
national laws and regulations, to cooperate [ ] to prevent and suppress actions
that risk human life and property at sea and with respect to alleged offenders'
(IWC 2007b).

The tactic by which activists place themselves as human shields between whalers and their prey creates powerful images. It was first employed in 1975, when
the ship *Phyllis Cormack* sailed from Vancouver to intercept the Soviet fleet in
the North Pacific (Brown and May 1991: 36–43). In the late 1970s the Greenpeace ship *Rainbow Warrior* tried to interrupt whaling outside Iceland and Spain
(Day 1992: 70). Greenpeace activists have also tried to place themselves between
whales and Norwegian whalers in the North Sea. Another strategy has been for
activists to chain themselves to harpoon cannons or crow's nests. In 1996 Greenpeace tried to interrupt the unloading of whale meat at Ålo in southern Norway,
an action that ended in a physical brawl in which activists were thrown off the
whaling vessels and into the water (Broch 2004).

Direct confrontations during the hunt constitute an important arena for the
task of bringing about a diversion of the commodity path. The confrontations
usually take place far from shore and therefore provide the activists with the opportunity to invent news—a role much appreciated by Greenpeace's cofounder
Robert Hunter (Pearce 1991: 20)—or to monopolize news coverage. They are
usually carefully staged, and the mass media play a crucial role in transmitting a
rather theatrical performance across the world. Although a nuisance to whalers,
these actions are not necessarily meant to result in an immediate termination
of whaling activities; rather, they are expressive acts that tell the world that the
activists are concerned about the environment, that the issue is urgent and cannot wait, and that they risk their lives in fighting powerful enemies at great odds.
The activists are always depicted as underdogs: the small inflatables going up
against the big catcher boat or a Japanese factory ship. The situation is ideally
suited for presenting an image of David fighting Goliath (Hunter 1979: 229)
(see Figure 3.1).

Skilful manipulation of the mass media engenders enormous sympathy for
their cause, which is one reason behind their success in removing whale meat
from the commodity state and placing the superwhale in its place. It matters little
that the picture might be contested. With environmentalism being a multi-billion-dollar industry, it is rather the whalers who are the weak party. The David-
and-Goliath image was reversed when a Greenpeace fleet of ships, headed by the

Figure 3.1 *Sea Shepherd trying to cripple a whaling ship by entangling a rope in the propeller. (courtesy by Institute of Cetacean Research, Tokyo)*

2,500-tonne *Solo* equipped with helicopter and water cannons, chased a tiny 40–50 feet fishing/whaling cutter. Such images are never distributed by Greenpeace or shown on its websites.

Other organizations have been more violent in their campaigns, and several whaling ships and facilities have been targeted by eco-saboteurs. In 1979, when these attacks climaxed, the ship *Sierra*, operating under a flag of convenience, was rammed and severely damaged by *Sea Shepherd* under the command of Paul Watson. The ship was later bombed and sunk while under repair in Lisbon. A few months later, in 1980, bombs sank two Spanish ships. A ship under the South African flag was razed by fire, which may have been an act of arson (Day 1992).

Direct action has always been Paul Watson's trademark—a militancy that brought forth his expulsion from Greenpeace. Sea Shepherd's most spectacular act was the sinking of two whaling vessels at Reykjavik harbour together with an assault on Hvalur's whale station at Hvalfjörður, Iceland, in 1986 (Scarce 1990: 97–113). Sea Shepherd has moreover made several assaults on Norwegian minke whalers; the first was the scuttling of the *Nybræna* during Christmas 1992 followed by the scuttling of *Senet* in 1994.[8] *Senet* was later set on fire in 1997, whereas a third vessel was subjected to an attempted scuttling in 1998.[9] It is uncertain whether Sea Shepherd was involved in the two latter cases, but Watson has promised a reward to anybody who destroys a whaling vessel. Once his vessel rammed into the Norwegian coastguard, and he has tried to interrupt Faroese catches of pilot whales. His expressed aim was to inflate insurance fees to a point where whaling became unprofitable.

Paul Watson and his Sea Shepherd took also a lead in the militant campaign against the resumption of Makah whaling in the late 1990s, when a poster read 'Save a whale, harpoon a Makah'. Forced to stop in the 1920s due to the decimation of the gray whale population, the Makah wanted to resume whaling to revitalize their culture after the gray whale population had recovered. Sea Shepherd claims that the seventy-year interruption in hunting proves that the Makah have no cultural need to whale and that what they really want is to get rich on exports to Japan. Although the protesters did not succeed in preventing the Makah from catching a whale in 1999, they have since then been more successful challenging the legality of the resumption of Makah whaling in court. The court case has dragged on, and in September 2007 five Makah men lost patience and killed a gray whale without a federal permit. They are now facing trial and risk imprisonment and fines.

Consumer Boycotts

Consumer boycotts organized by environmental and animal protection groups pose another threat to the commodity path. This strategy was first used in the 1960s, when twenty NGOs joined AWI's consumer boycott against Japan and the Soviet Union (Frøvik 1995: 160). Since then, the WDCS, EIA, EII, IFAW, HSUS, Greenpeace and Sea Shepherd have been among the most active organizers of boycotts. These organizations have pursued mainly two approaches: media advertisements that appeal to individual consumers, and pressure on large supermarket and restaurant chains not to purchase fish from whaling countries. Both approaches have been accompanied by demonstrations to enhance the media coverage. Consumer boycotts have been used against Canada, the Faroe Islands, Iceland, Japan, Norway and Caribbean states.

In 1988 Greenpeace targeted Iceland in an attempt to stop its scientific whaling programme, initiated two years before. The main fast food chains in the United States were pressed to cancel contracts with Icelandic fish exporting companies, and 150 school boards across the country decided not to buy Icelandic fish for school lunches. Two main German supermarket chains also decided not to buy Icelandic fish products (Ívarsson 1994). In response to the 1992 Norwegian decision to resume minke whaling, several NGOs announced their determination to organize boycotts not only of Norwegian fish, but also of a number of other Norwegian products and services, including the 1994 Winter Olympics, held in Norway. The tactics were the same as those used against Iceland. In 1996, the WDCS launched 'its biggest campaign ever' to 'kill the whale trade', mainly directed at the Faroe Islands, a small country that has been targeted by boycott campaigns organized by the EIA, IFAW and others several times since 1985. Japan has been threatened with boycotts on several occasions, as in 1985 when twenty-two organizations initiated a campaign against Japan Air Lines (Brown and May 1991: 108). Later, the EIA, HSUS and Greenpeace started a campaign to pressure Wal-Mart and Tesco to use their influence as large shareholders in Japanese supermarkets chains to ban trade of whale and dolphin meat in Japan (GRD 2004: 6). Several Caribbean states have been threatened with tourist boycotts in retaliation for their support of the Japanese position at the IWC, a campaign that has become so malicious that the IWC commissioners on several occasions have been forced to protest against the attacks on member countries.

These sanctions all have one aim in common: to close down whaling and turn the whale resources into a non-resource or a person. However, the effectiveness of these boycotts is difficult to assess. Even when contracts may have been cancelled for reasons of e.g. price or quality, blaming cancellations on whaling may gain favour among environmentally conscious consumers (Ívarsson 1994: 114). Moreover, products from whaling nations may have found markets elsewhere. The campaign against Iceland seems to have had the greatest impact, although the results were mixed: Icelandair noticed no effect of calls for boycott of the national airline, nor did the boycott have any impact on Icelandic sales in Britain. However, losses in Germany and the United States were significant (Ívarsson 1994: 83–134).[10] Although the boycott did not bring an end to Iceland's scientific whaling, which ended as planned in 1989, it is nonetheless likely that this experience is one reason why Iceland hesitated to resume commercial whaling. The impact on Norway, on the other hand, has been negligible. Despite Greenpeace's claim that Norway lost trade valued at NOK500 million (about US$ 80 million) in 1993, both fish exports and foreign tourist earnings reached all-time records in that year. The actual value of lost contracts was estimated at about US$ 1 million, mostly in Germany (Bjørndal and Toft 1994). None of these campaigns came close to the dramatic impact of the tuna boycott.

The campaign for 'dolphin-safe' tuna took largely two forms. A number of environmental and animal rights organizations, with the EII and HSUS playing key roles, lobbied politicians into proposing legislative measures and then took governmental agencies before the courts when they failed to enforce these laws. As early as 1974 a court ruling had ordered the authorities to end by-catches of dolphins by 31 May 1976 (Bonanno and Constance 1996: 129). Between 1988 and 1992 the EII and other groups filed several lawsuits to force the U.S. government to impose an embargo on imports. In August 1990 the judge ordered the administration to impose an embargo on tuna caught by foreign (i.e. Mexican) vessels until proof was provided regarding reduced dolphin kills comparable to U.S. levels (1996: 191). Later this embargo was extended to cover all nations that processed yellowfin tuna from Mexico, Venezuela and Vanuatu for reexport to the United States. The burden of proof remained with companies and countries: they were guilty until proven innocent (1996: 202). Mexico filed a protest with GATT (General Agreement on Tariffs and Trade) against the embargo in 1990, whereas the EU and more than twenty other countries filed a protest two years later. GATT ruled against the United States, but Mexico was reluctant to press the case in the midst of the NAFTA negotiations (1996: 202).

Consumer boycott campaigns were launched to bring additional weight to the legal measures. The first consumer boycott of canned tuna began in the early 1970s (1996: 189), but it was only when used in combination with political and legal measures that this strategy put strong pressure on the industry. In 1988 a coalition of environmental and animal welfare/rights organizations launched a consumer boycott of the three major tuna processors in the United States, which together controlled about 70 per cent of the domestic market. Later the same year this was expanded to include pet food. Several measures were introduced to reduce dolphin mortality, and The Dolphin Protection Consumer Information Act passed in 1990 set standards for the dolphin-safe label for tuna (1996: 188). That same year the companies announced that they would no longer buy tuna caught in nets that kill dolphins, and would put the dolphin-safe label on their tuna. In 1991 dolphin-safe tuna accounted for 95 per cent of U.S. sales of canned tuna.

The consequences of the campaigns against tuna purse seine fishing have been considerable. The implementation of the MMPA initially favoured operations from Latin American countries, but later embargos shifted the industry to Asia and the Western Pacific, where yellowfin tuna do not follow dolphins. Latin American fishers were unable to make this change due to financial constraints. The success of the NGOs put both fishers and processing workers, first in the United States and then in Latin America, out of work. Between 1982 and 1991 an average of 1,000 jobs were lost in the tuna processing industry in Puerto Rico alone. According to Bonanno and Constance, the fishing communities along the Eastern Tropical Pacific faced a 'devastating crisis' (1996: 239), and they blame the environmental movement for paying 'little attention to the economic consequences that its actions had on fishing communities and workers' (1996: 244). This has further marginalized labour to the benefit of transnational capital invested in the tuna industry, which has become more centrally controlled. In Mexico, Venezuela and elsewhere the campaigns were seen as U.S. protectionism and have fostered strong anti-environmental feelings among the local population.

Destroying the Market

Another strategy used by protectionist organizations has been to make the resources of no value to the whalers by destroying their markets, thus removing their products from the commodity state. This they have tried to achieve by turning the consumption of whale products into a barbaric act. With the widespread image of a superwhale, it has been rather easy at the rhetoric level to turn eating whale meat into an immoral act: 'Sickest dinner ever served: JAPS FEAST ON WHALE. VIPs tuck into its raw flesh' announced the British *Daily Star* over the front page, continuing on page 5: 'Greedy Japs gorge on a mountain of whale meat at sick feast' in a 'banquet of blood' (Perthen 1991: 1, 5). Apart from the racist tone ('Japs'), the paper's choice of words turns the event into an orgy of senseless eating of a luxury item only affordable to VIPs. Civilized people do not 'tuck into raw flesh' or 'gorge on a mountain of meat'. The focus on raw meat and blood underlines the lack of culture. This is how animals eat; people cook their food.[11] To some people, eating whale meat has been turned into something like cannibalism, and a U.S. professor in mathematics found 'cannibalism LESS offensive than the eating of whale meat' (quoted in *International Harpoon*, 20 May 1998, p. 8). Perhaps the British MP (and later sport minister) Tony Banks had such ideas when he suggested during a demonstration in Glasgow in 1992 that the Japanese and Norwegians eat each other rather than whales if they wanted something exotic to eat. Such claims turn consumption of whale meat into sensational events. For those who have a tradition of eating whale meat, these accusations are both humiliating and culturally imperialistic.

Today whale meat arouses aversion in more people than does almost any other kind of meat. In a survey of people's attitudes to whales in Australia, England, Germany, the United States, Japan and Norway; only seal meat met with the same level of disapproval as whale meat among the following alternatives: chicken, deer, horse (ranked third after whales and seals), kangaroo, lamb, lobster, and wildfowl (Freeman and Kellert 1992: 29). Both in Australia and in England 93 per cent answered that they cannot accept that people eat whale meat.

Recently, a new argument has been added to the anti-whaling rhetoric: whale meat might be harmful to human health. Several research projects have documented high concentrations of PCB and heavy metals in marine mammals, causing great concern to whaling societies.[12] The message is clear: not only are whalers killing warm-blooded and sentient whales, they are also destroying the health and the future of their own children in the quest for profit. Whalers have responded that their adversaries' sudden concern for the whalers' children is nothing but hypocrisy and that the contamination of the whales has been caused by the countries most opposed to whaling. The implication is that whale lovers should be more concerned about pollution than about whaling.

Parallel with moral condemnation of eating whale meat, several countries have employed legal means to turn their inhabitants against whale meat consumption, as when Norwegian catches of bottlenose whales ended after the U.K. banned imports of whale meat for pet food in 1972 (ISG 1992: 32). A number of other restrictions have been introduced on the trade of whale products. In the United States, the 1967 Endangered Species Act (ESA) and the 1972 Marine Mammal Protection Act (MMPA) both prohibited imports of marine mammal products, effectively destroying the Inuit handicraft market in whalebone and ivory carvings (RCSS 1986: 230, 238). The European Union introduced licenses for importing whale products into the community in 1981, and Australia banned imports of whale products the same year (D'Amato and Chopra 1991: 43).

International organizations have also made attempts to restrict trade in whale products. The Convention on International Trade in Endangered Species

(CITES), which was established in 1973, has listed all cetaceans (whether endangered or not), an action that severely restricts, and in many cases bans, international trade in whale products. As is the case with the IWC, however, countries that filed objections are not legally bound by this decision. In 1979, the
IWC adopted a resolution to end imports of whale products into member states
from nonmembers, and in 1986 it was decided that meat from scientific whaling should mainly be consumed locally, which means that no more than 49 per
cent can be exported. Although not legally binding, such resolutions are used—
against better knowledge—to claim that such trade runs counter to international
laws. Trade in whale products between Iceland, Japan and Norway is not illegal
according to the IWC and CITES regulations, but some countries imposed voluntarily restrictions in order not to provoke U.S. trade sanctions unnecessarily.
Norway has since lifted its export ban and sold whale meat to Iceland and is
prepared to resume exporting it to Japan, which has so far (as of 2008) failed to
lift its import embargo on whale products.

With international trade severely restricted, it should come as no surprise that
criminal elements have tried to go into the business of smuggling meat across
borders. The Japanese police have made several arrests, but some of the NGOs
have taken it upon themselves to make investigations in Japan and elsewhere,
timing the release of their reports to the IWC meetings. By analysing the DNA
in whale meat in Japanese stores, some NGOs have tried to prove illegal catches
and trade in protected whales. The Japanese, on the other hand, point out that
there is still frozen meat in storage. Moreover, when Japanese scientists wanted
to verify the findings of the NGOs, the tested meat was not available for verifica-
tion.[13] NGOs have also complained that dolphin meat has been mislabelled as
whale meat. Even though the labelling might be an attempt to misguide customers (who prefer whale to dolphin), it is doubtful whether such labelling is against
Japanese law as the term *kujira* (whale) includes *iruka* (dolphin) as a subcategory.
The opposite would have been worse: labelling whale meat as dolphin meat could
be taken as an attempt to conceal illegal whaling.

For thirty years anti-whaling activists have attempted to stop all consumptive use of whales. In addition to confrontations and insults there has been an
extensive marketing of non- and low-consumptive use of whales.[14] The two approaches are two sides of the same coin: actions against whaling would probably
not have received the economic and political support they have without there
having at the same time been a market for the superwhale.

Consuming the Superwhale

Whalemania was certainly a growth industry, as observed by Frederic Golden
(1989), the editor of a theme number of the scientific journal *Oceanus*. Today
the non- and low-consumptive value of cetaceans amounts to billions of dollar
per year. The superwhale, with all its cetacean and human qualities, has proved

to have enormous economic and political potential. What has turned this image into a commodity, however, is the emergence of a new demand among individuals, companies and governments to appear green. This demand has been created by the growing environmental awareness among people, fuelled by the crisis-maximizing strategies of many environmental groups. In the ecological discourse whales have come to play the role of a metonym for nature, and the image of an endangered whale has become a symbol for many people. Through the mass media the public is invited to participate as spectators to the tournaments of value, which may, moreover, be important marketing devices for low- and nonconsumptive use of whales. Tournaments allow millions of people to partake in the superwhale myth, where our relation to whales becomes a symbolic expression of our fundamental relations with nature. This provides the backdrop and raison d'être for whale watching, movies, coffee-table books and so on. But the superwhale is a symbolic type of commodity. What is consumed is not really the symbol itself, but human relations (Moeran 1992: 93), for which the superwhale is a metaphor. Therefore, feasting on the superwhale does not exhaust the superwhale but adds to its economic and political power, at least up to a certain point. Consuming the superwhale is seen as a means to change people's attitudes towards whales, which, it is hoped, will further stimulate campaigns against whaling.

Dolphinariums and Marine Theme Parks

One of the first low-consumptive uses of cetaceans appeared in dolphinariums and marine theme parks. These are still popular and have probably done more than anything else to foster a positive feeling toward cetaceans. The Flipper shows strengthened this image further. The HSUS claims that there are about 400 Atlantic bottlenose dolphins in captivity in the United States alone,[15] in addition to beluga, killer whales, false killer whales, Pacific white-sided dolphins and pilot whales (Mooney 1998). SeaWorld, which in 1994 operated four marine theme parks (in California, Florida, Texas and Ohio) with a combined budget of 164 million dollars (Mooney 1998: 26),[16] owned twenty-two of the forty-nine killer whales held in captivity worldwide. The park in San Diego has made Shamu—the name of a series of killer whales—its icon and trademark. Shamu has become Southern California's largest tourist attraction (Davis 1997). Through spectacular performances, SeaWorld wants to transmit love, caring and closeness between cetaceans and humans, where the audience can 'touch nature' and make 'contact with another world' (Davis 1997: 35). Children are invited to pet and feed the dolphins with expectations of receiving a splash in return, and a few chosen ones are invited to the 'Shamu Backstage' to touch the killer whale (1997: 104–5).

In the U.S., where boat owners may be fined several thousand dollars for giving food to wild dolphins, permission to keep whales in captivity is only given for the purposes of science, education, conservation and military. Theme parks therefore devote much rhetorical emphasis to education and work that generates a particular attitude towards nature—but in fact the marine theme parks are most of all money makers for the owners (Davis 1997: 127). To the WDCS they are nothing but circuses in disguise (Mooney 1998: 27). The number of voices against marine theme parks is on the rise. The WDCS, EII and HSUS are among the organizations that claim it is inhumane to keep whales in captivity. Even the largest pool does not satisfy the whales' needs for space. They are used to a life of freedom, where they can cover long distances and dive to great depths. Shallow pools force the whales to swim near the surface, increasing the danger of skin diseases. Close family and social relations are destroyed,[17] and mortality is said to be high (Mooney 1998; Williams 2001). Hence the dolphinariums are not completely nonconsumptive. Many animal advocates have turned against dolphinariums and theme parks, but most of the environmental groups have failed to campaign against the parks, perhaps because they recognize that parks still contribute importantly to the superwhale myth.

Whale Tourism

To view cetaceans in captivity is not regarded as authentic any longer. The real thing is to watch the whales in the wild, and more than nine million people reportedly spent more than US$ 1,050 million on whale watching activities in 1998, when whale watching was organized from 492 communities in 87 countries (Hoyt 2000: 5–6). Most of the whale watchers go by boats, but there are also organized tours from land and from the air. While whale watching people can observe whales first-hand, meet them, engage them and even touch them.

Some of the environmental and animal rights groups organize whale safaris, and those organized by the WDCS from London are probably among the most exclusive. In 1991 the WDCS organized tours from London to Alaska for £2,995, to Baja California for £2,070, to the Galapagos Islands for £3,260 and to the Antarctic and the Falkland Islands for £5,340 (ads in *Sonar* No.5: 23 and No.6: 17). In 1991, more than 200 commercial whale-watch operators offered more than 250 different tours in North America alone, ranging in duration from an hour to a fortnight with prices varying from US$7 to US$3,000 (Corrigan 1991: 7). The tours all offered special excitements: one operator invited tourists 'to reach out and touch nature' while 'travel[ling] in safety aboard a comfortable cruise vessel, in harmony with nature and at nature's own pace' (1991: 182). Some tours sought to enhance this oneness with nature by using small kayaks so as to be less separated from the water environment, while others preferred to observe nature through panoramic windows from a deluxe bar aboard a liner carrying 700 passengers. Many operators advertised tailor-made trips, which 'exactly suit the desires of the client', often with 'cultural highlights' such as visits to Indian and Inuit villages along the route. A Newfoundland operator brought 'people into our spectacular marine environment so that the whales can watch them!' (1991: 250). It is also interesting to note that many of the operators claimed that they operated in an 'area where whales abound' and were able to guarantee either sighting success or a new trip. This impression is underscored by Hoyt (1992: 1), who calms believers of these same organizations' rhetoric that whales are on the brink of extinction by stating that all 'the large whale species and many dolphins and porpoises can be seen regularly on a wide range of tours'.

Whale watching is seen as a means to educate people to perceive whales in the right way (Hoyt 1992; Ris 1993; Kemf et al. 2001). Most of the anti-whalers have therefore endorsed whale watching despite the negative impact this might have on the animals. The tours are carefully staged, and the participants are expected to behave and feel in a particular way. To be affiliated with a research centre gives added authority to the information whale watchers are given before and during tours. The Whale Centre in Andenes in Northern Norway is a case in point. One aim of the centre, which was opened in 1988 by the Swedish Centre for Studies of Whales and Dolphins with money from the WWF, was to change Norwegian views on whales: 'Located in the last stronghold of Norwegian whaling the centre plays an important role in changing attitudes towards whales', wrote two of the researchers at the centre (Similä and Ugarte 1991: 18). Before tours, participants are guided through the centre and given information about its nonlethal research. On the boat, tour guides—when I visited the centre as a consultant in 1992–94 most of them were foreign students opposed to whaling—offer interpretations of whale behaviour that please the spectators (cf. Peace 2005).

Figure 3.2   *Orca safari bus, Ketchikan, Alaska. (author's photo)*

Now tremendously popular, whale watching has been heralded as an alternative to whaling for small coastal communities. However, whale watching is not completely beneficial. The sea traffic may force the whales to change their behaviour and migration routes (Beach and Weinrich 1989; Hierta 1991; Richter, Dawson and Slooten 2003). Moreover, recently the U.S. National Oceanic & Atmospheric Administration (NOAA) has claimed that collisions with ships have become a serious threat to the future of whale stocks and ships carrying whale watchers pose the biggest risk, second only to ships from the U.S. Navy (Press release from the Public Employees for Environmental Responsibility, 15 July 2004). Whale tourism—unless conducted from land—is therefore not completely nonconsumptive, and the IWC has established a working group to examine all aspects of the whale watching industry. One report presented to this working group was critical also about the claimed economic benefits of the industry, indicating that the operators tend to exaggerate incomes and at the same time neglect the social (including health) and cultural benefits of whaling (Moyle and Evans 2001).

Swim with a Whale

Watching cetaceans from the deck of a ship does not satisfy everybody, and more and more people want to actually swim with cetaceans.[18] In Hong Kong people have broken into the Ocean Park at night in order to have a free ride on a dolphin (Carter and Parton 1992: 5), and in Western Australia people stand in line to be in the water with a group of dolphins (Winton 1992). Babies born in close proximity to dolphins are believed by some to be more harmonious and to develop exceptional talents (Dobbs 1990: 181), and it is thought that such children may even develop into *Homo delphinus*, 'a so-called new race or species of human babies born in water who exhibit dolphin traits' (Cochrane and Callen 1992: 30). In the United States there are about eighteen licensed dolphinariums with swim-with-the-dolphins (SWTD) programmes (HSUS 2002). According to the HSUS, tens of thousands of people may swim with captive dolphins in the U.S. every year, and a session with dolphins typically costs about US$ 100–125 (HSUS n.d.). Several of the institutions claim that their programmes are of therapeutic value for handicapped and distressed people, particularly for autistic children and patients suffering from Down's syndrome.

Animal protection groups like the HSUS and WDCS, however, believe the therapeutic value of such swim programmes is no greater than having contacts with domesticated animals. Dolphin assisted therapy can therefore not justify the suffering inflicted upon captive dolphins, a view also held by some scientists (e.g. Brensing 2006). Moreover, several participants in SWTD programmes have been seriously injured by dolphins, and there might be potential for disease transmission between humans and dolphins (Rose, Farinato and Sherwin 2006).

Some of those who oppose holding dolphins in captivity have taken these programmes into the wild. Most of the wild dolphins seeking human companionship are solitary, with the exception of the group of dolphins at Monkey Mia Bay in Australia. The few dolphins that voluntarily seek human companions attract crowds of people, some of whom are seeking therapy. To the initiate, these dolphins have become intimate friends and cult objects (Doak 1988; Cochrane and Callen 1992; McKenna 1992). Today there are many websites featuring SWTD programmes both with captive and wild dolphins.

One of the most celebrated dolphin therapists is Horace Dobbs, who holds a PhD in psychiatry in the U.K. In a series of books and movies he describes encounters with dolphins and the reactions among his depressed patients. Several of Dobbs's patients testify that they felt relaxed among dolphins. Being with the animal released them from the anxiety of having to perform or to live up to other people's expectations. Together with the dolphin one can behave naturally, as the following testimonial clearly shows (from Dobbs 1990: 82–83):

> I felt like a Princess being taken away to another land by her Prince . . . My Prince was taking me into his world beyond the realms of fantasy . . . We were together as one . . . I was him and he was me. Complete harmony and love . . . I did not speak, we communicated with our hearts. I was totally and completely in love . . . This beautiful dolphin loved me for what I was in my heart. It didn't matter whether I was old, young, fat or thin. I didn't have to impress him with a string of degrees. I was loved and accepted for myself, for the person I was . . . I did not have to compete, all the stresses of human values and life no longer existed.

Through such testimonials individuals share experiences and receive emotional support from a small group of like-minded people. To be rejected by a dolphin can thus imply rejection by the support group (Dobbs 1990: 95).

To swim with wild cetaceans is not unproblematic, however. The WDCS, which organized swimming with dolphins and pilot whales in the 1990s (WDCS 1992), has turned against such programmes for the same reason it is against SWTD programmes in pools: concern about the health of both animals and people,[19] a concern that has been reinforced through a survey recently conducted on behalf of the U.S. Marine Mammal Commission (Samuels and Bejder 2004).

Rehabilitation and Rescue

Some activists are not only against keeping cetaceans in captivity but want to release them, by legal or illegal means. To release dolphins can pose a serious threat to their safety, and it is against U.S. law to release captive dolphins without proper preparations. But rehabilitation is difficult, and several animals have been released before the authorities have issued permits. In 1999, for example,

Richard O'Barry—one of the trainers of the dolphins used in the Flipper television series—and his companions at Sugarloaf Dolphin Sanctuary in Florida were
fined US$ 59,500 for having illegally transported and released two dolphins that
were not properly prepared.

There exist reports of successful releases of dolphins. The most celebrated case
involved Echo and Misha, released in 1990 after two years in captivity (Howard
1995). But the great problems facing the rehabilitation work are well illustrated
by Keiko's history. Caught outside Iceland in 1979 at the age of two and sold to
Mexico in 1985, this killer whale became famous for his role in the movie *Free
Willy* (1993). The Free Willy Keiko Foundation—supported by the HSUS, EII
and others—was established in 1994 with large donation from Warner Bros. In
1996 Keiko was flown to Oregon, where he was trained to catch fish in a rehabilitation facility worth US$ 7.3 million. In September 1998 he was flown to
Iceland to continue training 'closer to home', and in 2002 he was finally released.
Two months later Keiko appeared in a fjord in western Norway, where he died of
pneumonia in December 2003 without having managed to become independent
of humans. The work to bring Keiko back to the wild lasted a decade and had
cost about US$ 20 million, without the aim being reached.[20]

Rescues of whales stranded, entangled in fishing nets or facing other kinds of
difficulties are another way people can show their concern and engagement with
whales. Most of the large stranded whales are sperm and gray whales, but the
great majority are small cetaceans like dolphins, pilot whales and killer whales,
which often beach themselves in groups.[21] Many cetaceans are moreover caught
in fishing gear every year. Networks to assist whales in difficulties have been organized in several countries. A U.S. network is composed of representatives from
the authorities (local, state and federal), academic and research institutions, rehabilitation centres, aquariums and NGOs, many of which are open around the
clock.[22] In 1992 the programme was incorporated under the MMPA—through
the Marine Mammal Health and Stranding Response Act—and reports and
manuals have been published about how stranded whales ought to be handled
(e.g. NMFS and FWS 1997; Geraci 2005).

The most spectacular rescue operation involved three gray whales that were
trapped in the ice off northern Alaska in 1988. In his book *Freeing the Whales*,
Tom Rose vividly narrates the US$ 5.8 million rescue operation in what he termed
'the World's Greatest Non-Event' (Rose 1989). Many actors took part. President
Reagan tried to shape up his environmental record, and the Soviet regime showed
a more humane face when a Soviet ice-breaker was redirected to save the whales.
The U.S. military provided material and personnel, the NOAA activated a new
satellite ahead of schedule in order to provide the Soviet Union with information
on ice conditions, the oil industry improved its image considerably (only to lose
much of the new-won goodwill in the *Exxon Valdez* oil spill five months later),
the Inuit were pictured as good-natured humans and not as greedy whale killers, and television companies competed to get the most spectacular shots in the

fight for higher market shares. Most important, all the calls from people want-ing to help made it possible for anti-whaling groups to capitalize on the event. To Greenpeace the event allegedly meant the biggest source of new money and members in its history.[23]

An important objective is to help individual animals back to deep water, if necessary after a period of rehabilitation. Animal welfare is high on the agenda. But the networks may also have conservational implications. Although rescue and rehabilitation is too infrequent to have significant direct impact on popu-lation levels—and despite humans' efforts, many of the animals die—medical research on dead and dying animals may throw light on infections and diseases and thereby tell us something about the health condition of the stocks in general. Such activities can moreover stir people's emotions and help them acquire a non-consumptive attitude towards whales.

Whale Adoption

Several organizations run whale adoption programmes both to change people's perceptions and to bolster finances. Jim K. McLay, a former New Zealand com-missioner to the IWC, is among those who see a clear potential in whale adoption and gives his full support:[24] 'The Whale & Dolphin Adoption Project encourages individuals, families and corporates to adopt a whale or a dolphin; thus creating an even closer relationship between New Zealanders and cetaceans. I strongly commend the Project's objectives and its fund-raising programmes. It provides even further support for New Zealand's strong conservation position at the Inter-national Whaling Commission and in other international forums.'

Some museums, aquariums and research institutions spend earnings from whale adoption programmes to cover research expenses. Among these are the Vancouver Aquarium Marine Science Centre, which offers killer whales for adoption in British Columbia,[25] and the New England Aquarium, which offers right whales off the U.S. northeast coast.[26] The Mingan Island Cetacean Study in Quebec offers blue whales at a price of US$ 100 for 'individual foster par-ents' or US$ 1,000 for a corporation for a two-year period to finance its blue whale research.[27]

These institutions, particularly the NGOs, see adoption programmes as a strategy in their work to protect whales. The WWF's adoption programme, con-nected to the whale watch centre at Andenes in Norway, has received consider-able attention. The indignation was strong in Norwegian coastal communities when it was disclosed that WWF-Denmark had earned more than £200,000 from corporations and people that 'adopted' sperm and killer whales appearing off the coast of Northern Norway in the second half of 1990. The price was about £4,500 for a sperm whale and £450 for a killer whale.[28] Despite numerous protests from the local population, these whales were still offered for adoption in 2001, but then through a local whale-watch operator.

The stated rationale for cetacean adoption programmes is mostly research and/or protection work. As with whale watching, there are many NGOs that stress contacts with researchers and research institutions in marketing their adoption programmes. Through such a relationship researchers can receive financial support for their studies, while the programmes get a varnish of being science. This applies to Whale Safari in Andenes and to Allied Whale, which uses ties to the College of the Atlantic in Maine to attract customers.

Whales offered for adoption are in general limited to a few species of animals that can be recognized by their colour patterning, flukes or scars, and therefore can be given individual names. Individual personality is important in relation to adoptions. Like the sponsor of a child in a Third World country, the whale sponsor may receive photos and regular progress reports on her or his whale. Allied Whale has therefore selected species 'that are favorites with whale watchers and biologists, or that have a long history of resightings',[29] making it possible to create life histories and pedigrees. The humpback whale, easily recognizable by its flukes, seems to be most popular. The killer whale, recognizable by the body's colour patterning, is also popular, and the Vancouver Aquarium has placed the 'family trees' of killer whales they offer for adoption on the Internet.[30]

Research, Conferences and Seminars

Cetology is a science with roots in the Enlightenment of the eighteenth century, and it developed quickly as a branch of biology at many academic institutions. Cetology is therefore not a new science, but the symbolic and political importance of whales today has unquestionably stimulated recruitment to the discipline. The ties between researchers and NGO activists are often close; frequently the researcher is also an activist. Research has also changed in focus. Early cetology at universities emphasized the large whales' physiology and life histories, a focus that was a response to the economic interests of the whaling industry. This kind of research depended to a large extent on the dissection of dead animals. Today most researchers have to work on living animals, with the exception of stranded whales, whose research value in many connections is undermined because these whales may not be representative of the stock. This has consequences for the research topics, which increasingly are restricted to nonlethal use of whales (dolphinariums, whale watching, swim-with-whale programmes, whale therapy, rehabilitation and release). This trend has been strengthened as much of the research is initiated, financed and/or conducted by NGOs and public offices.

This situation is mirrored in meeting programmes and publications. Many seminars and workshops, which often are important events for networking and policy making, focus on what whale protectionists may perceive as important, concrete problems. A typical example is a workshop on the bottlenose whale's sensitivity to anthropogenic noise, organized by the U.S. Marine Mammal Commission in April 2004. Also, larger international conferences organized by academic associations—e.g. the European Association for Aquatic Mammals (EAAM), the European Cetacean Society (ECS) and the Society for Marine Mammalogy (SMM)—are dominated by papers on small toothed whales (dolphins, harbour porpoises and killer whales) based on observed behaviour. At the ECS conference in 2000 there were thus more papers on vocalization (twelve included in the *Proceedings*) than on the whales' physiology and life stories together (four each). About 60 per cent of the papers focused exclusively on small toothed whales. A similar situation is reflected in journals like *Marine Mammal Science* (published by the SMM) and *Aquatic Mammals* (published by the EAAM), and increasingly even in the IWC's Scientific Committee.

A number of organizations and individuals run courses and seminars of varying length, scope and intention. At one end several universities offer courses in cetology to students at all levels, with the main focus on physiology, nourishment, ecology, behaviour and management. At the other end NGOs and private 'research institutions' offer shorter courses—often lasting a week or less—to participants without former experience. An example is the Coastal Ecosystems Research Foundation (CERF), a Canadian institution that offers weekend and 7-day courses in research methodologies.[31] In addition to learning 'field techniques first-hand from research biologists', participants have been offered instructions in sailing and kayaking—all at price of US$ 1,075 per week.[32] CERF's address was identical to that of the Adventure Spirit Travel Company, with whom they collaborated in developing ecotourism as a viable business.[33] CERF is among several operators who gain some legitimacy by having ties with universities. CERF has offered courses in collaboration with the University of California (Los Angeles), University of British Columbia (Vancouver) and University of Bath (U.K.).

In many cases the courses seem to be organized to finance research with the help of paying volunteers. The research is usually limited to photo identification and observation of behaviour, but may in fact be confined to preparing food and other miscellaneous work onboard (WDCS 1992). 'The trick here', writes Eric Hoyt, who is an activist and authority on whale watching, 'is to design a project in which volunteers will pay to participate and actually do some real work and not just require babysitting that distracts from the research' (Hoyt 1994: 7). Research undertaken by Italy's Tethys Research Institute seems to have been financed in this way.[34] But Tethys has another agenda as well: whale protection. The purpose of the courses is to help participants capture the charm of freely swimming whales and dolphins.[35]

The most spiritually inclined whale enthusiasts organize their own courses and seminars. In 2004, Joan Ocean and her Dolphin Connection could, for example, offer a seminar in the Azores, where 'Joan will share the most recent cetacean and extraterrestrial information', and several seminars in Hawaii, where the participants, through dolphinese consciousness, were invited to contact alien galactic cultures.[36] Jason Cressey, who has a PhD in psychology from Oxford and is a founder of People-Ocean-Dolphin (POD), offers a series of ninety-minute sessions—'dolphin vision quests'—that explore the participant's personal engagement with whales. POD also organizes a number of workshops for business leaders. Inspired by whales and dolphins, the participants at these sessions and workshops allegedly learn team-work and conflict resolution, enhance 'emotional intelligence' and interpersonal skills, define and pursue personal and corporate goals, strive for group harmony, and develop techniques to 'go with the flow' and reduce stress.[37]

Whales in Popular Culture

Whale adoption, conferences, lectures and courses catering to business leaders have taken us several steps from consumptive use towards nonconsumptive use of cetaceans. Other forms of nonconsumptive utilization are whales presented in text, form and music. A number of fictions about whales have been published since Herman Melville's famous novel *Moby-Dick* in 1851,[38] and they cover a number of genres. In her bibliography on whale literature, Trisha Lamb Feuerstein divided the works into a number of categories such as spy novels, horror, science fiction, romance (both between whales and between whales and humans) and nonfiction (Feuerstein 2001). In many of the books people and cetaceans—particularly dolphins—collaborate, but where they do not, the whales are the heroes. Lloyd Abbey's *The Last Whales* (1990) is in many ways typical for our time. In this love story between the two last blue whales on earth, all the characters are whales, but whaling is kept alive in their memories of great dangers and losses of dear ones to the harpoons. In this novel interspecies communication is common, and the oceans would have been a paradise had it not been for human beings and killer whales.

Some writers of science fiction are also intrigued by cetaceans. In *Startide Rising* (Brin 1983), for example, the spaceship *Streaker* is crewed by humans and 'neo-dolphins'; the latter are the product of genetic engineering and communicate among themselves in Japanese *haiku* verses. But probably the most widely read, and most entertaining, is the science-fiction novel *The Hitchhiker's Guide to the Galaxy* by Douglas Adams (1986), although the dolphins play a somewhat secondary role. From the poetic world, Heathcote Williams's ode to whales— *Whale Nation* (1988), combining exiting photographs and emotional poems— has become a classic, for whale lovers. *The Dolphin's Arc: Poems of Endangered Creatures of the Sea*, edited by Elisavietta Ritchie (1989), is but one of several published anthologies of whale poetry.

Most of the whale-related literature must be classified as nonfiction. There are thousands of scientific books, but most of them have a very limited market. However, a number of factual books are being published for the general readers. Some are encyclopaedic in style and coverage (e.g. Lyall Watson's *Whales of the World*, although its introduction leaves the reader in no doubt about the author's own opinion on whales and whaling); others focus on one species. Many books advance the author's personal views by combining value-laden texts and glossy photos in such a way that the protectionist message is clear. A good example is *Whales* by Jacques Cousteau and Yves Paccalet (1988).

New themes have recently been taken up. Books and articles are published about whale watching, both to meet the demand for information on travel destinations and to instruct tourists how to avoid disturbing the whales unnecessarily. Several guides have also been published on how to swim with dolphins.[39] Many books about friendly dolphins can best be regarded as examples of the dolphin cult and the New Age. In *Dolphins into the Future* (1997), for example, Joan Ocean takes readers on a journey together with dolphins through 'parallel realities and interdimensional localities' to the future world, whereas Tim Wyllie in *Dolphins, ETs & Angels* (1984) invites readers to swim with wild dolphins, 'encounter an ET and . . . expand and extend [her/his] consciousness to encompass the new energies sweeping our planet, heralded by angelic forces' (dustcover).

Typical of many of these books is that they weave together facts and speculation in such a way that it becomes difficult for the readers to know where facts end and fantasies begin. Moreover, the books often come in large formats and are illustrated with gorgeous, suggestive close-up photographs. Many of these books are attempts to stir wonderment towards the mysteries of the oceans, and are meant to influence—or educate—the readers in a special way. The same can be said about a large number of children's books. Feuerstein's bibliography includes more than a thousand English-language children's books on whales (Feuerstein 2005a). Meanwhile, a large number of the many educational packages offered to kindergartens and schools have been put together by anti-whaling organizations. Some dolphinariums in the United States offer educational packages to legitimize keeping cetaceans in captivity (Davis 1997).

Other kinds of artists have also turned to the world of whales. 'Whale music' exists in many forms, and several websites offer extensive lists of the whales' own songs, or of human music inspired by whales. Music cassettes and CDs feature 'singing' whales—foremost humpbacks, killer whales and some dolphins but also muter species like the minke whale. The album *Songs of the Humpback Whale*, produced by Roger Payne, has become a classic, and in 1979 extracts from the album were printed in 45 million copies and inserted in the *National Geographic Magazine*.[40] The song of the humpback whales also accompanies the two Voyager spacecrafts through space. In British Columbia, the Vancouver Aquarium opened the world's first Orca FM radio station in 1998, monitoring the live underwater communications of killer whales around Robson Bight. The old Greenpeacer Paul Spong has gone a step further in his project *Orca-live*. With support from the Japanese telecommunication giant NTT, among others, pictures and sound are transmitted via the Internet by the use of a network of underwater cameras and hydrophones. Registered members 'will receive email "alerts" about imminent events' (quoted in Feuerstein 2005b).

Stan Getz, John Denver, Olivia Newton-John, Herbie Hancock, Enigma, Judy Collins, Julian Lennon, Van Morrison and Lou Reed are only a few of the

many musical artists who have been inspired by whales. The New York Philhar-
monic is among those who have commissioned whale-inspired music. Much of
the music is influenced by the New Age and invites listeners to undergo healing
and spiritual experiences. *Dolphin Dreams: A Sonic Environment for Meditation
and Birth*, produced by Spirit Music in the U.S. state of Colorado, for example,
is designed with pregnant women, infants and people interested in interspecies
communication in mind. Others use didgeridoo and other ethnic instruments to
foster an illusion of a spiritual communion between indigenous peoples (particularly Australian Aborigines), whales and whale enthusiasts (Feuerstein 2005b).

A synthesis of whale sounds and human music constitutes an important subfield
within whale-related music. In *Symphony for Whales* (produced by Total Recording),
for example, 'the melodic and mysterious sounds' of humpback whales—whose
complex composition suggests a 'natural form of classical music'—are blended with
symphonies of Beethoven, Telemann and Haydn 'for a unique symphony from the
sea' (Feuerstein 2005b). Jim Nollman and his organization Interspecies Communication prefer to make the recordings not in studios but live. On *Orca's Greatest
Hits*, Nollman and his musicians play together with free-roaming killer whales. A
similar technique was used when Seattle's City Cantabile Choir held a concert for
killer whales, with the latter allegedly participating. Germany's Human/Dolphin
Research project has also made live recordings and released a CD with 'musical
conversation with "extraterrestial intelligence" culminating in an interactive reggae
session'. On track 4 one can hear the crew on the ship *Kairos* singing an Indian
Echo-song while pilot whales and common dolphins 'tune in'.[41]

'Whale artists' have produced paintings and drawings of whales and dolphins
for a large audience. Frank Stella (born 1936), an important figure within mini-
malism, has made a series of 266 paintings, prints, sculptures and metal relief
linked to the novel *Moby-Dick*, and an academic analysis of the series has been
published by the University of Michigan Press (Wallace 2000). Less renowned
but probably better known among whale enthusiasts is Wyland, who believes that
painting large whale murals might be the only way to save the whales (Wyland
and Doyle 1995: 35). He owns a chain of galleries, mostly located in Hawaii and
California, but his speciality is large murals of whales painted in their natural sizes.
His decoration of the circular conference centre in Long Beach (California) is the
world's largest mural painting, 378 metres long and ten floors high. The mural at
the entrance to the Reino Aventura Park in Mexico City includes a portrait of the
celebrated killer whale Keiko. The picture was painted on the condition that the
park released Keiko (Wyland and Doyle 1995: 145). In 2008 Wyland completed
his hundredth mural, in Beijing in connection with the Summer Olympics.[42]

Despite Wyland's claims, television and movies probably have a larger audience
and a stronger impact than Wyland's paintings. Long series of nature films have
been shown on such channels as the Discovery Channel, National Geographic
and BBC, and they are available on the video and DVD market as well as in educational packages destined for schools. Many of these films were made by NGOs

working against whaling. The close-ups of wild whales undoubtedly stir people's emotions and imagination, but the narratives accompanying the pictures make these films an even more efficient tool in combating whaling. The superwhale is presented in all its glory, and the focus is most often on the animals' intelligence, ability to communicate, peaceful friendliness and inscrutable mystique. Moreover, the experts and researchers interviewed are frequently themselves well-known activists with their own organizations—Dr. Robbins Barstow and Dr. Roger Payne appear repeatedly and are involved on both sides of the camera.

Some television programmes address the whaling issue directly, and although some programmes do try to present both sides of the divide equally, the great majority have an anti-whaling bias.[43] *Whale Wars*, produced by the BBC in 1993, for example, documented the work of the radical Environmental Investigation Agency (EIA), which is not particularly known for its objectivity, without asking any critical questions about the EIA. This programme allegedly had the highest ratings in the history of the BBC's Nature programmes (Feuerstein 2005c). The TV series *Flipper* may have contributed more to the whale cult than any other production, perhaps with the exception of the movie *Free Willy*. Many of these productions have a message that is very close to what we can find among the more spiritually oriented books. Titles like *Angels of the Sea* (Australia Channel 7) and *Dolphin Dreaming* (BBC) speak for themselves. Many videos are produced by New Agers.[44] Science-fiction movies like *Star Trek IV: The Voyage Home* also add fuel to the image of extraterrestrial intelligence.[45]

Finally, it should be mentioned that many NGOs offer a rich assortment of commercial products through their web pages or own shops. The most common products are richly illustrated books, movies, videos, whale music, art objects, stickers, posters, photos, stamps, bags, T-shirts, soft toys, pins, jewellery, computer games and so on, which all nourish and visualize people's commitment to the cause and thus help build a community of enthusiasts. Some have more special products to offer. One of the more curious products is the 'dolphin journey ointment' offered for sale by POD in 2000. The ointment which includes thistle, vervain and beeswax in an olive oil base, 'is a unique aid for those wishing to enhance meditation and visualization skills' when applied to the temples and 'third eye'.[46] Cetaceans have also invaded the world of computer games. In *Ecoquest 1: The Search for Cetus* the boy Adam and his dolphin friend Delphineus meet many dangers in their struggle to save the life of the whale Cetus from pollution and other hazards. The Sega group has released a series of games about a clever bottlenose dolphin named *Ecco*, who is young, intelligent and strong. The game is available both for PlayStation and Nintendo.

Selling Green Images

Individuals may go on whale-watching tours, pay for a swim with a whale, buy some of the many artefacts carrying whale symbols or send a check to one of the many anti-whaling organizations and get peace of mind, believing they have done something for the environment. Government agencies may also bolster their green image by supporting, and thus giving legitimacy to, the anti-whaling movement. In this section we shall focus on industrial firms, some of which constitute the greatest threat to marine life. In Chapter 4 we shall look more closely at the connection between NGOs and governments as it is manifested in the IWC.

Recent years have seen a green marketing boom in which companies try to take advantage of the ecological discourse. This can be done through totemic classification, which establishes a relationship between nature and a product (e.g. the Danish Dolphin TeleCom), or through eco-commercialism, by which a company creates an image of itself as aware of the environment (Moeran 1992: 197–98). One way to appear concerned about the environment is to advertise that the company plants a tree for each car sold, for example. Another path is that taken by the Anheuser-Busch beer company, which bought SeaWorld and used this chain actively in an attempt to appear green (Davis 1997: 27, 29). However, such claims are more credible if a known third party can endorse them. It is precisely here that the environmental and animal protection groups have a role to play. In the 1988 rescue of gray whales in Alaska, for example, oil companies and other industrial corporations worked side by side with NGOs (Rose 1989). Their work was transmitted worldwide for everybody to see. It is within this context that many of the transactions between NGOs and industrial concerns can best be understood.

Many people and firms are in need of a green image. Some people buy pins to wear on their jacket or a sticker for the car to tell the world that they care. Others may pay an environmental NGO for the use of its logos in marketing campaigns. The WWF, for example, has on several occasions been willing to sell green images to companies in need of one. In Denmark, the WWF allowed the Norwegian Statoil Company to use the WWF logo in advertisements and to announce that the oil company supported the WWF's work for endangered species, in order to get more Danes to use Statoil products in their cars. One million Danish kroner (about US$ 150,000) was considered a reasonable price to pay for the WWF's endorsement of advertisements for products that are harmful to the environment.

More companies than Statoil are in need of a green image, and these may be actively targeted by environmental and animal welfare organizations. In a letter to Danish business leaders, WWF-Denmark, after claiming that the whaling moratorium was about to be lifted and all known whales species were consequently about to be eradicated for all time, wrote:

> Therefore I send you this SOS for assistance in the WWF's fight for an extension of the moratorium. Here your company can give a cash contribution by sponsoring a whale for 50,000 kroner. The sponsorship will in a positive way connect your activities with

the WWF . . . Through a sponsorship your company has the opportunity to show your associates that it takes the environment and 'the green wave' seriously . . . I am sure that you will see the opportunities which a whale sponsorship will mean to your business. (WWF-Denmark 1990, author's translation from Danish)

The letter seems to have brought about the expected results, and one of the companies that decided to sponsor a whale was the Danish chemical company Brøste. In order to celebrate its 75-year anniversary, the company placed an advertisement in the *Børsen* (the Danish equivalent of the *Wall Street Journal*) stating: 'We bought a giant sperm whale from the WWF, Worldwide Fund for Nature, as a birthday present to ourselves . . . We know from the seller that he has more whales, in many sizes.' The advertisement asked those wishing to congratulate the company on its anniversary to donate money to the WWF rather than sending flowers, promising that their donations would be displayed at the birthday reception. Thus the chemical company mediated green images between the WWF and its own business partners.

In all the activities we have analysed, a feeling of belonging is created by partaking in the superwhale myth. This is most obvious on whale-watching tours and in SWTD programmes, but participation in whale saving operations and adoption programmes can also be a boost to company morale (cf. Rose 1989: 234). By displaying the proper buttons, T-shirts, jewellery, photos, bags and art objects, one's belonging to the movement is communicated to the world. Moreover, through books, movies and computer games consumers are educated to appreciate the qualities of cetaceans in the 'correct' way, a learning process that starts early in childhood. In the next chapter we will see some of the same processes at work in the International Whaling Commission, where its annual meetings provide the anti-whaling activists and governments with ample opportunities to display their emblems and commitment to the cause in their attempts to appropriate the whales for nonlethal purposes.

Notes

1. Wolfang Fischer, leader of the German section's anti-sealing campaign, on Bayrischer Rundfunk's TV programme *Live aus dem Schlachthof*, 15 January 1990 (my translation from German).
2. This is one reason why not-endangered harp seals hunted during a short season off Northeastern Canada make a better cause than does the endangered Mediterranean monk seal, slowly exterminated by pollution, tourism and military activities (Johnson 1988). In the case of the monk seal it is impossible to identify and give face to the enemy, and the forces behind the depletion of monk seals are powerful and influential. There is no face-to-face confrontation between the monk seal and the killer, no dramatic deaths and no blood.
3. This role was much appreciated by Robert Hunter, one of Greenpeace's founders and originally a professional journalist (Herscovici 1985: 79; Pearce 1991: 20): 'I was a traitor to my profession . . . Instead of reporting the news, I was in fact in the position of inventing the news, then reporting it' (Hunter 1979: 178).

4. This has created close ties between media and NGOs. By appointing spokespersons for each campaign, Greenpeace has further facilitated easy transfer of information to the media and made such ties even stronger (Hansen 1993: 168). This closeness may be one reason for the lack of scepticism against and sympathy for Greenpeace among many British journalists (see Hansen 1993; Linné 1993).

5. A mother ship with two or three catcher boats is still used in Japanese scientific whaling, making this an attractive target for Greenpeace and Sea Shepherd.

6. NGO reports are also extensively used as trustworthy sources of information by social scientists, at least in English-speaking countries. Paul Wapner's *Environmental Activism and World Civic Politics* is a case in point: the only reference used to support the claim that Iceland and Norway violate the moratorium is a paper written by the anti-whaling organization Earth Island Institute (Wapner 1996: 22).

7. *Brent Spar* was an oil storage and loading buoy operated by Shell U.K. in the North Sea. When Shell wanted to dispose of the structure on the seabed in 1995, Greenpeace—claiming the tank contained 5,500 tons of oil and many other pollutants—launched a campaign to have it dismantled on shore. Believing Greenpeace's claims, media, governments and the public forced Shell to change its plan. An independent investigation later proved that the Greenpeace figures were wrong and those of Shell mainly correct (DNV 1995). In September 1998 Greenpeace had to apologize to Shell. It should be added that dismantling the tank on shore might have exposed both workers and the environment to greater dangers (Wikipedia, 24 January 2006).

8. The scuttling of the *Nybræna* angered people in Northern Norway and housewives got together and established a new organization, Friends of the Harpoon, which has since been an active NGO at IWC meetings and other forums.

9. It should be added that in each case, all the Norwegian vessels were back in operation in time for the whaling season.

10. Ironically, some of these contracts went to Norway, another whaling nation, and, when Norway was the target of a similar campaign a few years later, losses in market share for Norwegian shrimp in the U.K. meant a gain for Iceland (Bjørndal and Toft 1994).

11. However, as Levi-Strauss has shown us long ago, food can be transformed from nature to culture by other means than heating, as in Japanese *sushi* and *sashimi*.

12. Thus, the authorities in the Faroe Islands have advised people not to eat liver and kidney of pilot whales—formerly regarded as great delicacies—and to reduce their daily consumption of meat and blubber. It remains to be seen whether this development will change people's perception of marine mammals as healthy food. From Canada, Poirier (1996) mentions that once Inuit from Nunavik were informed by the government about the pollutants in their traditional foods, the Inuit understood it to be poisonous. Out of fear they have periodically abstained from eating country foods, and some hunters have declined to use killed animals if they had even minor abnormalities. In Greenland the government urges the population to have a balanced diet and to consume country foods even though they may be polluted, as the health problems associated with the consumption of imported foods are considered more dangerous. See also Cone (2005).

13. Retrieved 8 April 2008 from www.whaling.jp/english/qa.html.

14. Often no distinction is made between the two terms. Strictly speaking 'nonconsumptive use' ought to be reserved for cases of indirect utilization (as a symbol, in novels, art and so on). Direct utilization of cetaceans through exposure at dolphinariums, swim-with-whales programmes, nonlethal research, whale watching and the like may not be entirely without negative effects on the animals—SeaWorld alone reported ninety-three dolphin deaths between 1971 and 2002 (retrieved 18 February 2008 from www.wspa-usa.org/pages/272_what_s_wrong_with_swimming_with_dolphins.cfm). Such direct utilization will therefore be termed 'low-consumptive use'.

15. Retrieved 19 July 2004 from www.hsus.org.

16. In another report the WDCS claims that SeaWorld, with about 10 million visitors a year (closer to 12 million according to Davis 1997: 27), earned 4–500 million dollars (Williams 2001: 67).

17. Such claims have been rebuffed by several researchers, e.g. Klinowska and Brown (1986); Brill and Friedl (1993); Duffield et al. (1995).

18. Swim-with-dolphins programmes dominate, but there are allegedly more than a dozen commercial programmes for swimming with large whales in the Dominican Republic, Tonga, Costa Rica, Niue, the Maldives, Australia, Galapagos, outside San Diego (U.S.) and Argentina, among others (Rose 2003).

19. Free-swimming dolphins can be dangerous, and in 1995 one swimmer was killed by a dolphin outside Rio's Copacabana. The dolphin was allegedly provoked by the swimmer and 'her response was totally justified' (Barbara A. Bilgree, Marmam@UVVM.UVIC.CA, 30 July 1996). Being tormented was also the justification for a dolphin killing a person in Mexico (Servais 2005: 228). At Eliat in Israel there have been problems with dolphins attacking people, and after several swimmers were harmed, the person-in-charge at Israel Nature and Park Authority asked via the Internet for advice, with the following words: 'We are concerned that continuation of these kinds of human-dolphin interactions could lead to harm to the dolphins. Obviously there is also real risk that a person could be seriously injured, and that is what could create more problems eventually for the dolphins' (Marmam@UVVM.UVIC.CA, 29 October 2002). See also Rose et al. (2006).

20. Although Keiko was not successfully brought back to a normal life, the Free Willy Keiko Foundation found that the money was well spent because Keiko 'inspired millions of children to get involved in following his amazing odyssey and helping other whales' (retrieved 28 August 2006 from http://www.keiko.com/history.html).

21. Many people have speculated why apparently healthy animals beach themselves in this way. A common explanation is that pollution has destroyed their ability to navigate, but whales were stranded long before pollution became a problem. Others have suggested that the whales voluntarily commit suicide, perhaps to follow a sick comrade in death. A few cases may have been caused by U.S. military operations and sonar tests. It has also been argued that 'seaquakes' or underwater earthquakes destroy the animals' ability to navigate.

22. See http://www.nmfs.noaa.gov/pr/health/networks.htm (retrieved on 7 December 2008) for a list of participants in the marine mammal stranding network.

23. Norwegian children in whaling communities were perplexed and thought the money would be better spent saving people. Discussing the incident in school they asked: 'But what about the people who are starving to death? What about the children starving, dying in mountains of garbage in various parts of the world?' (ISG 1992: 85).

24. Retrieved 19 August 2004 from www.adopt-a-dolphin.com/

25. Retrieved 8 April 2008 from www.vanaqua.org/conservation/kwap.html.

26. Retrieved 19 December 2005 from www.neaq.org/scilearn/research/rtwhale.html.

27. Retrieved 8 April 2008 from http://www.rorqual.com/.

28. Norwegian whalers asked what the 'parents' did for their adopted whales. 'Last year [1989] almost 30 dead sperm whales drifted ashore between Lofoten and Andenes [for unknown reasons]. They are polluting our shores. Why don't their adoptive parents come and give them a proper burial? Don't they have any obligations to their children? And let them pay for the food the whales eat every day! Parents are obliged to provide their kids with food!' (fieldwork).

29. Retrieved 22 December 2005 from www.coa.edu/html/adoptawhale.htm.

30. Retrieved 8 April 2008 from www.killerwhale.org/index2.html. Because most whales are promiscuous, it is only practically possible to trace relationship through females. If fatherhood is to be determined, it is necessary to perform DNA-analyses of males that often move over long distances.

31. Retrieved 8 April 2008 from http://cerf.bc.ca/courses. asp.

32. Retrieved 9 April 1996 from www.bcu.ubc.ca/~megill/cerf.
33. Retrieved 22 December 2005 from http://www3.telus.net/adventurespirit/page7.html.
34. Retrieved 22 December 2005 from www.tethys.org/tri_courses/courses_index_e.htm. The organization is also supported by the WDCS, IFAW, Apple and Canon, among others (http://www.tethys.org/index_e.htm, retrieved 8 April 2008).
35. Retrieved 1 June 1998 from http://www.tethys.org.
36. Retrieved 31 July 2004 from www.joanocean.com.
37. Retrieved 22 December 2005 from www.people-oceans-dolphins.com/Corporate/index.html.
38. *Moby-Dick* has itself become a research object, and many dissertations have been published on the book and its influence. An Internet Google search for 'Moby Dick' resulted in 5.5 million hits (28 August 2006).
39. One of the first of the genre was Japanese, and its title in translation is *Let Us Swim with Dolphins: The Complete 'DOS' Manual for All Dolphin-lovers* (where DOS stands for 'dolphin ocean swim').
40. This is allegedly the largest run done of any record.
41. Retrieved 5 July 1999 from www.snafu.de/~ulisses/kairosed.htm.
42. Retrieved 29 November 2008 from http://en.wikipedia.org/wiki/Wyland
43. There are also programmes that are biased in favour of whaling, for example *Survival in the High North*, produced by Magnus Gudmundsson from Iceland.
44. Among these are *Liquid Light: The Spiritual Wisdom of the Ocean* (by Serji Ayno), *Dolphin Connection* (Joan Ocean), *Dolphins, Angels and Mermaids* (Ashleea Nielsen, Dancing Dolphin Institute), *Oceania, the Promise of Tomorrow* (by ecofeminist and water birth advocate Estelle Myers) and *Orcananda* (about musical communication with cetaceans, by Jim Nollman).
45. In *Star Trek IV*, the earth is threatened in the twenty-third century by a space object that tries to contact humpback whales, assumed to be the most intelligent life form on Earth. At that time the humpback whale has already become extinct, but thanks to a time machine it is possible for the heroes to return to 1986 to fetch a humpback able to communicate with the space object and thereby prevent disaster.
46. Retrieved 25 April 2000 from www.People-Oceans-Dolphins.com/Shop.

Chapter 4

The International Whaling Commission (IWC)

At the forty-sixth Annual Meeting of the International Whaling Commission (IWC), held in Mexico in May 1994, Japan requested an interim quota of fifty minke whales to relieve the cultural, economic and social distress caused to four whaling communities by the moratorium on whaling for commercial purposes. Since the imposition of the moratorium in 1988, Japan had presented more than thirty reports, written by twenty-three social scientists from eight different countries, documenting this distress. Encouraged by the adoption by consensus at the 1993 IWC meeting of a resolution that 'recognizes the socio-economic and cultural needs of the four small coastal whaling communities in Japan and the distress to these communities . . . [and] resolves to work expeditiously to alleviate the distress' (IWC 1993), Japan presented an action plan that was designed to ensure that edible whale products were exclusively consumed in the local whaling communities (GoJ 1994). A management council was to be established, composed of representatives from national and local authorities, the industry and citizen groups. The nine licensed whaling boats—of less than 48 metric tonnes in size and with crews of about seven people—should be hired by the council, and meat and blubber were to be distributed without an eye to economic profit.

The response from the majority of the IWC delegations was negative. Delegations from Australia, New Zealand, the United Kingdom, the United States and other countries could not support the plan because the scheme was deemed commercial: meat was to be sold to the villagers for money in order to cover the expenses incurred during the hunt. The British commissioner strongly argued that it was, a priori, impossible to create a noncommercial sector in a commercial economy. Japan invited concerned delegations to further discuss how the last commercial elements could be removed, but despite this an overwhelming majority rejected the plan.

At the same meeting the Russian Federation requested a quota of 140 gray whales (down from 169) for its aboriginal population on the Chukotka Peninsula.

For the first time in several years the Russian delegation presented a short paper justifying the need for whale products. The annual consumption of the 7,000 coastal inhabitants was estimated to be 511 tonnes of whale meat. The inland aboriginals were expected to consume an additional 129 tonnes of meat. Moreover, each 'marine hunters's base' had an estimated need for one tonne of blubber on the average and reindeer herders at least 200 kg per tent for heating and lighting purposes. With the old quota of 169 animals, an estimated 773 tonnes of meat, 608 tonnes of blubber, 304 tonnes of innards, 152 tonnes of skin and 912 tonnes of bones were available to be used as fodder on state collective fox farms (Russian Federation 1994). The whales were to be caught using a 700-tonne whaling ship previously used in the Antarctic hunt and crewed solely by ethnic Russians. The Russian request met with a very positive response, and Australia, the Netherlands and the U.K., among other countries, expressed their gratitude to the Russian delegation for its 'detailed' report (IWC 1994a: 4). The Russian request was granted by consensus.[1]

In short, Japan's request for a quota of fifty minke whales—to be caught by villagers operating small vessels and to be consumed within local communities—was rejected because this form of whaling was considered commercial, whereas the Russian request for 140 gray whales—to be caught by ethnic Russians using a large vessel and to be distributed over a whole region, with large parts being used as fuel and feed in fur farming—was accepted because it was regarded as a form of 'aboriginal subsistence whaling'.[2] The fate these two requests met at the IWC meeting highlights the basic problem the commission is facing.

The IWC makes a major distinction between 'whaling for commercial purposes'—on which a moratorium has been imposed—and 'aboriginal subsistence whaling' (ASW), which is endorsed. However, this distinction has no background in the International Convention for the Regulation of Whaling (ICRW) but rather is a consequence of discursive changes within the IWC during the 1970s (Takahashi 1998). This distinction is based on the assumption that there is a fundamental difference between commercial and subsistence activities as well as between aboriginal and non-aboriginal peoples. It might be argued that this assumption is not warranted, as there are a number of difficulties with the IWC categories, which are defined for economic and political ends rather than for ecological ones. Nonetheless, the IWC's categories constitute the framework for the debate and hence are fundamental in order to understand what the issue is all about.

Aboriginal Subsistence vs. Non-aboriginal Commercial Whaling

In 1981, when the IWC decided to permit aboriginal subsistence whaling (ASW), defined as 'whaling for purposes of local aboriginal consumption carried out by or on behalf of aboriginal, indigenous or native peoples who share strong community, familial, social and cultural ties related to a continuing traditional dependence on whaling and the use of whales' (Donovan 1982:83), preferential treatment was given to aboriginal people. Considering the injustices inflicted upon them in the past, few voiced any objections to what seemed to be an attempt to put things right.

The IWC thus gave in to U.S. demands that a moratorium on Alaskan catches of bowhead whales should be lifted. In the 1970s there had been growing concern in the IWC's Scientific Committee because the catches had increased from an annual average of about a dozen whales before 1970 to more than thirty-two whales on average during the period from 1970 to 1977 (Huntington 1992: 110). One reason for this development was that new sources of cash flows—mainly due to petroleum explorations and settlement compensation related to land rights claims—made it possible for more people to outfit whaling crews (Gambell 1982: 1). At the same time, the number of whales struck but lost increased from ten in 1973 to seventy-nine in 1977, probably owing to lack of skill among some of the new whaling crews and a shift to new equipment that frequently failed (1982: 1). The IWC believed that with an estimated stock size of between 600 and 1,800 animals, the bowhead was the 'most endangered of all species despite forty years of protection from industrial exploitation' (Birnie 1985: 485, 500).[3] In 1977 the IWC therefore placed a moratorium on the Alaskan bowhead whaling, a moratorium that was lifted only half a year later because of strong pressure from the United States, where authorities believed that the hunt was not sustainable but demanded a period of grace 'to allow time for Eskimo attitudes to change' (Birnie 1985: 604).[4] In order to secure support for its position, the U.S. had to accept that ASW should include Greenland's catches of minke, fin and humpback whales and the Soviet Union's catches of gray whales. Japan expected a return of the favour for its support of the Inuit request, but after the quotas had been secured for the Inuit the U.S. government was no longer interested in compromises (Birnie 1985: 501) and could wholeheartedly work for a global moratorium on commercial whaling without fearing that this would have an impact on its own catches. The only moratorium suggested by the Scientific Committee was thus defeated by the IWC, which, on the other hand, imposed a moratorium its Scientific Committee found unnecessary.

This policy, which finds hardly any legitimacy in the ICRW, has several important consequences. First, whereas quotas in commercial whaling are based on complex mathematical models and extensive scientific research on whale stocks, quotas in ASW are calculated from people's perceived nutritional, cultural and social needs (cf. Huntington 1992: 114).[5] This has institutionalized a paradoxical management practice that can authorize hunting of endangered stocks while prohibiting hunting of more robust stocks (Frøvik 1995: 143).[6]

Second, as many Japanese delegates have observed, the IWC spends much more time criticizing commercial whaling than ASW for inhumane hunting methods. But in general the whales suffer much more under ASW due to less sophisticated equipment and difficult hunting conditions. Whereas 80 per cent die instantly in Norwegian minke whaling and the average time to death (TTD) is about 2 minutes (Knudsen 2005),[7] in 2002 it took the Chukotka whalers an average of 32 minutes to kill a gray whale and 41 minutes to kill a bowhead whale. An average of fifty-two bullets (down from sixty-four bullets in 2000) were used for each whale caught in addition to a number of darting gun projectiles and harpoons (IWC 2003a: 5). There was no available data on how many gray whales were struck and lost. I have not seen comparable data for the Alaskan hunt, but one whaling captain in Alaska described their (illegal) gray whale hunt in the following terms: 'Whalers like to sink five or six harpoons, each of which attaches a buoy to the animal, but chasing a gray whale can take a full day. It's a long, long chase. We let it run till it tires out, then we'll tow it home' (Gay 2002a). Moreover, at least 25 per cent of the bowheads are struck and subsequently lost, and there is good reason to believe that many of these meet a painful death. Yet this kind of whaling is referred to in morally more neutral ways than commercial whaling.

Researching the annual *Chairman's Report* from the IWC meetings for the period 1967–1987, the Japanese anthropologist Junichi Takahashi (1998: 245) found a consistent difference in wording. Whereas the term *kill* was often used in connection with commercial whaling (e.g. 'the killing of minke whales for commercial purposes'), this term was never used in regard to ASW. In its place the term *take* was frequently used (e.g. 'the taking by aborigines of minke whales').[8] It seems that the relatively inhumane hunt of the Inuit is more ethically acceptable to the majority at the IWC than the more humane commercial hunt.

Third, there are considerable differences regarding inspection and control between ASW and commercial whaling. Whereas there is extensive control of commercial whaling—in Norway there was a trained vet on each boat until electronic monitoring of the boats was introduced in 2005, and DNA 'fingerprints' are taken for each animal caught—there is little external control of the Alaskan hunt, which is only monitored by the whalers' own organ, i.e. the Alaskan Eskimo Whaling Commission (AEWC).[9]

Fourth, and this is the most important point if we want to understand the Japanese anger, the IWC recognizes that indigenous peoples—but not Japanese and Norwegians—have legitimate claims to their culture and identity. Japan was particularly annoyed when the U.S. used cultural arguments for the resumption of Makah whaling after a lapse of more than seventy years, whereas coastal Japanese whalers were denied cultural needs despite having hunted whales continuously. As will be argued in the next chapter, it is not only indigenous peoples who 'share strong community, familial, social and cultural ties related to a continuing traditional dependence on whaling and the use of whales.' In a situation where local people cannot claim, or do not want to claim, indigenousness, they have lost rights to their own culture and identity (cf. Chapter 6).

This difference in treatment does not become less peculiar when we recognize that the concepts of 'subsistence' and 'aboriginal' are both fraught with ambiguities and are nowhere defined in IWC documents. It nevertheless seems that peoples who qualify as aboriginal, indigenous or native—terms that seem to be used interchangeably—in the IWC context denote political and cultural minorities without elaborate political structures who have been oppressed by invaders for decades or even centuries. Moreover, they should possess only simple technologies, have little economic sophistication and be largely outside the market economy.[10] One may ask what separates the Greenlanders and the Faroese. Both enjoy home rule within the Danish Realm, so politically there is hardly any difference. Both people are affluent in the global context. Both catch whales, but whereas the Faroese catch pilot whales that are consumed locally, much of the minke and fin whale meat taken by Greenlanders reaches the market. Yet Greenland's minke whaling is termed 'aboriginal subsistence whaling' and endorsed by the international community, while the Faroese hunt is condemned for not being necessary.

Terms like aboriginal, native and indigenous have been used rhetorically by minority groups in order to muster support for their struggle to gain recognition as distinct peoples with their own cultures and rights to self-determination. But this can easily become a double-edged sword, because concepts such as ASW as used by the IWC imply a static view of a people and its culture. The IWC has authorized whale hunting, but only as long as it is conducted by small non-white minorities who are perceived as lacking unifying political institutions[11] and using simple technologies, and whose economic exchanges are believed to exist within the confinement of a noncommercial economy. A resolution from 1980 states that they 'shall document annually for the information of the Commission: the utilization of the meat and products of any whales taken for aboriginal/subsistence purposes' (quoted in Takahashi 1998: 243). It can be argued that Greenlanders and Alaskans at the annual IWC meetings have to stand trial before the IWC judges to testify to their own 'primitiveness'.

The untenable distinction between subsistence and commercial whaling has been pointed out by a number of social scientists during the last twenty years. It has been noted that the term 'subsistence' can be used in several ways (Freeman 1993). One interpretation is self-sufficiency, according to which people are supposed to produce no more than they need. Their products are supposed to be consumed locally to meet nutritional and cultural requirements and not enter the market (IWC 1981).[12] However, anthropologists have shown that there has hardly ever been a self-sufficient society and that whalers in Alaska, Greenland and Russia as well as in Iceland, Japan and Norway have been economically integrated into the world economy for a long time. A number of studies have pointed out the mixed economies of these societies, consisting of both subsistence and commercial elements (Usher 1981; Lonner 1986; ISG 1992; Kalland and Moeran 1992; Caulfield 1994, 1997; Freeman 2001; Kalland and Sejersen 2005). Secondly, subsistence can mean, according to *The Concise Oxford Dictionary*, 'a minimal level of existence'. In other words, subsistence might imply poverty, and many subscribe to the view that if the people are not poor, they are not engaged in subsistence activities. The condition of relative affluence is repeatedly used against Faroese, Icelandic, Japanese and Norwegian whalers. Such a view has important implications for aboriginals as well.

It has furthermore been pointed out that both subsistence and commercial whalers are imbedded in a web of social exchange: gift-giving, barter and exchange through the medium of money. Brian Moeran (1992) argues that there are no *logical* differences between the three forms of exchange and whale products must be regarded as commodities produced for exchange and consumption whether the hunt has been classified as ASW or as commercial. What might be different is people's *moral* evaluation of these various forms of exchange. In Japanese culture, for example, money is relatively unproblematic and has been used in gift-giving since ancient times. Today money rather than an object is the prescribed gift in Japan (Ohnuki-Tierney 1993: 72), whereas in Western societies there have long been two opposing views on money. To Adam Smith money was benign and provided the individual with the means to liberation and happiness. However, to Aristotle, Thomas Aquinas and Karl Marx money was held responsible for the destruction of community solidarity (Bloch and Parry 1989; Moeran 1992: 9). When it comes to whaling, as was argued in Chapter 2, commercialism in itself seems to be considered morally repugnant by the many of the contracting members of the IWC. It is ironic that this view is expressed by governments that otherwise are ideologically closer to Adam Smith than to Karl Marx and that usually are strong advocates of free trade and movement of capital.

As 'whaling for commercial purposes' has not been defined by the IWC, it must be taken as a residual category to mean 'non-ASW'. But empirical research has shown that 'small-type coastal whaling' (STCW) in Iceland, Japan and Norway is qualitatively different from both ASW and high-seas industrial whaling but, if anything, has more in common with the former than with the latter. A report to the IWC in 1992, for example, pointed out the many similarities between minke whaling in Greenland on the one hand and in Iceland, Japan and Norway on the other (ISGSTW 1992). The vessels used in all four countries are relatively small and operate from remote communities with few land-based resources but with a strong sense of community identity. Most of the boats are owner-operated and run under a domestic mode of production where household viability and social reproduction are the important rationales. The small crews are recruited through kinship and friendship connections; there is little specialization among them and they typically participate in a share system that also implies sharing the risk. The main product is whale meat, which is gifted, bartered and sold outside of the communities but at the same time is an important local source of nutrition and food culture. In contrast, industrial pelagic whaling was operated by large fleets and under a capitalist mode of production with a high return on investment as the primary goal. The highly specialized crews were often recruited through agents and the crewmembers received salaries. The main product was whale oil, for which there used to be a great demand. Hence, in terms of economic rationality the important dividing line between various types of whaling does not go be between ASW and commercial whaling, as implied by the IWC's usage of the concepts, but rather between ASW and STCW on the one hand and industrial pelagic whaling on the other.

It can be argued that linking whaling to the existence of a noncommercial mode of production and lack of overarching political organization has at least two important consequences. First, it denies aboriginal peoples their obvious right to define their own future as long as they wish to hunt whales. No culture is static, but the policy of anti-whalers has the effect of freezing the situation, turning evolving cultures into static museum objects. A concept used by ethnic minorities in order to protect their rights—and thus their cultures—has been used by the majority to impose their premises on other people's futures, clearly exemplified by the requirement placed on the aboriginal whalers to demonstrate their cultural needs and prove that they do not sell whale products on the market. I have elsewhere argued that ASW has been turned into a powerful concept in the hands of imperialism (Kalland 1992b). Second, the IWC categories mask important similarities between whaling regimes and create artificial dichotomies with little heuristic value. Commercial activities are not incompatible with a sound management of renewable natural resources per se, nor is indigenousness a precondition for sustainability. Hence, other criteria must be used if a proper management regime is to be formulated.

All concepts are cultural constructs that are continually contested and renegotiated. Through concepts the world is structured and given meaning. This applies, of course, also to the concepts discussed here. Concepts like 'commercial catch' and 'aboriginal whaling' had no position in the ICRW but were, as shown by Takahashi (1998), first used by the IWC during the 1970s. 'Commercial catch' was first mentioned in 1972, but only in reference to the UN Conference on Human Environment held in Stockholm at the time. The term 'aboriginal whaling' was first used by the IWC in 1973, but then apparently as a subcategory of commercial whaling. In a proposal for a moratorium it was stated that 'commercial whaling for all species of cetaceans should cease for a period of ten years . . . except aboriginal catches where they do not endanger the species' (quoted in Takahashi 1998: 240).

During the 1970s the IWC's rhetoric changed further, particularly after the Inuit catches of bowhead whales had been secured in 1977. 'The period between 1979 and 1982', writes Takahashi (1998: 244), 'is a very crucial period in which cognitive and linguistic schemes concerning various types of whaling, were firmly but in fact arbitrarily established by some native English speaking nations—notably USA, UK, and Australia'. The IWC began to describe aboriginal and commercial whaling in different terms: as we have already seen; commercial whalers *kill* whereas their aboriginal colleagues *take* whales. The employment of a series of semantic redundancies stressed that 'those whale fisheries are truly, genuinely or authentically aboriginal' (Takahashi 1998: 245).[13] A working group was also established to work out a regime for the Alaskan hunt, and in 1981 the concept 'aboriginal subsistence whaling' was defined. 'Whaling for commercial purposes' has never been defined but is taken to include everything from industrial whaling organized from factory ships in the Antarctic to minke whaling conducted by small fishing vessels in Iceland. The IWC rhetoric has consolidated a contrast between two extreme images: The Alaskan bowhead whaling as representative of indigenous peoples and the industrial whaling in the Antarctic representing commercial whaling.

The ASW–commercial whaling dichotomy structures the world and divides it into one mainstream, modern, industrial sector based on a market economy (i.e. 'we') and one peripheral, backward, traditional sector based on subsistence activities ('the other'). To confine whaling to aboriginal subsistence activities brands whalers as primitive or uncivilized and places them in the 'other' category. It seems that commercial whaling in this context is a threat to a totemic conceptualization of the world, rather than a threat to biodiversity. The IWC majority not only made themselves spokespersons for the totemic worldview discussed in Chapter 2, but since the 1970s have been actively creating it.

Despite lacking empirical and logical backing for the distinction between ASW and commercial whaling, this dichotomy has to a great extent laid the premises for what is going on within the IWC. There must therefore be other, more tangible reasons for the dichotomy upheld by the IWC. In order to understand these we have to outline the history of the organization and its present structure before we analyse the strategies employed within the IWC to end whaling.

The IWC: From Whalers' Club to Protectors' Club

Motivated primarily by the need to regulate the whale oil industry in Antarctica in the late 1920s, leading whaling nations took the initiative to develop multilateral agreements to manage the whaling industry. After two attempts in 1931 and 1938, fourteen countries signed (and later ratified) the International Convention for the Regulation of Whaling (ICRW) in 1946. The explicit purpose of the convention is, according to its preamble, to 'provide for the proper conservation of whale stocks and thus make possible the orderly development of the whaling industry'. The IWC was set up under the ICRW in 1949 as a global body for regulating whaling and related matters through a flexible set of rules (the Schedule). The IWC's raison d'être is, according to the ICRW, to decide catch quotas. Quotas, which require changes in the Schedules, are usually given annually, although ASW quotas are usually given for three or five years at a time. Article V.2 states that amendments to the Schedule require a three-fourths majority and '(a) shall be such as are necessary to carry out the objectives and purposes of [the] Convention and to provide for the conservation, development, and optimum utilization of the whale resources' and '(b) shall be based on scientific findings'. The Scientific

Committee was established to review biological and statistical data and to make recommendations to the IWC on research, quotas and status of whale stocks.

The IWC has been troubled with conflicts from the very beginning, and these conflicts can be traced through three distinct phases.[14] The first period—from 1949 to the late 1960s—was characterized by unsustainable exploitation of many whale stocks, and a few species were brought close to extinction. Several factors contributed to this development. First, the whaling industry was powerful and pressed the IWC to set quotas well above those recommended by its Scientific Committee. The influence of the scientists was seriously dwarfed by the Dutch members of the committee, who consistently cast doubt on the need to lower catch quotas by referring to scientific uncertainty (Tønnessen and Johnsen 1982; Schweder 1992; Heazle 2006).[15] Second, the quotas were defined in terms of the 'blue whale unit' (BWU) and did not specify species or stocks. The BWU was based on the amount of oil produced from one blue whale, which was defined as equal to two fin, 2.5 humpback, 6 sei or 30 minke whales. Hence it was rational—at least in the short term—to pursue the species that gave the most oil, and the blue whale was the first species to be depleted, followed by the fin and sei whales. In other words, the IWC sacrificed ecological considerations for the stable production of whale oil. Third, a total allowable quota (TAC) measured in BWUs was given in order to encourage competition. It was therefore important to catch whales as quickly as possible in order to capture as large a share of the total quota as possible, which led to overcapitalization of the whaling industry. Whether the species were endangered or not mattered little during this period, which has aptly been called 'Whaling Olympics'. The warnings of the Scientific Committee majority (all its members except the Dutch) fell mostly on deaf ears. One may get the impression that whales were looked upon as a nonrenewable resource that should be tapped as quickly as possible to maximize profits that could be invested in other enterprises (Clark 1981; Holt 1985; Frøvik 1995: 82).

Starting in the early 1960s the IWC moved slowly towards a new management policy. Three developments contributed to this change. First, it was by then obvious that the Antarctic resources were severely depleted and catches were declining faster than the quotas. Second, declining stocks in combination with falling prices for whale oil made the business unprofitable, and by the end of the decade the U.K., Australia, the Netherlands and Norway had all withdrawn from whaling in the Antarctic, leaving only Japan and the Soviet Union in the area.[16] And third, the U.K. and not least the Netherlands changed their policies after withdrawing from the hunt. Whereas they had earlier argued for high quotas in order to sell their fleets expensively to Japan, after the sales they no longer had an interest in keeping quotas high (Frøvik 1995: 155–56; Heazle 2006: 105–106).

These developments strengthened the Scientific Committee, and restrictions were gradually imposed. National quotas (as measured in percentage of TAC and first suggested by Norway in 1955) were introduced in 1962,[17] and humpback and blue whales were protected in 1963 and 1965, respectively. The quotas for the other species were increasingly set according to the recommendations of the Scientific Committee. The IWC began to manage whales as a *renewable* resource (rather than an extractive resource), and it was no longer legitimate to defend high quotas with reference to short-sighted economic interests (Frøvik 1995: 120). The TAC was gradually reduced but remained far higher than what the fleets managed to catch until 1972, when quotas for each species finally replaced the BWU. An international observer scheme—also suggested by Norway back in 1955—was introduced the same year to allow whalers to monitor each other's whaling operations. Moreover, a New Management Procedure (NMP) was intro-duced in 1974, and the following year saw the introduction of the precautionary principle that 'exploitation should not commence until an estimate of stock size has been obtained which is satisfactory in the view of the Scientific Committee' (Schedule amendment, 1975).

The NMP classified all stocks into three categories: (1) initial management stock if the stock was considered to be at or close to pre-harvest level; (2) sus-tained management stock if the stock was considered to be close to the maximum sustainable yield (MSY) level, assumed to be about 60 per cent of the initial level; and (3) protected stock if it was more than 10 per cent below the MSY level (or 54 per cent below the initial level), in which case no whaling should be done. It was labelled 'protected' because the Scientific Committee regarded the stock to be not endangered but at a level too low for its optimal utilization. With this categorization the committee aimed to rebuild the stock to a level where the *maximum* sustainable yield could be obtained. The NMP was developed with reference to the Antarctic hunt but was soon used also to manage other stocks of whales. It proved a step in the right direction with regard to sustainable manage-ment of whale stocks, and the 1970s were characterized by the increasing influ-ence of the Scientific Committee.

The period when management can be said to have been based on science was short, however. Quotas were given for each species and stock, but this procedure posed great challenges to the scientists. How could stock populations and MSY levels be determined, and how large must the current population be in relation-ship to the original before whaling could be allowed? Several ways to calculate both initial and current stock sizes were suggested. An early cleavage occurred in the Scientific Committee between scientists from whaling nations and a few anti-whaling scientists. Because the committee was unable to advice the IWC by consensus, almost any argument offered by a delegate could thus be scientifically legitimized. In such a situation it may be legitimate to choose the most restric-tive alternative, according to the precautionary principle. Again arguments about scientific uncertainty were used, but this time to the benefit of the resources and not of the whaling industry (Heazle 2006). A series of moratorium proposals were presented towards the end of the 1970s, and gradually a change came about in the IWC's attitude. The international environmental and animal rights move-ments had grown stronger, and whaling was one of the first targets of the activists.

Consequently, the IWC figured prominently in their strategies, and the meetings became more politicized. At the same time, new nations became members of the IWC with the sole aim of securing the three-fourths majority required to amend the Schedule and bring about a moratorium on whaling (Hoel 1986, 1992; Day 1992; Darby 2008). Even as the number of active whaling nations declined, the number of IWC members increased—from fourteen in 1972 to thirty-nine in 1982, when the proposal was backed by the required majority.

The Scientific Committee failed to recommend a blanket moratorium, but the IWC decided nevertheless to impose a moratorium (or zero quota, as the official term is) on all 'killing for commercial purposes' (Schedule 10[e]) until uncertainties regarding whale populations had been removed and a new, revised management procedure (RMP) had been adopted. It was also decided that the moratorium should be reviewed by 1990, but as of January 2009 this had not yet been done. In contrast to normal quotas, which are temporary, a new Schedule amendment with a three-fourths majority is needed to lift the zero quota. Although the justification of the moratorium was ecological, developments since 1982 have clearly shown that the IWC had entered its third and, so far, final stage. The IWC has become a preservation club (Hansen 1994) in which the scientists once again are largely ignored, this time not by the whaling industry but by the protectionists, who, in the eyes of the whalers, have hijacked the IWC.

Pointing to these inconsistencies, many delegates have claimed that the negotiations at the IWC have no scientific base but are a question of power relations. This became very clear at the IWC meeting in 2003, when it was decided to establish a 'conservation committee' with the purpose of strengthening the protective work further (IWC 2003b). There is no doubt that many IWC members want to introduce a *permanent* ban on all commercial whaling, and some delegates want to extend this to all cetacean species (including small toothed whales) and to ASW as well. The U.S. Marine Mammal Commission has suggested changing the ICRW to better reflect the view of the protectionists, who no longer regard whales as resource to be consumed. The negotiations at the IWC meetings are coloured by this, with regard to both the issues raised by the delegates and the character of the negotiations.

The Annual IWC Meetings and the Participants

Images of enemies and crisis predominate during the annual IWC meetings, which in the last thirty years have been turned into major events for whalers, protectionists and government agencies alike. The meetings have become the most important arena for the whale protectionists, taking the same position in the campaign against whaling as the ice floes outside Newfoundland have in the campaign against sealing (Kalland 1994). Although the outcome of the meetings in recent years has been more or less a foregone conclusion, the meetings themselves give concerned participants the opportunity to meet like-minded politicians, activists and journalists. Here activists can display their whale art objects and emblems on badges, T-shirts, posters and so on. Moreover, the IWC meetings make it possible to bring the whaling issue to the news headlines once a year. The meetings today can best be regarded as an arena for tournaments of value, where privileged participants compete for status, rank, fame and reputation by contesting central values in an attempt to diversify 'culturally conventionalized paths' (Appadurai 1986: 21). In the process a polarization has taken place, with the world being divided into an anti-whaling bloc (the so-called like-minded group) and a pro-whaling bloc of whaling nations and their friends.

Between thirty and forty member countries participated in the annual meetings of the 1990s, rising to seventy-three countries in 2007. As of 27 November 2008 the number of member countries had reached eighty-two. The members are a mixed bag of countries whose sizes are their most outstanding feature. Although we do find some of the largest countries among the members (China, India, the U.S., Russia, Brazil and Japan), many are tiny nations whose voices are usually not heard in the international community. Among these are Tuvalu (10,000 inhabitants), Nauru (13,000), San Marino (29,000), Monaco (33,000), Palau (20,000), St. Kitts and Nevis (39,000), the Republic of the Marshall Islands (62,000), Antigua and Barbuda (69,000), Dominica (69,000), Grenada (89,000), the Seychelles (81,000) and Kiribati (100,000). But in the IWC these tiny countries have found a forum where they can get considerable attention and international influence. Several of them have played important roles at the IWC meetings—St. Kitts and Nevis, Grenada and Monaco have even hosted meetings, and the Seychelles authored the moratorium proposal and suggested the sanctuary in the Indian Ocean. Another feature is that many member countries are landlocked (i.e. Luxembourg, Switzerland, Austria, Hungary, San Marino, the Czech Republic, Slovakia, Mongolia and Mali).

Unlike most international management bodies in fisheries, which usually are open only to nations with a historic interest in the resources in question, the IWC is open to all independent countries whether they have a history of whaling or not. In this sense the IWC is one of the few global management bodies. The majority of IWC members have never caught a whale, and many of them were brought into the IWC with the sole purpose of bringing whaling to an end, even though some of the most influential members are countries that relatively recently ceased whaling themselves (Australia, the Netherlands and the U.K.). Among active whaling members today we find Denmark (on behalf of Greenland, which despite home rule government does not qualify for membership in the IWC and thus may have less influence than San Marino), Iceland, Japan, Norway, Russia (on behalf of the Chukchi), St. Vincent and the Grenadines, and the U.S. (on behalf of its Eskimo and Makah populations). Whaling nations that are not members of the IWC include Canada, Indonesia and the Philippines. Meanwhile, a number of nations both inside and outside the IWC continue to hunt small whales.

Member countries send delegations ranging from the large Japanese and American ones, with dozens of delegates, down to the one-person delegation. Each delegation has one vote regardless of size. Whereas the Norwegian commissioner is a diplomat from the Foreign Ministry, many of the delegations from anti-whaling countries are headed by bureaucrats from less prestigious environmental ministries. In addition to diplomats and bureaucrats, delegations may also include scientists (mainly natural scientists but increasingly also social scientists),[18] whalers (in the case of whaling nations) and environmentalists and animal rights advocates (in the case of anti-whaling nations). The task of the scientists is to give scientific legitimacy to their countries' positions and to advise their delegations. Many of the questions discussed are complex and difficult to comprehend, not only for lay people but also for delegates. The Japanese anthropologist Masami Iwasaki-Goodman, who attended the meetings for many years, observed that the work of the Scientific Committee was poorly understood by the majority of delegations (1994: 154). IWC Secretary Ray Gambell has noted that 'some of the statements made by New Zealand in the Commission have caused concern amongst members of the Scientific Committee because they seem to demonstrate a lack of grasp of the science being developed in management' (quoted in Cawthorn 1999: 29).

A large number of NGOs are allowed to attend the proceedings without rights to vote or speak.[19] It was the U.S. government that in the 1970s encouraged NGOs and mass media to attend the IWC meetings, apparently in an attempt to mobilize international public opinion (Sumi 1989: 344) and to have its own 'greenness' reported to the electorate. The NGOs tend to form two major blocs. The largest, which at times numbers close to one hundred NGOs, is composed of environmental and animal rights groups, while the smaller is composed mainly of groups working for indigenous peoples or for sustainable whaling in general.

The NGOs have several tasks during the IWC meetings. First, they lobby delegates and try to convince the general public through the mass media that their world view is the correct one. Parallel with the negotiations in the meeting room, they organize a series of press conferences where protectionists with optimal press coverage can present 'shocking' reports about treatment of whales and dolphins, often accompanied by gory videos. This enables the NGOs to raise their own issues even when these are not on the agenda of the IWC. The annual demonstrations against whaling organized in connection with the IWC meetings, moreover, provide the media with attractive shots. Many anti-whaling NGOs collaborate closely, and about twenty groups jointly issue a publication called *Eco* during IWC meetings, while the pro-whaling High North Alliance (HNA) for a period published *The International Harpoon*.

Second, the NGOs monitor the proceedings and report their interpretations and evaluations of the delegates' performances to the media. Until 2000 the media had no access to the conference room but could only follow parts of the proceedings through loudspeaker systems placed in the pressroom. This put the

Figure 4.1 *Greenpeace and the Norwegian 'Friends of the Harpoon' (left) side by side in front of the IWC hotel, Dublin 1995. (courtesy by Institute of Cetacean Research, Tokyo)*

NGOs in a unique position to manipulate the flow of information by serving as intermediaries between the press and the delegations. Coffee breaks turned into intense press-briefing sessions where the media relied heavily on the services of the NGOs and some of the delegates.

Without the media, the IWC meetings would make a much less attractive arena. More than 200 media people were accredited for the meeting in London in 2001 (*HNA News*, 27 July 2001). Through the media, the NGOs are able to put pressure on national governments and politicians or endorse their opinions and statements, thus diminishing or enhancing their prospects of being reelected, and create lists ranking the most 'progressive' delegations and nations. The NGOs on both sides assume the role of judge and issue verdicts on delegations' 'progressive greenness' or 'care for local communities'. Herein lies perhaps the main reason for their influence. With anti-whaling NGOs in the majority, and with most of the media hailing from anti-whaling nations with strong anti-whaling populations, it should come as no surprise that anti-whaling sentiments dominate the newspaper columns and news broadcasts. The media willingly base reportage on the latest anti-whaling publications, particularly if they are sensational in character and grossly exaggerate crises.[20] In short, especially before 2000, the IWC meetings provided environmental and animal rights group a rare opportunity to get their message out to millions of people. In an attempt to reduce the influence of the NGOs, however, the media were given access to the conference rooms as of 2000, despite protests by some of the anti-whaling countries (Komatsu and Misaki 2003: 115), and reportage is now even distributed live via the Internet.

As long as the IWC provides an attractive arena to the environmental movement, its annual meetings will remain important to governments that need to bolster their green images. There is a swapping of legitimacy between NGOs and governments: activists are taken into inner political circles for a while in return for giving the relevant government a green stamp. By voting against whaling, governments can appear green and civilized before their constituencies. The U.S. government's concern for whales during the U.N. Conference on Human Environment in 1972 '[was not] the last time that a government adopted the whale as a convenient cause—a fig leaf for naked failures in environmental protection' (Darby 2008: 104). 'In Bourdieu's terms, this is where anti-whaling states reap the "symbolic profit" that accompanies a symbolic domination', writes Charlotte Epstein (2005: 217). Sometimes this is formally expressed, as when an IWC commissioner from the United States received the 'Schweitzer medal' for 'thwarting commercial whalers, reversing the Revised Management Procedure, and maintaining the moratorium on whale killing for profit'.[21] The odd alliance between states and NGOs has been forged because both sides—at least in the short term—benefit from the added legitimacy the cooperation gives both parties. This colours many of the issues discussed at these meetings.

The Agenda

Many who have attended IWC meetings might agree with the Icelandic commissioner who remarked in 1991 that there was no debate within the IWC between the two camps. A polarization had taken place, and there are reasons to believe that the presentations are more addressed to those on the same side of the divide than to those on the opposite side. Ottar Brox (2000) has used Gregory Bateson's (1958) notion of schismogenesis to understand polarized political debates as expressive competition. In such a perspective, not only do the two sides compete against each other, but there is a competition to express common shared values within each camp. The whale protectionists, whether NGOs or governments, compete with each other in expressing their opposition to whaling so as to appear more committed to environmental protection than the others. At IWC meetings opposition to whaling has often been expressed by drafting resolutions, which are not binding upon contracting governments but may nonetheless be annoying to whaling countries.[22] In such a situation both sides of the divide may be driven to extreme positions. By scrutinizing the issues on the agenda at the annual IWC meetings, we will see that most of them are characterized by such polarization, where little effort is made to find common ground. The attendance of NGOs and media has made this development possible.

The NGOs want to give the impression that they play important roles in the IWC, Representatives from NGOs have also become members of national delegations and even served as commissioners, and some of the official documents presented by national delegations have been written by them.[23] The HSUS has claimed to be an official NGO that participates in all aspects of IWC meetings, while Paul Watson claims that his Sea Shepherd is the unofficial police of the IWC. The truth is that NGOs have no official roles to play and attend only as observers and lobbyists. Sea Shepherd even has been expelled from the IWC since the 1980s.

The Moratorium (RMP/RMS)

The moratorium was, as already mentioned, imposed while the IWC awaited better knowledge on whale stocks and the development of a new, sophisticated management model—RMP (Revised Management Procedure)—which does not require detailed knowledge about either original or current sizes of whale populations. The crucial variable is how stocks change over time, which requires regular surveys to investigate. Consequently, scientists—particularly from whaling nations—initiated large research projects including both lethal research and sighting surveys. Simultaneously, the Scientific Committee initiated mathematical modelling for the development of the RMP. Then, at its meeting in Reykjavík in 1991, the Scientific Committee endorsed the assessment of the North Atlantic stock of minke whales and moreover accepted one of the most conservative of five RMP models presented. Among the seven scientists who voted against this model was Justin Cooke, who was its architect and affiliated with a number of anti-whaling organizations. The commission failed to adapt the RMP, requesting that more modelling be done. What the whaling nations regarded as foot dragging became more and more pronounced.

In 1993, when the IWC turned against its Scientific Committee for the third time and refused to endorse the RMP, the committee's chairman, Prof. Philip Hammond of Cambridge University, handed in his resignation with these words:

> [W]hat is the point of having a Scientific Committee if its unanimous recommendations on matters of primary importance are treated with such contempt? . . . I have come to the conclusion that I can no longer justify to myself being the organiser of and spokesman for a Committee whose work is held in such disregard by the body to which it is responsible (letter of resignation, 26 May 1993).

The IWC's credibility was at stake. The situation was particularly difficult for the U.S., which in other contexts argues for the principle that renewable natural resources ought to be managed according to the best scientific knowledge. To continue the argument about scientific uncertainty would undermine the legitimacy of science in resource management. A 'compromise' seems therefore to have been worked out between Norway and the U.S. the following year after several meetings between Norwegian Prime Minister Gro Harlem Brundtland and Vice President Al Gore. Among the delegates I spoke with during the IWC meeting in 1994 there was a widely shared assumption that the U.S. accepted the RMP and promised not to sanction Norway if Norway, in return, refrained from voting against the French proposal for the Southern sanctuary below 40°S.[24]

The RMP was thus finally accepted by the IWC, though only in the form of a resolution and not as a Schedule amendment. The IWC therefore did not endorse its use as a management tool, and it was shelved and not implemented. The RMP was no longer regarded as sufficient to lift the moratorium. From there, the IWC went from the RMP to the RMS (Revised Management Scheme). The scientific arguments for the moratorium had been exhausted, but the anti-whaling bloc argued that there were practical, nonscientific problems to solve (Simpson 1999: 341). Among the problems requiring a solution before the moratorium could be lifted was an international agreement on supervision and control.[25] Although whaling nations felt that necessary control mechanisms already existed, Norway invited the IWC to an intercessional meeting in Norway to speed up the process, but the meeting that was held in January 1995 made no progress. At the annual IWC meeting in 1999 a whole day was set aside to discuss RMS at the request of the Japanese, but the meeting was over before lunch because many of the delegates had not received any instructions from home (Simpson 1999: 341). Several meetings have been held since then, and a special Expert Drafting Group was established to draft the final text.

Today we are hardly any closer to an agreement on the RMS. Despite resolutions encouraging all participants to work expeditiously and in good faith to restore the IWC as an effective organization, new demands are made—apparently to delay commercial whaling under IWC quotas until the whalers give up or all oceans have been turned into a global sanctuary. One demand is that the control should cover not only the operations at sea but also the genetic monitoring of whale products in markets, a step that will infringe on member states' internal police and judicial systems. The last proposal, from the U.K., was to include data on whale 'killing methods and associated welfare issues' in the RMS. Japan's very firm reaction is stated in a letter to the IWC chairman, where Japan's Commissioner Morimoto writes: 'Japan has no intention to participate in a discussion on the details of matters concerning monitoring of markets and the incorporation of whale killing methods and associated welfare issues in the RMS since it is the position of the Government of Japan that such matters are outside the scope of the Convention' (letter to IWC Chairman Fernholm, 29 January 2001).[26]

It is becoming obvious to many observers that RMS has little to do with ecology and sustainable utilization of natural resources. In his opening address to the IWC meeting in 1999 Elliott Morley, the British minister of fisheries, said that 'the ultimate aim of the U.K. is the imposition of a permanent worldwide moratorium on all whaling other than ASW' (United Kingdom 1999). The U.K. is not alone having this objective.

Whaling for Scientific Research

Closely linked to the moratorium is the issue of scientific research. In line with Article V.2 of the ICRW, the 1982 moratorium decision called for an early review 'based upon the best scientific advice' (Schedule 10[e]). To provide such advice, Article VIII.1 of the whaling convention gives to any contracting government the right to grant its nationals 'a special permit authorizing that nationals to kill, take and treat whales for purposes of scientific research'. But when Iceland, Japan and Norway launched comprehensive research projects in order to provide the required scientific input for the RMP (Chapter 6), they were routinely rebuked. The IWC has adopted over thirty resolutions against special permit whaling since the imposition of the moratorium.[27] One of the arguments against scientific whaling is that newer research methods have made lethal taking of whales unnecessary (IWC 2003c). Japan, on the other hand, strongly argues that lethal taking of whales is necessary in order to collect some of the data required (e.g. Ohsumi 2000; Komatsu and Misaki 2003). Also the Scientific Committee admits that there are certain data that can only be obtained in this way, such as the age of an animal (obtained from earplugs) and the reproductive status and history of females (obtained from ovaries). This is important information when considering e.g. mortality and reproductive rates.

It is often pointed out that meat and other products from whales killed are sold at the market, and that scientific whaling—a term usually placed within quotation marks—therefore is 'commercial whaling in disguise'. Whaling nations find this criticism unfair, pointing to Article VIII.2, which states that whales taken under scientific whaling permits 'shall so far as practicable be processed and the proceeds shall be dealt with in accordance with directions issued by the Government by which the permit was granted'. The Japanese feel that they follow the letter of the whaling convention, and therefore regard all the resolutions against scientific whaling as illegal. As they see it, research should be the duty of any contracting member of the IWC (Sumi 1989: 359), as science is regarded essential to the management of whale resources. Moreover, Japan's income from such sales covers only a fraction of the expenditures and cannot justify the whaling economically. The IWC's opposition to scientific whaling is seen as proof that the IWC is insincere and disregards its own convention—in other words, that it has traded ecology and science for ethics.

Aboriginal Subsistence Whaling (ASW)

ASW seldom creates serious conflicts within the IWC. There do exist nuances in positions, from Australia wanting to end ASW at one extreme to the U.S.

wanting minimal interference with its own ASW at the other extreme. But in recent years several member countries—not least Japan—have been increasingly annoyed by what they perceive as the U.S.'s double standard and arrogance, and a more restrictive attitude towards indigenous whaling has emerged. Some delegates have complained about block quotas (quotas that are given for several years at a time) with the possibility of transferring quotas from one year to the next.[28] There are also complaints about the lack of proper external control of the Alaskan hunt. Indignation reached a peak when the United States requested a modest quota of five gray whales on behalf of the Makah Indians in Washington State. As the Makah have survived, physically at least, without hunting and eating whales for about seventy years, it was argued by some opponents that their whaling culture was no longer authentic and that they did therefore not qualify for ASW considerations. According to Schedule 13[b]2 only aborigines 'whose traditional aboriginal subsistence and cultural needs have been recognised' can catch gray whales. The U.S. interpreted this to mean that the IWC had endorsed the Makah hunt, but in fact the IWC had not recognized that the Makah needed to subsist on whales. In one of the rare dissonances within the like-minded group, Australia protested strongly against the U.S. interpretations. Whereas Australia opposed the U.S. because the country is against any kind of whaling, Japan—usually supportive of ASW—opposed a quota because of the perceived U.S. double standard. Many Japanese asked how the U.S. could argue for the cultural importance of an activity that had not been carried out for the last seventy years and at the same time deny the cultural importance of an uninterrupted coastal whaling tradition in Japan. When the U.S. failed to obtain a quota for the Makah, it struck a deal with the Russians. The Makah got some of the Russian quota of gray whales, whereas Russia got some of Alaska's bowhead quota. But such quota trade-offs are, according to the ICRW, only allowed when both parties have quotas (which the Makah did not have).

The frustration reached new levels in 2002 when the IWC failed to approve a new quota of bowhead whales for indigenous whalers in Alaska and Russia (Chukotka). Officially Japan was against quotas due to uncertainty about the size of the stock and the fact that the block quota period had been extended from three to five years. But it is no secret that Japan blocked the decision in retaliation against what the Japanese saw as double standard, and thus for the first time seriously and practically challenged the IWC-elaborated distinction between ASW and artisanal Japanese minke whaling. In the end the U.S. had its way at an extraordinary meeting called in great haste in October that same year.[29] Japan backed down, allegedly because the U.S. threatened to stop shipments of oil from Alaska to Japan (Roman 2006: 171, see also below).

Delegates from whaling nations hesitate to raise the question of ASW for fear of destroying the case for aboriginal peoples, and there is little willingness within the IWC to discuss the terms on which its management of ASW should be based. However, what seems to be clear is that if the IWC shall bear the responsibility of managing ASW—which is in no way obvious, as many hold the opinion that such a role is an example of the IWC's creeping jurisdiction—it is increasingly felt that the starting point must be the stock's size and demographic profile and not the whalers' need for meat. The Scientific Committee has therefore started work to develop a management regime for this kind of whaling. Meanwhile, nobody knows when, or whether, this regime will be completed and implemented. The U.S. is certainly not pushing the matter.

Infractions

The Infraction Sub-Committee discusses illegal catches of whales. The negotiations in this subcommittee are highly politicized. The delegates disagree both about species to be covered (and hence what kind of whaling) and what 'infraction' means in the IWC context. This has made it possible for whale protectionists to introduce issues that whaling nations think lie outside the subcommittee's mandate. The subcommittee has become an arena for insinuations and insults. Whalers feel that no opportunity is lost to cast doubt on their honesty and integrity, and again Japan is singled out for the worst beating. During the 1994 meeting, for example, the U.K. representative openly expressed distrust in the Japanese police, gravely insulting the Japanese delegation. Two other examples of issues taken up during the 1994 meeting will further illustrate the mode of work in this subcommittee.

Among the issues discussed was a small piece of blubber washed ashore in Alaska. After describing the piece,[30] the report from the United States goes on to say: 'Also found on the same day, farther up the bay, was a bottle with pelagic goose-neck barnacles on it. A glass float from a *foreign pelagic fishing fleet* washed ashore in the same area on that day, although there is no direct evidence that this was linked to the whale specimen. The objects on the beach suggest that this particular beach at this time was collecting objects from the high seas and that the piece may have come from the high seas as well' (USA 1994, emphasis added). There can be little doubt that the objective of this phrasing was to allude to a possible illegal catch made by foreigners. The other example also clearly shows the way in which the debate is conducted. Under the heading 'Infraction' in the document 'Summary of Infractions Reported by the Commission in 1993' (IWC 1994b) it is listed that St. Vincent and the Grenadines had taken one small whale, which is illegal if the calf is suckling. The following note was added: 'It is not clear if the . . . animal was a calf of the year but this *seems unlikely* as the female [also taken] was not lactating. It seems more likely, it is a yearling or older, then this would *not be considered* an infraction' (emphasis added). Yet New Zealand brought up the question again the following year. Rather we should ask why it was included in the first place. Similar allegations have been levelled since then against St. Vincent and the Grenadines.

One example of how some delegations try to extend the IWC's mandate to cover small toothed whales, is an intervention at the 2003 meeting when the

U.K. asked about a Greenlandic take of thirty-two killer whales the year before. Referring to the general prohibition on catching killer whales from factory ships (Schedule 10[d]) and the moratorium (Schedule 10[e]), the U.K. voiced the opinion that the catch was illegal. Denmark had to inform the meeting that the animals were not caught from a factory ship (such ships do not exist in Greenland) and that killer whales moreover are outside the IWC's area of competence and therefore not covered by the moratorium.

A controversial question is to what extent the IWC should involve itself in incidental catches of cetaceans in fishing gear. Whale protectionists think that everything should be done to save whales that become entangled in nets, and they are afraid that by-catch otherwise can motivate captures (e.g. IWC 2003d).[31] Further, they argue that all incidental catches should be reported to the Infraction Sub-Committee and criticize countries for not doing so. Iceland, Japan and Norway, on the other hand, think that such catches do not fall under the IWC's mandate,[32] and that what happens in the fisheries and how the carcasses are handled is up to the national authorities to decide.[33]

Another controversial issue that the committee tries to raise is trade in whale products. Japan, Norway and other countries have repeatedly protested against this point on the agenda, claiming that this question is outside the IWC's mandate and there are no paragraphs referring to trade in the ICRW. Such matters are more correctly discussed with reference to the provisions of CITES. But once this point is on the agenda, some anti-whaling delegates—often citing reports written by NGOs—miss no opportunity to cast doubt on the honesty and integrity of whalers and whaling countries. This has produced a series of resolutions particularly against Japan.[34] The country is repeatedly accused of smuggling, and Japanese supermarkets are accused of misinforming their customers and of selling the meat of endangered species.

Humane Killing Methods and Associated Welfare Issues

The issue of killing methods was firmly placed on the IWC agenda in the 1970s. In 1975 the Scientific Committee started to investigate killing methods in order to make whaling more humane. During the following years a number of recommendations were followed up with practical efforts, and a working group on humane killing was set up in 1983 (Mitchell, Reeves and Evely 1986; Donovan 1986). Since then this working group has also been given new tasks and has now become the working group for 'Whale killing methods and associated welfare issues'. Yet the IWC has been reluctant to discuss what 'humane' actually means (HNA 1995). When the group met in 2003, they discussed the criteria for death, how to put a whale that has been stranded or entangled in nets 'out of its suffering' (IWC 2003a: 11), to what extent whales feel stress during hunts, and how weather conditions may influence the hunt. New Zealand even informed the working group that 'grief counselling is an integral part of people management when whales are euthanased [sic]' (IWC 2003a: 7). There have been attempts particularly by the British to include animal welfare in the IWC's rules (and in the RMS), and in 2003 Japan left the meeting in protest of this point on the agenda.

This highly politicized working group has become one of the most annoying points on the IWC agenda to whaling nations, not least to Japan. It has not gone unnoticed by the Japanese that this working group has spent much time discussing to what extent the commercial hunt, with an average killing time of between two and three minutes, can be made more humane, without asking the same question when lack of proper technology means it may take several hours for a group of native whalers in Alaska to kill a bowhead whale. However, it should be added that since the 1990s the IWC has become increasingly interested in ASW and, through a resolution in 1997, urged aboriginal whalers to take steps to reduce the suffering of the whales (IWC 1997). Whaling nations have, on their side, tried to broaden the discussion to include the quality of the animals' entire life and not only the killing process. Norway has also wanted the discussion to include sport hunting of terrestrial animals for comparative purposes. However, the majority find such issues irrelevant to the discussion and have been reluctant to provide the working group with comparative material.[35]

Management of Small Whales

Another controversial issue has for many years been the meaning of the term 'whale'. Whereas some opponents of whaling argue that the term must cover all cetaceans, including dolphins and porpoises, nations with ongoing hunts of small toothed whales want to limit the term to the large baleen whales and the sperm whale, as these are the only species named in a nomenclature document included in the ICRW.

There have been a number of attempts to broaden the IWC's competence, and in 1972 the IWC established a subcommittee within the Scientific Committee for such cetaceans (Iwasaki-Goodman 1994: 216). So far these attempts have been unsuccessful. In 1991, when the IWC tried to include the Pacific Baird's beaked whale, Japan protested vigorously. The previous year the IWC had made a 'landmark' resolution (Simpson 1999: 249) requesting Japan to reduce its catches of Dall's porpoise. A similar resolution was passed in 1999—when Japan and seven other countries left the meeting room to protest what they perceived as the IWC's infringement of the sovereign rights of states (Komatsu and Misaki 2001: 87–88). Also Denmark has parried all the IWC's attempts to interfere with pilot whaling in the Faroe Islands. That Denmark nonetheless provides the IWC with information about this hunt is, according to Denmark, an expression of goodwill.

The tensions related to the management of small cetaceans are increasing. Many countries are of the opinion that these whales are best managed by regional bodies like the North Atlantic Marine Mammal Commission (NAM-MCO) and the Agreement on the Conservation of Small Cetaceans of the Baltic and the North Seas (ASCOBANS), and Japan points to the fact that only a few of the countries with populations of small whales are members of the IWC. But the hard core of anti-whaling countries make repeated attempts to extend the mandate of the whaling convention. Several NGOs have made the small cetaceans their main issue.

Whale Sanctuaries

The whaling convention endorses the establishment of sanctuaries, but adds that such amendments of the Schedule '(a) shall be such as are necessary to carry out the objectives and purposes of this Convention, . . . (b) shall be based on scientific findings; . . . and (d) shall take into consideration the interests of the consumers of whale products and the whaling industry' (Article V.2). One strategy in recent years has been to establish extensive sanctuaries, preferably covering all oceans, so that the moratorium can be lifted without any practical consequences. Several countries (e.g. Ireland, New Zealand and Australia) have established sanctuaries within their own economic zones, and the issue has become a permanent item on the IWC agenda.

The first successful attempt was the temporary sanctuary covering most of the Indian Ocean in 1979. This sanctuary has been prolonged indefinitely. In 1994 the IWC decided to establish a global sanctuary below 40° S, the so-called Southern Ocean Sanctuary.[36] Moreover, Australia and New Zealand have worked hard to have the South Pacific declared a sanctuary, and Brazil has made the same for the South Atlantic. These attempts have so far failed to get the required three-fourths majority, but one might wonder why new sanctuaries are needed. As the secretary of the pro-whaling High North Alliance observed, within this area the large whales are already protected in four ways: by the moratorium of 1982, by a 1981 moratorium on pelagic whaling, by the classification of whales stocks as protected and by the Southern Ocean sanctuary (Frøvik 1995: 139).

Whaling nations claim that the sanctuaries are illegal since they do not take the IWC's main objective into account, are not based on science and do not consider the interests of consumers. The Southern Ocean Sanctuary was established without considering whale populations, and Paragraph 7[b] of the Schedule now states: 'This prohibition [on catching whales] applies irrespective of the conservation status of baleen and toothed whale stocks in this Sanctuary.' A North American group of scientists concluded in 2004 that the sanctuary could not be ecologically justified (IWC/SC/56/SO55, quoted in Darby 2008: 173). Japanese scientists believe that by restricting lethal research the sanctuaries may prevent a proper understanding of the ecosystem to emerge and thus pose a serious threat not least to the recovery of the blue whale stocks (cf. Chapter 6).

Socioeconomic Consequences of the Moratorium

Since the moratorium closed down Japan's coastal minke whaling in 1988, Japan has spent much effort to convince the Commission of the cultural qualities of this activity. Despite a large number of scholarly reports and publications written by social scientists from a number of nations, the Japanese have repeatedly been asked to provide new information. In her doctoral thesis, Masami Iwasaki-Goodman (1994: 146), who attended the IWC meeting for a number of years, remarks that requests for more information and research are a commonly used stalling tactic within the working group as well as other areas of the Commission. It is likely that many delegates do not even bother to read the material provided, because the same people ask the same questions again and again (1994: 147).

While the Japanese stressed the cultural aspects for this working group, they also worked on plans to remove the last commercial elements from coastal hunts. Japan thought that their pleas were finally being heard in 1993, when the IWC by consensus adopted a resolution expressing the need 'to work expeditiously to alleviate the distress to [four small coastal whaling] communities' (IWC 1993). However, it soon became clear that this resolution was only an attempt to be nice to the host. When the Japanese presented a plan at the 1994 meeting detailing how meat could be distributed among the households within the communities concerned, they received little but scorn for their efforts. It was after denying an emergency quota to Japan that the Commission, without debate, gave a quota of 140 gray whales to Russia and increased the Alaskan quota of bowhead whales from fifty-one to sixty-eight animals, allegedly in consideration of dramatic increases in the human population of the Inuit villages. To the Japanese this policy was an outright act of racial discrimination against Japanese coastal whalers.

To speed up work the IWC decided to hold a workshop that should 're-view and identify commercial aspects of socio-economic and cultural needs'. In 1997 Japan therefore invited Japanese and foreign social scientists to discuss the issue at a workshop that was held in Sendai, Northern Japan. However, all hopes of a constructive meeting were dashed when the United States insisted that the chairman had to be one who knew the IWC from the inside. Countries like Australia, New Zealand, the U.K., Sweden and Germany moreover sent only low-ranking personnel from their Tokyo embassies. What was intended as a scholarly workshop to discuss the concept 'commercial' turned into a political meeting with presentations of the type 'it is my government's opinion that . . . ' The U.S. delegation even insisted that discussion of the relation between commerce and management was outside the meeting's terms of reference. The locked positions from the regular IWC meetings were imposed on the workshop (Kalland 1997).

Japan has still (as of 2008) not received any quota for its four local communities, despite new assurances from the IWC in 2001 that 'noting the widespread recognition in various UN covenants, conventions, and other documents, of the importance for communities to continue customary resource use practices on a sustainable basis, REAFFIRMS the Commission's commitment to work expeditiously to alleviate the distress caused by the cessation of minke whaling' (IWC 2001a).

Other Issues

New themes have been taken up for discussion in recent years. One theme is whale watching, and several member countries have expressed concern for the psychological impact these activities may have on the whales. The Scientific Committee has, on a request from the IWC, collected whale watch regulations from around the world and suggested general guidelines.

Another, and at first view more relevant theme, is the ecological situation in the oceans. Although this is not included in the mandate of the ICRW, it has been a permanent item on the agenda since 1998. But even here a polarization has occurred. It is symptomatic that a working group studying the chemical pollution of the seas met in Norway (in 1995), whereas a working group on the possible effects of the depletion of the ozone layer and of climatic change met in the U.S. (in 1996). While whaling nations are concerned about the direct impact of pollution of the seas, the whale protectionists are preoccupied with possible indirect factors that are much more difficult to map. Hence, research will drag on. Whaling nations are equally dismayed when protectionists discuss possible danger connected to eating contaminated whale products and bring this into the question of management. Japanese consider it hypocritical when some delegates suddenly express concern about the whalers' health.

At the end of the 1990s the 'Irish proposal' was a permanent item on the agenda and was even the topic for an intercessional meeting. Allegedly in an attempt to break the deadlock, and perhaps to save the IWC from collapse, the Irish chairman in 1997 tabled a proposal suggesting a kind of compromise. It allowed whaling nations to catch whales within their own economic zones (presupposing IWC quotas) while prohibiting whaling in international waters and all international trade in whale products. The hard core within the IWC was against this, as were most of the activists, as they are against commercial whaling whatever the conditions. Japan was also against the proposal because its whaling in the Antarctic would be outlawed. Norway too was against it because of the ban on international trade. Since the Irish chair's term in office came to an end, the proposal has silently died. The polarization of the IWC is deep and lasting.

Polarization of the IWC

One reason for the polarization of the IWC is that the two parties have very different interests. Whaling nations have instrumental and economic interests in the catch, although symbolic interests have become more important over the years. It is the question of people's livelihood, of viable coastal communities and of rational management of renewable natural resources. With the expectation of continuing a modest hunt, they have tried to meet their opponents through compromises (Chapter 6). The opponents of whaling, on the other hand, have foremost a symbolic interest in whaling. This is social capital they can carry with them to other issues. They need no compromise and can run the full course.

As I have already stated, many countries have become IWC members because of the symbolic importance of whales. Even though the moratorium was defended in ecological terms, it soon became clear that there were other considerations at work. The period since 1982 has clearly shown that the ethics have taken the front seat at the IWC, although the legitimacy of science still makes it necessary to clothe the discourse with a varnish of ecological rhetoric. The polarization is most apparent when in comes to whaling for commercial purposes. In discussions about the moratorium, RMP and RMS, and everything else connected to Icelandic, Japanese and Norwegian whaling operations, the IWC is clearly divided into two camps, and the anti-whaling bloc has so far been the larger. The dichotomization is less clear when it comes to the management of small whales, because some anti-whaling countries let their own citizens catch dolphins. But the hard core of the anti-whaling countries (Australia, New Zealand, the U.K., Sweden, Finland, the Netherlands, France, Germany and India, among others) wants the IWC to manage all cetacean species. A divide is emerging also regarding ASW, but so far only Australia is openly against it.

In order to understand the polarization that has emerged it will be useful to study the behaviour of delegates during the meetings. Negotiations are frequently moved out of the conference room and into closed rooms. The like-minded group meets both before and during IWC meetings to coordinate their positions so as to exploit their strength as a majority in the most effective way (Iwasaki-Goodman 1994), and countries may take the lead on different issues to spread diplomatic risk (Darby 2008: 160). An Icelandic delegate in 1991 expressed his frustration in the following terms: '[T]his organisation [IWC] is completely stultified [by] the automatic majority which can be developed around any particular proposal . . . there's no debate which takes place between that majority and the others who might have legitimate interests . . . The reason for that is that this discussion takes place in antechambers and the discussion here [plenum] is choreographed in those antechambers' (verbatim record 1991: 80–81, in Iwasaki-Goodman 1994: 261–62).

When discussions move into closed chambers, NGO observers can take a more active role. In the conference room the NGOs are restricted and occasionally not allowed to attend,[37] but in the back rooms the like-minded group makes its own rules and the NGOs can function more freely. The NGOs may even have helped move negotiations out of the conference room and into closed rooms (Iwasaki-Goodman 1994: 223). Contrary to Friedheim's (2001a: 10) claim that the attendance of NGOs opened up the negotiations at the IWC, NGOs have stimulated to their closure. Both in the closed rooms and during coffee breaks, a metamorphosis takes place where borders between roles are largely erased.

The NGOs have contributed importantly to the polarization by taking an active role and even have interfered directly in IWC negotiations. By being able to monitor the proceedings and report their interpretations and evaluations of the delegates' performances to their supporters or to the mass media back home, the NGOs have, as argued, been in a unique position to put pressure on national governments and politicians. There are indications that NGOs have been able to enforce changes in positions taken by some countries. Denmark's sudden about-face during the 1991 meeting springs to mind (Iwasaski-Goodman 1994: 94).[38]

Some pro-whalers regard many of the anti-whaling countries as mere puppets of the activists (cf. Komatsu and Misaki 2001: 80). This is probably going too far, because anti-whaling countries may have their own interest in keeping the conflict going.[39] There is little to loose from collaboration with the whale protectionists. And because citizens in anti-whaling countries are not themselves engaged in whaling, the costs can be externalized, i.e. the costs are born by whalers from distant countries. By going against whaling, governments acquire green images and appear environmentally progressive to their electorates, having embraced this perceived hallmark of civilization. An anti-whaling position is particularly attractive to governments with poor environmental records: 'there appears to be an inverse relationship between the support of these liberal, Western countries for the anti-whaling cause and their support for other global environmental treaties', writes Epstein (2005: 218). It was probably no coincidence that the moratorium on commercial whaling was strongly supported by conservative governments in Europe and the United States (e.g. those of Margaret Thatcher and Ronald Reagan), governments that in general were unresponsive if not openly hostile to environmental initiatives (Dalton 1994: 42–43). And it is probably no coincidence the hard core anti-whaling countries such as the United States, Australia and New Zealand are often large exporters of meat, eager to export both their farm products and their food hegemony complex (Epstein 2005: 223). Therefore, many of the anti-whaling countries have their own immediate interests in mind.

Many participants have called the IWC meetings a circus, where much of the time is spent manipulating texts. This is a game that favours the Anglo-Saxon bloc (Australia, New Zealand, the U.K. and the U.S.) at the expense of Japan in particular but also Iceland and Norway. None of the whalers today use English as their mother tongue, but four of the most influential countries within the IWC are English-speaking (Takahashi 1998). The exclusive use of English symbolically underlines the power relations in the IWC.[40] The discussions often concern preparations of reports, with phrasing and punctuation carefully chosen to express nuances that can be lost on delegates from non–English-speaking countries. Moreover, important concepts do not always translate into other languages easily. One example is the term 'aborigine', which has no counterpart in Japanese, a fact that has caused much misunderstanding and frustration among the Japanese.

The word used, *genjūmin*, can be translated as 'people who live in the same region as their original ancestors' (Takahashi 1998: 251); Japanese whalers therefore cannot understand why their whaling does not qualify as aboriginal whaling. Another example is the concepts of 'take' and 'kill' as described earlier. Things are not improved when resolution texts are distributed too late to allow delegates proper time to analyse them and grasp their full implications.

Another problem is that the chairs at times break the IWC's own rules of procedure. The majority forces a reluctant minority to accept consensus (to go against consensus always has a cost), or chairs, who usually come from the like-minded group, push decisions through despite strong opposition. 'The large anti-whaling block succeed in every instance in forcing an unwilling minority to join a consensus decision, or where a vote is taken, are able to defeat any initiative put forward by the whaling minority' (Iwasaki-Goodman 1994: 209). This is possible because consensus is highly valued in international forums, and most people give in upon realizing that they will lose a vote. Only in matters of vital importance will they insist on a vote and accept the social costs implied.

At present the polarization is tearing the IWC to pieces. Some observers have concluded that 'The Annual Meetings of the International Whaling Commission (IWC) are the most notorious and least decorous battlegrounds in international environmental law' (Burns, Wandesforde-Smith and Simpson 2001: 221). Rather than managing whaling in a sustainable way to the best interests of the industry and the consumer as the ICRW stipulates, most of the time allotted to the meetings is spent discussing the possible impact of whale watching on whale behaviour, rumours of infractions and smuggling of meat. During the meeting in 1997 the chairman acknowledged that the IWC is failing in its responsibility as an international whaling treaty. And in 1999, the IUCN warned in its opening statement to the IWC that 'IUCN . . . views the condition of the IWC with increasing concern . . . The IWC has shown little sign of an intention to resume its responsibility for the management of whaling . . . Each Commission meeting that passes without any concrete progress of the RMS further dents the credibility of the IWC and jeopardises its ability to re-assert its role as a serious management body' (IUCN 1999, quoted in INWR 2000).

Whales: A Global Resource?

In their critiques of the 'Tragedy of the Commons' paradigm (Hardin 1968), Ciriacy-Wantrup and Bishop (1975) pointed out the important distinction between common property and nobody's property. The former they defined as 'a distribution of property rights in resources in which a number of owners are co-equal in their rights *to use* the resource' whereas the latter refers to an open access situation to unowned resources. The difference is that of institutions. In a property situation there are rules of access and usage defined and sanctioned by one or more management bodies. I will argue that the whale protectionists have tried to change whales from an open access resource to everybody's property (or a common heritage of humankind) with rules of conduct laid down by a monopolistic management body, the IWC.

Feeny et al. (1990) suggest that two important features characterize any property regime. The first is excludability, i.e. the owners must be able to exclude non-owners from using the resource. They must sanction any encroachment on their property rights either themselves or, more commonly in modern society, via state authorities. The more expensive it becomes to defend a resource, the more open it tends to be. The second feature is subtractability, meaning that A's exploitation of the resource reduces B's exploitation of the same (as measured against unit of effort). This implies that there is a latent conflict of interests among the property holders. In order for a common property regime to work, the owners usually have to build institutions that can both control access to the resource and regulate the owners' use. Should institutions fail to address the first problem, the resource might *de facto* be open to everybody. If they fail to address the second, there might be no mechanism to prevent the owners from ruining the resource. In both cases a tragedy may occur.

Institutions, then, figure prominently in the large body of literature on common property resources. Perhaps this is one reason why most scholars have failed to consider common property regimes above the state level. It has proved difficult to establish international institutions to manage natural resources unless the contracting states are given the option to object to majority decisions that are deemed detrimental to their national interests. A member state lodging an official reservation within a certain period of time (i.e. ninety days in the case of the IWC) is not bound by such a decision, nor does the organization possess legal means of enforcement. Objections have frequently been lodged against decisions made by international management bodies, and Norway is currently whaling under this, what many have termed a 'loophole' of the ICRW.

Commercial whaling provides a good case study of the difficulties in creating viable international management regimes for natural resources. Since its beginning in 1949, the IWC has failed to establish a sustainable management regime for whales, going from one extreme in the 1950s and 1960s to the other extreme in the 1980s and 1990s. Part of the problem is that since the 1970s a well-orchestrated attempt has been made to transform whales from an open access resource owned by nobody (*res nullius*) to a global resource, a common heritage of humankind (*res communis*) (Hoel 1986: 28). This implies that everybody has the same right to participate in the management of whaling, whether one happens to live in Greenland or Switzerland, and that whales are seen as a common property resource under the sole management of the IWC. In order to achieve this, the whale protectionists first moved to eliminate whaling conducted by countries that were not members of the IWC, hoping that this would place all whale resources under one internationally recognized management body. Second, they tried to gain control over the IWC in order to impose a total moratorium on whaling for commercial purposes.

Creating an IWC Monopoly

One of the characteristics, or as some would say, weaknesses, of international treaties is that they are only binding on contracting governments. The ICRW is no exception to this. It applies only to 'factory ships, land stations, and the whale catchers under the jurisdiction of the Contracting Governments' (Article I). In other words, the ICRW does not apply to countries that are not members of the IWC. Nor do international agreements such as the *United Nations Convention on the Law of the Sea* (UNCLOS) and *Agenda 21* confine the management of whaling solely to the IWC. Nevertheless, both activists and anti-whaling countries try to give the impression that the IWC has an exclusive global mandate to manage at least all the large whales. Rhetoric is, as will be seen shortly, followed up by more tangible attempts to give the IWC a monopolistic position.

Several governments have, for various reasons, decided not to be a member of the IWC even though some of their citizens are engaged in whaling. Two examples are Indonesia and the Philippines. Other countries have withdrawn for shorter or longer periods of time, among them Norway and the Netherlands, which left the IWC temporarily in 1959.[41] Canada left in 1982 and remains a non-member although Canadian Inuit have taken up bowhead whaling after a lapse of several decades. Iceland left the IWC in 1992 but rejoined in 2002. Decisions made by the IWC are not binding on such governments. Whaling by nonmembers may undoubtedly diminish the effectiveness of IWC decisions, but it is hardly against international law.

Whaling activities conducted by nations outside the IWC in the 1970s met with little understanding or respect from countries like the U.S. and the U.K. Non-IWC whaling nations were therefore attractive targets for the activists who launched attacks on the whalers, calling them pirates and outlaws—although their whaling might have been perfectly legal according to international law. Several whaling ships were destroyed in 1979 and 1980 (Day 1992; Darby 2008). Such acts of sabotage, together with other forms of harassment as well as pressure from the United States (DeSombre 2001), brought most of the remaining whaling nations into the IWC. Whereas only eight of sixteen whaling nations were members of the IWC in 1972, the figure was nine out of ten in 1982 (Hoel 1986: 69). Hence the IWC had come a long way toward a *de facto* monopoly over the management of hunting large whales. To advance their goal of stopping all whaling, it remained for the anti-whalers to gain effective control of the IWC.

Controlling the IWC

The International Whaling Commission is open to all nations, whether they engage in whaling or not. This is one of its problems. Upon closing down their own commercial whaling activities for economic reasons, Australia, the Netherlands, the United States and the United Kingdom did not leave the IWC but became leaders of the anti-whaling bloc within the organization. The contradiction became even more apparent as new states opposed to the main objective of the ICRW (i.e. orderly development of the whaling industry) joined the IWC for the sole purpose of putting an end to whaling.

Although the number of active whaling nations declined, the number of IWC members increased from fourteen in 1972 to twenty-three in 1979, when the IWC made two important moves towards the cessation of whaling: the establishment of the Indian Ocean as a whale sanctuary and a moratorium on pelagic whaling by factory ships in the Antarctic (with the exception for minke whales). By 1982 IWC membership had soared to thirty-nine, establishing a three-quarters majority for the imposition of a moratorium on all killing of whales for commercial purposes. Ten new members attended an IWC meeting for the first time that year (Birnie 1985: 613; Holt 1985: 198; Frøvik 1995: 126).

Many of the new members were small states such as the Seychelles (member since 1979), Oman (1980), Costa Rica, Dominica, St. Lucia and St. Vincent and the Grenadines (all 1981), and Antigua, Belize and Monaco (1982). Anti-whaling NGOs were instrumental in this change in membership. A steering committee headed by Greenpeace and the WWF was established in 1978 in order to recruit anti-whaling members to the IWC (Danish TV documentary, *Manden i Regnbuen*). The operation had recruited at least half a dozen countries by 1982 (Spencer et al. 1991: 177). Apart from offering their services to small and newly independent countries, the activists spent millions of dollars paying for membership fees, expensive trips for the commissioners and 'grease' money (Cherfas 1989: 118).[42]

In his book *The Whale War* (1992) David Day—himself a whale saver—paints a picture of a small but coordinated group of Western activists lobbying these and other countries, who managed to place themselves in some of their delegations and in 1982 carried out 'what amounted to a *coup d'etat*' in the IWC (Wilkinson 1989: 272). The key strategists were allegedly David McTaggart, the director of Greenpeace International, and Sir Peter Scott of the WWF. Among the activists were Sidney Holt, who has been an adviser to a number of animal welfare and rights organizations including IFAW, and parapsychologist Lyall Watson. Holt and Watson engineered the Indian Ocean sanctuary scheme in 1979 and drafted the moratorium amendment while they represented the Seychelles (Day 1992: 118–20). The Frenchman Jean-Paul Fortom-Gouin, founder of the Whale and Dolphin Coalition (Day 1992: 30), became 'the driving force behind the delegation from Panama' (Cherfas 1989: 120), serving as that country's commissioner in 1978. Between 1987 and 1989 he was the alternate commissioner of Antigua and Barbuda. His friend Chris Davey headed delegations from St. Vincent and the Grenadines as well as from Costa Rica. The Colombian Francisco Palacio (a Greenpeace consultant) headed the delegation from St. Lucia in 1982; his friend and lawyer Richard Baron from Miami represented Antigua that year. Roger

Payne, who is most famous as a researcher of humpback 'songs', served as commissioner for Antigua and Barbuda between 1983 and 1987 (Spencer et al. 1991; *Manden i Regnbuen*).

The change in IWC policy came gradually. While still not strong enough to change the Schedule, the anti-whaling group managed to play whaling nations against each other. Proposals were watered down to make them acceptable to some of the whaling nations in order to secure the required majority. For example, Norway did not oppose a moratorium on hunting of sperm whales, and Japan did not object to the Indian Ocean sanctuary as long as its southern border was drawn in such a way as to minimize its impact on Japanese catches of minke whales in the Antarctic. In 1994, Denmark refrained from objecting to the Southern Ocean Sanctuary in return for quotas issued to Greenland's whalers, a decision that enraged Faroese delegates. Norway too declined to vote against the sanctuary—apparently in return for a guarantee that the United States would not impose trade sanctions—leaving Japan isolated and betrayed. Once again the protectionists had managed to split the whaling nations within the IWC.[43] Where such tactics were not feasible, they pushed for resolutions, which require only a simple majority. Although not binding on the members, many see them as soft laws that should be obeyed (Friedheim 2001b: 206). The resolutions legitimize, at least in the eyes of some anti-whalers, the imposition of sanctions.

The moratorium on whaling for commercial purposes was a major step, although not the final one, towards a global end to whaling. The moratorium will come up for review when a new management scheme has been accepted by the IWC. The strategy of the whale protectionists is on the one hand to make the RMS so strict that it will be virtually impossible to whale economically, and on the other to attempt persistently to delay its implementation until both whaling skills and equipment have been lost. Meanwhile they press for new sanctuaries that eventually will cover all oceans and for the inclusion of small toothed whales. Many would also like to see an end to aboriginal subsistence whaling.

In recent years Japan has taken up the challenge and worked hard to recruit friends to the IWC so that the organization, in their view, can resume its important role as a management body. Moreover, many small island states have changed sides since the imposition of the moratorium, and activists are no longer representing Caribbean countries or the Seychelles. Some NGOs have initiated smear campaigns against these nations, accusing them of having been bought with Japanese development aid (e.g. Caron 1995; Burns et al. 2001; Darby 2008), which they flatly deny.[44] The agitation has at times been so malicious that delegates have felt threatened. The Solomon Islands decided not to attend the important IWC meeting in 1994 after receiving hate mail from Australia and New Zealand (Caron 1995: 170), whereas that same year St. Lucia's commissioner was suddenly called to New York, preventing him from voting against the sanctuary. The delegation from the Solomon Islands allegedly again felt so threatened during the 2000 meeting in Australia that it returned home before important matters came to the vote

(Komatsu and Misaki 2003: 116). In 2003, pressure from Australia and New Zealand once more forced the Solomon Islands into silence (Epstein 2005: 242). The IWC has tried to intercede, for example during the 1994 meeting, when the campaign launched against the tourist industry in the small Caribbean states as well as against their delegations became so malicious that the IWC commissioners found it necessary to issue a protest against the attacks on member states. The same happened in 2001, when a resolution was passed that 'endorses and affirms the complete independence of sovereign countries to decide their own policies and freely participate in the IWC (and other international forums) without undue interference or coercion from other sovereign countries' (IWC 2001b). In order to protect these countries Japan has suggested secret votes, which anti-whaling countries oppose, allegedly in the name of transparency. Japan counters that secret balloting is a precondition for democracy.

In recent years both sides within the IWC have recruited new members to the IWC, and they have become more equal in strength. In 2006 a pro-whaling majority (of one vote) emerged for the first time since the early 1970s. However, the lifting of the moratorium will require a three-fourths majority, and there is no indication that the whaling countries will receive such a support in the near future. In fact, the anti-whaling majority was restored the following year. But to Japan and Norway even a small pro-whaling majority is important because it would at least temporarily make it possible to change the agenda and put an end to the practice of adopting anti-whaling resolutions that are used to legitimize attacks on whaling activities.

The IWC has moved in the direction of a *de facto* monopolistic position vis-à-vis whales, which is an important requirement in order to establish a common property resource with everybody as co-owner. In order for a common property regime to work, however, it is necessary to control access to the resource, regulate its use and not least to be able to sanction any encroachment on the property rights—by its own power or by relying on external support. It is to this question that we now turn.

Enforcement of IWC Decisions

The inability of the IWC to enforce its decisions upon reluctant members has been obvious to most observers. The main reason for this weakness is a clause (Article V) in the whaling convention that gives contracting governments the option to object to amendments. Ironically, this clause was included on the insistence of the United States and over Norway's protests (Cherfas 1989: 113), but it is this article that today allows Norway to continue commercial whaling within the framework of international law as represented by the ICRW.

The IWC has no power to sanction member states. The whale protectionists within the IWC have therefore been forced to rely on the powers of the United States and the NGOs to enforce its nonbinding decisions. The U.S. has more than once been willing to coerce whaling nations to comply with IWC decisions (Martin and Brennan 1989; DeSombre 2001). Under the 1971 Pelly Amendment to the Fisherman's Protective Act, the U.S. president is authorized to prohibit all imports of sea products from a country that 'diminishes the effectiveness of an international fishery or wildlife conservation agreement'. The 1979 Packwood-Magnusson Amendment to the Fisheries Conservation and Management Act requires the secretary of commerce to sanction such countries by reducing their access to fish within the U.S. 200-mile economic zone or to close the access altogether.

The United States has certified, or threatened to certify, whaling nations under the Pelly Amendment and the Packwood-Magnusson Amendment, thus in effect becoming the 'IWC's policeman' (Day 1992: 47). Japan and the Soviet Union were both certified as early as 1974 for objecting to and exceeding the 1973–74 minke whale quotas (Caron 1995: 158). In 1979 the U.S. put pressure on Japan to introduce a national law in adherence to IWC resolutions calling for a ban on imports of whale products from nonmember countries. In 1985 the Soviet quota for fish caught within Alaskan waters was halved because the Russians exceeded their quota of minke whales (Cherfas 1989: 189). But usually the threat of using this legislation has been sufficient to force whaling nations to comply (cf. DeSombre 2001: 190–91): South Korea, Peru, Chile and Spain all joined the IWC in 1978–79 after strong pressure from the United States (Siegel 1985: 584; Day 1992). This policy continued to be successful during the 1980s, when pressure was brought to bear on several whaling nations. Taiwan, a country that has been denied membership in the IWC, closed its whaling operations under threat of sanction (Birnie 1985: 601), Iceland did not object to the moratorium imposed on commercial whaling in 1982, and Peru withdrew its objection in 1984. Korea gave up scientific whaling for the same reason in 1986–87 (Day 1992: 111), and in July 1987 Norway announced a temporary halt in commercial whaling—without cancelling its objection to the moratorium—less than a month after the U.S. secretary of commerce had certified Norway for diminishing the effectiveness of the IWC (Hoel 1992: 24).[45] Finally, Japan withdrew its objection to the moratorium in an attempt to avoid being expelled from North American waters (Sumi 1989).[46]

It is, however, highly questionable whether these sanctions stand up to international law (Sumi 1989; McDorman 1991; Hoel 1992), and the United States has been criticized by a General Agreement on Tariffs and Trade (GATT) panel for its embargo of Mexican 'non–dolphin-friendly' tuna, though the U.S. did not change its policy for this reason. Nevertheless, this loss of prestige might be one reason why the United States has been slow to impose sanctions in several cases. Hence several environmental and animal rights groups sued the U.S. government for not sanctioning Japan in accordance with the Packwood-Magnusson Amendment, a case that they lost in the end, despite having enjoyed some initial successes (Sumi 1989). Moreover, once most of the foreign fishermen had been expelled from the U.S. 200-mile zone, the Packwood-Magnusson Amendment lost its teeth. It is therefore unlikely that U.S. sanctions alone will achieve much in the future. It is the environmental and animal welfare groups that will probably pose the biggest threat to the whaling nations.

The IWC is rather unique in that it is a global management body open to all independent countries in the world. It has therefore been crucial in turning whales from an open access resource into a common heritage of humankind, enabling NGOs and anti-whaling countries to become stakeholders and to introduce new concerns. The IWC has become an important arena where central values are contested, and over the years it has been transformed from a whalers' club to a preservationists' club. Whaling nations were slow to grasp that the main issue was no longer whether whaling could be conducted in a sustainable way but whether whaling should be done at all. Many people have asked why rich countries like Japan, Norway and Iceland continue to support an insignificant industry engaging a few hundred whalers despite all the international condemnation they receive. To answer that question we have to look at whaling from the whalers' point of view.

Notes

1.   The Russians were not able to conduct the hunt due to engine breakdowns, and the indigenous population has, with great difficulty and with assistance from the Alaskan Inuit, re-created the pre-Soviet way of whaling using simple technologies. This story is not retold here to put the indigenous population in Chukotka in a bad light—they were among the gravest victims of the Soviet regime—but to indicate the inconsistencies in IWC policy.

2.   It should be mentioned that neither species of whale is endangered. The Northwest Pacific stock of minke whales, from which the Japanese want to take the quota, was in 1989/90 estimated at about 25,000, and the total population of Eastern North Pacific gray whales was in 1997/98 estimated to be about 26,300 (www.iwcoffice.org/conservation/estimate.htm, retrieved 25 February 2008), which might well be the maximum population supported by the breeding grounds of this species.

3.   The stock has since been adjusted upwards a number of times, and in 2001 it was estimated at 10,500 animals, with a 95 per cent confidence interval between 8,200 and 13,500. The debate over whether the bowhead is endangered continues, however (e.g. Shelden et al. 2001, 2003; Taylor 2003).

4.   In 1978 the Alaskan Inuit received an annual quota of eighteen landed animals or twenty-seven struck animals. The quota has since increased; for the 5-year period 2003–2007 it was 280 landed animals, with no more than sixty-seven struck in any one year. The same figures apply for the years 2008–2112 (http://www.iwcoffice.org/conservation/catches.htm#aborig, retrieved 15 December 2008).

5.   When discussing ASW, the IWC uses a 'need' concept that is much broader than that used by animal protectionists like Singer and Regan. This has made social science research relevant to the IWC, a point I will return to in Chapter 6.

6.   Bowhead whaling is one example. More recently, the IWC gave West Greenland an annual quota of 175 minke whales from a population which at that time was estimated at 8,371 animals and nineteen fin whales from a stock with a 'best available abundance estimate' of only 1,096 (IWC 2003e: 4), but still refuses to give Norway a quota at all from an estimated stock of 174,000 minke whales.

7. TTD is another controversial concept in the IWC vocabulary, in 1980 defined as " . . . the time taken for the mouth to slacken, the flipper to slacken and all movements to cease" (quoted in Knudsen 2005: 42).

8. This last usage is similar to Japanese terminology. Japanese whalers use the term *toru* (take) when the killing is done to cover basic needs. The word *korosu* (kill) implies that they kill without reason (Takahashi 1998: 245).

9. The reason why the illegal hunt of a gray whale was discovered in Little Diomede, Alaska, in 2002 was that one of the whalers was killed when the whale overturned the boat. The AEWC expected a fine as low as US$ 100 'because of their desperate need to feed their people' and was willing to pay in lieu of the whalers (AEWC executive director, quoted by Gay 2002b). For the sake of comparison, since 1995 dolphin-feeding activities in U.S. waters have carried 'stiff civil and criminal penalties with fines ranging between US$10,000–$20,000' (retrieved 8 April 2008 from www.publicaffairs.noaa.gov/pr95/aug95/noaa95-r142.html).

10. When India asked for a clarification of terms in 1985, its commissioner suggested defining 'aboriginal subsistence whaling in terms of nineteenth century or earlier methods, equipment and utilization of products' (IWC 1986, in Takahashi 1998: 249). This echoes the attitude expressed in the 1931 whaling convention (see Chapter 2).

11. Leading experts on indigenous peoples (e.g. Dahl 1992) have started to question whether not some of the aboriginal peoples today have become autonomous to the extent that they might no longer qualify for this classification.

12. The term 'local' is not defined by the IWC either. Referring to Greenland's whaling, the term seems to mean the country as a whole plus Greenlanders living in Denmark. As long as the meat is marketed among Greenlanders, the IWC will accept this as subsistence. When it comes to Japan, however, the IWC seems to define local as within a village. Everything beyond is 'national'.

13. E.g. 'indigenous (aboriginal) people engaged in aboriginal/subsistence whaling' and 'aboriginal subsistence whaling to satisfy aboriginal subsistence need' (IWC 1983, in Takahashi 1998: 245).

14. For the history of the IWC, see e.g. McHugh (1974); Birnie (1985, 1989); Hoel (1986, 1992); Andresen (1989); Asgrimsson (1989); Freeman (1990); Hansen (1994); Heazle (2006).

15. Michael Heazle (2006: 42) goes as far as to give the Netherlands most of the blame for the collapse of stocks in the Antarctic: 'the Netherlands' entry into the whaling club [in 1946] would later prove to be a turning point, as the influence exerted by the Dutch government on the international regulation of whaling over the next fifteen years significantly contributed to the IWC's failure to conserve whales.'

16. The Japanese fleets were able to make money despite declining catches and oil prices because they produced cherished food. The Soviet Union was, because of its political system, not constrained by the same profit needs as the entrepreneurs from Western capitalist countries and did, moreover, underreport catches.

17. One reason for the delay was that national quotas were not endorsed by the ICRW 'because of the prevailing free-trade ethics and freedom of the seas doctrine in the postwar years, particularly favored by the United States' (Heazle 2006: 63).

18. Some of these are members of the Scientific Committee, which meets just before the IWC meeting. In addition to scientists from member nations, some scientists from other countries are invited to attend.

19. Three NGOs from each side were in 2008 invited to present short statements at the IWC meeting.

20. Even scholarly journals do this in reporting from the IWC meetings. In her report from the 1999 meeting, Karen Simpson writes that the WDCS and the Swiss Coalition for the Protection of Whales 'informed the IWC of particular threats posed to Japanese consumers'. The IWC was furthermore 'informed' that some meat was wrongly marked (Simpson 1999: 348). Her reference is BBC News. Hence, in a presumed scholarly report about the IWC meeting,

the author refers to the BBC's reference to an NGO report on a topic that was not on the IWC agenda.

21. Retrieved 15 February 2008 from http://www.awionline.org/schweitzer/

22. The adoption of resolutions has been used by, e.g., Paul Watson to legitimize his sinking of ships.

23. The U.K. has been forced to withdraw proposed documents directed against Japan because they included false allegations or because the information therein was obtained in ethically questionable ways.

24. Norway put itself in an awkward position. Since Norway was strongly against the sanctuary, it would send the wrong message to merely abstain. Hence, Norway refused to participate in the vote, arguing that the proposal was illegal because it was not based on the best scientific advice. With this move it became clear that the proposal, legal or not, would gain the three-fourths majority required to change the Schedule.

25. The deal between Norway and the U.S. definitely moved the management question from the table of the scientists to that of the politicians. To what extent a sovereign state can accept international bodies' control of its own citizens within its own borders, and who is to pay for this control, are political questions, not scientific. The Scientific Committee was given new tasks, among them to investigate possible impacts of whale watching.

26. Japan takes tissues of each whale for DNA analysis and voluntarily provides the IWC with the results but stresses that law enforcement is entirely an internal matter.

27. Japanese authorities regard these resolutions as illegal because they do not recognize the rights of sovereign member states to conduct whaling for scientific purposes, as enshrined in the convention. When whaling nations have proposed insertion in these resolutions of a sentence that the hunt is carried out according to Article VIII of the convention, this has been denied (Komatsu and Misaki 2001: 68–69).

28. The U.S. argument for this arrangement is the need for flexibility in a situation with considerable variations in weather and ice conditions. However, Greenlanders, with the same need for flexibility, only get annual quotas.

29. In such haste, in fact, that Norway questioned its legality as it was a breach of the IWC's own rules stating that the agenda shall be sent to the members at least hundred days prior to meetings.

30. The size of the blubber was 45 by 35 by 2.5 cm. The piece was registered and stored at Pratt Museum in Homer, Alaska, under the catalogue number P-1994–8.

31. A resolution from 2001 therefore proposed to ban marketing of products from incidental catches (IWC 2001c).

32. Japan has, however, offered to give such information bilaterally, though not to the IWC.

33. Japan has recently amended the law on this point and now allows marketing of incidentally caught whales on the conditions that the whale does not belong to an endangered species and that its DNA profile is submitted to the authorities (Komatsu and Misaki 2003: 15–16).

34. Although these resolutions are not binding, to a certain extent they legitimize sanctions imposed on countries involved in such trade. Greenpeace caused the seizure in 1987 of 170 tonnes of Icelandic whale meat shipped to Japan through Hamburg, and 197 tonnes were confiscated in Helsinki the year after (Day 1992: 167).

35. Making such a comparison caused Peter Sandøe (1993a), then chairman for the Danish Council for the Ethical Treatment of Animals, to state that he 'would rather be a whale than a pig or hen'. In 2000 he was elected the president of the European Society for Agricultural and Food Ethics (EurSafe). Alf Ring Pettersen (2004) from Naturvernforbundet, the largest environmental NGO in Norway, has expressed the same sentiment (http://www.naturvern.no/cgi-bin/naturvern/imaker?id=24300, retrieved 23 December, 2008).

36. The limit was set as far south as 60°S off South America and parts of the Pacific in order to secure the votes of South American and Pacific countries that needed guarantees that the sanctuary would not harm their own interests.

37. On at least one occasion a North American NGO observer attended an IWC session that was closed to observers. Japan objected and asked the person to leave, but when neither the U.S. nor the British chair took notice of the Japanese intervention, the Japanese delegation left the meeting in protest (Komatsu and Misaki 2001: 75).

38. In its opening statement Denmark had hinted that it might accept a temporary quota for Japan but then changed its mind and voted against it. Denmark was nonetheless expelled from the like-minded group and was not invited to write the resolution text on the RMP. In fact, Denmark did not receive the text within the deadline and protested vigorously against the behaviour of the like-minded group. The meeting was finally postponed so that Denmark could consult the government at home.

39. A paradox is that Norway probably has no interest in speeding up the process either. Any solution that is acceptable to the anti-whaling lobby will probably be so complicated and expensive that Norway prefers to whale under the present situation.

40. In recent years simultaneous translation into French and Spanish has been introduced and some documents are also translated into these languages.

41. Both withdrew due to disagreements about national quotas. But whereas the Netherlands withdrew because it did not get a higher quota, Norway withdrew because the TAC was not reduced. Norway rejoined the following year in order to continue negotiations for national quotas within the IWC, but the Netherlands demanded a quota first.

42. Greenpeace has repeatedly denied these accusations, but in the Danish documentary *Manden i Regnbuen*, Francisco Palacio admits to having received 4–5 million dollars through the French activist Jean-Paul Fortom-Guion—'the nearest thing to a saint the whale movement has yet produced' (Payne 1995: 288)—in order to entertain politicians and bureaucrats from potential new member states, paying all their expenses, first class, including about 300 dollars a day as 'pocket money'. He also paid for their wives or friends, a request he found reasonable. Asked whether this influenced outcomes in the IWC, he answered, 'Well, you know the result, that's the only thing to look at. Did the new countries support the cessation of commercial whaling? Yes. It is very simple, yes.'

43. The Irish proposal (see above) may be seen as the latest example of this strategy. Japanese whaling interests feared that this would further isolate Japan.

44. Japan points to the fact that the country gives development aid to 120 countries, several of which vote against Japan in the IWC. However, there is little reason to doubt that Japan—like other countries—tries to win the support of foreign countries through international aid.

45. Caron (1995) believes that the reasons Norway was not sanctioned when commercial whaling was resumed in 1993 were empathy with Norway's situation and the understanding that the moratorium was primarily directed at Japan.

46. Japan lost its access the following year anyway. The U.S. continued to penalize Japan for scientific whaling in 1988, 1995 and 2000, but without imposing trade sanctions.

Chapter 5

Whaling and Identity

We saw in the previous chapter that the IWC has tried to make a distinction between *cultural* aboriginal whaling (ASW) and *commercial* whaling apparently without cultural values. For many years Norwegian authorities shared this understanding and justified its own minke whaling with reference to biological and economic arguments only. Whaling was seen as an industry, and the problems caused by the moratorium were unemployment and rural depopulation. In contrast to Japan, which has always used cultural arguments to defend its coastal minke whaling, Norway began to use the cultural argument only in 1992, when the report *Norwegian Small Type Whaling in Cultural Perspectives* (ISG 1992) was presented at the IWC meeting and Norway's resumption of whaling was announced. In order to understand local responses to the international campaigns against whaling, it is necessary to recognize that the hunt is much more than an economic activity.

In this chapter we will see that whaling implies a way of life and is the foundation of culture as well as economically viable households and communities. It will be argued that whaling forms an important aspect of people's identity, whether they are from Alaska, Japan or Norway. The dichotomy between ASW and commercial whaling—or Western and non-Western perceptions—masks more than it explains. The whalers see themselves, and are regarded by their neighbours, as honest people engaged in honourable work in the service of society at large and even as role models for the young—not as brutal barbarians possessed by greed and the desire to hunt whales to extinction.

Perceptions of the Ocean Ecosystem

A comparison between Western and non-Western perceptions of nature will reveal several differences. The notions of parallel animal societies and of animals giving themselves up to humans are alien to Western whalers. However, in Inuit and Japanese cosmologies humans and animals are partners linked in webs of reciprocity, each endowed with souls. The animal-human relationship is one of equality. European whalers, on the other hand, may see marine mammals as created by the Lord for people to harvest. The relationship is one of dominance. Much of the environmentalist literature takes it for granted that the latter view is at the root of most environmental problems.

A superficial dichotomy between Western and non-Western perceptions of nature glosses over important nuances, however. It ignores that Judaeo-Christian doctrine not only gives man mastery over nature, but also demands wise stewardship. Svend Foyn was among the many who believed that whales were gifts from God and therefore required full utilization in respect to God and his creation.[1] Today, such an attitude is typically attributed to non-Western hunters. Moreover, in Northwest European communities it is often argued that the Protestant world view deems an unlimited exploitation of the sea and its resources as morally unjustifiable greed. Thus, contrary to what is often claimed about the influence of Christianity on environmental ethics (cf. White 1967), there is also recognized need for conservation of the natural environment to the benefit of current and future generations, expressed as a concern for the survival of nature and respect for life (Eder 1996: 1). It is no coincidence that the environmental movement first emerged in communities dominated by Protestant ethics.

The Inuit are among the peoples often portrayed as ecologically noble savages. Various taboos and practices have been interpreted by observers as strategies to secure—although unconsciously, perhaps—a sustainable way of life. Inuit and non-Inuit alike often point out the myth of the sea woman Sedna as proof of the ecological insight of traditional Inuit, interpreting the mythical relationship between human action (observing taboos) and ecological consequences (lack of animals) as a traditional way of living sustainably. Even though such a perception implies that humans can interfere in the presence of animals and thus make a difference, the ritual practices are based on a spiritual rather than an ecological understanding of the world.

Today, there is a large anthropological literature questioning this notion of the noble savage (e.g. Broch 1977; Ellen 1986; Redford 1991; Edgerton 1992; Burch 1994; Conklin and Graham 1995; Kalland 2000; Sejersen 2000). The critique is partly empirical (there are many cases of depletion) and partly theoretical (if resources are not depleted, it may be a result of low population density and simple technologies). It should not come as a surprise that the Inuit are also reported to have overkilled resources (e.g. Krupnik 1993a; Burch 1994). The idea that the more one gives away the more one will receive, coupled with idea that animals will be reborn if proper rituals are performed, does not necessarily work in the interests of sustainable use of natural resources. Neither does the obligation to use all parts of the animals prevent waste: narwhals have been hunted solely for their *mattak* (the fatty skin of whales), and ice cellars in Alaska have to be emptied of old meat before the new whaling season starts: 'the old meat was simply thrown away into garbage pits or abandoned houses' (Krupnik 1993b: 232).[2] We should therefore not expect that non-Western hunters a priori conserve the resources on which they depend, as this concept here has been defined.

The introduction to this volume presented a model suggested by Thompson et al. (1990) and Douglas (1996), who identified four basic perceptions, or myths, of ecosystems. They can be seen as (1) robust and able to take a heavy blow, (2) relatively robust but only within certain limits, (3) capricious and beyond control, or (4) fragile and easily destroyed by pollution or overharvesting. Such myths variously inform and legitimize resource use. Douglas argues that there can be no moral judgment between these values when it comes to how they serve adaptation arrangements. The myths represent preferences and assessments of the outside conditions and attitudes for achieving different kinds of results (Douglas 1996: 90). But those who expect to find whalers firmly subscribing to one of the above myths will be disappointed. It is often claimed that fishers—and most whalers must be included in this category—believe in the 'nature as robust' myth, but realities are much more complex. A multitude of perceptions seem to be present. The diversity encompasses different emphases on the importance of human influence of animal presence, as well as different reasons for fluctuations in animal numbers.

Some whalers seem to be rather fatalistic and feel that they only play a very small or even no role in the fluctuations occurring in the environment. This is an understanding that is often uttered when they are on the lookout for mammals or searching for fish. Others put more emphasis on the role of human agency and argue for environmental stability using concepts also encountered in Western discourses on sustainable development. For them, environmental and social stability is linked to the control of human activities and allocations of access to animals among different user groups. Many clearly see the necessity of implementing catch quotas, and voices have even been heard among these fishers that the quotas of fish may be too high. Other fishers may acknowledge the influence of human agency on the presence of animals, but believe that the richness of the sea can easily sustain extensive hunting. These different views have little in common with the environmental movement's preoccupation with perceived human excesses and ecosystem collapse. Few whalers and fishers believe in this 'nature as fragile' myth, at least not in terms of their own impact on the marine ecosystem. But they fear industrial pollution, including that from oil extraction installations and radioactive disposals as well as air- and seaborne pollutants. High concentrations of heavy metals detected in marine mammals have added to this fear.

Rather than thinking about the ecosystem as robust or fragile, many whalers see the availability of prey as a function of social relations. In the discourse on sustainable development, the concept 'resource' takes up an important position, involving a rather well defined and demarcated group of animals that it is possible to quantify. A consequence of adopting such a concept is that fluctuations in observations may be used to indicate fluctuations in the population as such. Numerical concerns quite similar to the ones of biologists can undoubtedly be found among whalers, but whalers seldom use well-defined and demarcated populations as a framework for understanding fluctuations in the presence of animals. Commonly, whalers do not work with the concept of 'population'; rather, they see the animals as either present or not present (Thomsen 1993). If they are not present, they must be somewhere else. The number of animals observed at one location is not believed to represent an index for the overall population. Whalers tend to refer to qualitative aspects that can influence the presence of animals: wind, ice, temperature, feeding conditions, noise, smell, boat traffic, fishing activity and hunting. Although availability is not strictly associated with the idea of population in a numerical sense, hunters are well aware that fluctuations in animal numbers occur.

This perception of a dynamic ecosystem also informs whaling strategies, for whalers must live with inherent unpredictability and arrange their lives accordingly. Hence their adaptation is adjusted to strategies for handling unpredictability (Maurstad 1994: 34–35), which does not completely accord with any of the myths of nature outlined above. When there is plenty of prey, they may try to catch as much as they can in order to establish savings for possible bad periods to follow. In Greenland, where animals traditionally were considered active person-like beings who offered themselves to the hunter, it could, as was also the case in the Faroe Islands, be considered a sign of disrespect if one did not accept their generous offer.

Whalers' perceptions of cetaceans are complex, contextualized and often changing. Although the marine environment itself might be regarded in some sense as vulnerable and easily polluted by outsiders, marine resources are in general seen as robust in relations to one's own technology—if overharvesting occurs, it is thought to be caused by other people using different technologies. The disappearance of resources is usually accounted for by nature's unpredictability (natural fluctuations), as among most Norwegian whalers, or in terms of social relations (insulted the animals), as among some Inuit whalers. The best remedies for such a situation are resource flexibility and proper rituals.

Flexible Use of Natural Resources

One of the salient features of contemporary whalers, with the sole exception of the Japanese, is that they may also be fishers, sealers, trappers, hunters of terrestrial animals, farmers or, more recently, office clerks and oil workers. They utilize what we may term a generalized niche, consisting of several resources; the latter are defined as those 'components of an ecosystem that provide goods and services useful to man' (Gibbs and Bromley 1989: 22). A specialized niche, in its most extreme form, would consist of one resource, such as cod or iron ore. A household or a community dependent on such a specialized niche is fragile, for if that resource is lost it will have to go through a complete readjustment, or it may face disintegration (ISG 1992). Japanese whaling communities come close to this position. Most whalers were laid off and had considerable difficulties finding new employment (Kalland and Moeran 1992). To assist the coastal minke whalers, the Japanese authorities increased the quotas for Baird's beaked and pilot whales—two small species not covered by the moratorium. After the implementation of the moratorium on minke whaling, only a few whalers have managed to switch to these species or crew the Japanese scientific whaling fleet.

A household or a community based on a generalized niche can, on the other hand, increase the exploitation of the other available resources within the niche and thereby more easily compensate for the loss of one resource. A resource does not have any qualities sui generis—the qualities are constructed out of the social, cultural and economic contexts. Nor is the niche a static entity; rather, it narrows or expands due to ecological fluctuations, overexploitation, technological innovations, imposition of access restrictions to resources or changes in the market, among other reasons. Such a community is more versatile and able to adapt to both ecological changes and political upheavals. At the household level, generalized niches facilitate flexibility in people's relationship with their environment, a flexibility that is further enhanced by the multiple ways the catch can be distributed (e.g. eaten by the household or sold on the market).

Unlike in Japan, whalers in Norway can be said to make use of more generalized niches. The boats used in minke whaling are fishing vessels, and Norwegian whalers catch a number of other marine species, such as cod, herring, capelin, shrimp and basking shark. During the early days of modern minke whaling, Norwegian whalers furthermore relied heavily on terrestrial resources such as birds, eggs, down and peat, as well as on small farms with a few cows and sheep. Today this resource base has narrowed considerably, partly in response to government policies (Brox 1966), and as a consequence whaling has become relatively more important. During the two- to three-month whaling season, a vessel can make from 50 to 70 per cent of its annual revenue (Mønnesland et al. 1990: 47; ISG 1992: 44). Minke whales are a very predictable resource and may serve as a buffer during periods when other fisheries fail, thereby safeguarding the viability of many local communities (Broch 1994: 203). The seasonal fisheries are much less predictable but can nevertheless be attractive options, as minke whaling does not overlap with the important cod and herring fisheries.

The situation in Iceland is not very different from the one in Norway, and minke whalers typically also engage in fisheries for cod, lumpsucker and shrimp (Sigurjónsson 1982: 288). The moratorium on minke whaling was therefore not as destructive for Norwegian and Icelandic whalers as for their Japanese colleagues, who could not fall back on fisheries. Yet even for the Europeans, the loss of an important resource all the same implies a narrowing of their niche, which—in addition to economic losses—makes the whalers and their local communities more vulnerable to ecological changes and fluctuations in the future.

The Inuit have also typically exploited generalized niches, although there are considerable local variations in the composition of these niches. In Greenland, much of the time can be spent catching ringed seal to obtain food for the family and cash to buy necessary equipment, but the household may also engage in capelin fishing or beluga whaling, both of which can be very rewarding in terms of food supply and cash income alike. Sea birds, porpoises, caribou, musk oxen, walruses, polar bears, large cetaceans (minke and fin whales) and different species of fish constitute seasonal resource alternatives. The generalized niche may comprise work on a cutter or trawler, social welfare programmes, unemployment assistance, subsidies and tourism (Kalland and Sejersen 2005). The situation among the Inuit in Canada and Alaska is not much different from that in Greenland, although the exact combination of resources varies, with marine fish playing a smaller role. In Clyde River, Canada, for example, narwhals, wolves, polar hares and ptarmigan were among the prey being hunted (Wenzel 1991). In Northern Alaska the bowhead whale is the most important prey in many communities, whereas the gray whale holds that position in Siberia.

Thus, one of the conspicuous features of most coastal societies is that only by exploiting several marine and terrestrial resources have the inhabitants been able to form viable households and communities. Harvests of marine resources are typically seasonal activities, with different seasons giving people different opportunities and constraints. Although resources are seasonal, people's activities remain to a certain extent open to individual strategies (Kleivan 1964). The strategies vary between households, between local communities and from one year to the next depending on access to technology, resources and markets as well as on individual economic and cultural priorities. Strategies also vary as to how the prey is utilized, i.e. whether it is eaten by the household or distributed fresh or processed through sharing or the market. This flexibility has long been under attack, and since World War II Norwegian governments have encouraged specialization to the point that the farmer-fisher is almost history. The introduction of licenses and quotas has further caused a kind of monoculture within the fisheries. Marketing trends work in the same direction. The flexibility allowed by the numerous alternative ways the catch can be distributed and marketed has come under attack as modernization programmes have stimulated more capital-intensive extraction of natural resources to pay for better and more efficient technologies. Because viable households and coastal communities depend on access to flexible generalized niches,[3] specialization can easily be seen as a threat to their future. It is on this basis that we have to understand some of the whaling nations' resistance to anti-whaling campaigns. Whaling has become a symbol also to the whalers and their friends. Whalers ask each other, 'This time whales, what will they [the environmentalists] target next? Cod?' Such a scenario is frightening, and to many people whaling has therefore become a question of survival.

Whalers' Perceptions of Whales

It is probably no surprise that whalers' perceptions of whales differ significantly from those of most protectionists. But it is too simplistic to claim, as has frequently been done, that whalers take a one-sided view of whales as a natural resource, valuing whales only as a means to their own enrichment. Their perceptions of their environment—whether involving individual animals or whole ecosystems—are complex and far from static. Profound changes can, as in the case of the Norwegians, be traced through written sources back a millennium or more. A rather factual, utilitarian approach to whales characterized the thirteenth-century *King's Mirror*, in which the author described more than twenty species of whales. This undoubtedly reflects the high value placed on some species of whales as resources at that time. Whereas some humpback and right whales were regarded as dangerous to ships, the *fiskreki* (lit. 'fish-driver', probably a rorqual) was considered beneficial. It was widely believed that these whales protected people and ships and drove shoals of fish towards land, 'as if appointed and sent by the Lord' (Whitaker 1986: 5). In return for this service, the fishers should keep peace on the fishing grounds; if fights and bloodshed occurred among the fishers the whales would drive the fish back into the open sea. Anybody killing such a whale during the herring fishery was, according to a ninth-century Norwegian law codex, fined.

However, by the late medieval period fabulous tales of sea monsters had become dominant. 'These marine animals seem to have been created to inflict pain on humans' wrote Diderik Brinch in 1676 (quoted in Lindbekk 1978: 327, my translation). By this time, cetaceans had largely ceased to be regarded as a natural resource in Scandinavia, which negatively influenced people's knowledge about these animals. Although it was still believed that some whale species could be beneficial in driving fish towards shore, it was generally held that they were a nuisance and even a pest, and several methods, from making noise to more magic ones, were designed to keep them away. But the writings of Brinch and his contemporaries signalled a new interest in natural history and economic development, and in the following centuries a great number of geographical and natural history books and reports were published. Once more whales became a valuable resource, and by the early nineteenth century cetology had become an established branch of science. Scientific knowledge about whales accumulated rapidly, and by the end of the nineteenth century scientists had challenged the old notion of beneficial whales driving fish towards land (e.g. Hjort 1902). In Norway this caused a heated debate between fishers who opposed whaling because they blamed whaling for poor catches of fish, and scientists who claimed the disappearance of fish was due to natural fluctuations. The conflict peaked in 1903 when between 1,000 and 1,500 angry fishers attacked and destroyed Svend Foyn's whaling station at Mehamn in Finnmark.[4] For the first time, though not the last, the perceptions of the fishers and the scientists were clearly at odds.

Today marine mammals are seen as natural resources, and many whalers subscribe to the Judaeo-Christian notion that they were created for people to utilize. In this view whales have no intrinsic value. Neither are whales considered particularly smart, although whalers do recognize idiosyncrasies among whales. Some are curious and seek out the boat (*søkjar*, 'seekers');[5] others are *trollat* (naughty and unpredictable) and impossible to outsmart. The animals are seen as sentient beings that can suffer, and for this reason they should be killed as quickly and painlessly as possible. It has long been prestigious among Norwegian whalers to deliver *dauskudd* ('death shots') that kill the whales instantly (ISG 1992: 47). With the introduction of the expensive penthrite harpoon, economic incentives to deliver death shots have been added.

Others take a less prosaic view on whales. In Oceania, along the Amazon, on the Northwest Coast of North America and in the Arctic there are stories and legends about cetaceans living in marine societies where they behave almost like humans. People and animals inhabit parallel worlds. Whales have even been termed 'underwater people'[6] and are perceived as sentient persons, our equals who share the world with us (Wenzel 1991: 138). A similar view is prevalent in Japan, where whales often are perceived as manifestations of the fisher-deity Ebisu, who, according to legend, can be seen disguised as a whale on the way to Shinto shrines to worship on festival days.

Metamorphism is a common theme in whale legends. According to Greek mythology, the first dolphins were created when the wine god Dionysus sailed between the islands. Having discovered that the crew intended to sell him as a slave, he turned the oars into snakes. In their panic the crew jumped into the sea, but Poseidon took pity on them and turned them into dolphins. On another occasion Apollo turned himself into a dolphin to save seafarers in a storm. In both the Amazon and Kiribati, people are reported to believe that dolphins can take human forms to attend village festivals (Slater 1994; Cressey n.d.), and on several Pacific islands people believe that they may turn into dolphins when they die. Among the Haida of British Columbia it is thought that people may turn into killer whales upon death, and the killer whale is recognized as a totem animal among the Kwakiutl. From here it is only a short step to regard cetaceans as ancestors or protectors. In Vietnam whales receive funerals just as human beings do and are reborn as angels of the sea (Kemf 1993).

At first sight these perceptions seem to resemble those held by many environmentalists. This is, however, to ignore one fundamental difference. According to the world views of Inuit and Japanese whalers, among others, the spirituality of the whales creates webs of reciprocity linking whales and whalers. Whereas their view helps to bridge the divide between animal and human realms, the logic of Western environmentalists tends to do the opposite. This is particularly the case with animal rights advocates such as Tom Regan, who claims that whales have rights not to be disturbed in any way, whether for commerce, research or recreation. The final connection between human and animal worlds is thereby broken. Not even beached whales may be utilized. The Maori, an indigenous people of New Zealand, have been denied access to stranded whales, which they regard as theirs by treaty rights. Seen as gifts from Tangaroa—God of the Ocean—beached whales have long been utilized for their meat, oil, teeth and bones, and access to them has become a symbol in the Maori struggle to safeguard their rights as indigenous people. Their hosting of the 3rd General Assembly of the World Council of Whalers, in 2001, underlined the importance of the issue to the Maori.

Figure 5.1   *Divided views on beached whales in New Zealand.*
(courtesy by Garrick Tremain)

In many hunting societies there is a perception that animals give themselves to the hunter, a view that is common among Inuit in Alaska, Canada and Greenland (e.g. Boas 1901; Lantis 1938; Spencer 1959; Fienup-Riordan 1983; Bodenhorn 1988; Turner 1990; Nuttall 1992), as well as in Japan (Kalland and Moeran 1992). Through this sacrifice a relationship of interdependence is established between hunter and prey, and the animals are thereby brought into the social realm of human beings. Not only do animals give themselves to the hunter, but their societies are also renewed through hunting. In Inuit cosmology hunting means rebirth, not death (Fienup-Riordan 1983: 189), and the hunt may be seen as a semisacred act that unites animals and human beings in webs of reciprocity (Kalland and Sejersen 2005).

In order to attract a whale, the whaler and his household have to prove that they are worthy of such a gift. The whales are believed to harbour great knowledge about people and to have the ability to smell, see and listen over large distances. They are therefore able to distinguish a good and generous person from a stingy one. Because whales are said to dislike conflicts, noise, sudden movements, dirt, blood and death, these have to be avoided, or else the whales will stay away. The whalers must also observe a number of taboos affecting preparations for the whaling season, the hunts themselves and the butchering and distribution of the meat. Some of these are shared with other whaling cultures. Boats and equipment must be repaired, painted and cleaned before the season can commence, and new clothing prepared. We have already seen that among the Alaskan Inuit it is also important to clean the cellar where whale meat has been stored. Old meat is either given away or thrown out. During hunts, whalers may observe taboos pertaining to food, clothes, shelter and behaviour. Among the Inuit as well as in Norway, land should be clearly separated from the sea: Inuit may refrain from eating caribou and berries during the whaling seasons and in the past did not bring dogs to the ice at this time. The Norwegian whaler will not bring waffles, goat cheese or rucksacks aboard the vessel. Nor should a whaler mention terrestrial animals by their proper names. In Lamalera, Indonesia, this prohibition extends to places, whales and persons as well (Barnes 1996: 295).

Women may also be regarded as a threat. Some people in Norway—as well as in Japan—still have problems accepting women on a whaling boat because they allegedly bring misfortune.[7] In Alaska, taboos extend to family members on land, not least to wives of whaling captains. But women may also have positive roles to play. A wife of a Norwegian skipper used to spit three times on the harpoon-gun before her husband's boat left harbour, and sexual intercourse before departure is still said to be beneficial to the catch. As the land-base or 'ground crew' (Gerrard 1983), she may take responsibility for much of the day-to-day management of the operations. In Alaska the whaling captain's wife is believed to play a crucial role, to the extent that captains are known to say that it is the wife who is the great hunter. Before the season she may perform a ceremony directed to the moon asking for whales, and in another rite she may represent a whale symbolically being harpooned—it has even been suggested that she *is* the whale. The close association between the wife and whale is also expressed during the hunt. Details vary, but women have been, and sometimes still are, severely restricted in their movements while their husbands are out whaling. Wives of Alaskan whalers will still remain quiet and move cautiously during the hunt. Similar beliefs have been reported among the Makah and Nootka further to the south. Researchers are divided over whether to interpret this behaviour as imitative magic acts meant to calm or attract the whale.

If all the preparations have been properly done—taboos observed, appropriate charms and songs performed, and the captain's generous wife stationed quietly at home, at peace with the community—the whale is believed to come and give itself as food to the people. But the hunter-whale relationship does not end there. The whale carcass must be handled with great care and respect. In Northern Alaska this means that a successful catch initiates a ritual period similar in length to the mourning period for humans,[8] during which time no sharp implement should be used for fear of hurting the whale's shade. In a ceremony to welcome the whale to the community, the captain's wife makes the first ritual cuts and offers the whale a drink of water. She is given the flipper to keep for the whaling festival. The head is, at times with great ceremony, returned to sea so that the spirit can reincarnate and return as a whale (Lantis 1938; Taylor 1985; Turner 1993).

In return for the whales' gift of themselves to the hunters, people are morally obliged not only to make the fullest possible utilization of the carcasses but also to share it with others. Generosity and sharing are among the highest values in most hunting societies, and the whales will know to reward the generous. Among the Inuit in particular, there is a notion that the more one gives away, the more will come—which together with a belief in whale reincarnation is not necessarily conducive to sustainable use of the resource. The whaling captain and his wife will feast the people several times during the year. The most important event is the whaling festival (*nalukataq*) held in June after the end of the bowhead whaling season. Held inside a sacred ring, this three-day feast is a major social event among the Inuit. Intended to thank and honour the whales caught, the event is a reenactment of the hunt itself. The meals mark a communion with the whale's soul, thus uniting people and whales spatially and temporally. Hence the feast not only marks the end of one whaling season but begins the preparations for the next. The ritual distribution of meat is an invitation for the whales to come again the following year.

There can be no doubt that whales are important to the Inuit. But perceptions can be equally elaborate among Japanese whalers. Whales have been hunted and eaten by the Japanese for centuries, and whaling activities are intimately bound up with religious beliefs and practices. According to a widespread Japanese view that stresses the interdependence of supernatural, human and animal worlds, the whale is seen as manifestation of Ebisu, the patron deity of fishing. The belief that whales sacrifice themselves for the benefit of humans is strong also in modern Japan, and in return the whalers should utilize the carcass to the fullest—waste is seen as an insult to the whale—and take care of their immortal souls. Impurity is also offensive, and menstruating women have particularly been regarded as offensive to whales.

Poor catches and misfortunes are frequently explained as the results of neglecting to perform proper rituals or breaking taboos. In the Japanese whaling town Taiji more than one hundred whalers lost their lives to a gale in 1878 when whalers broke a taboo and hunted a right whale with a calf. A similar story is known from Ukushima, north of Nagasaki, where seventy-two whalers lost their lives in 1715 after having attacked a blue whale with calf, allegedly while the whales were heading to a Shinto shrine to pray (Kalland and Moeren 1992: 150–51).[9] Such catastrophes have become parts of the cultural heritage of these communities and underline their unique identity. But the accidents also strengthen the taboos—which, probably unintentionally, may have some conservational value.

In times of poor catches, whalers may perform magic rites. The Lamalera whaler may 'turn the luck' by washing his mouth with holy water, formerly with blood (Barnes 1996: 299), whereas Norwegian whalers used to burn gunpowder around the harpoon gun in order to 'burn the devil' (Eriksen 1964: 159–60).

Japanese whalers may try to turn the luck (*mannaoshi*) by getting drunk on sacred sake (*omiki*) (Kalland and Moeran 1992: 153). Sometimes magic may involve deliberate breaking of taboos. A Norwegian whaler, who for a long period of time had been stuck in port due to adverse weather conditions, smeared horse excrement (doubly defiling because the dung came from a farm animal) on the cannon, the most sacred place onboard. According to one of the crew members, this was done in a spirit of fun, but the storm calmed and the crew caught a minke whale just outside the harbour (ISG 1992: 83).

As in Alaska, a number of rituals are performed in Japan to repay the great personal sacrifice made by the whale and thereby also to secure good catches and safe voyages in the future. The boat owners gather the whalers and their wives both before and after the season, and in some communities the wives may perform pilgrimages to local shrines. While their husbands are away the wives may also perform daily rituals both before the house altar (*kamidana*) and at the local shrine. Short rituals are held on the boats for each whale caught, with a part of its tail offered to the boat's Shinto altar.

Important rituals are performed at Buddhist temples after the season. To prevent a killed whale turning into a 'hungry ghost' (*gaki*) that may cause accidents and disease, it may receive a funeral similar to a human being's. The whale is given a posthumous name (*kaimyō*) that is inscribed on a memorial tablet (*ihai*) and registered in the death register (*kakochō*) of a Buddhist temple. Moreover, memorial rites (*kuyō*) are held where temple priests recite from the sacred *osegakikyō* sutra, which is also recited for human beings lost at sea (Kalland and Moeran 1992). At least twenty-five memorials and festivals (*matsuri*) are held every year in Japan to honour killed whales. Tombs and memorial stones for whales exist in forty-eight locations at least, from Hokkaido in the north to Kyushu in the south. A tomb in Kōganji (a temple dedicated to whales in Yamaguchi prefecture) marks the burial site of whale foetuses and has been declared a national historical monument. Towards the end of April, several temple priests read sutras for several days and nights to help the whales be reborn in a higher existence. Such rituals have several meanings. The priests perform the rites in the belief that the whales will be released from the yoke of reincarnation and thereby enter paradise as a Buddha (*hotoke*). Some local representatives believe that the whales will be reborn so they can be caught a second time. Finally, the memorials are held to tell the whalers—and particularly the harpooner—that they are released from the burden, or sin, inflicted by taking life. The memorials have therefore a special importance to the harpooners, who upon returning home often go straight to the temple to pray for the whale's soul (Kalland 1989a; Kalland and Moeran 1992: 152–55).

Rituals tie whalers and their families to each other and to the whales. Rituals also tie them to a place and give the local community a distinct identity first and foremost defined by the local Shinto shrine with its tutelary deities (*ujigami*). The deities differ from place to place, as does the annual cycle of rituals, but they are all variations on a common theme based on an idea that whales are creations with immortal souls and a world view that underlines the mutual interdependence between spirits, human beings and the animal world. Rituals, whether Buddhist or Shinto, create shared meaning and a cultural heritage that is expressed and strengthened in festivals, songs, dance, art objects and local cuisine (see below).

It is difficult to argue—as the majority long did in the IWC—that whaling culture is more important to the Inuit in Alaska than to whalers in Japan. In both cases there is a rich repertoire of perceptions about whales, and both peoples have developed a broad spectrum of rituals. Although details may vary, whalers in Alaska and Japan share the notion that the whales give themselves to the hunters and that this gift establishes a mutual relationship of dependency between humans and whales. Both the Inuit and the Japanese have used mainly cultural arguments to support whaling, though with very different results, as we saw in Chapter 4. In other whaling societies—those practising ASW and others—such perceptions can be weaker or absent. Perceptions and rituals are considerably richer among the Inuit in Alaska than in Eastern Canada and Greenland, and in both Greenland and Norway whaling has to a great extent been deritualized (Kalland and Sejersen 2005). But even here we may find some beliefs and practices similar to those found in Alaska and Japan.

Whereas whalers in Alaska and Japan are indebted to whales, the common notion according to Christian doctrine is that the whale is a gift from God, towards whom one is placed in a position of indebtedness. Svend Foyn and his counterparts in Alaska and Japan felt equally morally obliged to make optimal use of the gift. In most societies, declining a gift is taken as an insult, a signal that one does not want to enter a relationship. Therefore there is a universal duty to accept gifts (Mauss 1954). Among the Faroese it is taken as not only laziness not to attack a passing pod of pilot whales but as a sin for not having accepted God's gift (Joensen 1988: 3). One of the strongest obligations upon whalers is to share the catch.

Sharing the Catch

Whaling not only creates a relationship between people and the physical environment, it creates relations between people. As already mentioned, sharing is a significant moral code and activity in most hunting societies, and the practice among the Inuit has been described at great length (e.g. Damas 1972; Bodenhorn 1988; Dahl 1989; Nuttall 1991a; Wenzel 1991, 1995). A survey conducted in Greenland shows that half of all the households in Qeqertarsuaq reported that they always or often were involved in sharing with households within as well as outside the community (Caulfield 1993, 1997: 66–71). From an economic point of view, sharing provides many households with valuable products that otherwise would have to be purchased in shops, although the exact monetary value of the meat shared is difficult to estimate.

A wide range of sharing practices has been reported among the Inuit (Damas 1972; Nuttall 1992; Wenzel 1995; Collings, Wenzel and Condon 1998). One important factor is the size of the catch. Products from large whales have a much wider distribution than those of ringed seals. There are many local and idio-syncratic differences, but whalers participating in a successful hunt invariably receive a share of the catch. Rules to guide the distribution of shares among the participants are complex, vary between regions and are changing to adapt to new contexts (Sejersen 2001). Very often, other hunters claim a share just by arriving at the scene and by touching the dead animal (Nuttall 1992: 143). Specific and well-defined parts of the animal are distributed to the hunters depending upon the order of their arrival at the scene. Beyond this primary distribution among the hunters, shares now enter a complex secondary system of sharing. Very often this secondary distribution is made by the hunter's wife. Meat is shared out to relatives and partners according to rules, obligations and probably also social strategies (e.g. as a means to gain prestige). In the eastern Canadian Arctic, the head of the extended family used to supervise the division and redistribution of the meat on certain occasions (Damas 1972: 233). Sharing could also take the form of communal meals (Collings et al. 1998). Today, many Inuit moreover send meat gifts to friends and relatives living in faraway communities or abroad.

Sharing is often believed to be less important among Euro-Americans and Scandinavians. In a study of a mixed Inuit and settler community in Labra-dor, Barnett Richling (1989: 55) argues that settlers have been more successful in adapting to new technologies precisely because they are more individualistic. However, we should not make overly sweeping generalizations from this case study. Wage employment and new technologies have created social differenti-ation in many Inuit communities, which in turn has brought about a moral conflict between sharing and the need for cash (Nuttall 1991a; Sejersen 1998). However, this impact of a monetary economy is not inevitable, as the distribu-tion and sharing of meat and blubber from pilot whales in the Faroe Islands well illustrates. Although the distribution of meat obtained from a pod of whales (*grind*) has changed considerably since settlers came to the islands more than a thousand years ago, 'the rules for distributing the *grind* provide a kind of Faroese social history in miniature' (Wylie and Margolin 1981: 120). Sharing is still of great importance in this Western, industrialized society. Today the distribution of the *grind* may vary slightly between the nine *grind* districts into which the Faroe Islands are divided. But as soon as a *grind* has been beached and the ani-mals have been slaughtered, an assessment of the catch is invariably undertaken in order to distribute the meat between participants, caretakers and villagers ac-cording to customary rules. Each whale is valued in terms of the *skinn*, a unit averaging about 38 kilos of meat and 34 kilos of blubber (Bloch et al. 1990: 42). In general, the person who discovers the pod is entitled to the largest whale or a certain number of *skinns*, and some *skinns* are given to those administering the hunt and distribution (i.e. the whaling foremen, the sheriff, the measuring men and the guards). A few of the whales are auctioned off to pay for repairs to boats and equipment damaged during the hunt; the rest is usually distributed to all the inhabitants registered in the whaling district in which the hunt took place, whether they participated in the hunt or not. Small pods, however, may be shared between the participants (Joensen 1976, 1990; Wylie and Margolin 1981). Tickets indicating the exact share to which each individual is entitled are then distributed, and people sharing a carcass will come together to butcher it (Bloch et al. 1990: 42). Most of the whales are distributed within the whaling district, and only a small amount reaches the market.

In Norway as well, there were elaborate regulations as to how minke whales caught in the whaling bays outside Bergen should be distributed among the participating farms (Kalland and Sejersen 2005: 81). Moreover, before the imposition of the moratorium in 1987 it was not uncommon among Norwegian minke whalers to take an extra whale (a *kokfisk*, 'fish for cooking', i.e. taken home for dinner). As these whales could not easily be sold at the market, they were shared locally with neighbours, friends and relatives.[10] Even today, not all the meat reaches the commercial market. Usually a whaler brings home a chunk or two of choice meat after the season, some of which may enter an exchange system in which various products and services circulate.

It is well known that in traditional Japanese society, relationships between main and branch households as well as between neighbours were continually cemented by formal and informal exchanges of gifts. In the modern economy too, gift giving forms an important means by which not only employees within a company, but whole companies themselves are linked to one another. It is not surprising, therefore, to find that in fishing villages, net or boat operators used to distribute a part of each catch to their crews. Similarly, in the whaling industry whale meat was frequently used both as a form of payment in kind and as a product that could then be exchanged among households having kinship and neighbourhood ties to those closely involved in the whaling industry.

Whaling companies developed a system of meat distribution whereby all those on board a catcher boat were supplied with a fixed amount of whale meat for every whale spotted and killed. In large-type coastal whaling (LTCW) and pelagic whaling, the distribution depended to some extent upon the position of each crew member, with gunners being paid twice as much as boat captains and chief engineers, who in turn received more than the rest of the ship's crew. Moreover, those working on catcher boats tended to receive more than those working on the factory vessel. These amounts could be substantial: one gunner in Arikawa recalled that during the heyday of whaling he received about 100–120 kg—mostly salted blubber—after one season in the Antarctic. In small-type coastal whaling (STCW), however, the distribution among crew members was equal, amounting to between 1 and 2 kg of high-quality meat from every whale caught. At the same time, a distinction was maintained between those working on the boats and those who flensed the whale on land, with the latter generally receiving less meat than the former. The quality of the meat also differed: while those working on the catcher boats were paid in regularly shaped blocks of high-quality meat, those working on the shore station tended to be given irregular or blemished pieces that would not fetch such high prices on the market (see Akimichi et al. 1988: 42–43). Indeed, in some cases, workers not usually employed at the shore stations but taken on temporarily during very busy periods were paid entirely in kind.

It was not only those directly involved in the hunting and processing of whales that received meat. The community as a whole also benefited from gifts of meat. In the old days, whaling groups often paid part of their compensation to the host village with meat. For example, in 1730 a whaling group in Arikawa promised to give red meat 'to the six coastal villages of Arikawa' three times during the season (Fujimoto et al. 1984: 662), while more recently, STCW boat owners in Ayukawa have frequently given whale meat to local institutions such as the Community Centre, the Old People's Club, local schools, the Children's Association, and the Fire Brigade, as well as to local temples and shrines (Akimichi et al. 1988: 46–47). In short, whale meat has been an important focus of community identity in those villages where whaling companies have operated, and often local inhabitants have been closely involved in whaling activities.

Another important example of this noncommercial distribution of whale meat among those living in a whaling community is to be found in the activities surrounding what is known as *hatsuryō*, or the first catch of the season. In Japan, one frequently comes across people exchanging fruits and vegetables because they are both freshly in season and rare, and whale meat is no exception to this general rule of reciprocity. In Ayukawa, for example, it is reported that during the several days between the start of the whaling season and the taking of the first whale, gifts known as *omiki* and consisting primarily of sake are given to people involved in whaling (see Akimichi et al. 1988: 43–51).[11] Local inhabitants give bottles of sake to whalers because they wish to share in the distribution of whale meat following the first catch. For every gift of sake received, the vessel owner is obliged to make a return gift of whale meat. This return gift is not limited to a single instance, but frequently takes place a number of times during the whaling season, so that in exchange for a bottle of sake someone may receive up to five gifts of whale meat, each weighing close to one kilogram. In April 1986, one of the boat owners in Ayukawa received a total of 156 bottles of sake, together with a few bottles of whiskey and crates of beer and Coca-Cola. During the season he returned about 200 kg of meat to eighty-six people in 242 transactions.[12] Using market prices, the return gifts were between 1.5 and 2 times higher in value than the original presents. In this network of exchange through noncommercial distribution of whale meat, relatives were valued more highly than friends and neighbours, who themselves were placed on a slightly higher level of reciprocity than were business associates. The data suggest that balanced reciprocity has been customary with business associates, while a more generalized reciprocity (Sahlins 1972) has been practised towards friends, neighbours and in particular relatives.

At the same time, gifts are also presented to the whaling vessels and their crews. Although exact records of these transactions are not available, it is clear that each boat may receive as many as fifty bottles of sake every year, and that these gifts are returned by members of the crew, who receive from their employer large pieces of meat weighing 30 or 40 kg, which they then redistribute among their own network. It is known that upon receiving gifts of whale meat, local inhabitants then used to redistribute these gifts in smaller quantities to relatives, neighbours and friends, so that at the beginning of every whaling season communities such as Ayukawa were involved in one vast cycle of gift exchange. It is hardly surprising, therefore, that local inhabitants of whaling communities have commented that whale meat is not for buying, but for exchanging with others. In other words, the distribution of whale meat in a whaling community such as Ayukawa is closely connected to long-term ongoing ties between the individuals and households therein. To eat whale meat thus becomes an important metaphor for social exchange, and for community identity as a whole.

Food and Identity

It is well known by anthropologists that few things are as symbolically laden as food, and local cuisine is one of the strongest markers of social identity throughout the world. Not only do special foodstuffs constitute a significant part of many rituals, but everyday food is also of great cultural significance. In many households and communities whale meat may be regarded as 'super food' due to its double role as both being 'highly valued culturally and as a staple' (Manderson and Akatsu 1993: 210).[13] Besides being a staple, whale meat may be an indispensable part of all types of community gatherings and celebrations, being extensively served at festive occasions. Food systems—defined as a 'repertoire of particular daily menus and the rules that dictate when each is appropriate in terms of social audience and event' (Freeman 1996: 46)—tell us what to eat, when and with whom. The importance of eating the right food with the right people is stressed again and again in the literature, not least because food is seen as a medium through which social relations can be expressed. Not only are these foodstuffs the right thing to eat to express and live out one's identity, the food is also seen as particularly healthy and clean.

The perception of local food as healthy is partly confirmed by research, and several studies show the nutritional significance of marine mammals (e.g. Dyerberg 1989; Borré 1991; Nordøy, Nordøy and Lyngmo 1991; Freeman et al. 1998). The Home Rule of Greenland therefore urges Greenlanders to consume more locally produced foods because they are more nutritious than imported foods, a position also advocated by the Canadian and Japanese governments. Japanese parents have given evidence that their children with allergies perform remarkably well on a diet of whale meat. It has repeatedly been pointed out that whale meat is rich in protein, iron and omega-3 polyunsaturated fatty acids that offer protection from cardiovascular diseases and also contain antioxidants that work to reduce the content of blood cholesterol. Foremost among these antioxidants is selenium, which is found in particularly high concentrations in *mattak* (Freeman et al. 1998: 47). Selenium may also offer protection against health hazards caused by the heavy metals and chemicals like PCB and DDT that are increasingly found in marine mammals. Contamination is a source of great concern in several North Atlantic countries (Egede 1995; Freeman et al. 1998; Cone 2005). Thus the authorities in the Faroe Islands have advised people not to eat the livers and kidneys of pilot whales—formerly regarded as great delicacies—and to reduce their daily consumption of meat and blubber. It remains to be seen whether this development will change people's perception of marine mammals as healthy food, however.

Despite the scientific evidence indicating high levels of pollutants in some marine mammals—especially in East Greenland—the notion that wild game hunted in peoples' own backyards is healthier than nonlocal foods from domesticated animals is widespread and certainly not unique to the Inuit. The notion is primarily to be understood in cultural terms, as an attempt to celebrate and demarcate one's own way of life as the right way to live. Some of this attitude to domestically produced food is summed up in the Faroese proverb *søtur er sjálv-givin biti* ('sweet is the food one can provide for oneself'). The Inuit draw a clear distinction between Inuit foods and white people's foods (Petersen 1985; Kleivan 1996; Roepstorff 1997). Thus, products from marine mammals are not only appreciated dishes; they have become national or ethnic symbols. Consumption of whales is a way to underpin and thus strengthen one's own identity, way of life and political arguments (Sejersen 1998).

Whale meat—as well as blubber, skin, cartilage, flukes, intestines and genitals—has for centuries been cherished as food in Japan. Whale meat recipes have been included in Japanese cookery books since at least 1489, when it was mentioned as superior food. The importance of whale meat in Japan has given rise to a rich culinary tradition. The quality of the meat is finely graded, and various parts are regarded as suitable for different dishes. In 1832 a special whale cookery book, *Geiniku chōmihō*—dividing the whale into seventy named parts, each with detailed information about methods of cooking and nutritive value—was published in Hirado, north of Nagasaki. According to this source, roasted red meat (*akami*) can 'taste better than geese and ducks' and *unagi* (the outer side of the upper gums near the baleens) is tender and has a noble taste, whereas the trachea (*nodowami*) is 'given servants in the countryside' and the duodenum (*akawata*) is eaten by the poor. What part of the whale people ate thus signalled their social position in the community and therefore carried important symbolic significance. In 1989, the only wholesaler in Arikawa, not far from Hirado, still dealt in sixty categories of whale meat, although he had run out of stocks for twelve of these (Kalland 1989a: 111).

Regional food preferences have emerged as a result of the history of whaling in particular communities. Such preferences exist not only as a result of the particular species traditionally caught, but also in terms of the method of cooking. In Arikawa in the south, for example, the most cherished whale meat in the past came from right whales. Because this meat is no longer available, salted blubber of fin whale has become a new favourite. This was the meat many of the local whalers brought home at the end of each season's whaling in the Antarctic. In Taiji, southeast of Osaka, on the other hand, people have developed a special liking for pilot whale, which is often eaten raw as *sashimi*. In Wadaura, outside Tokyo, a local speciality consists of dried, marinated slices of Baird's beaked whale, but people in Arikawa find this meat offensive because of its allegedly strong smell. Baird's beaked whales are not eaten in Abashiri (Hokkaido) or Ayukawa (northeast Japan) either, and when landed there they used to be sent to the Wadaura area for processing and consumption. However, the market has changed considerably since coastal minke whaling ceased in 1988, and demand for Baird's beaked whale has expanded. The inhabitants of Abashiri and Ayukawa prefer raw red minke whale meat. A special New Year's dish in Abashiri is soup boiled from salted blubber. Sperm whale meat is preferred in some areas of Northeastern Japan, while Arikawa people find sperm whale meat fit to eat only when dried or in fish paste (*kamaboko*).

Similar variations also apply to dolphins. Dolphin meat is extensively eaten in some communities in the southwest, particularly in Taiji and in Arikawa, where it is salted and dried, pickled or boiled and used in *sukiyaki* (Kalland and Moeran

Figure 5.2   *A quick meal of whale meat at a restaurant in Arikawa, Japan. (author's photo)*

1992: 149). However, there is little demand for this kind of meat in many other parts of Japan, and on Iki Island—not far from Arikawa—dolphin meat is regarded as non-food (*tabemono ja nai*). Marketing has posed a serious problem for those attempting to develop dolphin hunting in Hokkaido. One of the reasons for some people's low regard for this kind of meat might be a lack of proper knowledge about how best to prepare the meat. But there are reasons to believe that psychology also plays its part. The meat finds a better market when sold as whale (*kujira*) rather than as dolphin (*iruka*).

During the first postwar years whale meat accounted for 47 per cent of the animal protein intake by the Japanese, many of whom are convinced that whales saved them from a major famine. Indeed, some of their attachment to whales and whale meat possibly stems from this belief. The use of whale meat in school luncheons has also made a lasting impression among many people. With today's scarcity, however, prices have soared, and whale protectionists nowadays claim—wrongly—that whale meat is a luxury only served in expensive Tokyo restaurants. In fact, much of the meat is consumed locally, and the meat from scientific research is distributed across the nation according to the pre-moratorium consumption pattern. Because Ayukawa has received special consideration, meat has been offered to all households in the community. In Arikawa, many people try to eat a small amount of whale meat daily, 'just to get the flavour of it', and whale meat is an indispensable part of all types of celebrations. It is extensively used for weddings, funerals and memorials for ancestors, as well as to celebrate the building of new houses, the first day at school and so on. It is typically served at the New Year; indeed, about a fifth of the annual sale of whale products in Arikawa occurs during that season. August, which is also marked by high sales of whale meat, is the month when *Bon* (All Soul's Day) is celebrated, bringing many people back to Arikawa to visit relatives and ancestors. It is worth mentioning that August and December are also months when there is an extensive exchange of gifts for Bon and the New Year, respectively, and a significant amount of salted blubber and skin is sent out of the township on these occasions. A third peak in whale meat sales, which is becoming less and less apparent, occurs in late March/early April and reflects an old but dying tradition in Arikawa of celebrating 'girls' day' in combination with a flower-viewing event (*hanami*). Special three-layered lunch-boxes (*jubako*) are prepared with cherished food: rice on the lower layer, dishes of whale and dolphin in the middle, and cakes on the top layer in case of children, or snacks to be eaten with sake in the case of adults (Kalland 1989a: 110–13).

Local cuisine is one of the strongest markers of social identity in Japan, and food often figures in special products. Many railway stations sell lunch boxes (*eki-ben*) with local specialties. Food is used actively to make a positive image of the local community. Whale meat serves that purpose in whaling communities and is an important element in developing tourism, and various ways of preparing whale meat have become important means by which whaling communities express their identity. Whalers from different parts of Japan often discuss local whale cuisine, and people travel to whaling communities in order to eat their special products. When Ayukawa was allowed to buy some of the minke meat obtained during research whaling in the Antarctic, a substantial part of it was channelled to hotels, inns, restaurants and other institutions catering to tourists, including the famous shrine on the offshore island of Kinkazan, which received a share so that it could continue to serve whale dishes to pilgrims there. Similarly, many of the customers of the main whale restaurant in Arikawa are local inns that order plates of aesthetically arranged whale meat prepared in various ways at the request of their guests. The inns also place orders directly with the wholesaler and with the main fish retail shop.

The symbolic importance of whale meat is also apparent in Inuit societies, where its significance is explicit on several social occasions. Inuit foods are among the most important markers of ethnic identity and personal well-being, reflected not only in daily habits of consumption, but also on special occasions like festivals, birthdays, confirmations, weddings and seasonal feasts.[14] On these occasions people in Greenland often invest large amounts of money on 'country' foods if they are not able to produce it themselves or receive it through sharing relationships. The category of 'country' foods positions them in a sociocultural sphere separate from the one imported foodstuffs occupy. The latter are seldom shared and do not embody the same cultural values that country food does (Roepstorff 1997: 6–7). In Greenland, serving a snack of chips and cookies, for example, is hospitality; serving snacks prepared from Greenlandic resources is hospitality *par excellence*, linking hosts and guests to a common cultural frame of reference. If some of these foods are difficult to procure, this adds to the festive mood and marks the occasion as a particularly Greenlandic one (Kleivan 1996: 154; see also Petersen 1985: 299). Sharing country foods links not only members of a community, but also the hunter and the animal through continuous reciprocal relationships. The involvement in these relationships is important in the definition of what it means to be Inuit. Using the old aphorism 'You are what you eat', Ingmar Egede, himself a Greenlander, outlines the significance of country foods in Inuit self-perception:

If [the proverb] is true then those who eat Inuit foods must be Inuit. Our foods do more than nourish our bodies. It feeds our souls. When I eat Inuit food, I know who I am. I feel the connection to our ocean and to our land, to our people, to our way of life. When I travel outside our homeland, my metabolism often goes wrong. Coming home and turning to Inuit foods I am all right again, within hours. While many other things in our lives are changing, our foods remain the same, and it makes us feel the same as it has for generations. Maybe that is even more true today, since we see so many influences from outside, and we think more often about what it means to be an Inuk. (Egede 1995: 2)

Whale meat has important symbolic meanings also in the Faroe Islands, Iceland and Norway. In Iceland, for example, pickled blubber (*súr hvalur*) and putrefied whale meat (*kæstur hvalur*, meat buried or marinated in whey) together with putrefied Greenland shark (*kæstur hákarl*) are important ingredients of the 'traditional cuisine' eaten during the winter feast, Thorrabót. Probably dating back to pre-Christian times, these feasts gained new significance with the emergence of Icelandic nationalism in the mid nineteenth century, and are today major events where the participants' Icelandicness can be fully expressed and confirmed (Stefánsson n.d.). In the Faroe Islands whale meat and blubber are first of all regarded as everyday food and are not to be served on Sundays. But Faroese whale cuisine is nonetheless rich, at least when compared to other Scandinavian countries, and whale meat and blubber are among the favourite foods. Fresh meat may be boiled and served with blubber and potatoes. Meat and blubber are also salted or wind-dried, and the hang-dried meat of pilot whales frequently served as snacks has been associated particularly with the Faroes. In Norway, few whalers consider whale meat the best food they get, and most people can easily mention other dishes they prefer. Still, whale meat is a very special dish in many homes. While it is being eaten, and particularly when guests are entertained, sooner or later the conversation turns to whale meat. The whaler always knows from which whale the meat was cut, and he may narrate that particular hunt and how they finally outsmarted the whale. Thus, when whale meat is served the whaler's position as important family provider and skilled hunter is strengthened, or at least confirmed, and local gender roles are underlined.

Whether the meat is served as steak on a Norwegian whaler's table, boiled with *mattak* among the Inuit or enjoyed as *sashimi* in Japan, the eating of the meat signals that whales are recognized as being culturally important animals (Freeman et al. 1998: 25). In this way whale meat becomes an important ingredient in shaping local identity, and as a food it affects the whaling community in a number of ways. Whale meat gives the community an image that is now needed in order to promote tourism, for example. Furthermore it gives the village an identity—an identity that may be different from those of both other villages in the vicinity and other whaling villages. Whale meat also helps the villagers to mark time, for it is used to emphasize important events in the life cycle as well as in the annual cycle. Whale meat, then, is used in communication, both within each community and with the outside world, and in many ways symbolizes what it means to grow up in a whaling community.

Growing up with Whaling

Most of the whalers live in small communities where neighbours are often relatives, colleagues and friends. These are moral communities, with strong networks providing good role models to follow. The way fishers and hunters talk about the physical environment reveals a complex and rich sense of belonging. The construction of land- and seascapes is closely interwoven with community identification, experiences and interactions with the physical environment. Traces of past use are left in the landscape itself as well as in the memories of community members. Mark Nuttall (1991b) introduces the concept of memoryscape to emphasize people's mental images of the environment, with particular emphasis on places as *remembered* places. Memoryscapes evolve as people, no matter their cultural background, accumulate experiences and encounters in the physical environment. Events, whether contemporary, historical or mythical, that happened at certain points in the local area tend to become integral elements of those places.

Hunting, fishing, pastoralism and agriculture are all activities that tie the practitioners to a locality and to a great extent give people an identity and define who they are. The identification with the place is confirmed and reproduced through one's daily activities and narratives, and it is precisely these activities and narratives that transform the physical environments into meaningful landscapes (Basso 1996). Should these activities cease, serious consequences would affect how people relate to the place and to their identity. In the widest sense whaling is a question about lifestyle: not only to survive economically but to be able to maintain one's social network of relatives, friends and neighbours and to transmit one's cultural heritage to coming generations. Although economic arguments are used to defend whaling, these are often followed by arguments about rural depopulation and destruction of local communities and the cultural landscape. A sustainable community depends not only on ecological and economic adaptations to the environment, but also on a sustainable culture.

Socialization processes are of vital importance to the whaling culture—and to how people perceive themselves and their environment—on two main levels. First, children who are brought up from infancy in a whaling environment acquire an understanding of the hunt and consumption of wild animals as integral parts of their culture. By watching adults at work from an early age they begin to learn needed skills that might be an important prerequisite if the craft is to be properly mastered (Joensen 1988: 8). And by listening to stories about events that happened at a certain locality, children acquire insight into the norms and values of the whaling community, while at the same time ideals and role models are established (Hauan and Mathisen 1991: 37; Mathisen 1995). Moreover, the children become knowledgeable in reading the landscape, a skill that is particularly emphasized by parents who continuously test their children's geographical knowledge (Nuttall 1992: 69–71). Acquisition of skills directly related to whaling activities (such as handling of vessels and weapons, knowledge about prey, sea and ice conditions) constitutes the second level. Whereas usually only boys taken on whaling trips acquire second-level hunting skills, a much larger group of people, including girls, are socialized into the hunting culture at the first level.

Where whaling is conducted close to home, as is often the case with the Faroese pilot whaling, or from hunting camps where families accompany whalers, as among the Inuit, youngsters may be exposed directly to hunting activities from an early age (Condon 1987: 62; Chance 1990: 98; Condon and Stern 1993). In Greenland, boys as young as four years old may accompany their fathers on shorter fishing and hunting trips (Nuttall 1992: 73). By the age of ten, a boy may have killed his first seal. In the Faroe Islands, boys are not allowed to participate in the pilot whale drives before their late teens, although 15- and 16-year-old boys may in the past have been allowed to partake in the killing (Taylor 1997). Before reaching this age, however, boys helped with miscellaneous tasks, and today they are—to the great horror of many foreign observers (Sanderson 1992)—still seen playing at the site of the killing, collecting whale teeth and satisfying their general curiosity by examining the dead bodies. They also help in collecting meat and blubber for their families (Sanderson 1990: 19).

In Norway, where whaling is generally conducted far from home, socialization to a whaling way of life may take more indirect means. In the old days boys made small wooden boats and 'flensed' small fish and crabs on their decks (ISG 1992: 85), or they rigged small, beached boats with crow's nests and wooden harpoons, thus imitating their adult heroes in a very realistic way. If there is a processing plant in the village, as in Skrova, children may do odd jobs (ISG 1992: 84). But training may also take more direct forms. In Lofoten, for example, a six-year-old boy had his own corner in his grandfather's workshop, fully equipped with a small lathe and other tools, and below the house he had his own dinghy with an outboard engine. Children will also be taken on board during short voyages near home, giving them a first real encounter with their fathers' occupation. What the children learn in this way is valuable when they in the future become *skårunge* (greenhorns). In Japan, where all aspects of whaling have been professionalized for centuries (Kalland 1995), children are excluded from participation, although some kids undoubtedly get in touch with whaling by observing flensing on shore and—if we are to judge from old illustrations— occasionally pilfering some meat or blubber. But whaling figured importantly in their play (see Figure 5.3).

Skills develop when children make their first appearance as a whaler. The circumstances vary from society to society and from case to case, but often the first voyage or catch marks an important rite of passage for boys (Kalland, Sejersen and Broch 2005). Invariably it takes time to become a good whaler, and the first years may be looked upon as an apprenticeship. A number of tasks are essential, concerning both the operation of equipment (e.g. steering the boat, keeping the engine running, mending boat and gear, etc.) as well as the handling of the prey (e.g. searching for, shooting, and flensing the whales). Some are trained for particular tasks, such as caring for the engine or serving as skipper. The most crucial task of all is to shoot the whales. Training gunners has traditionally been rather informal, but gunners in Greenland, Japan and Norway are now licensed and required to pass shooting tests regularly. A license may also be required for the skipper. But in most cases there is little specialization in coastal whaling, and individuals may perform a number of tasks. On the small crews on minke whalers in Greenland, Iceland and Norway the gunner might also be the skipper and owner of the boat, while the youngest and least experienced crewman might be the cook. The whole

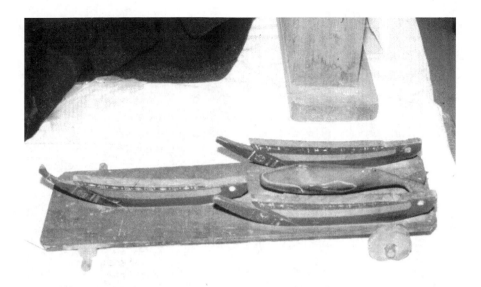

Figure 5.3 *A toy from Arikawa, Japan; a whale in tow by three whaling boats. (author's photo)*

crew looks out for whales and participates in flensing,[15] although young crew members are the first to be sent to the crow's nest to look for whales.

Training is more than just mastering skills, however. It is also a question of human relations. The young whaler must become accustomed to working long and irregular hours under often strenuous conditions. He—for as was indicated earlier, whalers are typically male—must be able and willing to adjust to the other crewmembers' personalities and peculiarities because teamwork is essential. Finally, he has to become familiar with the way things are done on the vessel and on shore, as well as with taboos and lore connected to whaling. Gradually, the apprentice becomes more experienced, until he reaches the status of an experienced man, although only a few finally become whaling captains or gunners.

Generally, children look at their parents as models for moral comportment and are prone to idealize them as loving persons whom they can trust as basically good. In most families the members seek to mirror themselves in the others. Thus the whalers are given moral support and recognition by their wives and children, who explicitly acknowledge their arduous labours at sea or on the ice in order to provide for their common livelihood. This support is expressed in different ways. Norwegian whalers were relieved when they got supportive telephone calls from home after they engaged in a fight with Greenpeace activists (Broch 2004). Less dramatic are the school essays written by daughters, full of pride and praise for their whaler fathers (e.g. ISG 1992: 118–19). In one Norwegian whaler's home a small fired and glazed clay sculpture representing a minke whale was placed in a prominent niche. It was a gift to the father from one of his daughters. Drawings by Inuit children often portray the hunting and fishing activities of their fathers (cf. Briggs 1970: 72), which can be seen as celebration and admiration of their fathers' occupation, as can the many Inuit students' supportive statements about whaling and the value of whale meat (e.g. Freeman et al. 1998: 33–53). The anti-whaling campaign poses a serious threat to both their world view and the interpersonal values that are held high in whaling communities. In the following chapter we will take a closer look at their responses to this threat.

Notes

1. Foyn's whaling fleet nevertheless seriously depleted many whale populations in the North Atlantic.
2. It can be argued that it was necessary to hoard meat for strategic reasons in an unpredictable environment with scarce resources. But it seems that beliefs encouraged whalers to abandon the previous year's meat *before* new provisions had been secured (cf. Turner 1990: 43).
3. Some new resources—e.g. tourism and employment—have been added. Even in cases where these new activities do not collide in time with the old ones and to a certain extent meet the economic needs, they usually imply considerable social and cultural costs (Sejersen 2003).
4. The angry fishers in Northern Norway also voted the first socialists into the Norwegian parliament. National unity was at stake at a time when Norway was moving towards independence from Sweden. The parliament banned hunting of baleen whales in Northern Norway in 1904, a prohibition that was extended to the whole country in 1914. For the conflict, see e.g. Hjort (1902); Kamsvåg (1956); Johnsen (1959); Olsen (1982) and Alvestad (1999).
5. Some Norwegian whalers think that the seeker is looking for a mate and mistakes the boat for a whale. At least one whaler tried to paint the scull in the colours of the minke whale, but his boat failed to attract more whales.
6. The parallel marine and terrestrial worlds may also create pairing of land and sea creatures, a common idea in much of the Pacific. The ritual pairing of taro and whales seems to be particularly common in Micronesia and on the Woleai atoll in the western Caroline Islands. One interpretation is that whales and taro constitute important binary oppositions symbolizing the dualities of land versus sea and male versus female. Similar pairing has been reported for killer whales and wolves among the Siberian Chukchi and Native Americans of the Northwest Coast. In some cases each marine species has a counterpart on land.
7. This attitude is now changing, at least in Norway, where many of the whale inspectors are women.
8. Similar beliefs and practices have been reported elsewhere. On the Woleai atoll in the Caroline Islands, for example, an eight-day period of taboos and rituals is imposed after a pod of dolphins have been caught, and during this time many of the gender roles are reversed. In Japan Buddhist memorial rites for whales may resemble those for human beings (see below).
9. In both cases the whalers had long been troubled by poor catches, and this might have been the reason why taboos where broken despite misgivings from some of the whalers.
10. In recent years it is impossible to catch an extra whale because of stricter control.
11. *Omiki* is a word that is used to refer to Japanese sake (rice wine) when used in a ritual context, in which the wine is first offered to the deities before being drunk by those participating in the

ritual concerned. Sake itself has important ritual connotations in Japanese culture, especially as a means of purification, and the use of the term *omiki* here indicates the importance that those living in a whaling community attach to this particular form of gift giving.

12.   In March 1987, when the owner launched a new boat, he received gifts of sake from 134 people and—regardless of the quantity received—he gave 2 kg of whale meat on two occasions to everyone except relatives, to whom he gave meat every time he caught whales that season. The next year the moratorium was imposed.

13.   This use of the term should not be confused with the popular notion of superfood as especially healthy food.

14.   This is not to say that other markers are unimportant or that Inuit-ness *has* to be expressed through the consumption of Inuit foods.

15.   In Icelandic large-type whaling, however, the carcasses are flensed by professional flensers on land, as is also the case with small-type coastal whaling in Japan. But in this latter case they are often assisted by women and retired men who are compensated with a small share of the catch.

Chapter 6

Local Responses to Global Issues

Whalers and whaling nations have tried to respond to global environmental discourses in many ways, and this chapter will focus on how they have met the challenges imposed by the anti-whaling campaigns. It will be argued that they have done so in two main ways. First, they have tried to accommodate the discourses by interpreting their adversaries in terms of the International Convention for the Regulation of Whaling (ICRW). By actively participating in a number of international management bodies, they have presented scientific reports supporting their view that some whale stocks are large enough to be exploited. Moreover, they have done considerable work to improve killing methods and thus reduce animal suffering. Second, they have contested the views advanced by their adversaries by actively defending their *rights* to exercise self-determination and to harvest their traditional resources in a sustainable manner. This they have done rhetorically, by bringing in statements from several global discourses and by working through existing international bodies as well as new ones. In addition, they have sought to strengthen their own sense of identity, whether it takes place at the level of the national, ethnic or local community, without reducing their claim to being full members of the global community.

Accommodating the Global Eco-discourse

For many years both governments and lay people in whaling nations believed that the protests against whaling rested on ecological arguments. Whaling nations have therefore spent large amounts of money and energy on science to convince anti-whalers that some whales stocks can be exploited sustainably. When the arguments against whaling switched to ethical ones, whaling nations responded by introducing new regulations and technologies to make the hunt more 'humane'. They have produced a large amount of informative material, aimed at the media as well as the general public, on both ecological questions and the cultural context of the hunt. Hence 'sustainable use' and 'humane killing' have become key themes in the pro-whaling narrative. Moreover, they have attended a number of international and bilateral discussions to present their view and win support for their position—mostly with little success, as we shall see.

Scientific Investigation

Natural sciences have been assigned key roles by the intergovernmental organizations established to manage utilization of natural marine resources, and the IWC is no exception. The ICRW states that amendments to its Schedule (and quotas require such amendments) shall be based on science, and the IWC has its own Scientific Committee for this purpose. Whaling nations long took it for granted that the IWC would stick to its mandate, believing, perhaps naïvely, that science would in the end remove all uncertainty and give a true representation of reality.

Because the argument to impose a moratorium on whaling for commercial purposes allegedly was based on a grave concern about the conditions of whale stocks, it was important for whaling nations to provide data in support of sustainable whaling. Although research had been conducted on whales caught during the commercial hunt, it was felt that this research was not comprehensive enough and failed to address new issues whaling countries were facing. The most important management questions were whale abundance and whale stock identity. Most whaling nations therefore inaugurated extensive sighting programmes. Greenland, the Faroe Islands, Iceland and Norway, together with Spain, launched an extensive shipboard sightings programme, the North Atlantic Sightings Survey in 1987. A similar international sighting programme in the Antarctic started as early as 1978–79 under the leadership of a South African biologist, and since 1990 Japan has carried out sighting programmes in the South Pacific and in more recent years also in the North Pacific. These projects have provided scientists with quantitative information on a number of whale species (cf. Sigurjónsson 1990: 69–70).

However, sighting surveys could not provide all the answers that scientists felt they needed. To map age and gender distribution, fertility and mortality rates, stock identity and the whale's roles in the marine ecosystem it has been necessary to kill whales (cf. ICR 1991: 1). With commercial whaling prohibited, scientists could only obtain the data they needed through research whaling. Article VIII of the convention authorizes contracting governments to issue special permits to their own citizens, and the start of Icelandic, Japanese and Norwegian scientific whaling coincided approximately with the enforcement of the moratorium. This connection between the moratorium and scientific whaling has caused whale protectionists to claim that scientific whaling is an attempt to keep a dying industry afloat (cf. Chapter 4).

From 1986 to 1989 Iceland caught 362 fin and sei whales; meanwhile, the intention to catch minke whales was abandoned due to international pressure (Ívarsson 1994: 128). Norway killed 289 minke whales in the period 1989–1994

as a part of an extensive marine mammal project. The project, which was motivated by the moratorium and by a devastating invasion of Greenland seals in
Northern Norway, has produced hundreds of scientific publications—among
which one-third deal with minke whales (Blix, Walløe and Ulltang 1995; Haug
et al. 1998). In 1987 the Institute of Cetacean Research (ICR) was founded in
Tokyo to carry out Japanese research. Besides counting whales, their catches of
minke whales in the Antarctica have gradually increased from 300–400 whales
annually to 800–900 since scientific whaling commenced in 1987. Since 1994
research whaling has also been conducted in the North Pacific, where Japan has
taken a hundred minke whales annually. In 2002 this project was broadened;
it now includes a maximum of 150 minke whales, 50 Bryde's whales, 50 sei
whales and 10 sperm whales per year.[1] So far more than 11,000 whales have
been caught in Japanese research whaling. The scope of the programme has
made it easy to level accusations that research whaling is nothing but 'commercial whaling in disguise'.[2]

Also nations not directly affected by the moratorium have felt a need to legitimize their whaling activities using scientific data. Early in the 1980s the Faroe
Islands took thirteen fin whales for research purposes (Olafsson 1990: 132),[3]
and in 1986 they began an extensive research programme to map the pilot whale
population in collaboration with UNEP and IWC. Thousands of pilot whales—
sometimes whole pods—have been investigated by scientists from the Faroe Islands, Denmark, France, Spain and the United Kingdom in order to identify
stocks and to study their social structure, reproductive history, feeding patterns
and vulnerability to contamination by heavy metals and pollutants (Desportes
1990; Sanderson 1991). Research has also been extensive in Canada and Greenland and has included sightings projects, photo identification, satellite tracking
and DNA analyses, along with more traditional biological research (McLaren
and Davis 1983; Born 1991; Heide-Jørgensen et al. 1993, 2001; Larsen 1994a,
1994b; Kalland and Sejersen 2005).

Whaling nations have used the whaling convention to argue for the importance of science for management purposes. The importance of science is embedded in most international management treaties and texts. Whaling nations long
believed that other members of the IWC saw management in the same light and
therefore expected that the anti-whaling countries would see reason, as soon as
they were convinced by science. In 1991, when the IWC continued to question
new scientific evidence and upheld the moratorium, Iceland decided to leave
the organization. Canada had withdrawn back in 1982 because the IWC had
already, according to the Canadian government, ignored science in its management politics.

Japan and Norway have remained unhappy members, but their situations are
very different. Norway objected to the moratorium in 1982 and is therefore not
bound by it. Hence Norway was legally free to resume whaling in 1993 despite a
storm of international protest. Japan, on the other hand, withdrew its objection

to the moratorium after strong pressure from the United States, and Japan therefore does not share the legitimacy that allows Norway to resume commercial whaling. To continue whaling under the special permit clause was the least problematic option.

The great research efforts have produced little effect. Nothing indicates that the IWC is about to open up to commercial whaling in the near future. It is a long way from the small pro-whaling majority that emerged in 2006—which in 2007 again was turned into a minority—to the three-quarters majority needed to change the Schedule. In its minke whaling activities, Norway uses the most conservative quota-model designed by the IWC's Scientific Committee, has engaged trained vets as inspectors on all whaling vessels, takes DNA profiles of each whale caught and has imposed strong sanctions for infractions—yet none of this has softened the international critique. Nor, as we shall see, have the whaling nations enjoyed success by accommodating the criticism of their killing methods.

Humane Killing

Animal welfare and animal rights advocates have, as we saw in Chapter 2, painted a bloody picture of whaling. No killing is pleasant to the eye and mind, hence the isolation and lack of visibility of abattoirs in many societies (Vialles 1994). There can be little doubt that whales occasionally suffer considerable pain before they are killed, particularly in indigenous hunts where old technologies are still employed. But although Alaskan bowhead whaling may cause more stress and pain to the whales than does modern, commercial whaling, it was the latter that was targeted when the animal welfare issue was firmly placed on the IWC agenda in the late 1970s. The IWC is particularly concerned about the *time* it takes the animal to die after being hit (i.e. time-to-death, TTD) and about the killing being *humane*. The IWC tends to see these as two sides of the same coin: a quick and painless death is regarded as more humane, in line with modern people's utilitarian view of pain.

When Iceland, Japan, Norway, Brazil and the Soviet Union in 1981 objected to banning the cold harpoon in the minke whale hunt,[4] it was not because they disagreed in principle but because they wanted more time to develop alternative methods (Donovan 1986: 141). In that year Norway initiated a research programme to test a number of killing methods such as electrocution, drugs and gases, but found an explosive penthrite grenade to be most efficient. This technology was made mandatory in Norwegian minke whaling starting in the 1984 season (Øen 1993: 95) and in Greenland after 1989. A similar grenade was developed in Japan. In 1993, Norway introduced compulsory shooting tests for all the gunners in an attempt to further improve performance. These steps have shortened the average TTD, and the majority of whales are now killed instantly (Øen and Walløe 1996). A new penthrite grenade was introduced in 1999, which has further improved performance (Knudsen 2005).

The humane killing discourse has primarily targeted commercial whaling, but aboriginal whalers too have gradually come under pressure to utilize more humane killing methods. The Alaskan Inuit have begun to employ a smaller, handheld version of the penthrite grenade in their bowhead hunt, and the Greenland government prioritizes grants of minke whale quotas to modern whaling vessels equipped with penthrite grenades at the expense of hunters only using rifles. Even hunters of small cetaceans have been affected, although these animals fall outside the legal competence of the IWC. The government of the Faroe Islands introduced new regulations in 1986 to reduce stress and pain during the drives (Olafsson 1990). Spears and harpoons were among the equipment that was banned, in most cases. Some landing sites considered unfit for whaling were closed, whereas others had to be improved in order to be authorized as whaling bays. Moreover, the whales must be properly secured and killed by severing the major artery in the neck, and alternatives to the gaff (used to haul ashore animals that do not beach themselves) were to be used (Sanderson 1991: 16–17).

Whaling countries have tried to meet their critics by attempting to develop more humane killing methods, even though this issue, strictly speaking, is not an ecological question but one of ethics and therefore, in their view, outside the competence of the convention (Frøvik 1995: 141–42). They have tried to compare pain inflicted on whales with pain inflicted on domesticated animals, and on game during sport hunting. But they have no more successfully silenced their critics on the issue of humane killing than on sustainable whaling. As better killing methods were developed, new concerns were aired. IWC delegates have become increasingly concerned about animals being stressed during the hunt and now demand that this question must be investigated before quotas can be given.

Members of the 'Global Village'?

Several international organizations have been established and many initiatives taken to improve the management of whaling. Some of these—e.g. the IWC, IUCN and CITES (Convention for International Trade in Endangered Species)—are global in scope. Others have a stronger regional orientation. A recent creation is the North Atlantic Marine Mammal Commission (NAMMCO), established by the Faroe Islands, Greenland, Iceland and Norway as an alternative to the IWC for the management of whaling and sealing in the North Atlantic region. Moreover, there are a large number of multilateral and bilateral treaties to consider. Whaling countries participate actively, often with large delegations, in a number of international forums in order to secure their national interests. They pay membership fees, prepare discussion papers and take on leadership roles. For small countries with few inhabitants and resources, like the Faroe Islands, Greenland and Iceland, participation is costly as well as taxing on human resources. At times, participation has also been politically difficult, for example in the IWC, where the Faroe Islands and Greenland are not represented by own delegations but have to work within the Danish delegation, which has not always been easy.

Despite all the financial, personal and political difficulties, whalers and authorities in whaling countries have sat down with their critics to share views and opinions and to work out possible solutions and compromises. In view of the effort they have made to respond in what they consider constructive ways to issues raised by individuals and organizations, it can be concluded that they have accomplished very little in terms of creating a more positive international attitude toward whaling. The moratorium has not been lifted; rather, new demands have been raised. Recommendations from the Scientific Committee are still largely ignored, even after its British chairman resigned in protest in 1993. The prohibitions against imports of marine mammal products into the European Union and the United States are upheld—regardless of the abundance of the species in question, or the hardship imposed on the whalers by these trade barriers.

During the annual IWC meetings delegates openly claim that whales are unique and that it is immoral and unethical to kill these animals regardless the size of their populations or how humanely the hunt can be conducted. Several countries have for years tried to change the convention to make the moratorium permanent (e.g. Burke 2001; Stone 2001). At the IWC meeting in 2003 the like-minded group took another large step in that direction when it secured a majority vote for 'strengthening the conservation agenda' (IWC 2003b).[5] But only Australia has gone so far as to withdraw from the work on the RMS, a project that is seen as a step towards the resumption of commercial whaling.

To most whalers, whatever their cultural background, it is difficult to grasp why it should be morally worse to kill a whale for food than to kill a kangaroo, cow or pig for the same purpose. They are convinced that the enforcement of the moratorium is no longer motivated by science or the opposition to animal suffering. The opposition to whaling goes deeper. Power relations on the global arena have made it possible for activists to turn whales into symbols for larger environmental and animal rights issues. Against this background it is not surprising that whalers have achieved little through a strategy of accommodation. What progress the whalers have achieved can largely be ascribed to the other strategy employed: openly contesting the cultural and political premises of the campaigns against hunting whales.

Contesting the Global Eco-discourse

Pro-whalers have challenged their adversaries in several ways. First, they have tried to question the cultural and political premises for the hegemonic anti-whaling discourse, and they have tried to define some of the premises themselves. Second, they have questioned the real motives of the anti-whalers, and in so doing have made their own contribution to a polarized world. Third, they have united and organized themselves locally and, not least, internationally.

Ecological Arguments for Whaling

The ecological arguments for whaling fall mainly into two categories. One set of arguments states that catching whales is *possible* because some whale stocks are abundant and can be utilized in a sustainable manner. Whalers stress that they are the last people who want to overexploit whale stocks, as this would undermine their own way of life. This might at first glance look convincing, but it is not difficult to find people who have overharvested their natural resources in the past and in the present (Edgerton 1992; Kalland 2003; Diamond 2005). To governments, such romantic claims from whalers themselves are not good enough, and because the moratorium was justified by ecological uncertainties it became paramount to bring hard, scientific facts to the table. The authorities in whaling countries thereby took a modernist approach to management—often going against the whalers themselves—which has occasionally caused great resentment among whalers. But as I have stressed several times already, there is now little doubt that some stocks can tolerate a limited and monitored harvest. The problem is to get this message out to the public in the protectionist countries.

The other set of arguments concerns whether whaling is *desirable*. 'No', say Greenpeace and the WWF, referring to arguments about the ethical treatment of animals. They are supported by governments in e.g. Australia, New Zealand, the U.K., Sweden and the U.S. 'Yes', say supporters of whaling, who continue with ecological arguments. In their opinion whaling is ecologically desirable because it helps maintain the ecological balance in the oceans. Marine mammals are seen as potential competitors for fish. To continue fishing while protecting predators at the top of the food chain will undermine the ecosystem and create imbalance. An important aim of research whaling is therefore to learn more about what these animals eat. It is estimated that cetaceans consume somewhere between 300 and 500 million tonnes of fish, krill and other marine biomass a year. If we include what seals and other marine mammals eat, the total consumption may reach 700 million tonnes (Komatsu and Misaki 2003).[6] For the sake of comparison, the world's total fisheries amount to about 90 million tonnes a year. Norwegian scientists have tried to calculate the cost of this competition in terms of potentially lost income to the fisheries (e.g. Flaaten and Stollery 1996). Similar arguments can be heard in other countries, and Japan in particular argues strongly that we need to use marine resources to feed the growing global human population. It is not surprising that local communities make use of such calculations in their arguments for whaling. Nor is it surprising that the same calculations have caused whale protectionists to charge that Japan and Norway want to exterminate the whales to maximize profits from fisheries.

Figure 6.1   *Stomach content (Pacific saury) from a minke whale.*
(courtesy by Institute of Cetacean Research, Tokyo)

Pro-whalers claim that exploitation of whale resources for food has several ecologically sound consequences. First, they have put great efforts into stressing the nutritious qualities of whale meat. It has repeatedly been pointed out that whale meat is rich in protein and iron and has a high percentage of unsaturated fatty acids, which lower the cholesterol level and reduce the risk of blood vessel diseases. Moreover, whale meat is seen as local food. Japan is gravely concerned about the question of food security. With a food self-sufficiency of only 41 per cent in terms of calories Japan, like other whaling countries, needs to import much of her food. It is argued that shortage of food makes a country vulnerable to external pressure and may in the end jeopardize the sovereignty of a state. Japan and Norway heavily subsidize their agriculture, both to lower their dependency on imports and as a measure to decentralize the population. Both aims are claimed to be in the interest of biodiversity and the environment.

Whaling is also seen as a most energy-efficient way to produce food for an increasing global population (Freeman 1991; Nagasaki 1993; Misaki 1996). One study has shown that Japanese minke whaling is one of the most energy-efficient fisheries in the world, consuming only one-tenth of the energy North American and British fishermen spend to land the same amount of protein. The average North

American beef farmer spends thirty times more energy per Kcal produced than Japanese minke whalers. Second, a switch to meat from farm animals—as desired by the large meat exporting countries Australia, New Zealand and the U.S.—implies that more land must be cleared to produce animal feed, with the consequences this may have for e.g. forests and the global climate (Komatsu and Misaki 2001).[7] Moreover, emissions of the greenhouse gas carbon dioxide (CO_2) equivalents per kilo of meat produced are considerably lower for whale meat than for meat from terrestrial animals (HNA 2008). Finally, emissions of methane from farm animals already constitute an important greenhouse gas; in New Zealand they comprise the largest component in the country's total release of greenhouse gases (*Guardian*, 5 September 2003). According to Milton Freeman (1991), the 'world opinion' is working to close down energy-efficient, sustainable production of high-quality food in favour of an ecologically more problematic one. Unless one has a vegetarian frame of mind, it can be argued that it is ecologically irresponsible to fight against sustainable whaling. We must, according to pro-whalers, take the ecosystem as the starting point and consider all species in relation to each other. By protecting charismatic animals at the top of the food chain, we not only create imbalances in the ecosystem but we also deny people access to cheap and healthy food.

Many Japanese scientists are moreover concerned about the possible interplay between the various species of cetaceans in the Antarctic ecosystem (Kojima 1993: 42), arguing that one reason for the slow recovery of the blue whale stocks since the 1960s might be the rapid growth of the minke whale population. The minke whale has, the argument goes, taken over the blue whale's niche (Komatsu and Misaki 2001). It is therefore necessary, they claim, to catch minke whales in order to help the blue whale population to recover.

Hunters are very aware of global discourses on sustainable development, animal welfare, animal rights and human rights. These issues are used to underpin the (self-) image of indigenous peoples as possessing traditional culture and an 'ecological mind'. Whalers use the same eco- and human rights discourses to support their identity construction (Broch 1994). In their rhetoric on sustainable whaling—a rhetoric partly appropriated from the global environmental discourse—it is the whalers who harbour the proper green values. They honour many of the ideals usually promoted by environmentalists. They live in small communities and engage in small-scale operations. They try to exploit generalized niches and switch from one natural resource to another before a resource has been severely depleted. In a somewhat romantic perspective they think they have always lived in harmony with nature by harvesting from renewable marine resources and have thereby contributed to society through hard and honest work. To overexploit their resources would be the same as to undermine their own future. But the moratorium has caused a narrowing of the niches and further specialization within the fisheries (cf. Chapter 5), thus making them more vulnerable to ecological fluctuations (ISG 1992).

The Japanese refer to their long (and by implication, sustainable) history of coastal whaling and strong religious sanctions against waste. As a leading fishing nation of the world, Japan is not only concerned about obtaining marine products for its own inhabitants, but also claims to be concerned about the global food security in the future, which can only be achieved via optimal exploitation of marine resources using a multiple-species management approach (Komatsu and Misaki 2003). This is not only Japan's view. According to Article 61 of UNCLOS (the United Nations Convention on the Law of the Sea), the coastal state is obliged to utilize the marine resources within its exclusive economic zone in an optimal way, or leave these resources to other countries to exploit. An exception has been made for marine mammals, however, in that the coastal state can choose to keep its whale resources untapped (Article 62). But this article does not empower nations to disallow a coastal state to exploit cetacean resources within its own economic zone.

From Economic Problems to Cultural Values

During the first years after the moratorium was adopted in 1982, whaling nations used mainly ecological and economic arguments against the decision. Norwegian authors, for example, tried to calculate how many man-years that were lost in a report, presented to the IWC, on the economic implications of the moratorium (Mønnesland et al. 1990). This and other reports (e.g. ISG 1992) emphasized that given a dearth of available work alternatives, the moratorium may create rural depopulation. Pro-whalers were not slow to point out that this consequence is hardly in the interests of the environment. Japan has also used such arguments and refers to a particularly steep population decline in communities that were once engaged in whaling (Akimichi et al. 1988; Kalland 1989a; Kalland and Moeran 1992). Job loss and rural depopulation have been among the most common arguments for whaling among local authorities and not least among whalers themselves.

It is not surprising that economic arguments carry little weight in the IWC, where many of the delegates come from countries with millions of people out of work. They claim, correctly, that Iceland, Japan and Norway are affluent societies that can easily compensate the economic losses imposed on their whalers. It is also difficult to measure the impact of the moratorium on depopulation, which is a general trend in most rural areas of the industrialized world.

Since the late 1980s *cultural* values have come more to the fore. As early as 1981 ASW was legitimized for its cultural significance to the Alaskan Inuit (Bockstoce et al. 1982; also see Chapter 4 in this volume). Others have been impelled to promote their whaling in a similar way. In addition to presenting a large number of scientific publications to IWC's Scientific Committee, Greenland presented at least thirty-six documents to the IWC between 1979 and 1994 on the sociocultural, technological and management aspects of its whaling (see Stevenson, Madsen and Maloney 1997).

This approach opened the IWC to the humanities and social sciences, and anthropologists in particular have been engaged in documenting cultural aspects of whaling, legitimizing indigenous catches of whales and estimating indigenous peoples' needs for whale meat. It is against the background of whale foods' nutritious and cultural importance to local communities that we have to understand Japan's attempts to have its coastal minke whaling defined as ASW. To underline this point, twelve social scientists (mostly anthropologists) from six countries were invited to Japan to study the cultural importance of coastal whaling in Japan. The group concluded that coastal minke whaling shared features with both ASW and commercial whaling (Akimichi et al. 1988). Japan therefore suggested to the IWC that a separate category be defined for small-type coastal whaling (STCW). This has not been adopted, but a working group was established to discuss the implications of the moratorium on coastal communities, and Japan has presented a large number of documents attempting to obtain an emergency quota of fifty minke whales.[8] Comparative studies have concluded that the distinction between ASW and commercial whaling is untenable (e.g. ISGSTW 1992; Moeran 1992; Freeman 1993). Norway, after first distancing itself from the Japanese strategy, tabled a report in 1992 focusing on the cultural importance of minke whaling (ISG 1992). Also the Faroe Islands have repeatedly used cultural arguments defending pilot drives.

With the focus on cultural values, indigenous peoples have been presented in a positive light—to the point of romanticism, in some cases. By stressing the interconnection between family, religion, identity and economy it is possible to claim that the closure of ASW would undermine both the fundament of existence and the culture of these communities. For the Inuit, the value of cultural arguments in the global management discourse has proven to be fruitful and they have been able to obtain quotas for minke, fin, gray, humpback and bowhead whales. But although Icelandic, Japanese and Norwegian small-type whalers have added cultural arguments to their quota claims, they have failed to persuade the IWC to issue even limited quotas for minke whales based on scientific investigations. One of the reasons for this disparity seems to be that the IWC does not ascribe legitimate cultural significance to 'commercial' whalers.

One reason why indigenous peoples have been more successful than other whalers using this line of argumentation is that they have been able to exploit the global discourse on cultural diversity and the rights of indigenous peoples. The emphasis on preserving cultural diversity is an attempt to counter the process of homogenization of cultures dominated by politically and economically strong metropolitan centres of influence. Preserving cultural diversity is seen as a strategy to secure the rights of indigenous peoples and local groups to control their own development. Phrased simply, it proclaims that people have a right to be different.

Culture has become a powerful weapon on the global political battlefield. Cultural arguments have become politically correct, and 'real' or 'pure' culture is perceived to be good. This elevation of culture within global politics has made it possible for local peoples to enter the global political arena and to a certain extent reclaim their rights to life, land, resources and self-determination. However, in order to be successful they are often forced to present their cultures as virginal, untouched by modernity. This interest in pure or authentic culture is a consequence of postmodernity and global decentralization (Friedman 1992). Very often, indigenous peoples' cultures have been singled out as possessing exactly this pristine quality. The IWC's dichotomy between ASW and commercial whaling shows the anti-whalers' need for a clean and authentic culture. In order to continue whaling, Alaskan whalers must document to the world that they do not sell whale products on the market. In other words, to continue whaling the ASW whaler is forced to live up to the image of a savage who is ascribed an ecological mind sheltered from the influence of the world market.

The positive connotation of culture and nature in global politics has forced indigenous peoples to present their cultures in an explicit way to gain acceptance and rights. In some contexts it has become acceptable, in the case of whaling even attractive, to be identified as indigenous. Environmentalists have often drawn a picture of ecologically minded indigenous peoples who represent the opposite of the modern industrial society (Kalland 2003), and in this view there is no room for culture or ecological reasoning in local communities in Japan or Northwestern Europe. Hence, although several international reports such as *Our Common Future* and *Agenda 21* argue for local participation in natural resource management, this has not improved the international understanding of Faroese, Icelandic, Norwegian or Japanese whaling.

When indigenous peoples—and other local groups—are believed to possess ecological knowledge and cultures founded in premodern traditions,[9] it is sometimes difficult for them to be accepted as equal or even relevant players in a dynamic modern world. Therefore, a narrow focus on knowledge and culture may often be disadvantageous, for people may be stripped of their humanity by the postmodernists, and their culture as well as their knowledge may be perceived as being static. As long as they remain primitive and authentic they may hunt, but if they become part of the modern world, this right to hunt must be denied them (Kalland 1992b). As the leader of the Whale and Dolphin Conservation Society stated: 'We see tradition, certainly in the case of whaling, as going back to the old days, how things used to be, how they used to do things. And if they want to kill whales in the traditional way, that's fine by us, *if* nothing else about their way of life, significantly anyway, has changed' (quoted by Nauerby 1996: 162, original emphasis). So far this argument has mostly been used against Faroese, Icelandic, Japanese and Norwegian whalers, but it could easily be applied to whaling by Alaskan Inuit as well. They are not only able to hunt bowhead whales and engage in offshore oil drilling operations at the same time; they also use money from modern oil activities to outfit whaling crews using modern weapons.

Ethical Arguments for Whaling

In preceding chapters we have seen that ethical arguments against whaling have gained in importance since the moratorium was imposed, and many environmental and animal welfare/rights organizations and several IWC member countries today openly work for a permanent ban on whaling for ethical reasons. Rhetorically they use arguments from both the animal welfare and animal rights discourses. Three issues are of special concern to many: how long time it takes from the whale is hit to its death, to what extent the whale suffers stress during the chase before it is hit and how the hunt breaks social relations between whales. Some people are prepared to go a step further and ban whaling because whales, like humans, have rights. Whalers and their supporters strongly oppose such ethical arguments, not least because the protection of individual animals is not necessarily in the interest of the ecosystem. Ethical considerations for individual animals can easily come into conflict with a more holistic environmental ethics (Gillespie 1997).

Giving special rights to whales, as D'Amato and Chopra (1991) want to do, implies a perception that whales are uniquely special. Being our equals in the oceans, they are different from other animals to such an extent that they deserve the same legal protection as human beings. We have seen how they have been portrayed as intelligent, sentient beings living in close family units and caring for each other. But whalers and their supporters have repeatedly stressed that this image is false. It was argued in Chapter 1 that while there are immense differences between the many species of cetacean, most species do not live in close family units. Baleen whales like minke whales are rather asocial and leave their calves after only a few months. Most species, if not all, are moreover promiscuous. Nor are there any indications that cetaceans are more aware of their existence and have a richer emotional life than many other animals. The difficulty of documenting such claims has, as we saw in Chapter 1, caused Payne to conclude that 'therefore, in the absence of evidence to the contrary . . . whales are aware of their lives and of their interests, simply because that seems to be the most parsimonious conclusion' (Payne 1991: 21). Georg Blichfeldt (1993: 14), then secretary of the High North Alliance (HNA, an NGO working for the rights of coastal communities to harvest whales and seals), observes that the same claim can be made for most animals. Again, there is no objective reason to single out cetaceans for special rights.

It would be more consistent to bestow rights on all animals. Whalers see several problems with such a position, however. First, the logical consequence of animal rights is vegetarianism, but only few anti-whalers seem prepared to take this step. Whalers are not alone in having pointed out the inconsistencies of being against whaling for ethical reasons while at the same time supporting consumption of pork, beef and turkey as Australia, New Zealand and the U.K. do (e.g. Gillespie 1997). Second, it is practically impossible to give all life forms—e.g. viruses, bacteria, fleas, rats—right to life, and a dividing line must for practical reasons be made somewhere, but where? To bestow rights only on animals that are sentient beings and able to feel pain does not solve the problem of drawing boundaries, which always will remain unsolved because we cannot penetrate the animals' minds.

Third, according to the Danish philosopher Peter Sandøe there is a fundamental difference between humans and whales (as well as other animals) because whales are less self-conscious than man. They do not worry about the future to the same extent, and one does not violate the whale's future plans by killing it. Also, the social implications of killing whales are fewer than those of killing people (Sandøe 1993b, 1993c).[10] Moreover, as Greenlandic pastor Finn Lynge (1992) points out, rights are closely connected with duties, but whales do not have duties. Whales are not moral actors and do not know the difference between right and wrong. They are innocent. That infants, the senile and mentally handicapped humans have rights without matching duties does not challenge this because, both Sandøe and Lynge claim, rights are extended to such people partly in respect for their families and partly to prevent a discussion about what kind of people should be denied the right to live.

Animals have no rights, but people have an obligation to treat them with kindness, says Lynge (1992: 13). But what does this mean? Animal protectionists and the like-minded group within the IWC are preoccupied with pain, not least at the moment of death, and think that the hunt is painful and therefore inhumane. The whalers think this is too narrow a view for two reasons. First, such a view is ethnocentric. It is reasonable to assume that our perception of animals' pain is coloured by the way we experience our own pain, which is culturally dependent. Implied in the anti-whalers' notion of 'inhumane treatment' is a perceived lack of consideration for or kindness towards the animal among whalers. But, as Milton Freeman (1992) argues, most whalers show great compassion for the animals they kill. In the previous chapter we saw how whalers in both Alaska and Japan honour such whales. The whalers are indebted to the whales that have given themselves to the whalers, who in return are obliged to make full use of the carcasses and perform the proper rituals. People's behaviour may be strictly curtailed before and during the hunts, and the meat must be shared after a successful hunt.

Second, whaling nations want to place whaling within a larger context and compare the suffering of whales with that inflicted on other animals. Does whaling inflict more pain than sporting hunts do on elk, deer or fox? Certainly many more elk and deer are struck and lost than whales in commercial and scientific whaling, and whalers never miss the opportunity to stress the cruelty of the British fox hunt. And what about the suffering of domesticated animals in captivity and during transportation, in addition to pain inflicted at the slaughterhouse? How should one compare the suffering of one minke whale to that of ten cows or 2,000 chickens? And how do we compare pain inflicted during the slaughtering process with pain inflicted during 'imprisonment'? In this way pro-whalers seek to shift the focus away from whaling to the treatment of farm and game animals. Such comparative research is relevant in the eyes of pro-whalers in order to reveal double standards and ethnocentrism on the part of the anti-whalers. The majority in the IWC, however, does not want to discuss these issues, claiming that the sufferings of domesticated animals do not justify harm being inflicted also on whales, and that comparative research therefore is irrelevant.

To whalers, animal welfare and animal rights are two entirely different matters. Whereas animal rights are not compatible with whaling, whalers have long offered to discuss welfare issues and humane killing methods; although they think it is outside the competence of the IWC. Whalers claim that they are among those most concerned about humane killing methods, and in most hunting cultures a high value is placed on swift and painless killing. A 'death shot' gives the gunner added prestige. Whalers are convinced that whales enjoy a much better quality of life than do most farm animals. Therefore the HNA has claimed to be an animal welfare organization. The hunters have appropriated the animal welfare discourse in the same way that they have appropriated the global environmental discourse. What they protest is linking the issues of animal welfare with sustainable utilization of natural resources.

Another way animal welfare advocates have addressed the problem of animal suffering is to take the utilitarian approach of Peter Singer, i.e. that people shall not inflict unnecessary pain on animals. This is a view most whalers can support. But what is 'necessary'? As mentioned in Chapter 2, Singer had human nourishment in mind. And because the Faroe Islands, Iceland, Japan and Norway are affluent societies where people can afford to buy Australian and North American beef, it follows that there is no need to kill whales. To emphasize this, anti-whalers often claim that whale meat and blubber are luxury foods (e.g. Greenpeace 2002), which is a gross exaggeration (see Chapter 5). But this rhetoric has made the Japanese ask why it is immoral to eat expensive food.

Supporters of whaling raise several questions about needs. Why does the IWC accept that affluent Alaskan whalers who have reaped considerable benefits from the petroleum industry have not only nutritious but also cultural and social needs? We saw in the previous chapter how whaling has important implications not only in Alaska and Greenland but also in the Faroe Islands, Japan and Norway. Don't the latter have the same right to a culture as the Alaskan Inuit? How can we compare material and cultural needs? And moreover, who decides people's needs? Is there a greater need to eat turkey than to eat whale meat? To the British, yes, but not to the Japanese. 'Would it be ethically commendable of the Norwegian coastal population to renounce a local resource like minke whale and import pork from other areas instead?' asks Blichfeldt (1993: 13). This kind of evaluation will always be subjective and can easily be ethnocentric.

International Law and Whaling

We saw in Chapter 4 that the whale protectionists have tried to give the IWC a monopoly on the management of whaling. Whaling conducted in nonmember countries is easily condemned as illegal. The most recent example is the case of Inuit bowhead whaling in Canada. The U.S. has even used the 1971 Pelly Amendment to sanction its northern neighbour for diminishing 'the effectiveness of an international fishery or wildlife conservation agreement', an agreement Canada does not recognize. Also Japan and Norway have repeatedly been accused of illegal whaling. With references to the moratorium and a long series of resolutions, Japan has been accused of illegal research whaling and Norway of illegal commercial whaling. Whaling countries view these accusations and resolutions as infringing on the rights of sovereign states.

The whaling nations have objected to these accusations and claim they have international laws on their side. First, they point out, the whaling convention applies only to 'factory ships, land stations, and the whale catchers under the jurisdiction of the Contracting Governments' (Article I). It therefore does not apply to Canada and other nonmembers of the IWC. But according to UNCLOS, coastal states are obliged to cooperate in management where marine resources move between national economic zones, as many of the whale species do. Whaling nations argue, however, that such cooperation need not necessarily be carried out within the IWC. What UNCLOS states is that 'in the case of cetaceans [states] shall in particular work through the international *organizations* for their conservation, management and study' (Article 65, emphasis added). The IWC is not even mentioned by name, and Article 65 clearly opens the field for more than one organization to be considered an appropriate management regime (Hoel 1992; Burke 1997, 2001). This phrase has moreover been included in paragraph 17.76 of *Agenda 21*, which mentions the IWC as one of several possible organizations. According to Paragraph 17.90, states recognize:

(a) The responsibility of the International Whaling Commission for the conservation and management of whale stocks and the regulation of whaling pursuant to the 1946 International Convention for the Regulation of Whaling;

(b) The work of the International Whaling Commission Scientific Committee in carrying out studies of large whales in particular, as well as of other cetaceans;

(c) The work of other organizations, such as the Inter-American Tropical Tuna Commission and the Agreement on Small Cetaceans in the Baltic and the

North Sea under the Bonn Convention, in the conservation, management and study of cetaceans.

In other words, the IWC is given the responsibility to implement the ICRW (which is legally binding only on member countries), and the work of its Scientific Committee is recognized—as is, according to (c), the work of other organizations (Hoel 1992: 50). The phrase 'such as' must furthermore mean that there are organizations other than those mentioned here, for example NAMMCO (see below).

Japan and Norway have repeatedly denied that they are violating the ICRW. Norway legitimizes its commercial whaling activities by referring to its two objections to the moratorium and to the classification of the Northeast Atlantic minke whale stock as protected. According to Article V.3 Norway is therefore not legally bound by these decisions, and Robert L. Friedheim, professor of international relations at the University of Southern California, has claimed that Iceland and Norway 'have scrupulously avoided deliberate breaches of international law in the action they have taken in response to IWC policies they deemed illegal.' (Friedheim 1996: 22) The accusations are nonetheless levelled again and again.[11]

Japan withdrew its objections to the moratorium in the face of strong U.S. pressure and is therefore bound by the decision unless it can be proven before an international court that the U.S. has used force or fraud. However, it is easier for Japan to claim rights to conduct whaling for research purposes, as Article VIII.1 of the ICRW explicitly stresses that such whaling is outside the mandate of the IWC.[12] Japan has therefore launched research programmes that are more comprehensive than earlier research programmes. Whereas only 840 whales were killed by Japan for scientific research between 1954 and 1987, more than 11,000 whales have been killed in such whaling since 1988, when the moratorium was imposed.[13]

Whaling nations feel they have followed international law (Caron 1995; Friedheim 1996), but they ask to what extent the IWC has done so. I have already discussed several procedural irregularities occurring at IWC meetings (Chapter 4). Meetings have been called and resolutions adopted without consideration for deadlines; member countries' calls to bring resolutions to a vote have been denied; a resolution was mistakenly written into the Schedule;[14] Iceland was denied the right to vote whereas anti-whaling countries that failed to pay the membership fees for years have been allowed to vote;[15] observers have been admitted to closed meetings; and so on and so forth.

In January 1996 U.S., Canadian and Japanese experts on international law met in Tokyo to discuss the legal aspects of the IWC's behaviour. The meeting, which was chaired by Robert L. Friedheim, concluded that whereas the moratorium was legal, its maintenance probably is not. The whaling convention is clearly built on the principle of sustainable whaling, and it is stated in the 1982 decision that the moratorium should be revised no later than in 1990 according to scientific advice. When the majority in the IWC ignored this advice and turned the IWC into a de facto protectionist organization, this was not only a violation of the ICRW, which says amendments to the Schedule 'shall be based on scientific finding' and 'shall take into consideration the interests of the consumers' (emphasis as in Friedheim 1996: 36), but also a violation of Article 40 in the Vienna Convention on the Law of Treaties (Friedheim 1996: 32–36). The lawyers were even clearer in their judgment on the Southern Sanctuary, which they found to be illegal because it did not meet the requirements stated in the ICRW (Friedheim 1996: 15–16): the decision was not 'necessary to carry out the objectives and purposes of this Convention and to provide for the conservation, development, and optimum utilization of the whale resources', nor was it based on the best scientific advice, nor did it take into consideration the interests of whalers and consumers.

The legal experts also found that pressure, including threats to impose sanctions, and vote manipulation might have been against international law. However, the problem is not to have the law on one's side but to get a valid verdict. One of the weaknesses of the ICRW is that it has no mechanism for conflict solution or imposition of legal sentences. This means that the whaling countries must find an external court that the IWC is willing to recognize. Japan has long considered a lawsuit against the IWC (Komatsu and Misaki 2001: 111). Whaling nations are also of the opinion that some of the IWC's demands for the RMS may be in violation of international law. They find it intolerable to give international observers enforcement power over whaling vessels operating within national waters, as this runs against the universally accepted rights of sovereign nations (Hoel 1992: 64; Komatsu and Misaki 2001: 165). The same can be said about foreigners meddling in domestic market prerogatives such as distribution, pricing and monitoring (Komatsu and Misaki 2003: 92–93). Whaling nations see these attempts as serious infringements on national sovereign rights.

It is today a widely held notion that access to natural resources is best regulated when local communities that depend on these resources for their nutritional, economic, social and cultural needs are brought into active participation, a principle incorporated into the report *Caring for the Earth: A Strategy for Sustainable Living* (IUCN et al. 1991). This principle of self-management is laid down as a right both in the International Covenant on Civil and Political Rights (ICCPR) and in the International Covenant on Economic, Social and Cultural Rights (ICESCR), both parties to the International Bill of Human Rights. According to these covenants:

> All peoples have the right to self-determination: by virtue of that right they freely determine their political status and freely pursue their economic, social and cultural development (Article 1(2))
> All peoples may, for their own ends, freely dispose of their natural wealth and resources without prejudice to any obligations arising out of international economic co-operation based on the principle of mutual benefit,

and international law. In no case may a people be deprived of their means of subsistence (Article 1(2))

The bill is in general supportive of a people's right to harvest natural resources in order to meet their basic needs 'of personal security, food, shelter, clothing and medicine—in short, a guarantee of cultural survival' (Ward 1993: 27). Moreover, the ICESCR acknowledges the 'right of everyone to the enjoyment of the highest attainable standard of physical and mental health' (Article 12). ILO (International Labour Organization) Convention No.169 addresses the rights of indigenous peoples in a more direct manner. Article 15, for instance, speaks of the need to safeguard their rights to natural resources, including the right to 'participate in the use; management and conservation of these resources', and Article 23(1) states that 'hunting, fishing, trapping and gathering shall be recognized as important factors in the maintenance of their cultures and their economic self-reliance and development'. A number of other international declarations, treaties and conventions stress that their social and cultural identities, customs, traditions and institutions shall be treated with respect (Ward 1993).

However, only nineteen countries have so far (as of 26 March 2008) ratified ILO-Convention 169, and Australia, New Zealand, the U.K. and the U.S. are not among these. Indigenous peoples therefore seem to have a long way to go before their rights are firmly secured. Meanwhile, the rights of non-indigenous whalers appear to be even more distant because, as has already been pointed out, their culture is not recognized by the IWC.

'Crazy Greens'

The whalers and their supporters have difficulty understanding the campaigns against whaling. They feel they have shown without reasonable doubt that some whales can be hunted sustainably and that modern technology has made this hunt more humane than the modern breeding of farm animals and many other forms of hunting. Moreover, they have argued that they have international law and a powerful global discourse on cultural diversity on their side. But their arguments fall on deaf ears, and anti-whaling campaigns continue unabated. Two sets of answers to this puzzle are offered by whalers. One is that anti-whalers are not rational; the other is that they have a hidden agenda (i.e. money and votes).

One of the characteristics whalers most often attribute to whale savers is that they are ignorant people living in big cities. They are depicted as living a life far from nature, which they know only from books and movies. 'They don't have the intimate relationship which indigenous people have with animals and the land', says co-ordinator for Inuit Tapirisat in Canada Peter Williamson. Susan Watkins, from the same organization, is less diplomatic: 'These people are so ignorant, so arrogant, so patronizing, so stupid; they know nothing about aboriginal peoples' (Beinart 1995). The argument that whale savers do not have proper knowledge about nature and local people is frequently also levelled against resource managers, scientists and bureaucrats.

Accusations about ignorance are often traded in environmental conflicts, but in most such cases knowledge of indigenous or local users of natural resources is pitted against that of national authorities, scientists and professional managers. Indigenous knowledge (IK), or traditional ecological knowledge (TEK), is often seen as being more holistic and organic than science. The scholarly debate on science versus other knowledge systems is indeed very extensive but has hardly been brought up in this book. The reason is that the whaling issue has not primarily been cast in these terms. The whalers have mostly employed a scientific discourse, both because the whaling convention demands it and because scientists have been on their side. However, tensions are always just under the surface. There have been conflicts of knowledge between Inuit and scientists as to the stocks of bowhead, beluga and narwhals. During the self-imposed Norwegian moratorium between 1988 and 1993, Norwegian minke whalers had little but scorn for the research whaling conducted, and Norwegian marine biologists were accused of collaborating with British scientists who worked for Greenpeace. Regional management bodies like NAMMCO and the Joint Commission on Conservation and Management of Narwhal and Beluga (JCCMNB) now try to build bridges between science and other systems of knowledge.

Much effort is expended to portray the whale savers as irresponsible and irrational people who in fact pose a threat to the environment. After a brawl between Greenpeace activists and Norwegian whalers in 1996, one of the skippers had this to say: 'The activists were largely young girls. Most of them were worse than wild cats. Scratching and biting. To say it bluntly; they were nothing but brats (*udisiplinerte drittunger*) . . . The organization has little knowledge about whaling and the members are guided by irrational feelings' (Olsen 1998: 8). To point out that many activists are young girls makes them more suspect, as women allegedly are more emotional and less rational than men, while likening activists to wildcats may evoke associations with sexy girls in cheap crime literature. The play on the theme of sex is taken further by Norwegian papers that frequently underline that one of Sea Shepherd's leaders once was *Playboy*'s model of the month. Many of the activists are said to be foreigners. Through such rhetoric pro-whalers try to undermine the credibility of the activists, who are portrayed as being too removed from nature and too young to understand complicated ecological processes.

The juxtaposition of rationality and emotion is a frequent one among the pro-whalers. Japan, like Iceland and Norway, has strongly argued for the principle of sustainable utilization of natural resources and for the need to base natural resource management on science instead of taking an 'emotional approach' (Sumi 1989: 319). This is the message also of the report *Our Common Future* (WCED 1987), and science was, to Gro Harlem Brundtland—chair of the WCED—a strong symbol and the foundation for sustainable use of resources when she as prime minister decided to resume commercial whaling in Norway. Science is seen as the only knowledge system of universal value. To protect whales because they are special and have intrinsic value and/or personhood would mean to give in to the values of particular groups, or to the green 'crazies' or 'lunatics' as some whalers like to call them. It would imply making moral judgments and ranking cultures according to how they treat whales. Pro-whalers see this as ethnocentric, a case of cultural imperialism and an act of eco-colonialism.

Whalers often claim that whale lovers anthropomorphize whales, which are given human values and desires and regarded as the humans of the sea (cf. Chapter 1).[16] Closely related to this is the question of cetaceans' high intelligence, a claim whalers find hilarious. Whales are regarded by whalers as a natural resource that ought to be utilized, not a person to befriend. If activists can be portrayed as emotional, it follows in this rhetoric that they have no legitimate role to play in resource management. Hence, they are often depicted as driven by emotions: 'the emotions of the anti-whalers take the upper hand' and 'this case is solely about emotions, not about being rational' are typical expressions from Norwegian newspapers in 1993. Environmentalists are even accused of being against knowledge. Under the heading 'Aversion to knowledge' (*Uvilje mot viten*), Ketil Falch (2000: 2) writes that 'this propaganda machine [the anti-whaling campaigns] is driven by an urban way of thinking based on emotions'. Emotions are not only irrelevant; they are presented as potentially dangerous. In a newspaper article entitled 'The terror of emotions' (*Følelsesterror*), Norwegian writer Michael Grundt Spang (1992) writes that 'it ought to be possible to resist the life-threatening danger of a world governed by unjust (*urettsmessige*) waves of emotions'. At times the opponents to whaling are even said to be motivated by religious zeal: Sir Tipene O'Regan, former [Maori] Waitangi Fisheries Commission chairman, called whale savers 'environmental ayatollahs' who were 'practicing a new form of millennium religion' (Christian 2000: 1).

One of the most common accusations made against activists is that not only do they accidentally misinform the public, but they do so deliberately as well. They are pictured as hypocritical liars despite better knowledge. Makah Tribal Council and Makah Whaling Commission writes (2005: 5): 'But we are also aware that much of this opposition has been whipped up deliberately by organized groups who have put out a blizzard of propaganda attacking us and urging the public to oppose us. Unfortunately much of this propaganda contains misinformation, distortion, and outright falsehoods.'

Most pro-whalers are convinced that the purpose of such misinformation and lies is to earn money. Chief Happynook, chairman of the World Council of Whalers (WCW), has 'witnessed the environmental movement evolve from individuals who were truly concerned about the environment to a protest industry which is now a multitude of multi-million dollar corporations' (Goddard 1999). The chairman of the HNA, a whaler himself, has pointed out that the WWF and Greenpeace are motivated by money: they are 'thieves in the same market' (Münster 1998: 14). Komatsu Masayuki, an alternate IWC commissioner for Japan, links lies and money more forcefully: 'Once misguided by the anti-whaling pro-paganda, the gullible public has donated generously to these NGOs . . . The more they misguide the public, the more money flows into their coffers' (Komatsu and Misaki 2001: 119). By presenting anti-whaling NGOs as a multi-million dollar protest industry, pro-whalers hope to dismantle the image of activists altruisti-cally devoted to saving nature and replace it with an image of activists fighting for their own economic interests.

This accusation is not directed only against anti-whaling NGOs but against governments as well. Pro-whaling advocates repeatedly accuse especially New Zealand, Australia and the U.K. of spreading misinformation and lies. In No-vember 2005, to take a trivial example, the New Zealand minister of conserva-tion stated in a press release that 'the fleets of Japan *and other Northern Hemi-sphere nations* are once again travelling outside of their own waters and all the way down to Antarctica to kill their scientific quota' (emphasis added). New Zealand authorities know very well that only Japan has hunted whales in Ant-arctica during the last twenty-five years. One may join the secretary of the HNA in wondering whether this was said to make matters *sound* worse.[17]

Economic interests might be one motivation for such misinformation. Whereas most of the countries that support whaling are coastal states with con-siderable fishing interests to consider,[18] most of the countries against whaling have strong agricultural sectors. Among the most uncompromising anti-whaling countries we find the largest exporters of meat—the U.S., Australia, New Zea-land and Brazil—and at least Australia and New Zealand have seen an end to whaling as an opportunity to increase their own exports of farm meats. Australia launched an aggressive export drive in Japan, and by the mid 1990s Japan had become its main market (Epstein 2005: 223).

But symbol-politics is probably more important still. Anti-whaling countries want to appear to be civilized states that care about nature. The leading Norwe-gian newspaper *Aftenposten* writes in an editorial that 'governments that attack [Norway] use these attacks as a handy means to bolster their own environmen-tal image at home. The moratorium does not cost them anything but helps to distract attention away from their own environmental negligence' ('Hykleri om hval', 27 July 2001: 6). According to Heidi Sørensen, then the leader of the Norwegian NGO Nature and Youth (affiliated with Friends of the Earth) and at present deputy environmental minister from the Socialist Leftist Party, 'the whal-ing issue provides the rich, major polluters with a cheap way of buying a green alibi' (1993: 30). Komatsu links the U.S. moratorium proposal in 1972 directly to their use of 'Agent Orange' and other defoliants in Vietnam. At the time there was worldwide criticism of the use of such chemicals in the war (Komatsu and Misaki 2001: 60).

To drive the point home, the HNA and others have assembled cases to show what they perceive as hypocrisy among whale savers (e.g. HNA 2000: 3). Their message is clear: anti-whaling countries operate with double standards and have dubious scores both regarding the environment and animal welfare. In Australia, Environmental Minister Robert Hill—dubbed 'Minister of Double Standards' by the HNA—in 2000 'passed death sentences on some 5.7 million kangaroos' (HNA 2000: 1). A large number of these animals are culled in an inhumane way, according to the Royal Society for the Prevention of Cruelty to Animals (RSP-CA). New Zealand spends millions of NZ$ annually to cull millions of possums and stoats, earning the Department of Conservation the nickname 'Department of Culling' (Epstein 2005: 246). Many of the possums are killed with poisoned baits and suffer painful deaths as their internal organs fail. To Norwegian whalers, the most 'spectacular' example of double standards was long the British fox hunt, and the most provocative individual—next to Paul Watson of Sea Shepherd—was probably John Gummer, formerly the U.K. minister of the environment as well as agriculture. He was against whaling because 'there is no humane way of killing a whale' (press conference in Glasgow, May 1993), yet he maintained that '[f]ield sport [i.e. fox-hunting] is a basic human freedom' (at a 1990 meeting of the Field Sport Society). The British fox hunt has since been outlawed, but executions of convicts that continue in the U.S. despite international protests, are also a popular target for Norwegian whalers (see Figure 6.2), whereas the Japanese are most outraged at what they see as double standards in the U.S.'s behaviour at the IWC (cf. Chapter 4).

A final accusation levelled against whale savers is that they frequently are perceived as fanatics who are prepared to resort to sabotage and terrorism. In the words of Prime Minister Helen Clark (n.d.), New Zealanders are 'passionate' about whales and take that 'passion' with them into the IWC. The problems start when one is blinded by one's passion to the point that the end justifies the means. That Clark has embraced Greenpeace has, by whalers and their advocates, been taken as proof that 'the New Zealand government supports violent actions . . . in breach of the maritime safety rules' (Komatsu and Misaki 2001: 133). Attempts to interrupt whaling at sea, which have lead to collusions, have been characterized by Clark as 'brave', but Takehiro Takayama, the president of the company operating the whaling ships, is of another opinion: 'This sabotage and harassment is terrorism . . . Calling [Greenpeace] an environmental group is an insult to those who work sincerely for our environment' (*HNA News* 9 December 1998).

Whether Greenpeace can be termed a terrorist organization is controversial and has been contested in courts. But if by 'terrorism' we mean 'the use of organized intimidation to force one's will upon others by means of fear' there can be little doubt that at least Sea Shepherd is an international terrorist organization.[19] Paul Watson has repeatedly bragged about the whaling vessels he and his group have scuttled and has promised monetary rewards to those who destroy whaling boats. Yet despite his apparently criminal activities, the Canadian Paul Watson has, from the whalers' point of view, been taken under the protective wing of the U.S. government. He operates from Seattle but he has not been extradited to stand trial.

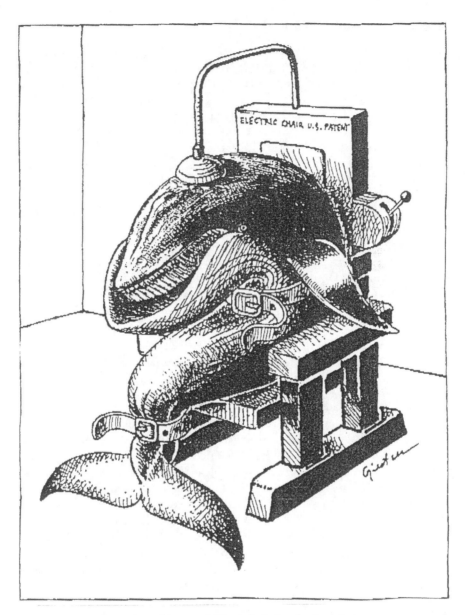

Figure 6.2   *Humane killing of whales, the American way.*
(courtesy by Karl Gustav Gjertsen)

Marine Mammals and Identity

I argued in Chapter 5 that whaling has had, and still has, important ramifica-
tions for the ways whalers define themselves and their communities. Values and
attitudes are internalized through socialization. They are particularly expressed
in rituals that enable people to reflect upon what it means to be e.g. Inuit,
whaler, woman or elderly. But these values and attitudes can also be highlighted
when they are challenged. As we saw in Chapters 2 and 3, whalers and their
supporters have been bombarded with accusations. This has caused a reaction
among the Inuit as well as in the Faroe Islands, Iceland, Japan and Norway. In
all these countries attacks on whaling have nourished nationalistic sentiment
(Kalland et al. 2005). Deep ecologist David Rothenberg therefore deplores Paul
Watson's rhetoric and his acts of terrorism because he believes that Watson has
united the Norwegians in 'defending whaling as patriotically as ever!' (Rothenberg 1995: 217).

Reactions have been particularly strong when the criticism was directed against
the whalers' culture, and the critique of the consumption of whale meat has not
passed unchallenged. Attempts by environmental and animal rights activists to
move whales from the category of edible resource to that of inedible pets (cf.
Introduction) have caused a passionate reaction among pro-whalers, who on several occasions have termed whales 'rats' or 'cockroaches' of the sea (e.g. Burns et
al 2001: 222), thus moving whales into the pest category. But, as was argued in
Chapter 5, consumption of whale meat may also be a way to underpin and thus
strengthen one's own identity and way of life. For people facing criticism, consumption of whales has acquired new meaning as a way to consume the totem
animals of the environmental movement. It was no coincidence that a large whale
meat barbecue was held in Northern Norway on 4 July, the U.S. Independence
Day. In Iceland and Norway in 1992–93, criticism of this sort triggered a T-shirt
campaign, with people donning shirts with slogans like 'I love whales—for dinner'
(Figure 6.3) and 'Intelligent food for intelligent people'. For the same reason, a
number of whale festivals—several of them new—are being held in many places,
among them Ulsan in South Korea, where people can learn whale recipes and
have a free meal of whale meat (INWR 2003a: 2). Paradoxically, anti-whaling
campaigns have at least temporarily turned whale meat into a symbol for local and
national cultures, and eating whale meat has become a ritual act through which
the partakers express their belonging to a place or the national tribe.

Whaling has, therefore, maintained and gained new significance. Facing new
challenges in an ever-changing world, whaling is a way to express, sustain and
act out historical continuities, social and cultural values and distinctiveness,
and to exercise one's sovereignty and rights. Inuit youth in Alaska and Canada
have shown new interest in participating in bowhead whaling, and Makah Indians are reviving the old gray whale hunt. In many communities hunting is
still considered an important part of successful socialization and coming of

Figure 6.3   *From a T-shirt campaign, Norway 1993. (author's photo)*

age. Whaling is embedded in a social and cultural system of fundamental importance to the cultural integrity. This sociocultural system is the very fabric of many communities. Thus, an attack on their hunting activities is an attack on their culture and sovereignty.

   This process can be observed in many countries. Faroese pilot whaling is a case in point, as its significance as a national symbol has changed over the last decades. Pilot whaling has increasingly acquired a more specific significance for the Faroe Islands as a symbol of their traditional lifestyle, a special coexistence and dependence on nature, and as a symbol of national sovereignty challenged by the outside world. The global environmental movement and the international attention given to pilot whaling have paved the way for turning the hunt into a strong national symbol that the Faroe Islanders can live out in praxis during the communal hunt, around the dinner table and in the use and exhibit of symbols associated with the hunt. Nauerby argues that the impetus for the transformation of pilot whaling into a national symbol came from outside to a great extent, because the process of transformation took place at an international level (Nauerby 1996: 146; see also Joensen 1976, 1990, 1993). Similar processes have been observed in Iceland (Brydon 1990) and Norway (ISG 1992) but the reactions have been particularly strong in Japan, where the anti-whaling campaigns have been interpreted as Western racism and Japan-bashing.

The whaling controversy has caused the Japanese to ask themselves a number of questions that bear directly on their relations with the rest of the world. One of the questions frequently asked by officials and whalers alike is why the hunting of non-endangered minke whales in Japanese waters was prohibited when the Alaskan Inuit were allowed to harvest bowhead whale at a time when it was considered to be extremely endangered. And why is Japanese STCW, with all its cultural qualities, denied the status of ASW and an interim quota of fifty minke whales—to be consumed within the communities—when the Russians were allowed under the ASW category to take a larger quantity of gray whales to feed foxes in state-owned fur farms? Again, why should the Japanese not be allowed to carry out scientific whaling when it is provided for in the ICRW? Claiming that Japan is the only member nation that obeys the IWC decision, Misaki (1993: 34, 27) asks how 'this absurd situation [i.e. that Japan is perceived as a villain by the Western public] ever [has] been created'.

The international critique of the Japanese consumption of whale meat is seen as evidence that the anti-whaling campaign is directed against Japanese culture in general, since food is seen as an important cultural symbol in most societies. Most Japanese do not understand why it is more morally wrong to kill a whale for food than to kill a cow or a pig for the same purpose. Indeed, they think it is worse to kill a domesticated animal than a wild one. 'How can people kill an animal they have fed?' is a rhetorical question often heard in Japanese whaling communities. Yet in the Western media, eating whale meat is seen as barbaric, an act close to cannibalism. The Japanese react with dismay to such reports—and the anti-Japanese feelings behind them—which they regard as an insult to their national culture. The sentiment expressed by Mutsuko O. is quite representative: 'this is like telling your nextdoor neighbor not to eat his dinner because you don't like his food. That is awfully rude, isn't it?' (quoted in Takahashi 1988: 96.)

Many Japanese today are convinced that the squabbles over whaling are neither ecological nor ethical questions at all. Rather, some see the whaling issue in a broader perspective in which trade friction and security questions also play important parts. 'The more economic progress Japan achieves', the novelist Shichibei Yamamoto wrote in 1986, 'the more the whaling issues escalates'. Misaki (1994: 31) points out that an image of Japan as 'inhabited by millions of untiring workaholics, in an inhuman land' fits perfectly with another image of Japan as the 'environmental public enemy No. 1'. The whaling controversy, then, is seen in light of Japan-bashing in general. In the words of Kazuo Sumi (1989: 344), a professor of international law in Yokohama, 'the U.S. government has taken advantage of the whaling issues as a political means of stirring up mistrust of Japan'. The whaling issue has triggered a national discourse in which the Japanese are victims of Western racial prejudices.

Clearly, we should not take such claims at face value. After all, the Faroe Islands, Iceland and Norway have also been criticized for whaling. But the Japanese nonetheless seem to have a point. They have, more than the Norwegians who openly hunt whales for commercial purposes, been singled out for attacks at IWC meetings. One commissioner told me that he 'did not like the Japanese attitude', and another confessed that 'many western delegates oppose or throw suspicions on whatever the Japanese say at the IWC meetings', adding that in the IWC Japan was punished for what these Westerners perceived as the outrageous behaviour of Japanese loggers and fishers around the world. There is a widespread belief among Japanese, but also elsewhere, that the moratorium was aimed first and foremost at Japanese whaling (Caron 1995).

There has developed a sense of mutual distrust between Western countries opposed to whaling and Japan, and it is sometimes a small step from verbal abuse to physical violence. Being the most physically recognizable group among the representatives of whaling countries, Japanese delegates have more than once been spread by red paint or been spat at during IWC meetings—in 1978 accompanied by yells of 'you bloody whale eaters!' (Iwasaki-Goodman 1994: 11). In 1992 a Korean delegate, mistaken for being Japanese, was attacked by a mob outside the conference hotel. 'While these insults are certainly irritating', writes Shigeko Misaki (1994: 24), who has been both dyed red and spat at, 'they are no more than the top of an enormous iceberg'. The insults are important factors in understanding prevailing Japanese attitudes towards the IWC and their perception that the campaigns against whaling to be racist.

The Western cultural critique may hurt the pride of some Japanese, but it also fuels an internal Japanese discourse, *nihonjinron*, e.g. that the Japanese are uniquely special. We are, for example, repeatedly told that the Japanese are unique in having a whale cuisine, and it is even argued that whale meat 'suits the constitution of Japanese people'.[20] But the Japanese are not unique in eating whale products. Nor can whale meat be said to constitute a traditional food for all Japanese or be said to have had a special place in the Japanese *national* culture. Traditional whale cuisine was largely confined to certain regions where there developed strong, local preferences about species to consume and methods of preparing the meat (Akimichi et al. 1988; Kalland 1989a; Kalland and Moeran 1992; Manderson and Akatsu 1993). With the spread of the whaling industry towards the northeast as of the early twentieth century (cf. Kalland 1989b; Kalland and Moeran 1992), new regions in Tohoku and Hokkaido took to eating whale meat, and new local preferences emerged.

Three developments stimulated whale consumption at the national level: the use of canned whale meat by the military in the prewar period, food shortages during the first postwar years, and the use of whale meat in school lunches. But what has turned whale meat into an important ingredient of the national cuisine is the symbolic value of the meat. The anti-whaling campaigns have turned whale meat into a symbol for Japanese culture, and eating whale meat has acquired a new meaning: it has become a ritual act through which the partakers express their belonging to the Japanese tribe, not only to a local community as before. Eating whale meat sets the Japanese apart from others; that some other people do eat such meat is simply ignored in this context. The Japanese thus become unique, and the whaling issue serves to strengthen the cherished Japanese myths about their identity, which themselves help fuel one form of Japanese nationalism. Certainly the whaling issue has been used for the purpose of stirring national sentiments in Japan, just as it has been used for a different kind of nationalism in the United States.

The moratorium has affected Japanese whaling communities in different ways. Each of the whaling communities has had unique experiences with whales and the anti-whaling campaigns, and these are being integrated into community histories and ritual life. Some communities have taken up the challenge and managed to appropriate part of the anti-whaling rhetoric to their advantage, giving whales and whaling new symbolic meanings. Japanese communities look to their past in an attempt to create a sense of *furusato* ('my old home town') and revitalize their communities. Communities like Ayukawa and Taiji are promoting themselves as 'whale towns' (*kujira-no-machi*), and Katsumoto—made infamous for killing large pods of dolphins around 1980—bills itself as a 'dolphin town' (*iruka-no-machi*). They have invested heavily in whale museums, 'whale-lands' and other whale-related attractions to draw tourists to their towns. Whales and dolphins adorn bridges, gateways, post offices, fire stations and manholes; festivals, music and dances have been reinvented to attract tourists (Takahashi 1987; Kalland and Moeran 1992). No doubt, the international anti-whaling campaigns have created a market not only for whale watching but for whaling-related tourism as well. However, in order to survive in this competitive market the towns have to live up to their image. This means that if they are to continue to be seen as a whale town, they must at least enable the visitors to eat whale meat at their hotels and inns, rather than simply gaze at invented festivals and whale-images on manholes.[21] In the absence of whaling, this has created a new demand for small cetaceans like dolphins and pilot whales.

Consensus is not the same as majority dictatorship. Consensus is, at least as it is understood in Japan, a historic process with its own memory. Decisions are not seen in isolation but in relation to each other. Those who sacrificed their interests to achieve consensus will be remembered, and it is expected that they will get something in return on a later occasion (see Kalland 1981). But the global community—and here the IWC is a prime example—does not seem to operate with such an understanding. The Japanese therefore complain more and more that they never get anything back for all their compliance, and many feel that enough is enough. 'We are not going to cave in any more. It is their turn now, not ours, to consider compromise with us' (Komatsu and Misaki 2001: 166). Similar frustrations are felt in other countries. Whalers have therefore recognized the need to organize themselves in order to challenge the anti-harvest campaigns and fight for the rights given them on paper by many international agreements.

Getting Organized

Whalers have organized themselves in a number of ways to defend their access to natural resources and the international market. Some of these organizations predate the whaling controversies; others have been established more recently in response to international anti-use campaigns. Support for these initiatives is based on a number of criteria, such as ethnic affiliation, place of residence, occupation and so on. Some are confined to a country, or regions thereof, whereas others transcend national borders and are international or intergovernmental organizations. In general, these organizations can be categorized as either management institutions that formulate management policies, or as groups of activists and lobbyist who in various ways seek to influence public opinion as well as the decision making process.

Management Institutions

Since its establishment in 1949, the IWC has been widely recognized as the main international body for regulating catches of large whales. But several whaling nations have become dissatisfied with the organization, claiming that it has been taken over or 'hijacked' by protectionists. Two management organizations have so far been established as a direct response to developments within the IWC. The first was the Alaska Eskimo Whaling Commission (AEWC) in 1977, and the second was the North Atlantic Marine Mammal Commission (NAMMCO) in 1992 with the Faroe Islands, Greenland, Iceland and Norway as members and Canada, Denmark, Japan and Russia as observers.

The AEWC was established when the IWC tried to stop the Alaskan Inuit catches of bowhead whales (Huntington 1992). At that time the Inuit had a considerable amount of money from the petroleum industry at their disposal, and the AEWS was therefore able to bring in experts needed to handle questions related to the management of whaling. Beyond purely legal aspects, the Inuit maintain that their specific historic, cultural and economic relationship with the bowhead whales strengthens their claims to be the rightful managers. The AEWS takes it upon itself the full control over resources, whatever the IWC or the U.S. government may think: 'Despite their recourse to action in federal courts, from the initial ban down to this day, Alaskan Eskimo whalers have never capitulated to federal or international claims to regulation of whaling, staunchly asserting that their aboriginal sovereign unextinguished right to whale also means the right to self-regulation' (Langdon 1984: 45). In practice, however, the AEWC plays a co-management role, with responsibility for managing the bowhead hunt and allocating quotas established by the IWC (Freeman 1989). The Alaskan whalers have also assisted whalers in Chukotka (Russia) in restoring their traditional hunt. One step in that direction was the establishment of the Association of Traditional Marine Mammal Hunters of Chukotka. This body has attempted to document their indigenous knowledge and cultural dependence on gray and bowhead whales, and since 1996 it has participated in the Russian delegations to the IWC and NAMMCO (INWR 2003b: 2).

Whereas the AEWC is a national organization working with quotas and conditions decided by the IWC, NAMMCO is an intergovernmental organization that some member states—particularly Iceland—hoped should 'emphasize a rational approach to marine mammal management' and become a regional alternative to the IWC. NAMMCO—with its secretariat in Tromsø (Norway) and its own scientific committee—is both broader and narrower in scope than the IWC. It is narrower in the sense that it is confined to the North Atlantic (although Japan has observer status) and only regional countries can apply for membership, which can be denied by the existing parties (Sanderson 1994: 132). It is broader than the IWC in that it aims at managing hunts of seal, walrus, whale, dolphin and porpoise, rather than just the catches of the large whales. So far, NAMMCO has primarily busied itself with management questions not covered by the IWC, i.e. management of the hunting of small cetaceans and pinnipeds. However, NAMMCO as a possible alternative remains a threat to the IWC. Japan has aired the possibilities with South Korea, Russia and Canada of establishing a similar body for the Northern Pacific, but the time is not yet ripe.

Another regional organization, the Eastern Caribbean Cetacean Commission (ECCO), was established in 2000, and its aim 'shall be to contribute . . . to the conservation, rational management and research of cetaceans in the Eastern Caribbean'. One objective is to survey the stocks of humpback whales, but there is little doubt that a major objective is to venture into the management of small cetaceans and thereby prevent the IWC from doing so. ECCO receives considerable scientific assistance from Japan and Iceland; Norway and NAMMCO have also offered help (INWR 2001: 1–2).

The Joint Commission on Conservation and Management of Narwhal and Beluga (JCCMNB) is narrower still both in terms of area and species covered. Established by Canada and Greenland in 1991, this organization applies to stocks of narwhal and beluga that move between the two countries. Its Scientific Working Group provides advice on the status of these stocks, including estimates of current population size and trends, stock definition, current and historical population harvest and so on. JCCMNB discusses, evaluates and coordinates Canadian and Greenlandic hunting restrictions and management systems and has advised

Greenland to reduce the hunt of beluga. The terms of reference of the Scientific Working Group moreover specify that Inuit knowledge will be incorporated into the management processes, further linking the commission firmly to local co-management arrangements (Goodman 1997).

Although both the AEWC and JCCMNB are regional bodies for the management of Inuit whaling, they are very different. The AEWC is a typical ethnic organization that handles quotas set by the IWC, which involves the AEWC in local as well as international questions in a different way than does JCCMNB. The AEWC has been very successful in its scientific work and management functions (Freeman 1989; Huntington 1992), which may be due to its solid support in each of the bowhead whaling communities. The AEWC has clear management responsibilities, whereas the JCCMNB has more of an advisory role to two national governments in the management of beluga and narwhal hunting.

Interest Groups and Lobbyists

In most countries whalers are organized in hunters' or fishers' associations. Some of these are well established and have for years worked to address a broad spectre of questions related to the members' economic concerns, health, rights and identity. Moreover, some of them actively engage in resource management and may attend IWC meetings as members of national delegations. Among these are the Organization of Fishermen and Hunters in Greenland (*Kalaallit Nunaanni Aalisartut Piniartulla Kattuffiat*, KNAPK), the Pilot Whaler's Association (*Grindemannafelaget*) in the Faroe Islands, the Minke Whaler's Association (*Félag Hrefnuveiðimanna*) in Iceland and the Norwegian Small-Type Whaling Association (*Småkvalfangerlaget*). In Japan whalers engaged in pelagic whaling are organized in the Japan Whaling Association, whereas small-type coastal whalers are organized in the Japan Small-Type Whaling Association and dolphin hunters in local fishing cooperatives. The whalers in St. Vincent and the Grenadines were the last to organize; they established the Bequian Indigenous Whalers' Association in 2002 with the objectives of harmonizing relationships between whalers and community, being an informative and educational force in keeping the island whaling cultural heritage alive in the school system, improving the shore station, insuring improved processing of the whales and enhancing the historical cultural sites associated with the whaling industry (INWR 2002: 2).

The hunters' and fishers' associations are examples of rather traditional political organizations for cooperation and negotiations within a given national framework. However, the international anti-whaling movement has forced these organizations into new roles that they are often not designed or trained to perform. Therefore, new international organizations have been established to respond to the anti-hunting movement. The Inuit Circumpolar Conference, Indigenous Survival International, the High North Alliance and the World Council of Whalers are such organizations.

Threats to the arctic environment and the need to improve the security of the 100,000 Inuit living in Alaska, Canada, Greenland and the Soviet Union brought the Inuit together to form a pan-Inuit organization in 1977, the Inuit Circumpolar Conference (ICC). The objectives of the ICC were twofold: first, to promote and actively participate in long-term management and conservation of arctic and sub-arctic wildlife; and second, to strengthen and support Inuit rights, interests and well-being. To attain these goals, the ICC has developed an environmental policy strategy called the Inuit Regional Conservation Strategy (IRCS). Work on the IRCS started in 1986 and represented the first attempt by an indigenous organization to develop an overall strategy that considers the needs of both modern development and traditional values. In 1988, the ICC received the Global 500 Award from UNEP for significant environmental achievement through the IRCS.

Although the ICC has done much to counter the campaigns of animal rights organizations, a number of other circumpolar indigenous peoples joined with the Inuit to form Indigenous Survival International (ISI) in 1984 to become better able to fight anti-hunting and anti-trapping campaigns and thereby protect their ways of life and livelihoods. ISI actively worked to promote sustainable use of natural resources and contributed an indigenous peoples' perspective that is included in the IUCN/UNEP/WWF World Conservation Strategy. Both the ICC and ISI have worked together with international human rights organizations, including the International Work Group for Indigenous Affairs (IWGIA), and have gained a distinctive position within international conservation organizations such as the IUCN.

More recently, two organizations with members drawn from diverse groups have formed to create an international response to attacks on marine mammal hunters. The High North Alliance (HNA, until March 1992 known as Survival in the High North) is an umbrella organization formed in 1990 that now represents the interests of fishers, sealers and whalers in Canada, the Faroe Islands, Greenland, Iceland and Norway. The main objective of the HNA is to defend what it sees as fundamental rights of coastal communities and settlements on the basis of rational utilization of living marine resources according to the sustainable development principles established by the Brundtland Report (WCED 1987). The HNA has fought the anti-harvest movement on a broad front. It is an active NGO during the CITES and IWC meetings (where it published its newsletter *The International Harpoon*). Through a number of public hearings, organizing and participating in conferences and debates with opponents, as well as its web pages and publications, the HNA tries to provide a broad audience with an understanding of the problems that coastal people face on the periphery of Europe and North America.

The other organization to be mentioned is the World Council of Whalers (WCW). Whereas the HNA is limited to the North Atlantic region, WCW is truly global. Growing out of a series of informal meetings between 1992 and

1996, the WCW was formally established in 1997. Its third general assembly, held in Nelson (New Zealand) in 2000 on the invitation of the Maori,[22] was attended by more than 200 people from more than twenty countries, many of them representing indigenous peoples who want to utilize whales, dolphins, porpoises and dugong for nutritious, cultural or economic purposes. Whaling countries like Canada, Greenland, Iceland, Japan, the Faroe Islands, Norway and Russia were represented by both whalers and government officials. Scientific presentations are a central feature of the general assemblies and reflect one of the main objectives of the organization, which is to disseminate information of importance to the public as well as to the whalers themselves. Other objectives are to enhance respect for whaling communities and their cultures, to assist indigenous peoples who want to resume whaling with information and support, and to provide a forum for whalers, governments, researchers and managers to discuss issues related to the sustainability of whale use and whaling societies. The WCW has, for example, provided the Kingdom of Tonga with scientific material on whales and whaling, thus breaking the de facto monopoly on information Australia for many years had enjoyed.[23]

The anti-whaling campaigns have aroused whalers in many different ways. Not only have whaling communities reinterpreted the meanings of their whaling activities and what constitutes a good life, but the anti-whaling campaigns have also caused them to organize themselves along, and across, professional lines both nationally and internationally. Furthermore, whalers have increasingly extended their network to associate with fishers and loggers in the United States, with rural peoples in Zimbabwe and Namibia (fighting for their rights to hunt elephants and seals) and to the global indigenous rights movement. Armed with reports like *Our Common Future* (WCED 1987), *Caring for the Earth* (IUCN et al. 1991), and *Agenda 21* (UNCED 1992), they think they make a strong claim for the legitimacy of sustainable use of natural resources and for their right to take an active role in the management of these resources. Their societies' futures depend on the success of their educational and political endeavours. But the mobilization among the whalers has undoubtedly served to polarize the situation further. Both sides stereotype and demonize their opponents. This will be one of the main focuses of the final chapter.

Notes

1. Of estimated populations of about 25,000 minke whales, 22,000 Bryde's whales, 28,000 sei whales and 102,000 sperm whales in the Northwest Pacific (Komatsu and Misaki 2003: 141–42).

2. Japan has denied such charges, claiming the research is genuine, and refers to an extensive number of scientific reports presented during meetings in the Scientific Committee. For more popular presentations of Japanese research efforts and findings, see e.g. ICR 1989, 1991, 1993, 1995 and *Isana* No.10 (1994). The latter is published by the Japan Whaling Association and reviews the possible interaction between the depleted blue whale stocks in the Antarctic and

the increasing stocks of minke whales, crab-eater seals and penguins. The programme was evaluated in 2006 by the Scientific Committee, which concluded that while the research is not required for management under the RMP, it has the potential to improve management of minke whales in a number of ways (IWC 2008: 39). Furthermore, when anti-whalers take the marketing of meat as proof that this whaling is done for a commercial purpose, the Japanese refer to Article VIII.2 of the ICRW which states that 'any whales taken under these special permits shall so far as practicable be processed and the proceeds shall be dealt with in accordance with directions issued by the Government by which the permit was granted.' Moreover, the income from these proceedings covers only half the research expenses.

3. The Faroes had taken a small number of fin whales for local consumption, but ceased this fishery due to Danish pressure (Olafsson 1990: 132).

4. Large whales were shot by 'hot' harpoons that exploded inside the whales. The reasons for not using such grenades in minke whaling were that a considerable part of the meat on the relatively small animals was destroyed, and that such harpoons were both expensive and dangerous to handle.

5. The wording used here exploits the ambiguity of the term 'conservation' (rather than to use 'preservation') in an attempt not to alienate environmentalists interested in sustainable *use* of resources.

6. It is hotly debated how much of this biomass could be made available for human consumption.

7. As an illustration, it is calculated that Japan must convert almost 7,100 hectares to cattle feed to replace the meat from the 2,260 minke whales Japan caught annually before the moratorium (Frøvik 1995: 64).

8. Most of these documents are included in GoJ (1997). One document that is not included is Akimichi et al. (1988).

9. See Kalland and Sejersen (2005) for a discussion of native and other local peoples' ecological knowledge.

10. One may ask whether such a claim can be documented or whether Sandøe too will be forced to argue á la Roger Payne, though conversely: '[I]n the absence of evidence to the contrary, I will conclude that whales do not make plans for the future, have weaker social relations, and are not as conscious as human beings.'

11. The same claims are put forwards regarding international trade in whale meat. An example is the British minister of fisheries who said, against better knowledge, that Norway's 'attempts to export the meat are illegal' (*BBC News* 13 June 2003). The export is not illegal because Norway objected to the decision to place the minke whale on CITES's list—a point the minister had acknowledged the year before.

12. Article VIII.1 says: 'Notwithstanding anything contained in this Convention any Contracting Government may grant to any of its nationals a special permit authorizing that national to kill, take and treat whales for purposes of scientific research subject to such restrictions as to number and subject to such other conditions as the Contracting Government thinks fit, and the killing, taking and treating of whales in accordance with the provisions of this Article shall be exempt from the operation of this Convention.'

13. See http://www.iwcoffice.org/_documents/table_permit.htm (retrieved 26 April 2008).

14. In 1987 a resolution that made new demands on research whaling was adopted and illegally written into the Schedule as pt.30 (Hoel 1992: 26). The IWC has, with reference to this point, adopted several resolutions against Japanese and Norwegian research whaling (Hoel 1992: 27).

15. Point 1.3.2 of the Chair's Report from the special IWC meeting in October 2002, which details the voting procedure taken when Iceland's voting right as a member was challenged for the third time. This should be read by anyone who wonders why the IWC has gone astray (IWC 2003f: 2–6).

16. They seem to forget that many whalers, particularly along the northern shores of the Pacific, also anthropomorphize whales. Whales and people live in parallel worlds where they worship the same deities and communicate with each other in various ways.
17. See letter to New Zealand, retrieved 5 April 2008 from www.highnorth.no/Library/Policies/cont-nat.htm).
18. The exceptions are landlocked Mali and Mongolia, which became IWC members in 2004 and 2005, respectively. Landlocked members against whaling are Austria, the Czech Republic, Hungary, Luxembourg, San Marino, the Slovak Republic and Switzerland.
19. Greenpeace may also play the fear card and provoke fights (e.g. *The International Harpoon*, no. 2, 25 June 1996; see also Broch 2004).
20. *Culture of seafood: Let's take a new look at healthy whale meat.* Pamphlets published jointly by the Beneficiaries of the Riches of the Sea and the Institute of Cetacean Research, both Tokyo.
21. This is the closest one gets to a whale totem among whalers. Among whalers in Norway it is whaling that is the important symbol, not whales. The old centre of whaling, Sandefjord, is therefore known and promoted as a 'whaling town', not as a 'whale town' as in Japan. Whales are clearly used as emblems, but even in Japan there is no obligation to protect the whales, no homology by which sociocultural differences are expressed through perceived natural differences, and whales do not function metonymically for nature as a whole.
22. The National Museum in Wellington was scheduled to be the venue for the meeting because of its rich collection of Maori artefacts, but the museum changed its mind due to pressure from environmentalists. Public servants among the Maori were furthermore discouraged from attending, lest they risk losing their jobs. The Maori do not intend to start whaling but are seeking to exercise their treaty rights to utilize stranded whales at a time when New Zealand wants to interrupt almost any use of these animals.
23. Tonga caught humpback whales until 1978. In 1999 a wounded humpback was killed and distributed in the capitol Nukualofa. The bones were distributed to craftsmen (INWR 1999).

Chapter 7

Conclusion

International management of renewable natural resources has in recent decades been increasingly influenced by low- and no-use philosophies. The management of whales is an excellent example of this trend. In the 1970s, when the international environmental and animal welfare movements gained momentum, whaling was among the activists' first targets, and the IWC figured prominently in their strategies to put environmental issues on the international agenda. Once said to be a 'whaling club', this shift in focus has turned the IWC into a 'preservation club' (Chapter 4). Today there is a strong lobby within the IWC that wants to exclude cetaceans from all lethal usage. According to this view, whales are uniquely special and should not be available for human consumption in any way. At the IWC this view is most forcefully promoted by Australia and New Zealand.

The whale protectionists have achieved this apparent success through two partly overlapping strategies: first to secure for the IWC a de facto monopoly over management of whales, and then to take control over the IWC itself. The former was attained by bringing whaling operations by nationals of countries outside the IWC to an end. Control over the IWC was attained by recruiting new, anti-whaling nations to the IWC in order to obtain the three-quarters majority required to make the necessary Schedule amendments to impose the whaling moratorium (adopted in 1982) and to establish the Southern Sanctuary (adopted in 1994). These have been important steps in turning whales into a common property resource.

To claim that whales are a global resource or a common heritage of humankind constitutes the final stage in the appropriation of whales by non-whalers, a process that started centuries ago with a gradual appropriation by national authorities. With this idea of whales as a common, global resource rather than an open, free resource, landlocked countries like Switzerland as well as the environmental and animal rights activists can legitimately claim the same rights to participate in managing cetaceans as peoples for whom whaling is a way of life.

As a matter of fact, Switzerland, Austria and other nations that have never caught a single whale may have more influence in the IWC than indigenous peoples, who are not even recognized as contracting partners to the whaling convention and must therefore be represented by their 'colonial' governments (i.e. Denmark, Russia and the United States).

In this book I have aimed to investigate how this transformation has been achieved. I have argued that cetaceans have symbolic significance in many cultures (1) because they are difficult to fit into our broad schemes of (mainly) terrestrial mammals and marine fish, (2) because some species have special physical traits (size and form), and (3) because they move in a medium that is both clean in ritual context (salt water) and unknown (allowing for fantasies and mystification). This starting point has been used to construct a 'superwhale' that combines traits taken from many different cetacean species. The superwhale has been endowed with human characteristics (anthropomorphized) and has been used as a cultural critique against modern society. It is too special to be hunted and therefore, as pointed out by Heazle (2006: 173), the superwhale has also downgraded the relevance of science.

The anti-whaling movement is complex and brings together individuals with very different perspectives and aims, ranging from people who are genuinely worried that whales may be exterminated, to people who think that whales should simply be left in peace, to those who regard cetaceans as messengers from space. Despite their different perspectives and strategies, they share the objective of protecting cetaceans. And to a certain extent they have succeeded, by combining arguments from a variety of discourses on ecology and on animal welfare/rights. But among whale savers there has been a shift from an ecological perspective to a focus on animal welfare and rights. Among the pro-whalers there has been a similar transition from economic to cultural arguments. There are at least two reasons for these shifts. First, it has become more difficult to defend the moratorium on commercial whaling on ecological grounds. Second, it is difficult for rich countries with low unemployment rates to defend whaling in economic terms. These shifts in arguments have further contributed to the polarization of the conflict.

Schismogenesis

The polarization emerges in several ways. Whalers have been targeted for verbal and physical abuse, and a totemic world view has been constructed in which whalers are cast as greedy and brutal enemies of nature while whales and their protectionists defend everything that is good. Even as whale savers organize boycotts and try to change people's attitudes in order to destroy traditional markets for whale products, the superwhale symbol is marketed through whale tourism, literature, movies, theme parks, adoption programmes and research. Appadurai refers to this situation as 'diversion of commodities from their preordained path' (1986: 26). One such kind of diversion is theft, and many whalers see sales and adoptions of whales—and here they include the sales of whale images that have contributed so importantly to the finances of environmental and animal rights groups—as theft: not only of the whales, which they feel belong to them through several generations' involvement in whaling, but theft of their livelihood, pride and culture.

The polarization is not least apparent in the IWC, which for all practical purposes has ceased to work as intended. In almost all matters being discussed the assembly is divided into two blocs opposing each other: the like-minded group that works for a permanent ban on whaling for commercial purposes, and the pro-whaling faction that accepts sustainable use of whale stocks. Bateson (1958: 175) has defined schismogenesis as 'a process of differentiation in the norms of individual behaviour resulting from cumulative interaction between individuals'. This can cause a vicious circle. A's action toward B triggers a reaction from the latter, which in turn further adds to A's action, and so on. An arms race (e.g. between the U.S. and the Soviet Union) can be viewed as a *symmetric* schismogenesis: each rearms because the other does. The vicious circle can only be broken through negotiations or if one of them gives up. The other can then choose between disarming (in which case the situation remain symmetric) or exploiting the situation by using its new relative strength to subdue its adversary. In such a *complementary* schismogenesis a situation may arise where one party grows increasingly arrogant and the other increasingly subdued. (The relations between the U.S. and Russia in the first years after the collapse of the Soviet Union can serve as an example.)

The development within the IWC during the 1970s can be viewed as a complementary schismogenesis. Whale protectionists became increasingly influential in the organization, and most of the new members at the time were against whaling. Whaling nations were slow to recognize the threat and were inclined to compromise in order to build goodwill and understanding. Only after the vote for the moratorium in 1982—and particularly after 1990, when it became clear that the moratorium would not be lifted as originally believed—did whaling nations really mobilize. The number of NGOs working for the whalers has increased since the enforcement of the moratorium; many new countries supportive of whaling have been recruited to the IWC, and some countries originally recruited by anti-whaling NGOs in the late 1970s and early 1980s have changed sides. The schismogenesis has become more symmetric, which has opened what Ottar Brox has called 'expressive competition', in which people and groups of people *within* each position try to outdo each other in expressing commitments to common shared values (Brox 2000: 389). Most of the rhetoric is not meant for the opponents but aims to tell that the speaker is more committed to the cause than his or her fellow adherents are.

We have seen that whalers and whale protectionists have partly used similar arguments. Discourses on both sides can be seen as bundles of more specialized discourses, which partly overlap. The discourse against whaling has mainly been carried out with arguments from discourses on biodiversity, animal welfare and rights, and international law, whereas the discourse in favour of whaling has fetched arguments from discourses on biodiversity, animal welfare, cultural diversity and international law. It is obvious that there is no common ground between whalers and animal rights advocates, but most whale protectionists are not animal rights supporters. On the other hand, both environmentalists and whalers stress the importance of sustainable use of natural resources and biodiversity. And both sides believe that animals should be treated humanely. Hence, some basic values are apparently shared and a dialogue ought to be possible.

All major Norwegian environmental organizations support Norwegian minke whaling, recognizing that it can be done sustainably and legitimately according to international law. Many international NGOs as well as leading IWC member countries, on the other hand, continue their campaigns against whaling. They do this partly by using arguments of scientific uncertainty and the precautionary principle and partly by changing their own rhetoric in order to undercommunicate what both sides can agree upon. Moreover, rather than an understanding being built on shared values, there has evolved a conflict about ownership of these values. An important element in this competition is that each side denies the other legitimate access to these values and discredits the other in many ways. They not only undercommunicate common ground, but they strongly deny that shared values in fact exist. 'It is indeed a common social process that people separate very completely their own ways of behaviour and values from those of members they oppose' (Broch 1994: 211). Whaling is no longer solely a question of sustainability, but it now extends to identity management (Kalland 2001). Indeed, Robert Hunter, one of the founding fathers of Greenpeace, was of the opinion that the ability to see the other's point of view only weakens one's commitment to the cause (cited in Milton 1993: 7). Let us summarize the rhetoric used.

Whereas whalers like to present themselves as ecologically concerned citizens engaged in honest productive work for the common good of society, some anti-whalers do their utmost to present a different image. They claim that whalers are ecologically ignorant (see Broch 1994: 204) and deny that whalers are engaged in sustainable activities, portraying them as greedy butchers 'willing to wipe out the world's last whales for profit' (*Today* 28 May 1991). Moreover, anti-whalers may paint a negative picture of whale products. The meat, which is said to be dangerously contaminated, is presented as a luxury for the privileged few who have no legitimate need of it. Moreover, some activists claim that whalers are pirates and poachers breaking international laws—although some have recognized that Iceland, Japan and Norway follow the ICRW to the letter—and view whaling countries as exploiting loopholes in the convention.

The whalers' argument about cultural diversity is also refuted by the whale protectionists. Whereas most NGOs accept that indigenous peoples hunt whales to meet cultural needs, they deny that non-indigenous peoples have such needs.

Japanese and Norwegian whalers have become an anachronism in the modern world. To say 'no' to whaling is to be civilized. Several leading figures within the anti-whaling movement seem to believe in a unilinear evolution, from primitive societies that need to catch whales to survive, to civilized society that can let the whales live. This rhetoric depicts whalers as very different from the image they themselves try to convey. In an attempt to monopolize the discourses on bio-diversity and animal welfare, whale protectionists refute that whalers have any concern for resource depletion and animal welfare, or indeed, that commercial whalers have any culture at all. Instead whalers are presented as being motivated only by a narrow quest for money.

We can discern a similar process in the other direction. Environmentalists and animal rights advocates like to present themselves as protectors of biodiversity and animal welfare. 'When the Earth is sick the animals will begin to disappear. Then the rainbow warriors will go out and save them', proclaimed a Danish Greenpeace poster. It is exactly this image that whalers try to destroy, by questioning whether whale protectionists really are motivated by concern for biodiversity and animal welfare and by casting doubt on their integrity. 'Crazy greens' is the term whalers often use for the activists.

Perhaps the most common accusation against the whale protectionists is that they are irrational and led by emotions, whereas sustainable resource management must be built on science. Pro-whalers claim that by protecting 'charismatic megafauna'—animals that often are at the top of the food chain—the activists in fact create an imbalance in the ecosystem. According to whalers, biodiversity is best achieved by using multi-species management models where all levels in the chain are harvested. They also question to what extent the activists are genuinely concerned about animal welfare. When Greenpeace managed to cut a harpoon line, preventing the whalers from killing an animal quickly, the Norwegian press wrote about the immense suffering this action may have caused. The defenders of whaling claim that whaling in many ways is more humane than modern husbandry of pigs and chicken, a view supported by the chairman of the Danish Ethical Council Concerning Animals, Peter Sandøe, who would rather be a harpooned whale than a pig on a modern farm. He argues that we have to take the quality of the animal's whole life into consideration instead of focusing solely on the slaughter.

In this way whalers and others who defend whaling try to discredit their adversaries' real intentions and deny them ownership of discourses on biodiversity and animal welfare. The whale protectionists are depicted as animal rights villains and/or cynical profit-seekers employed by multinational concerns like Greenpeace and the WWF to earn money by exploiting people's well-meaning environmental concerns. Meanwhile, anti-whaling advocates are accused of cultural imperialism and racism. Both Greenpeace and particularly Sea Shepherd are accused of terrorism and putting animals before people. Finally, the integrity of individuals may be questioned, as when the Norwegian tabloid press repeatedly pointed out that a prominent activist has a past as nude playmate in *Playboy* magazine. Both sides of the divide, then, reduce the others to stereotypes.

Even if there is agreement as to how nature should be valued, a conflict may emerge as to the ownership of those values. Both environmentalists and people who harvest from nature, therefore, emphasize aspects mirroring values that are believed to be shared by most people: sustainable use of natural resources, biodiversity, decentralization, tradition and cultural diversity. The actors on both sides compete for ownership of these values, partly by telling about their own excellence and partly by portraying the other side as solely motivated by economic self-interest. In this way two meganarratives about whaling are constructed. According to one, which until recently was hegemonic, whales are threatened with extinction, it is impossible to manage whaling in a sustainable manner and the hunt is inhumane. Whales are depicted as very special animals—to many they are the humans of the oceans—that deserve rights comparable to those enjoyed by human beings. The heroes in this narrative are the whales and their human protectors, whereas the villains are the whalers and the whaling nations. The narrators are environmental and animal rights advocates in the industrial Western world, part of the international media (including Hollywood) and about half the governments represented at the IWC.

In the other narrative, whaling is depicted as humane, at least compared to other forms of hunting and to modern animal husbandry. It quotes science to the effect that some whale stocks can be harvested sustainably, and claims that the whalers are the first to value conservation. The bad guys in this narrative are the international environmental movement, foreign press and governments, particularly those of the U.S., the U.K., Australia and New Zealand. The heroes are the whalers, who are portrayed as environmentally conscious and knowledgeable practitioners of a trade that produces healthy food (as least until the oceans became polluted by emissions from the very same countries that are against whaling) who thus contribute to the prosperity of local communities and national security. Alongside the whalers themselves, the narrators of this story are governments, media and the majority of the people living in whaling countries. In Norway all the major environmental NGOs are also among the tellers of this narrative.

There are other, more balanced narratives that probably would be attractive to most people. But these narratives are given little space in the media and remain largely unorganized and unarticulated. We are therefore left with two very distinct and mutually exclusive narratives, where arguments and motives of the other side are demonized and stereotyped. A feature that has strengthened this tendency is the rare alliances formed in the whaling conflict. In most environmental conflicts we find authorities and industrialists opposed by environmental and animal rights activists. However, in the case of whaling alliances are formed across these lines. This is quite apparent during the IWC meetings, which are divided into two camps of almost equal size. On one side is the like-minded group of anti-whaling countries supported by most of the international NGOs and media. On the other side are the whalers, their governments and most of the national NGOs and press.

A Contest over Symbols

Peoples' perceptions of nature have undergone radical changes, particularly in the Anglo-American world. Nature has increasingly been associated with wilderness, the part of the physical environment that is believed to remain undisturbed by human beings: rainforests, African savannahs, the Arctic and the depths of the oceans. These are often depicted as Edenic gardens (Slater 1995) where animals, plants, birds and rocks coexist in blissful harmony, idylls that are vulnerable to human encroachment. In such a world view human beings are evil and should therefore be kept out of the garden. The solution is to protect parts of nature by establishing national parks, nature reserves, sanctuaries or biosphere areas. Similarly, it is possible to enclose certain species through protective legislation.

The IUCN, WWF and other international organizations have worked hard to promote preservation of species and habitats, urging the establishment of national parks and sanctuaries in Third World countries, which are often tempted by attractive proposals to develop tourist facilities. Eco-tourism is seen as a new promising source of foreign capital by many poor countries in Africa, Asia and Latin America. Governments have also established parks and nature reserves for the sake of national pride and to partake in a global trend. However, because restrictions are often imposed on traditional use of the areas and resources in question, nature preservation not infrequently conflicts with the interests of the local people (e.g. McNeely and Pitt 1985; Dasmann 1988; Homewood and Rodgers 1988; Poole 1989; West and Brechin 1991; Wenzel 1991; Lynge 1992; McNeely 1993; Harper 2002; Brockington 2002; Igoe 2003; Satterfield 2003; Walley 2004).

The many people who make a living from using natural resources are vulnerable to political decisions influenced by environmental and nature rights ideologies. This applies in particular to non-indigenous people. Hence Faroese, Icelandic, Japanese and Norwegian whalers are condemned, whereas the attitude towards Inuit and Makah whalers is more ambivalent. The romantics have often expressed a feeling of sympathy for indigenous peoples, who are seen as part of nature, at least as long as they do not produce for the market and partake in the world economy. But as we have seen, many environmentalists hold indigenous peoples' rights to nature to be incompatible with modern technology and development. 'Sure, natives should have a place in the wilderness, *but should they be allowed* to bring their rifles and snowmobiles with them?' asks Patrick Moore of Greenpeace (Pearce 1991: 43, emphasis added). This quote underlines how one of the organization's leaders (and certainly leaders of many other environmental and animal welfare/rights organizations) believes outsiders have a right to make decisions about how people are to organize their lives. The nature romantics thus place indigenous peoples in an impossible dilemma: we accept that you hunt, as long as you behave like an ecological savage. Hence indigenous whalers may gradually lose environmentalists' sympathy once they claim rights to participate in the world economy and to develop on their own terms, according to their own values (e.g. Conklin and Graham 1995). Indigenous peoples are becoming humanized with desires and priorities consciously made upon cultural values and not dictated by natural instincts. No longer regarded as noble savages in the world view of the nature romantics, they are losing their innocence and thereby their right to reside in the Garden of Eden.

Nowadays, anti-whaling campaigns, as the whalers see them, are not aimed at saving whales from extermination. Even among the campaigners many know that most whales are no longer threatened. But whales and whaling have become symbols for both parties. I have repeatedly argued that whales easily are given symbolic significance, and industrial whaling has an ugly history that makes it a powerful symbol of our overexploitation of natural resources. Whaling has become a metonym for all our problematic relations with nature. To fight against whaling has become a measurement of being civilized (Chapter 2). That the costs are externalized—i.e. are paid by others who live in distant countries—makes the whaling issue popular among politicians and governments without whalers to consider. To many activists a whale is no longer regarded as a natural resource but as a person (Milton 2002). A Norwegian colleague of mine has argued against whaling because whales have become symbols to many people, and we ought to respect their symbol. Moreover, he claims that this symbol has contributed positively to higher environmental awareness among large groups of people worldwide. Similar sentiments are held by many whale protectionists.

Of course the notion that we ought to respect each other's symbols is widely held. Defilement of national symbols, such as burning a flag, is a powerful expression of anger and protest. Similarly, eating whale meat, i.e. eating the totem animal of environmental and animal rights groups, has for some people become a means to express their indignation about what they conceive as outsiders' infringement on their customary rights to harvest not only whales but marine resources in general. For many years Norwegian fishers have had the feeling that they are losing influence over local resources to the national bureaucracy and increasingly to international bodies. For them, whaling has become a symbol of their right to harvest local resources in a sustainable way. They repeatedly ask themselves and each other: 'If we give up whaling, what will be next?'

Thanks to the international campaigns, whaling has become invested with symbolic significance far beyond the ranks of the whalers. Some people have claimed that the Norwegian decision in 1992 to resume whaling was motivated by domestic politics: the government needed to strengthen its electoral base in Northern Norway before the parliamentary elections in 1993 and the EU referendum the following year (e.g. Clifton 1994). To start whaling amidst foreign protests certainly indicated firmness and national sentiment and was a sure winner. More important, however, is that whaling has become a symbol of both national sovereignty and the principle of sustainable use of natural resources. These two symbolic fronts have been at the forefront of the pro-whaling advocates' rhetoric. National authorities and scientists are more likely to emphasize the importance of sustainability. If we are to understand why such an insignificant industry has received so much attention in Japan and Norway, these larger issues must be considered. To people depending on marine resources as well as to the authorities, the principle of sustainable use has been important. In this *anthropocentric* perspective, whaling and lethal research are both legitimate activities. To governments of whaling nations, whaling has become a symbol of national sovereignty. Thus whales and whaling have taken on new symbolic meanings to the whalers and the whaling nations as well. For many people whaling spurs nationalistic sentiments, particularly when one's country is threatened with sanctions from abroad (Brydon 1990; Joensen 1993; Kalland 1998). For many Norwegians and Japanese, defending whaling becomes a question of patriotism (Rothenberg 1995: 217).

This does not mean that whales and whaling were not loaded with symbolic significance before the anti-whaling campaigns were launched. On the contrary, whales and whaling have long been powerful symbols to whalers in Alaska (Braund, Armstrong and Stroker 1984), Canada (Freeman, Wein and Keith 1992; Freeman et al. 1998), the Faroe Islands (Wylie and Margolin 1981; Joensen 1990), Greenland (Sejersen 1998), Japan (Kalland and Moeran 1992) and Norway (ISG 1992). In all whaling societies, rules govern how the animal shall be shared or the profit used in order to reproduce the social and cosmic order (Moeran 1992). At a more general level, whaling is a way of life and must be seen 'as a process whereby hunters mutually create and recreate *one another*, through the medium of their encounter with prey' (Ingold 1986: 111). Whales typically constitute multi-vocal symbols in that they convey several meanings simultaneously, and no particular meaning deserves a priori more respect than the others.

The superwhale might have contributed to a higher environmental awareness among people, but we have to ask at what cost. The campaigns against whaling have triggered nationalistic sentiments in Iceland (Brydon 1991) and Japan (Kalland and Moeran 1992), have turned coastal people against environmental organizations and have turned whale eating into ritual consumption of the enemies' totem animal. Worse, the campaigns have distracted attention from issues of greater importance to the global environment to produce a symbol that individuals and corporations can afford to buy. The totem is for sale, and one can buy a place in the sun, as well as green legitimacy, by joining the flock of 'converts'.

The Common Heritage of Humankind

During the last twenty or thirty years we have witnessed the emergence of a new discourse on property rights, i.e. that some natural resources are the 'common heritage of humankind' (CHH). Among the first to express the idea that resources can belong to everybody was the Argentine lawyer José León Suárez, who in 1927 on behalf of the League of Nations proposed that marine life—and whales in particular—belong to humankind (*patrimoine de l'humanité*) (Société des Nations 1927: 123). But it is Arvid Pardo, Maltese ambassador to the UN, who is given the credit for taking up the term when he suggested at the UN General Assembly in 1967 that resources from the high seas should be conceptualized as CHH. The rationale at the time was to prevent all the benefits being reaped by the handful of powerful countries that possessed the technological and economic strength to harvest these resources. He argued that all nations, whether coastal or landlocked, should benefit equally (Pardo 1993). According to Tullio Scovazzi (2006), professor of international law, the concept implies a third kind of regime in addition to sovereignty, which applies in territorial waters, and the scheme of freedom, which applies on the high seas. When the concept was incorporated into the UN Convention on the Law of the Sea (UNCLOS) its applicability was, however, limited to commercial exploitation of minerals located on the deep seabed. Living resources were explicitly excluded. The International Seabed Authority was established to organize and control the extraction activities. As of February 2007 ISA had 153 member countries, and the U.S. was the only power that had not ratified UNCLOS and hence was not a member of this truly global management body.

The CHH concept was first coined to address management problems related to *res nullius* situations—i.e. resources that had not been claimed and were under nobody's jurisdiction: the exploitation of outer space, seabed beyond national economic zones and Antarctica. The concept was picked up by UNESCO in its work to preserve sites that are not only of national interest but have important cultural or natural value to humanity at large. Such sites, however, are located within national borders and are therefore managed by national bodies. The concept is today not limited to *res nullius* situations and the UNESCO World Heritage list but has, according to Rusen Keles (1997), Director of Environmental Studies at Ankara University, become one of the most widely pronounced concepts in modern environmentalism.

Most people hardly reflect over what the concept means or implies. It is taken as a positive recognition that some resources or sites are particularly valuable, and most people feel a sense of national pride when a site in their country is added to the UNESCO list. Contrary to Pardo's intention to ensure that extraction of natural resources benefits all, it can be argued that CHH has become an important rhetorical device for appropriating resources at other people's expense. A problem with the concept is that it opens up natural resources for new kinds of interest groups. If a resource like a rainforest or a type of whale belongs to everybody, everybody is potentially a stakeholder and has a legitimate right to participate in its management. As a consequence local communities have lost influence over, and even access to, the natural resources on which they have depended.

Whales are no longer a local resource that is meaningful only to whalers but have acquired symbolic significance for millions of people, most of whom have never seen a whale. Indeed, whales are increasingly regarded as a CHH that should be managed by international organs. Whale protectionists therefore try to establish the IWC as the sole body for the management of cetaceans, which is a prerequisite for a global appropriation of whales. But unlike nation states that possess means to expropriate individual rights and claims to resources with references to a common good, the IWC at present lacks such means. Direct actions carried out by NGOs and U.S. threats of trade sanctions against any country that 'diminishes the effectiveness of an international fishery or wildlife conservation agreement' have forced most whaling countries to comply.

It is the concept of CHH that, in the eyes of the protectionists, legitimizes their actions and coercion. Whales have become our common heritage through the same processes by which physical environs in many countries have been transferred from a local to a national level. Whales were attractive as CHH because an intergovernmental body for management of whaling (the IWC) already existed, because whales move largely in deterritorialized space outside national control and because whales can easily be given symbolic significance. Industrial whaling has a history of reckless depletion of many stocks and has come to represent human greed towards nature. A general mystique has been spun around whales. Whales are good to think with. They are widely described in scientific and popular literature, and they glide across television screens while narrators tell of their intelligence and social life. Through numerous websites people can buy books and movies in addition to 'whale music', T-shirts, soft toys and other whale emblems (Chapter 3). Whales have become a resource for the 'global village'. And as with sites of national significance, people penetrate the world of whales via whale tourism, swim programmes and rescues. In this way images of whales are produced that are quite different from those held by the whalers.

Redefining a resource from open access to CHH invites new stakeholders— or outsiders, as they are perceived by traditional users—who may demand full participation in its management, often based on alternative values. They may be motivated by economic interest, as in the case of ecotourism, by aesthetic and recreational considerations or by the desire to safeguard biodiversity. When a CHH resource—which means that it is also *mine*—is pictured as endangered, its loss thereby threatening the life quality of *my* descendants, this may legitimate *my* intervention in other people's access to the same resource. Whalers have been confronted by new and, to them, incomprehensible ways to claim rights to whales, through other people's rules and sanctions. They have been displaced because the new and more powerful stakeholders have not been content to offer new ways to appreciate whales but demand a closure of the old ways, i.e. demand a full diversion of the whale's commodity path.

This raises important questions about participation and democracy. At the national level, a majority can, through 'democratic' processes, decide how natural resources are to be used. And because most people live in cities, the interests of rural people are often pushed aside. However, the political process may take time, and when a resource is held to be threatened we are often told that the matter is urgent and we have no time to waste. Democracy can easily be viewed as a luxury in such a scenario, and most environmental NGOs are fundamentally undemocratic in their organization.

This is even more pronounced at the international level where political processes are slower. At this level, democracy may be understood in two ways: either one nation, one vote or one person, one vote. In the IWC each member nation has one vote, whether it is a whaling country or not. This gives landlocked countries like Switzerland, Mali, Mongolia and San Marino more influence than whaling nations like Greenland, the Faroe Islands and the Alaskan Inuit, who have no delegations of their own and therefore have no voting rights. However, Roger Payne, a well-known researcher of humpback songs and the former IWC commissioner for Antigua, argues for a global democracy where each person has one vote. In this perspective Iceland becomes very small indeed, as for each Icelander there are 21,000 non-Icelanders (Payne 1995: 296). Payne continues this line of reasoning by making a list of 136 cities in India and China with larger populations than Iceland.[1] When New Zealand, in the opening statement to the 1994 meeting, justified its resistance to commercial whaling with reference to 'world opinion' (New Zealand 1994) it is unclear whether the world opinion referred to the situation in the IWC (where only a minority of the countries in the world are members) or to democracy in Payne's sense.

No study actually tells us what the world opinion is. How is world opinion defined, and how is it formed? A minority of the world's nations are members of the IWC, and other international bodies with larger memberships have not taken the IWC's position. A majority at CITES has voted for a declassification of the Northeast Atlantic minke whale, and both UNCLOS and UNCED 1992 recognize whales as a natural resource. Moreover, opinion polls in major anti-whaling countries show that people are not overwhelmingly against whaling if they are informed that the whale stocks in question are not endangered. In 1998 the U.S.-based public opinion survey firm Responsive Management released a survey showing that 71 per cent of U.S. respondents endorsed regulated catches of minke whales when they were told that this can be done sustainably. The similar figures for Australia, United Kingdom and Germany were 53, 61 and 63 per cent (cited in Aron, Burke and Freeman 1999, 2000). To most Japanese this 'world opinion' means the opinion of some Western activists who, for dubious reasons, are supported by certain governments. But if a majority of the people on earth were opposed to whaling—and no survey indicates that this is the case—it does not follow that this majority has the right to enforce its perceptions on the minority. To impose this opinion on the rest of mankind is, according to the view of most whalers, cultural imperialism.

The attempt to turn whales into a global resource under the sole management of the IWC has so far been a qualified success. If a CHH regime is to work properly, it is necessary to make compromises and seek consensus. Democracy— whether the IWC's one nation, one vote or a global system of one person, one vote—is ill suited to handle such situations. Any institution that harbours ambitions to manage the utilization of natural resources must secure the interests of the minorities. This is where the IWC has failed. The majority, with its many new stakeholders, has made it almost impossible to make compromises that could have secured multiple usages of whale resources.

The appropriation of whales by outsiders, although it has gone further than for any other natural resource, is but a part of a more general trend. Since the dawn of the industrial revolution, the industrial world has laid claim to more and more of the world's natural resources, not only through their extraction—by way of mining, fishing, cattle ranching, food export, and so on—but through nature preservation as well. The process started with the emergence of the nation state, which has been very apt at defining itself as a commons exactly because it possesses institutions that by force can both control access to and regulate the use of resources. The process gained momentum in the twentieth century as the state appropriated more and more of the natural resources even as they were opened to new groups of users. This process has continued at the international level, particularly regarding rainforests, large terrestrial animals and marine mammals.[2] But there is one fundamental difference: the global community lacks the power of the nation state to enforce its decisions on dissidents and must rely on the willingness of external powers like the United States and environmental and animal welfare/rights activists to enforce its will on what to many looks like a neocolonial attempt to appropriate other people's natural resources for their own ends.

Notes

1. The irony here is that this argument comes from a person who has represented one of the smallest countries in the IWC, which, after the moratorium decision in 1982, failed to pay its membership fees until 1994, when the anti-whaling bloc needed its vote to establish the Southern Sanctuary.
2. The trade in CO_2 quotas can be seen as the most recent example of the industrial world's infringement on Third World countries.

Bibliography

Aanes, G. 2001. 'Sakseierskap og strategiske posisjoner i medienes miljødekning', in A. Kalland and T. Rønnow (eds), *Miljøkonflikter: Om bruk og vern av naturressurser*. Oslo: Unipub, pp. 201–20.

Aasjord, B. 1991. 'Fredning av vågehval, miljøvern eller etikk?' *Ottar* 184: 48–50.

———. 1993. 'Hvaldebatten og Naturvernforbundets rolle', in N.C. Stenseth, A.H. Hoel, and I.B. Lid (eds), *Vågehvalen—valgets kval*. Oslo: ad Notam-Gyldendal, pp. 167–72.

Abbey, L. 1990. *The Last Whales*. London: Doubleday.

Adams, D. 1986. *The Hitch Hiker's Guide to the Galaxy: A Trilogy in Four Parts*. London: William Heinemann.

Akimichi, T. et al. 1988. *Small-Type Coastal Whaling in Japan*. Edmonton: Boreal Institute for Northern Studies.

Alpers, A. 1960. *A Book of Dolphins*. London: John Murray.

Alvestad, S. 1999. '"We Are Fighting for our Existence": Striden om hvalfangsten i det nordøstlige Atlanterhav 1880–1914', MA (hovedfag) thesis. Bergen: University of Bergen.

Anderson, A. 1993. 'Source-Media Relations: The Production of the Environmental Agenda', in A. Hansen (ed.), *The Mass Media and Environmental Issues*. Leicester: Leicester University Press, pp. 51–68.

Andresen, S. 1989. 'Science and Politics in the International Management of Whales', *Marine Policy* 13(2): 99–117.

Anker, P. 2002. 'Den antiliberale dypøkologien', in P. Anker (ed.), *Miljø og menneske: Kritiske innspill*. Oslo: Gyldendal Akademisk, pp. 53–65.

———. 2007. 'Science as a Vacation: A History of Ecology in Norway', *History of Science* 45(4): 455–79.

Ansolabehere, S. and S. Iyengar. 1994. 'Riding the Wave and Claiming Ownership over Issues', *Political Opinion Quarterly* 58(3): 335–57.

Appadurai, A. 1986. 'Introduction. Commodities and the Politics of Value', in A. Appadurai (ed.), *The Social Life of Things: Commodities in Cultural Perspective*. Cambridge: Cambridge University Press, pp. 3–63.

Aron, W. 1988. 'The Commons Revisited: Thoughts on Marine Mammal Management', *Coastal Management* 16(2): 99–110.

Aron, W., W.T. Burke and M.M.R. Freeman. 1999. 'Flouting the Convention: The Ongoing Campaign to Ban all Commercial Whaling is Driven by Politics rather than Science, and Sets a Terrible Precedent', *Atlantic Monthly* (May): 22–29.

————. 2000. 'The Whaling Issue', *Marine Policy* 34: 179–91.

Asgrímsson, H. 1989. 'Developments Leading to the 1982 Decision of the International Whaling Commission for a Zero Catch Quota 1986–90', in S. Andresen and W. Østreng (eds), *International Resource Management: The Role of Science and Politics*. London: Belhaven Press, pp. 221–31.

AWI (The Animal Welfare Institute). 2007. 'Animal Welfare Institute Positions on Aboriginal Subsistence Whaling Issues at IWC59', campaign material.

Bakhtin, M. 1986. *Speech Genres and Other Late Essays by M.M. Bakhtin*. Austin: University of Texas.

Barnes, R.H. 1996. *Sea Hunters of Indonesia*. Oxford: Clarendon Press.

Barstow, R. 1989. 'Beyond Whale Species Survival: Peaceful Coexistence and Mutual Enrichment as a Basis for Human/Cetacean Relations', *Sonar* 2 (Autmn): 10–13.

————. 1991. 'Whales are Uniquely Special', in N. Davies et al. (eds), *Why Whales?* Bath: WDCS, pp. 4–7.

Barzdo, J. 1981. 'The Slaughter of Whales'. Report. Horsham, Sussex: The Royal Society for the Prevention of Cruelty to Animals.

Basso, K.H. 1996. *Wisdom Sits in Places: Landscape and Language among the Western Apache*. Albuquerque: University of New Mexico Press.

Bateson, G. 1958. *Naven*. Stanford, CA: Stanford University Press.

————. 1973. *Steps to Ecology of Mind*. Frogmore: Paladin.

Beach, D. and M.T. Weinrich. 1989. 'Watching the Whales: Is an Educational Adventure for Humans Turning Out to Be Another Threat for Endangered Species?" *Oceanus* 32(1): 84–88.

Beinart, P. 1995. 'Activism: Watching the Fur Fly', *The Globe and Mail* (9 December).

Bentham, J. 1960 [1789]. *An Introduction to the Principles of Morals and Legislation*. Oxford: Basil Blackwell.

Benton, T. 1993. *Natural Relations: Ecology, Animal Rights and Social Justice*. London: Verso.

Berzin, A.A. 2008. 'The Truth About Soviet Whaling: A Memoir', *Marine Fisheries Review* 70(2) Special Issue. Washington DC: U.S. Department of Commerce.

Birnie, P. 1985. *International Regulation of Whaling: From Conservation of Whaling to Conservation of Whales and Regulation of Whale-watching*. New York: Oceana.

————. 1989. 'International Legal Issues in the Management and Protection of the Whale: A Review of Four Decades of Experience', *Natural Resources Journal* 29(4): 903–34.

Bjørndal, T. and A. Toft. 1994. 'Økonomiske verknader av boikottaksjonar mot norsk næringsliv grunna norsk kvalfangst [Economic effects of boycotts of Norwegian industry due to Norwegian whaling]', Report to the Norwegian Foreign Ministry.

Blichfeldt, G. 1993. 'An Insight into the Ethical Arguments', in G. Blichfeldt (ed.), *11 Essays on Whales and Man*. Reine, Norway: High North Alliance, pp. 12–15.

Blix, A.S., L. Walløe and Ø. Ulltang (eds). 1995. *Whales, Seals, Fish and Man*. Amsterdam: Elsevier Science B.V.

Bloch, D., G. Desportes, K. Hoydal and P. Jean. 1990. 'Pilot Whaling in the Faroe Islands: July 1986–July 1988', *North Atlantic Studies* 2(1–2): 36–44.

Bloch, M. and J. Parry. 1989. 'Introduction: Money and the Morality of Exchange', in J. Parry and M. Bloch (eds), *Money and the Morality of Exchange*. Cambridge: Cambridge University Press, pp. 1–32.

Boas, F. 1901. 'The Eskimo of Baffin Land and Hudson Bay', *Bulletin, American Museum of Natural History* 15(1): 1–379.

Bockstoce, J. et al. 1982. 'Report of the Cultural Anthropology Panel', in G.P. Donovan (ed.), *Aboriginal/Subsistence Whaling*. Cambridge: IWC, pp. 35–49.

Bodenhorn, B. 1988. 'Whales, Souls, Children, and Other Things that are "Good to share": Core Metaphors in a Contemporary Whaling Society', *Cambridge Anthropology* 13(1): 1–19.

Bonanno, A. and D. Constance. 1996. *Caught in the Net: The Global Tuna Industry, Environmentalism, and the State*. Lawrence: University Press of Kansas.

Bonner, R. 1993. *At the Hand of Man: Peril and Hope for Africa's Wildlife*. New York: Alfred Knopf.

———. 1994. 'Western Conservation Groups and the Ivory Ban Wagon', in M.M.R. Freeman and U.P. Kreuter (eds), *Elephants and Whales: Resources for Whom?* Basel: Gordon and Breach Publishers, pp. 59–71.

Bookchin, M. 1982. *Ecology of Freedom: The Emergence and Dissolution of Hierarchy*. Palo Alto, CA: Cheshire Books.

Booth, W. 1989. 'Unraveling the Dolphin Soap Opera', *Oceanus* 32(1): 76–79.

Born, E.W. 1991. 'Studies of Walrus and Polar Bears', in I. Egede (ed.), *Nature Conservation in Greenland*. Nuuk: Atuakkiorfik, pp. 31–49.

Borré, K. 1991. 'Seal Blood, Inuit Blood, and Diet: A Biocultural Model of Physiology and Cultural Identity', *Medical Anthropology Quarterly* 5(1): 48–62.

Braund, S., H. Armstrong and S. Stroker 1984. *Subsistence Study of Alaska Eskimo Whaling Villages*. Report to the U.S. Department of Interior. Washington D.C.: Alaskan Consultant Inc. and Stephen Braund and Associates.

Brensing, K. 2006. 'Expert Statement on "Swim with the Dolphin Program and Dolphin Assisted Therapy"', 3rd Meeting of the Scientific Committee, Cairo 14–17 May 2005, ASCOBANS Sc3/Inf10.

Briggs, J.L. 1970. *Never in Anger: Portrait of an Eskimo Family*. Cambridge, MA.: Harvard University Press.

Bright, C. 1992. 'A Fishy Story about Whales', *Wildlife Conservation* 94(4): 62–69.

Bright, M. 1989. *There are Giants in the Sea. Monsters and Mysteries of the Depths Explored*. London: Robson Books.

Brill, R.L. and W.A. Friedl. 1993. 'Reintroduction to the Wild as an Option for Managing Navy Marine Mammals'. Report. San Diego, CA: US Navy/NRaD.

Brin, D. 1983. *Startide Rising*. New York: Bantam Book.

Broch, H.B. 1977. 'Den økologiske "harmonimodell" sett i lyset av jegere og sankere, eller de såkalte naturfolk', *Naturen* 3: 243–47.

———. 1994. 'North Norwegian Whalers' Conceptualization of Current Whale Management Conflicts', in M.M.R. Freeman and U.P. Kreuter (eds), *Elephants and Whales: Resources for Whom?* Basel: Gordon and Breach Publishers, pp. 201–18.

———. 2004. 'The Battle of Ålo, 1996: A Descriptive Analysis of a Confrontation between Greenpeace Activists and Norwegian Minke-Whalers', *Folk* 45: 177–206.

Brockington, D. 2002. *Forest Conservation: The Preservation of the Mkomazi Game Reserve, Tanzania*. Bloomington: Indiana University Press.

Brown, M. and J. May. 1991. *The Greenpeace Story*. London: Dorling Kindersley.

Brox, O. 1966. *Hva skjer i Nord-Norge?* Oslo: Pax Forlag.

———. 2000. 'Schismogenesis in the Wilderness: The Reintroduction of Predators in Norwegian Forests', *Ethnos* 65(3): 387–404.

Bryden, M.M. and P. Cockeron. 1989. 'Intelligence', in R. Harrison and M.M. Bryden (eds), *Whales, Dolphins and Porpoises*. New York: Fact on File Publication, pp. 160–65.

Brydon, A.E. 1990. 'Icelandic Nationalism and the Whaling Issue', *North Atlantic Studies* 2(1–2): 185–91.

———. 1991. 'The Eye of the Guest Microform: Icelandic Nationalist Discourse and the Whaling Issue', Ph.D. dissertation. Montreal: McGill University.

Bryld, M. and N. Lykke 2000. *Cosmodolphins: Feminist Cultural Studies of Technology, Animals and the Sacred.* London: Zed Books Ltd

Burch, E.S., Jr. 1994. 'Rationality and Resource Use among Hunters', in T. Irimoto and T. Yamada (eds), *Circumpolar Religion and Ecology: An Anthropology of the North.* Tokyo: University of Tokyo Press, pp. 163–85.

Burns W.C.G., G. Wandesforde-Smith and K. Simpson. 2001. 'The 53rd Meeting of the International Whaling Commission and the Future of Cetaceans in a Changing World', *Journal of International Wildlife Law and Policy* 4(3): 221–37.

Burke, W.T. 1997. 'Whaling and International Law', in G. Pétursdottir (ed.), *Whaling in the North Atlantic: Economic and Political Perspectives.* Reykjavik: Fisheries Research Institute, University of Iceland Press, pp. 113–22.

———. 2001. 'A New Whaling Agreement and International Law', in R. Friedheim (ed.), *Towards a Sustainable Whaling Regime.* Edmonton: Canadian Circumpolar Institute Press, pp. 51–79.

Butterworth, D.S. 1992. 'Science and Sentimentality: Commentary', *Nature* 357(18 June): 532–34.

Caron, D.D. 1995. 'The International Whaling Commission and the North Atlantic Marine Mammal Commission: The Institutional Risks of Coercion in Consensual Structures', *American Journal of International Law* 89(1): 154–74.

Carter, J. and A. Parton. 1992. 'Park in Flap over Swims with Flipper', *Sunday Morning Post* (29 November): 5.

Caulfield, R,A. 1993. 'Aboriginal Subsistence Whaling in Greenland: The Case of Qeqertarsuaq Municipality in West Greenland', *Arctic* 46(2): 144–55.

———. 1994. 'Aboriginal Subsistence Whaling in Greenland', in M.M.R. Freeman and U.P. Kreuter (eds), *Elephants and Whales: Resources for Whom?* Basel: Gordon and Breach Publishers, pp. 263–92.

———. 1997. *Greenlanders, Whales, and Whaling: Sustainability and Self-Determination in the Arctic.* Hanover, NH: University Press of New England.

Cawthorn, M.W. 1999. 'The Changing Face of New Zealand's Whaling Policy', in S. Ohsumi (ed.), *Whaling and Anti-whaling Movements.* Tokyo: ICR, pp. 17–30.

Chance, N.A. 1990. *The Iñupiat and Arctic Alaska: An Ethnography of Development.* Fort Worth, TX: Holt, Rinehart and Winston.

Cherfas, J. 1989. *The Hunting of the Whale: A Tragedy that Must End*, new edition. Harmondsworth: Penguin Books.

Christian, P. 2000. 'Attack on "Ayatollahs"', *The Press* [NZ], 17 November, p.1

Ciriacy-Wantrup, S.V. and R.C. Bishop. 1975. '"Common Property" as a Concept in Natural Resource Policy', *Natural Resources Journal* 15(4): 715–27.

Clark, C.W. 1973. 'The Economics of Overexploitation', *Science* 181: 630–34.

———. 1981. 'Economic Aspects of Renewable Resource Exploitation as Applied to Marine Mammals', in J.G. Clark (ed.), *Mammals in the Seas.* Rome: FAO, pp. 7–19.

Clark, H. (n.d.). 'New Zealand Foreign Policy', Address at Oxford Union.

Clark, S.R.L. 1977. *The Moral Status of Animals.* Oxford: Clarendon Press.

Claudi, E. 1988. *Greenpeace: Regnbuens krigere.* Copenhagen: Tiderne skifter.

Clifton, M. 1994. 'Whales for Missiles', *Animal People* 3(6): 1, 8–9.

Cochrane, A. and K. Callen. 1992. *Dolphins and their Power to Heal*. London: Bloomsbury.

Collings, P., G.W. Wenzel and R.G. Condon. 1998. 'Modern Food Sharing Networks and Community Integration in the Central Canadian Arctic', *Arctic* 51(4): 301–14.

Condon, R.G. 1987. *Inuit Youth: Growth and Change in the Canadian Arctic*. New Brunswick: Rutgers University Press.

Condon, R.G. and P.R. Stern. 1993. 'Gender-Role Preference, Gender Identity, and Gender Socialization among Contemporary Inuit Youth', *Ethnos* 21(4): 384–416.

Cone, M. 2005. *Silent Snow: The Slow Poisoning of the Arctic*. New York: Grove Press.

Conklin, B.A. and L.R. Graham. 1995. 'The Shifting Middle Ground: Amazonian Indians and Eco-Politics', *American Anthropologist* 97(4): 695–710.

Corrigan, P. 1991. *Where the Whales Are: Your Guide to Whale-Watching Trips in North America*. Chester, CT.: The Globe Pequet Press.

Cousteau, J.-Y. and Y. Paccalet. 1988. *Whales*. New York: Harry N. Abrams, Inc.

Cracknell, J. 1993. 'Issue Arenas, Pressure Groups and Environmental Agendas', in A. Hansen (ed.), *The Mass Media and Environmental Issues*. Leicester: Leicester University Press, pp. 4–21.

Cressey, J. (n.d.) 'Making a Splash in the Pacific: Dolphin and Whale Myths and Legends of Oceania', mimeograph.

Czordas, T. (ed.). 1994. *Embodiment and Experience: The Existential Ground of Culture and Self*. Cambridge: Cambridge University Press.

Dahl, J. 1989. 'The Integrative and Cultural Role of Hunting and Subsistence in Greenland', *Etudes/Inuit/Studies* 13(1): 23–42.

———. 1992. *Indfødte folk [Indigenous Peoples]*. Copenhagen: IWGIA.

Dalton, R.J. 1994. *The Green Rainbow: Environmental Groups in Western Europe*. New Haven and London: Yale University Press.

Damas, D. 1972. 'Central Eskimo Systems of Food Sharing', *Ethnology* 11(3): 220–40.

D'Amato, A. and S.K. Chopra. 1991. 'Whales: Their Emerging Right to Life', *American Journal of International Law* 85(1): 21–62.

Darby, A. 2008. *Harpoon. Into the Heart of Whaling*. Cambridge, MA: Da Capo Press.

Dasmann, R. 1988. 'National Parks, Nature Conservation, and "Future Primitive"', in J.H. Bodley (ed.), *Tribal Peoples and Development Issues: A Global Overview*. Mountain View; CA: Mayfield Publishing Company, pp. 301–10.

Davies, B. 1990. *Red Ice: My Fight to Save the Seals*. London: Methuen.

Davies, N., A.M. Smith, S.R. Whyte and V. Williams (eds). 1991. *Why Whales?* Bath: WDCS.

Davis, S.G. 1997. *Spectacular Nature: Corporate Culture and the Sea World Experience*. Berkeley: University of California Press.

Day, D. 1991. *The Eco Wars: A Layman's Guide to the Ecological Movement*. London: Paladin.

———. 1992. *The Whale War* (revised edition). London: Grafton.

Denmark Radio 1991. *Manden i regnbuen*. TV program.

DeSombre, E. 2001. 'Distorting Global Governance: Membership, Voting, and the IWC', in R. Friedheim (ed.), *Towards a Sustainable Whaling Regime*. Edmonton: Canadian Circumpolar Institute Press, pp. 183–99.

Desportes, G. 1990. 'Pilot Whale Research in the Faroe Islands: Presentation of Preliminary Research', *North Atlantic Studies* 2(1–2): 47–54.

Devall, B. and G. Sessions. 1985. *Deep Ecology: Living as if Nature Mattered*. Salt Lake City, UT: Gibbs Smith, Publisher.

Diamond, J. 2005. *Collapse. How Societies Choose to Fail or Succeed*. New York: Viking Books.

DNV (Det Norske Veritas). 1995. 'Brent Spar Disposal Contract c48870/95/db9 Inventory Study'. Høvik (Norway): DNV.

Doak, W. 1988. *Encounters with Whales and Dolphins*. Auckland: Hodder & Stoughton.

Dobbs, H. 1990. *Dance to a Dolphin's Song*. London: Jonathan Cape.

———. 1992. *Journey into Dolphin Dreamtime*. London: Jonathan Cape.

Dobson, A. 1990. *Green Political Thought: An Introduction*. London: Unwin Hyman.

Donovan, G.P. 1982. 'The International Whaling Commission and Aboriginal/Subsistence Whaling: April 1979 to July 1981', in G.P. Donovan (ed.), *Aboriginal/Subsistence Whaling*. Cambridge: IWC, pp. 79–86.

———. 1986. 'The International Whaling Commission and the Humane Killing of Whales, 1982–1986', in E. Mitchell, R. Reeves and A. Evely (eds), *Reports of the International Whaling Commission*. Cambridge: IWC, pp. 141–53.

Douglas, M. 1966. *Purity and Danger: An Analysis of the Concept of Pollution and Taboo*. London: Routledge and Kegan Paul.

———. 1990. 'The Pangolin Revisited: A New Approach to Animal Symbolism', in R.G. Willis (ed.), *Signifying Animals: Human Meaning in the Natural World*. London: Unwin Hyman, pp. 25–37.

———. 1996. *Thought Styles: Critical Essays on Good Taste*. London: Sage.

Duffield, D.A., D.K. Odell, J.F. McBain and B. Andrews. 1995. 'Killer Whale (*Orcinus orca*) Reproduction at Sea World', *Zoo Biology* 14: 417–30.

Dumond, D.E. 1995. 'Whale Traps on the North Pacific?'in A. McCartney (ed.), *Hunting the Largest Animals: Native Whaling in the Western Arctic and Subarctic*. Edmonton, Alberta: Canadian Circumpolar Institute, Occasional Publication No. 36, pp.51–61.

Dunlop, R. and A. Mertig. 1992. *American Environmentalism: The U.S. Environmental Movement 1970–1990*. Washington. D.C.: Taylor and Francis.

Durkheim, E. 1976. *The Elementary Forms of Religious Life*. London: George Allen & Unwin.

Dyerberg, J. 1989. 'Coronary Heart Disease in Greenland Inuit: A Paradox. Implications for Western Diet Patterns', *Arctic Medical Research* 48(2): 47–54.

Eckersley, R. 1992. *Environmentalism and Political Theory: Towards an Ecocentric Approach*. London: UCL Press.

Eder, K. 1996. *The Social Construction of Nature: A Sociology of Ecological Enlightenment*. London: Sage.

Edgerton, R.B. 1992. *Sick Societies: Challenging the Myth of Primitive Harmony*. New York: Free Press.

Egede, I. 1995. 'Inuit Food and Inuit Health: Contaminants in Perspective', *Avativut/Ilusivut Newsletter* 2(1): 1–3.

Elias, N. 1978. *The History of Manners*. Oxford: Basil Blackwell.

———. 1982. *State Formation and Civilization*. Oxford: Basil Blackwell.

Ellen, R.F. 1986. 'What Black Elk Left Unsaid: On Illusory Images of Green Primitivism', *Anthropology Today* 2(4): 8–12.

Epstein, C. 2005. 'The Power of Words in International Relations: Birth of an Anti-Whaling Discourse', Ph.D. dissertation. Cambridge: Cambridge University.

Eriksen, E. 1964. 'Folketro på hvalfangst', in A. Bakken and E. Eriksen (eds), *Hval og hvalfangst: Vestfoldminne*. Tønsberg: Vestfold Historielag, pp. 146–64.

Eyerman, R. and A. Jamison. 1989. 'Environmental Knowledge as an Organizational Weapon: The Case of Greenpeace', *Social Science Information* 28: 99–119.

Falch, K. 2000. 'Uvilje mot viten', *Fiskaren* (5 April): 2.

Feeny, D., F. Berkes, B.J. McCay and J.M. Acheson. 1990. 'The Tragedy of the Commons: Twenty-two Years Later', *Human Ecology* 18(1): 1–19.

Ferry, L. 1995: *The New Ecological Order*. Chicago: University Of Chicago Press

Feuerstein, T.L. 2001. 'Cetacean Bibliographies, Audiography, and Videography', http://www.helsinki.fi/~lauhakan/whale/literature/fic_main.html. Retrieved 29 November 2008.

———. 2005a. 'Cetacean Children's Bibliography: Fiction, Non-fiction, and Other Resources', www.helsinki.fi/~lauhakan/whale/literature/children/biblioc.html. Retrieved 29 November 2008.

———. 2005b. 'Cetacean Audiography: CDs, Tapes, LPs, Online Sound Clips', www.helsinki.fi/~lauhakan/whale/literature/audio/audiogra.html. Retrieved 29 November 2008.

———. 2005c. 'Cetacean Videography: Films, Videos, Visual CDs, DVDs, Television Programs, Computer Games, Online Clicks', www.helsinki.fi/~lauhakan/whale/literature/video/videogra.html. Retrieved 29 November 2008.

Fichtelius, K-E. and S. Sjölander. 1973. *Man's Place: Intelligence in Whales, Dolphins, and Humans*. London: Gollancz.

Fienup-Riordan, A. 1983. *The Nelson Island Eskimos: Social Structure and Ritual Distribution*. Anchorage: Alaska Pacific University Press.

Firth, R. 1930–31. 'Totemism in Polynesia', *Oceania* 1(3): 291–321.

Flaaten, O. and K. Stollery. 1996. 'The Economic Costs of Biological Predation: Theory and Application to the Case of the Northeast Atlantic Minke Whale's (*Balaenoptera Acutorostrata*) Consumption of Fish', *Environmental and Resource Economics* 8(1): 75–95.

Foreman, D. 1980. 'Memo To: The Leading Intellectual and Literary Lights of EARTH FIRST!', Draft, Statement of Earth First! principles and membership brochure, 1 September.

Fowler, R. 1991. *Language in the News: Discourse and Ideology in the Press*. London and New York: Routledge.

Fox, J. 1991. 'The Business of Greenpeace', *The Financial Post (Toronto)* (7 January).

Franklin, A. 1999. *Animals and Modern Cultures: A Sociology of Human-Animal Relations in Modernity*. London: Sage Publications.

Freeman, M.M.R. 1989. 'The Alaska Eskimo Whaling Commission: Successful Co-management under Extreme Conditions', in E. Pinkerton (ed.), *Co-Operative Management of Local Fisheries: New Directions for Improved Management and Community Development*. Vancouver: University of British Columbia Press, pp. 137–53.

———. 1990. 'A Commentary on Political Issues with Regard to Contemporary Whaling', *North Atlantic Studies* 2(1–2): 106–16.

———. 1991. 'Energy, Food Security and A.D. 2040: The Case for Sustainable Utilization of Whale Stocks', *Resource Management and Optimization* 8(3–4): 235–44.

———. 1992. 'Why Whales? Do Ecology and Common Sense Provide Any Answers?' in Ö.D. Jónsson (ed.), *Whales and Ethics*. Reykjavik: University of Iceland, pp. 39–56.

———. 1993. 'The International Whaling Commission, Small-Type Whaling, and Coming to Terms with Subsistence', *Human Organization* 52(3): 243–51.

———. 1996. 'Why *Mattak* and other *Kalaalimerngit* (Local Foods) Matter', in B. Jacobsen (ed.), *Cultural and Social Research in Greenland 95/96: Essays in Honour of Robert Petersen*. Nuuk: Ilisimatusarfik/Atuakkiorfik, pp. 45–53.

———. 2001. 'Is Money the Root of the Problem? Cultural Conflicts in the IWC', in R.L. Friedheim (ed.), *Towards a Sustainable Whaling Regime*. Edmonton: Canadian Circumpolar Institute Press, pp. 123–46.

Freeman, M.M.R., L. Bogoslovskaya, R.A. Caulfield, I. Egede, I.I. Krupnik and M.G. Stevenson. 1998. *Inuit, Whaling, and Sustainability*. Walnut Creek, CA: AltaMira Press.

Freeman, M.M.R. and S.R. Kellert. 1992. *Public Attitudes to Whales: Results of a Six-country Survey*. Edmonton and New Haven, CT: Canadian Circumpolar Institute/School of Forestry and Environmental Studies.

Freeman, M.M.R., E.E. Wein, and D.E. Keith. 1992. *Recovering Rights: Bowhead Whales and Inuvialuit Subsistence in the Western Canadian Arctic*. Edmonton: Canadian Circumpolar Institute Press, University of Alberta.

Freud, S. 1960. *Totem and Taboo*. London: Routledge & Kegan Paul.

Friedheim, R.L. 1996. 'Executive Summary: The International Legal Workshop'. Workshop organized by the Institute of Cetacean Research, Tokyo, 7–9 January.

———. 2001a. 'Introduction: The IWC as a Contested Regime', in R.L. Friedheim (ed.), *Towards a Sustainable Whaling Regime*. Edmonton: Canadian Circumpolar Institute Press, pp. 3–48.

———. 2001b. 'Negotiating in the IWC Environment', in R.L. Friedheim (ed.), *Towards a Sustainable Whaling Regime*. Edmonton: Canadian Circumpolar Institute Press, pp. 200–34.

Friedman, J. 1992. 'Past in the Future: History and the Politics of Identity', *American Anthropologist* 94(4): 837–59.

Frøvik, R. 1995. 'Hval og politikk: En studie av kommersielle fangstkvoter i regi av den Internasjonale Hvalfangstkommisjon'. MA (hovedfag) thesis. Bergen: University of Bergen.

Fujimoto T., K. Kubota, K. Kita and K. Hara. 1984. 'Arikawa kujira-gumi shiki hōtei', I and II. *Fukuoka daigaku shōgaku ronsō* 28(3): 225–60 and 28(4): 633–85.

Fuller, K.S. 1995. 'President's Note', *WWF Conservation Issues* 2(2): 2.

Gabriel, T. 1991. 'Slow Boat to Trouble', *Outside* 9 (September): 54–60, 128–33.

Gambell, R. 1982. 'The Bowhead Whale Problem and the International Whaling Commission', in G.P. Donovan (ed.), *Aboriginal/Subsistence Whaling (with Special Reference to the Alaska and Greenland Fisheries)*. Cambridge: International Whaling Commission, pp. 1–6.

Gay, J. 2002a. 'Diomede Will be Fined for Illegal Whaling', *Anchorage Daily News* (9 July).

———. 2002b. 'Little Diomede Man Dies after Gray Whale Flips Boat', *Anchorage Daily News* (27 June).

Gay, J.T. 1987. *American Fur Seal Diplomacy: The Alaskan Fur Seal Controversy*. New York: Peter Lang.

Geraci, J.R. 2005. *Marine Mammals Ashore: A Field Guide for Strandings*. Baltimore: National Aquarium in Baltimore.

Gerrard, S. 1983. 'Kvinner—fiskerinæringas bakkemannskap?' in B. Hersough (ed.), *Kan fiskerinæringa styres?* Oslo: Novus Forlag, pp. 217–41.

Gibbs, C. and D. Bromley. 1989. 'Institutional Arrangements for Management of Rural Resources: Common Property Regimes', in F. Berkes (ed.), *Common Property Resources: Ecology and Community-Based Sustainable Development*. London: Belhaven Press, pp. 22–32.

Gillespie, A. 1997. 'The Ethical Question in the Whale Debate', *Georgetown International Environment Law Review* 19: 355–87.

Goddard, J. 1999. 'James Swan's Christmas Whale', *WCW News* 9 (December). Retrieved 29 November 2008 from http://www.worldwhalers.com/publications/newsletters/9.htm.

GoJ (Government of Japan). 1994. 'Action Plan for Japanese Community-Based Whaling (CBW): Distribution and Consumption of Whale Products', 46th Annual Meeting of the IWC, Puerto Vallarta, Mexico, 23–27 May (IWC/46/31 Rev.2).

———. (ed.). 1997. *Papers on Japanese Small-Type Coastal Whaling Submitted by the Government of Japan to the International Whaling Commission, 1986–1996*. Tokyo: ICR.

Golden, F. 1989. 'Facts and Fantasy', *Oceanus* 32(1): 3–4.

Goodman, D. 1997. 'Land Claim Agreement and the Management of Whaling in the Canadian Arctic', in Hokkaido Museum of Northern Peoples (ed.), *Proceedings of the 11th International Abashiri Symposium: Development and Northern Peoples*. Abashiri, Hokkaido: Association for the Promotion of Northern Cultures, pp. 39–50.

GRD (Gesellschaft zur Rettung der Delphine). 2004. 'Online Petition: Stop Japanese Supermarkets Selling Whale and Dolphin Meat!', *Delphinpost* 2–2004.

Greenpeace International. 1992. 'A Whale Sanctuary for Antarctica'. Mimeo campaign material. Amsterdam: Greenpeace International.

———. 2002. 'Science, Culture or Commerce? The Truth about Japanese Whaling'. Greenpeace Briefing (May). Amsterdam: Greenpeace International.

———. 2006. *Annual Report 2005*. Amsterdam: Greenpeace International.

Guha, R. 1989. 'Radical American Environmentalism and Wilderness Preservation: A Third World Critique', *Environmental Ethics* 11: 71–83.

Gulland, J.A. 1988. 'The End of Whaling?' *New Scientist* 120(1636, 29 October): 42–47.

Gylling-Nielsen, M. 1987. 'Havets mennesker', *Greenpeace Magasinet* (1): 10–11.

Hall, S. 1997. 'The Work of Representation', in S. Hall (ed.), *Representation: Cultural Representations and Signifying Practices* (Culture, Media and Identities series). London: Sage Publications, pp.13–74.

Halverson, J. 1967. 'Animal Categories and Terms of Abuse', *Man, N.S.* 11: 505–16.

Hansen, A. 1993. 'Greenpeace and Press Coverage of Environmental Issues', in A. Hansen (ed.), *The Mass Media and Environmental Issues*. Leicester: Leicester University Press, pp. 150–78.

Hansen, H. 1994. 'The International Whaling Commission: The Transition from a "Whaling Club" to a "Preservation Club"', *International Politics STV 561*. Lund: Department of Political Science, University of Lund.

Hardin, G. 1968. 'The Tragedy of the Commons', *Science* 162: 1243–48.

———. 1972. *Exploring New Ethics for Survival*. New York: Viking Press.

Harper, J. 2002. *Endangered Species: Health, Illness, and Death among Madagascar's People of the Forest*. Durham, NC: Carolina Academic Press.

Hatt, J. 1990. 'Enigmatic Smiles', *Harpers & Queen* (December): 244–52.

Hauan, M.A. and S.R. Mathisen.1991. 'Småkvalfangst og lokalkultur i Skrova', *Ottar* 184: 31–38.

Haug, T. et al. 1998. *Sjøpattedyr: Om hval og sel i norske farvann*. Oslo: Universitetsforlaget.

Heazle, Michael. 2006. *Scientific Uncertainty and the Politics of Whaling*. Seattle and London: University of Washington Press/Edmonton: Canadian Circumpolar Institute Press.

Heide-Jørgensen, M.P., H. Lassen, J. Teilmann and R.A. Davis. 1993. 'An Index of the Relative Abundance of Wintering Belugas, *Delphinapterus leucas*, and Narwhals, *Monodon monoceros*, off West Greenland', *Canadian Journal of Fisheries and Aquatic Sciences* 50(11): 2323–35.

———. 2001. 'Surfacing Times and Dive Rates for Narwhals (*Monodon monoceras*) and Belugas (*Delphinapterus leucas*)', *Arctic* 54(3): 284–98.

Heilbroner, R. 1991. *An Inquiry into the Human Prospect: Looked at Again for the 1990s*. New York: W.W. Norton.

Herscovici, A. 1985. *Second Nature: The Animal Rights Controversy*. Toronto: CBC Enterprises.

Hierta, E. 1991. 'Troubled Waters', *National Parks* 65: 26–31.

Hjort, J. 1902. *Fiskeri og hvalfangst i det nordlige Norge*, (special issue of *Aarsberetning vedkommende Norges Fiskerier*). Bergen: Grieg

HNA (High North Alliance). 1995. 'Humane or Inhumane: That is the Question', *The Inter-national Harpoon* 5 (2 June): 4.

———. 2000. 'Searching for Cheap Green Points', *The International Harpoon* (3 July): 3–4.

———. 2008. 'Low Carbon Whale Meat', *HNA News*, retrieved 7 April 2008 from www.highnorth.no/news/siste.asp.

Hoel, A.H. 1986. *The International Whaling Commission, 1972–1984: New Members, New Concerns*, 2nd edition. Lysaker: The Fridtjof Nansen Institute.

———. 1992. *Internasjonal forvaltning av kvalfangst: Bakgrunn for dagens situasjon og bet-ingelser for endring*. Tromsø: Norwegian College of Fisheries Science Report Series.

Hollander, R. 1984. 'The Man Who Loves Animals', *Town and Country* (March): 200–50.

Holt, S. 1985. 'Whale Mining, Whale Saving', *Marine Policy* 9(3): 192–213.

Homewood, K.M. and W.A. Rodgers. 1988. 'Pastoralism and Conservation', in J.H. Bodley (ed.), *Tribal Peoples and Development Issues: A Global Overview*. Mountain View, CA: May-field Publishing Company, pp. 310–20.

Howard, C.J. 1995. *Dolphin Chronicles*. New York: Bantam Books.

Hoyt, E. 1992. 'Whale Watching Around the World: A Report on Its Value, Extent and Pros-pects', *International Whale Bulletin* (WDCS) 7: 8.

———. 1994. 'Whale Watching Worldwide: An Overview of the Industry and the Implica-tions for Science and Conservation'. Paper prepared at European Cetacean Society, Mont-pellier, France, 4–6 March.

———. 2000. *Whale Watching 2000: Worldwide Tourism Numbers, Expenditures, and Expand-ing Socioeconomic Benefits*. Crowborough: International Fund for Animal Welfare.

HSUS (Humane Society of the United States). 2002. 'Why You Shouldn't Swim with the Dolphins', *All Animals* 3(4, winter). Retrieved 3 May 2008 from www.hsus.org/press_and_publications/

———. (n.d.). 'Swim-with-the-dolphins attractions'. Retrieved 8 April 2008 from http://www.hsus.org/search.jsp.

Hunter, J. 1787. 'Observations on the Structure and Oeconomy of Whales', *Philosophical Transactions of the Royal Society* 77: 371–450.

Hunter, R. 1979. *Warriors of the Rainbow: A Chronicle of the Greenpeace Movement*. New York: Rinehart and Winston.

Huntington, H.P. 1992. *Wildlife Management and Subsistence Hunting in Alaska*. London and Cambridge: Belhaven Press.

hy. 1992. 'Norway: Death to Moby Dick', *Fish International* (October): 6–11.

ICR (The Institute of Cetacean Research) (ed.). 1989. *The Research on the Whale Stock in the Antarctic: The Result of the Preliminary Study in 1987/88*. Tokyo: ICR.

———(ed.). 1991. *Japanese Research on Antarctic Whale Resources*. Tokyo: ICR.

———(ed.). 1993. *Whaling Issues and Japan's Whale Research*. Tokyo: ICR.

———(ed.). 1995. *Sustainable Use of Wildlife and International Regime, with Special Reference to Cetaceans*. Tokyo: ICR.

IFAW (International Fund for Animal Welfare). 2006. 'Saving Lives. Annual Report July 1, 2005–June 30, 2006', Yarmouth Port, MA: IFAW.

Igoe, J. 2003. *Conservation and Globalization: A Study of National Parks and Indigenous Com-munities from East Africa to North Dakota*. Belmont, CA: Wadsworth Publishing.

Ingold, T. 1986. *The Appropriation of Nature*. Manchester: Manchester University Press.

INWR (International Network for Whaling Research). 1999. 'Tongans Distribute Whale Meat', *INWR Digest* 18 (December), http://www.ualberta.ca/~inwr/DIGEST/digest18.html#6.

———. 2000. 'IUCN Expresses Concern about IWC', *INWR Digest* 19 (May), http://www.ualberta.ca/~inwr/DIGEST/digest19.html#3.

———. 2001. 'The Eastern Caribbean Cetacean Commission (ECCO)', *INWR Digest* 21 (May), pp. 1–2.

———. 2002. 'Bequian Indigenous Whalers' Association Established', *INWR Digest* 22 (July), p. 2.

———. 2003a. 'Korean Whaling Festival', *INWR Digest* 25 (June), p.2.

———. 2003b. 'Chukotkan Whalers' Organization', *INWR Digest* 25 (June), p.2.

ISG (International Study Group for Norwegian Small-Type Whaling). 1992. *Norwegian Small Type Whaling in Cultural Perspectives.* Tromsø: Norwegian College of Fisheries.

ISGSTW (International Study Group for Small-Type Whaling). 1992. 'Similarities and Diversity in Coastal Whaling Operations: A Comparison of Small-Scale Whaling Activities in Greenland, Iceland, Japan and Norway', in S. Ward and B. Moeran (eds), *Symposium on Utilization of Marine Living Resources for Subsistence.* Tokyo: ICR, pp. 1–22 (also as IWC/46/SEST 6)

IUCN ((The World Conservation Union). 1999. 'Opening statement', 51th Annual Meeting of the IWC, Grenada, 24–28 May (IWC/51/OS IUCN).

IUCN (The World Conservation Union), UNEP (United Nations Environment Programme), and WWF (Worldwide Fund for Nature). 1991. *Caring for the Earth: A Strategy for Sustainable Living.* Gland, Switzerland: IUCN/UNEP/WWF.

Ívarsson, J.V. 1994. *Science, Sanctions and Cetaceans: Iceland and the Whaling Issue.* Reykjavik: Centre for International Studies, University of Iceland Press.

Iwasaki-Goodman, M. 1994. 'An Analysis of Social and Cultural Change in Ayukawa-hama (Ayukawa Shore Community)', Ph.D. dissertation. Edmonton: University of Alberta.

IWC (International Whaling Commission). 1981. *Report of the Ad Hoc Technical Committee Working Group on Development of Management Principles and Guidelines for Subsistence Catches of Whales by Indigenous (Aboriginal) Peoples.* Cambridge: IWC.

———. 1993. 'Resolution on Japanese Community-Based Minke Whaling', 45th Annual Meeting of the IWC, Kyoto, 10–14 May (Resolution 1993–3).

———. 1994a. 'Report of the Sub-committee on Aboriginal Subsistence Whaling', 46th Annual Meeting of the IWC, Puerto Vallarta, Mexico, 23–27 May (IWC/46/13).

———. 1994b. 'Summary of Infractions Reports Received by the Commission in 1993', 46th Annual Meeting of the IWC, Puerto Vallarta, Mexico, 23–27 May (IWC/46/6).

———. 1997. 'Resolution on improving the humaneness of Aboriginal Subsistence Whaling', 49th Annual Meeting of the IWC, Monaco, 20–24 October (Resolution 1997–1).

———. 2001a. 'Resolution on Japanese Community-Based Whaling', 53rd Annual Meeting of the IWC, London, 23–27 July (Resolution 2001–6).

———. 2001b. 'Resolution on Transparency within the International Whaling Commission', 53rd Annual Meeting of the IWC, London, 23–27 July (Resolution 2001–1).

———. 2001c. 'Resolution on the Incidental Capture of Cetaceans', 53rd Annual Meeting of the IWC, London, 23–27 July (Resolution 2001–4).

———. 2003a. 'Report of the Workshop on Whale Killing Methods and Associated Welfare Issues', 55th Annual Meeting of the IWC, Berlin, 7–9 June (IWC/55/Rep 5).

———. 2003b. 'The Berlin Initiative on Strengthening the Conservation Agenda of the International Whaling Commission', 55th Annual Meeting of the IWC, Berlin, 7–9 June (Resolution 2003–1).

———. 2003c. 'Resolution on Whaling under Special Permit', 55th Annual Meeting of the IWC, Berlin, 7–9 June (Resolution 2003–2).

———. 2003d. 'Report of the Infractions Sub-Committee', 55th Annual Meeting of the IWC, Berlin, 7–9 June (IWC/55/Rep 4).

———. 2003e 'Report of the Aboriginal Subsistence Whaling Sub-Committee', 55th Annual Meeting of the IWC, Berlin, 7–9 June (IWC/55/Rep 3).

————. 2003f. 'Chair's Report of the 5th Special Meeting, 14 October 2002', Cambridge: IWC. Retrieved 28 March 2008 from http://www.iwcoffice.org/_documents/meetings/CHREPSM02.pdf.

————. 2007a. 'Annex I: Catches by IWC Member Nations in the 2005 and 2005/06 Seasons'. Cambridge: IWC (19 January).

————. 2007b. 'Resolution on Safety at Sea and Protection of the Environment', 59th Annual Meeting of the IWC, Anchorage, 28–31 May (Resolution 2007–2).

————. 2008. 'Chair's Report of the 59th Annual Meeting, 28–31 May 2007, Anchorage, Alaska'. Cambridge: IWC.

IWGIA (International Work Group for Indigenous Affairs) (ed.). 1991. *Arctic Environment: Indigenous Perspectives*. Copenhagen: IWGIA.

Jalakas, I. 1993. 'Gentle Killers', *Scanorama* (September): 46–52.

Jamieson, D. and T. Regan. 1985. 'Whales are not Cetacean Resources', in M.W. Fox and L.D. Mickley (eds), *Advances in Animal Welfare Science 1984*. Boston: Martinus Nijhoff Publishers, pp. 101–11.

Joensen, J.P. 1976. 'Pilot Whaling in the Faroe Islands', *Ethnologia Scandinavica* 6: 5–42.

————. 1988. 'The Pilot Whale in the Old and Modern Society'. Paper presented at the conference *Man and the Animal World*, Berg en dal, Nijmegen, Holland, 22–23 September.

————. 1990. 'Faroese Pilot Whaling in the Light of Social and Cultural History', *North Atlantic Studies* 2(1–2): 179–84.

————. 1993. 'Den færøske grindehvalefangst som social organisation, nationalt symbol og international kulturkonflikt'. Paper presented at the conference *Antropologien og naturen: Den kulturelle dimension i forholdet mellem naturressourcer og samfund*, Tórshavn 28–30 October.

Johnsen, A.O. 1959. *Den moderne hvalfangsts historie. Oprinnelse og utvikling. Første Bind: Finnmarksfangstens historie 1864–1905. [History of modern whaling. Origins and development. Vol.1: History of Finnmark's hunt 1864–1905]*. Oslo: H. Aschehoug & Co.

Johnson, W. 1988. *The Monk Seal Conspiracy*. London: Heretic Books.

Kalland, A. 1981. *Shingu: A Study of a Japanese Fishing Community*. London: Curzon Press.

————. 1986. 'Pre-modern Whaling in Northern Kyushu'. In E. Pauer (ed.), *Silkworm, Oil, Chips . . .* (Proceedings of the Economic and Economic History Section of the Fourth International Conference on Japanese Studies, Paris, September), *Bonner Zeitschrift für Japanologie*, Band 8, Bonn, pp.29-50.

————. 1989a. 'Arikawa and the Impact of a Declining Whaling Industry', *NIAS Report 1989*: 94–138.

————. 1989b 'The Spread of Whaling Culture in Japan', Cambridge: IWC (TC/41/STW3). Reprinted in ICR (ed.), *Papers on Japanese Small-Type Coastal Whaling Submitted by the Government of Japan to the International Whaling Commission, 1986–1995*. Tokyo: ICR, pp. 137–50.

————. 1992a. 'Whose Whale is That? Diverting the Commodity Path', *Maritime Anthropological Studies* 5(2): 16–45.

————. 1992b. 'Aboriginal Subsistence Whaling: A Concept in the Service of Imperialism?' in G. Blichfeldt (ed.), *Bigger than Whales*. Reine, Norway: High North Alliance, pp. 18–20.

————. 1993. 'Management by Totemization: Whale Symbolism and the Anti-Whaling Campaign', *Arctic* 46(2): 124–33.

————. 1994. 'Seals, Whales, and Elephants: Totem Animals and the Anti-Use Campaigns', in N.D. Christoffersen and C. Lippai (eds), *Responsible Wildlife Resource Management: Balancing Biological, Economic, Cultural and Moral Considerations*. Brussels: European Bureau for Conservation and Development, pp. 31–44.

———. 1995. *Fishing Villages in Tokugawa Japan*. Surrey: Curzon Press.

———. 1997. 'Some Reflections after the Sendai "Workshop"', *Isana* 16: 11–15.

———. 1998. 'The Anti-Whaling Campaigns and Japanese Responses', In S. Ohsumi (ed.), *Japanese Position on Whaling and Anti-whaling Campaign*. Tokyo: ICR, pp. 11–26.

———. 2000. 'Indigenous Knowledge: Prospects and Limitations', in R. Ellen, P. Parkes and A. Bicker (eds), *Indigenous Environmental Knowledge and its Transformations: Critical Anthropological Perspectives*. Amsterdam: Harwood Academic Publishers, pp. 319–35.

———. 2001. 'Fiendebilder i hvalfangstdebatten', in A. Kalland and T. Rønnow (eds), *Miljøkonflikter: Om bruk og vern av naturressurs*. Oslo: Unipub, pp. 183–200.

———. 2003. 'Environmentalism and Images of the Other', in H. Selin (ed.), *Nature Across Cultures: Views of Nature and the Environment in Non-Western Cultures*. Dordrecht, Boston and London: Kluwer Academic Publishers, pp. 1–17.

———. 2005. 'Religious Environmentalist Paradigm', in B. Taylor (ed.), *The Encyclopedia of Religion and Nature*, vol. 2. London and New York: Thoemmes Continuum, pp. 1367–71.

Kalland, A. and B. Moeran. 1992. *Japanese Whaling: End of an Era?* London: Curzon Press.

Kalland, A. and F. Sejersen. 2005. *Marine Mammals and Northern Cultures*. Edmonton: CCI Press.

Kalland, A., F. Sejersen and H.B. Broch. 2005. 'Hunting, Selfhood and National Identity', in Kalland, A. and F. Sejersen (eds), *Marine Mammals and Northern Cultures*. Edmonton: CCI Press, pp. 91–130.

Kamsvåg, K.E. 1956. 'Hvalsaken og dens betydning for den politiske utviklingen i det nordlige Norge', MA (hovedfag) thesis. Oslo: University of Oslo.

Keles, R. 1997. 'The Common Heritage of Mankind and the New Concept of Responsibility'. Paper presented st seventh B.I.O. conference, Bratislava, June 1997. Retrieved 27 April 2008 from www.biopolitics.gr/HTML/PUbS/VOL6/HTML/keles.htm.

Kellert, S.R. 1988. 'Human-Animal Interactions: A Review of American Attitudes to Wild and Domestic Animals in the Twentieth Century', in A.N. Rowan (ed.), *Animals and People Sharing the World*. Hanover, NH, and London: University Press of New England, pp. 137–75.

Kemf, E. 1993. 'Vietnam's Guardians of the Islands', in E. Kemf (ed.), *Indigenous Peoples and Protected Areas: The Law of Mother Earth*. London: Earthscan Publication, pp. 29–35.

Kemf, E., C. Phillips and K. Baragona. 2001. *Whales in the Wild: A WWF Species Status Report*. Gland, Switzerland: WWF.

Kleivan, H. 1964. 'Acculturation, Ecology and Human Choice: Case Studies from Labrador and South Greenland', *Folk* 6(1): 63–74.

Kleivan, I. 1996. 'An Ethnic Perspective on Greenlandic Food', in B. Jacobsen (ed.), *Cultural and Social Research in Greenland 95/96: Essays in Honour of Robert Petersen*. Nuuk: Ilisimatusarfik/Atuakkiorfik, pp. 146–57.

Klinowska, M. 1988. 'Are Cetaceans Especially Smart?" *New Scientist* (15 October): 46–47.

———. 1992. 'Brains, Behaviour and Intelligence in Cateceans', in Ö.D. Jónsson (ed.), *Whales & Ethics*. Reykjavik: Fisheries Research Institute, University of Iceland, pp. 23–37.

Klinowska, M. and S. Brown. 1986. *A Review of Dolphinaria*. Report to the Department of Environment, United Kingdom.

Kojima, T. 1993. 'Japanese Research Whaling', in F. Nagasaki (ed.), *Whaling Issues and Japan's Whale Research*. Tokyo: ICR, pp. 37–56.

Knudsen, S.K. 2005. 'A Review of the Criteria Used to Assess Insensibility and Death in Hunted Whales Compared to Other Species', *The Veterinary Journal* 169: 42–59.

Komatsu, M. and S. Misaki. 2001. *The Truth Behind the Whaling Dispute*. Tokyo: ICR.

————. 2003. *Whales and the Japanese*. Tokyo: ICR.

Krupnik, I.I. 1993a. *Arctic Adaptations: Native Whalers and Reindeer Herders of Northern Eurasia*. Hanover, NH, and London: University Press of New England.

————. 1993b. 'Prehistoric Eskimo Whaling in the Arctic: Slaughter of Calves of Fortuitous Ecology', *Arctic Anthropology* 30(1): 1–12.

Lacépède, B. 1804. *Histoire Naturelle des Cetacées*. Paris: Plassan.

Lakoff, G. and M. Johnson. 1980. *The Metaphors We Live By*. Chicago: University of Chicago Press.

Lamb, F.B. 1954. 'The Fisherman's Porpoise', *Natural History* 63(5): 231–32.

Langdon, S.J. 1984. *Alaskan Native Subsistence: Current Regulatory Regimes and Issues*, vol. 19. Anchorage: Alaska Native Review Commission.

Lantis, M. 1938. 'The Alaskan Whale Cult and its Affinities', *American Anthropologist* 40(3): 438–64.

Larsen, F. 1994a. 'Abundance of Minke and Fin Whales off West Greenland, 1993', *Reports of the International Whaling Commission* 45: 365–70.

————. 1994b. 'Forvaltningsrelaterede undersøgelser af våge-, fin- og pukkelhvaler ved Grønland', Report. Greenland Fisheries Research Institute.

Lawrence, E.A. 1989. 'Neotony in American Perception of Animals', in R.J. Hoage (ed.), *Perception of Animals in American Culture*. Washington D.C.: Smithsonian Institution Press, pp.57–76.

Leach, E. 1964. 'Anthropological Aspects of Language: Animal Categories and Verbal Abuse', in E.H. Lenneberg (ed.), *New Directions in the Study of Language*. Cambridge, MA: The MIT Press, pp. 23–63.

Lee, M.F. 1995. *Earth First! Environmental Apocalypse*. Syracruse, NY: Syracruse University Press.

Leopold, A. 1949. *The Sand County Almanac*. Oxford: Oxford University Press.

Lévi-Strauss, C. 1962. *Totemism*. London: Merlin Press.

————. 1966. *The Savage Mind*. Chicago: The University of Chicago Press.

Lilly, J.C. 1967. *The Mind of the Dolphin: A Nonhuman Intelligence*. New York: Doubleday.

————. 1978. *Communication between Man and Dolphin: The Possibilities of Talking with Other Species*. New York: Crown Publishers.

Lindbekk, K. 1978. *Lofoten og Vesterålens historie: 1500–1700*. Svolvær: Kommunene i Lofoten og Vesterålen.

Linné, O. 1993. 'Professional Practice and Organization: Environmental Broadcasters and their Sources', in A. Hansen (ed.), *The Mass Media and Environmental Issues*. Leicester: Leicester University Press, pp. 69–80.

Lonner, T.D. 1986. 'Subsistence as an Economic System in Alaska: Theoretical Observations and Management Implications', in S.J. Langdon (ed.), *Contemporary Alaskan Native Economies*. Lanham, MD: University Press of America, pp. 15–28.

Lorenz, K. 1981. *The Foundations of Ethology*. New York: Simon and Schuster.

Lovejoy, A.O. and G. Boas. 1935. *Primitivism and Related Ideas in Antiquity*. Baltimore, MD: Johns Hopkins.

Lynge, F. 1990. *Kampen om de vilde dyr*. Copenhagen: Akademisk Forlag.

————. 1992. *Arctic Wars: Animal Rights, Endangered Peoples*. Hanover, NH: University Press of New England.

Löfgren, O. 1985. 'Our Friends in Nature: Class and Animal Symbolism', *Ethnos* 50(3–4): 184–97.

Makah Tribal Council and Makah Whaling Commission. 2005. 'The Makah Indian Tribe and Whaling: Questions and Answers', information sheet. Available at http://www.makah.com/makahwhalingqa.pdf (retrieved 29 November 2008).

Malinowski, B. 1954. *Magic, Science and Religion and Other Essays.* New York: Anchor Books.

Manderson, L. and H. Akatsu. 1993. 'Whale Meat in the Diet of Ayukawa Villagers', *Ecology of Food and Nutrition* 30: 207–20.

Manes, C. 1990. *Green Rage: Radical Environmentalism and the Unmaking of Civilization.* Boston: Little, Brown and Company.

Manning, L. 1989. 'Marine Mammals and Fisheries Conflicts: A Philosophical Dispute', *Ocean and Shoreline Management* 12(3): 217–32.

Martin, G.S., Jr. and J.W. Brennan. 1989. 'Enforcing the International Convention for the Regulation of Whaling: The Pelly and Packwood-Magnusson Amendments', *Denver Journal of International Law and Policy* 17(2): 293–316.

Mathisen, S.R. 1995. 'Kvalfangst og kulturell identitet. Eksemplet Skrova', *Museumsnettverket* 5: 89–108.

Maurstad, A. 1994. 'Fisker og forsker i samme båt', *Ottar* 200: 34–48.

Mauss, Marcel. 1954. *The Gift: Forms and Functions of Archaic Societies.* London: Cohen and West.

McCormick, J. 1989. *Reclaiming Paradise: The Global Environmental Movement.* Bloomington: Indiana University Press.

McDorman, T.L. 1991. 'The GATT Consistency of U.S. Fish Import Embargoes to Stop Driftnet Fishing and Save Whales, Dolphins and Turtles', *The George Washington Journal of International Law and Economics* 24(3): 477–525.

McHugh, J.L. 1974. 'The Role and History of the International Whaling Commission', in W.E. Schevill (ed.), *The Whale Problem: A Status Report.* Cambridge, MA: Harvard University Press, pp. 305–35.

McIntyre, J. (ed.) 1974. *Mind in the Waters: A Book to Celebrate the Consciousness of Whales and Dolphins.* Toronto: McClelland and Stewart.

McKenna, V. 1992. *Into the Blue.* London: Aquarian Press.

McLaren, P.L. and R.A. Davis. 1983. 'Distribution of Wintering Marine Mammals off West Greenland and in Southern Baffin Bay and Northern David Strait, March 1982', No. LGL Limited, Toronto, Ontario, for Arctic Pilot Project, Petro-Canada Explorations Inc.

McNeely, J.A. (ed.). 1993. *Parks for Life: Report of the IVth Congress on National Parks and Protected Areas, 10–21 February 1992.* Gland, Switzerland: IUCN (The World Conservation Union).

McNeely, J.A. and D.C. Pitt (eds). 1985. *Culture and Conservation: The Human Dimension in Environmental Planning.* London: Croom Helm.

Melchett, P. 1994. 'United against Whaling', Letter to *Daily Mail*, 19 May.

Melchior, H.B. 1834. *Den danske Stats og Norges Pattedyr.* Copenhagen: Gyldendalske Boghandlings Forlag.

Menninger, K.A. 1951. 'Totemic Aspects of Contemporary Attitudes Toward Animals', in G.B. Wilbur and W. Muensterberger (eds), *Psychoanalysis and Culture: Essays in Honor of Géza Róheim.* New York: International Universities Press, pp. 42–74.

Merchant, C. 1992. *Radical Ecology: The Search for a Livable World.* New York: Routledge.

Midgley, M. 1983. *Animals and Why They Matter.* Harmondsworth: Penguin.

Milton, K. 1993. 'Introduction: Environmentalism and Anthropology', in K. Milton (ed.), *Environmentalism. The View from Anthropology.* London: Routledge, pp. 1–17.

————. 1996. *Environmentalism and Cultural Theory: Exploring the Role of Anthropology in Environmental Discourse*. London: Routledge.

————. 2002. *Loving Nature: Towards an Ecology of Emotion*. London: Routledge.

Misaki, S. 1993. 'Japanese World-view on Whales and Whaling', in F. Nagasaki (ed.), *Whaling Issues and Japan's Whale Research*. Tokyo: ICR, pp. 21–36.

————. 1994. 'Whaling Controversy is the Name of the Game', in F. Nagasaki (ed.), *Public Perception of Whaling*. Tokyo: ICR, pp. 21–39.

————. 1996. 'Responsible Management of Renewable Resources: Case for Whaling', in ICR (ed.), *Whaling for the Twenty-First Century*. Tokyo: ICR, pp. 13–26.

Mitchell, E.D., R.R. Reeves and A. Evely. 1986. *Bibliography of Whale Killing Techniques*. Cambridge: IWC.

Moeran, B. 1992. 'The Cultural Construction of Value: "Subsistence", "Commercial" and other Terms in the Debate about Whaling', *Maritime Anthropological Studies* 5(2): 1–15.

Mooney, J. 1998. 'Captive Cetaceans: A Handbook for Campaigners'. Bath: WDCS.

Moore, L. 1991. 'Whale Killers Defend Their Crime', *Today* 28 May.

Morgan, Elaine. 1990. *The Scars of Evolution: What Our Bodies Tell Us About Human Origins*. London: Souvenir Press Ltd

Mowat, F. 1990. *Rescue the Earth: Conversations with the Green Crusaders*. Toronto: McLelland and Stewart.

Moyle, B.J. and M. Evans. 2001. 'A Bioeconomic and Socio-Economic Analysis of Whale Watching with Attention Given to Associated Direct and Indirect Costs', IWC Document IWC/53/SC/WW8. Cambridge: IWC.

Münster, Torill. 1998. 'Store verdier står på spill', *Fiskeribladet* (24 September): 14.

Myers, E. 1997. 'The Politics of Creation (Birth) and Captive Cetacea (Whales, Dolphins): What is the Connection?' Paper presented at the World Futures XV Conference, retrieved 3 May 2008 from http://members.tripod.com/~rainbowdolphins/futures_final.html.

Mønnesland, J., S. Johansen, S. Eikeland and K. Hanssen. 1990. *Whaling in Norwegian Waters in the 1980'ies: The Economic and Social Aspects of the Whaling Industry, and the Effects of its Determination*. Oslo/Alta: NIBR (Norwegian Institute for Urban and Regional Research).

Naess, A. 1972. 'The Shallow and the Deep, Long-range Ecology Movement', *Inquiry* 16: 95–100.

————. 1989. *Ecology, Community and Lifestyle*, Cambridge: Cambridge University Press.

Nagasaki, F. 1993. 'On the Whaling Controversy', in F. Nagasaki (ed.), *Whaling Issues and Japan's Whale Research*. Tokyo: ICR, pp. 5–20.

Nash, R.F. 1989. *The Rights of Nature: A History of Environmental Ethics*. Madison: The University of Wisconsin Press.

Naturvernforbundet. 1991. 'Vågehval—forvaltning og forskning', *Dyrenes Forsvarer* [*Defender of Animals*] 5(2): 10.

Nauerby, T. 1996. *No Nation is an Island: Language, Culture, and National Identity in the Faroe Islands*. Århus: SNAI-North Atlantic Publication, Aarhus University Press.

Neubacher, H. 1992. 'Pet Killing', *Fish International*, October, p. 2.

New Zealand. 1991. 'Statement on Cetaceans', UNCED Prep.Comm. III, Working group II, Item 2. Geneva, 12 August.

————. 1994. 'Opening statement'. 46th Annual Meeting of the IWC, Puerto Vallarta, Mexico 23–27 May (IWC/46/OS NZ).

Nicholson, M. 1987. *The New Environmental Age*. Cambridge: Cambridge University Press.

NMFS (National Marine Fisheries Service) and FWS (Fish and Wildlife Service). 1997. *Draft Release of Stranded Marine Mammals to the Wild: Background, Preparations and Release Criteria*. Washington, D.C.: NMFS/FWS.

Nollman, J. 1990. *Dolphin Dreamtime: The Art and Science of Interspecies Communication*. New York: Bantam Books.

Nordøy, A., E.S. Nordøy and V. Lyngmo. 1991. 'Hvalkjøtt: Delikatesse med helsemessige fortrinn', *Ottar* 184: 53–59.

Norris, K.S. 1974. *The Porpoise Watcher*. London: John Murray.

Nuttall, M. 1991a. 'Sharing and the Ideology of Subsistence in a Greenlandic Sealing Community', *Polar Record* 27(162): 217–22.

———. 1991b. 'Memoryscape: A Sense of Locality in Northwestern Greenland', *North Atlantic Studies* 1(2): 39–50.

———. 1992. *Arctic Homeland: Kinship, Community and Development in Northwest Greenland*. Toronto: University of Toronto Press.

O'Barry, R. 1991. *Behind the Dolphin Smile*. New York: Berkley Books.

Ocean, J. 1997. *Dolphins into the Future*. Kailua, HI: Dolphin Connection.

Odent, Michel. 1990. *Water and Sexuality*. London: Arkana (Penguin Books).

Ohnuki-Tierney, E. 1993. *Rice as Self: Japanese Identities Through Time*. Princeton, NJ: Princeton University Press.

Ohsumi, S. 2000. 'Why is Necessary the Japanese Whale Research Program?' in S. Ohsumi (ed.), *Misinformation: The Protest against Japan's Whale Research Program*. Tokyo: ICR, pp. 15–29.

Olafsson, A. 1990. 'Faroese Whale- and Whaling-Policy', *North Atlantic Studies* 2(1–2): 130–37.

Olsen, B. 1982. 'Mehamn 1903: Fiskeropprør mot kvalfangstnæringa', *Ottar* 138 (5): 26–30.

Olsen, T.E. 1998. 'Fedje's siste hvalfanger?' *Nordisk Aqua & Fiskeriblad* 16: 8.

Orbach, M.K. 1977. *Hunters, Seaman, and Entrepreneurs: The Tuna Seinermen of San Diego*. Berkeley: University of California Press.

O'Riordan, T. 1981. *Environmentalism*. London: Pion.

Ottaway, A. 1992. *The Whale Killers*. London: Greenpeace UK.

Pálsson, G. 1991. *Coastal Economies, Cultural Accounts: Human Ecology and Icelandic Discourse*. Manchester: Manchester University Press.

Pardo, A. 1993. 'The Origins of the 1967 Maltese Initiative', *International Insights* 9(2): 65–9.

Payne, R. 1991. 'Is Whaling Justifiable on Ethical and Moral Grounds?' in N. Davies et al. (eds), *Why Whales?* Bath: WDCS, pp. 20–22.

———. 1995. *Among Whales*. New York: Charles Scribner's Sons.

Peace, A. 2005. 'Loving Leviathan: The Discourse of Whale-Watching in Australian Ecotourism', in J. Knight (ed.), *Animals in Person: Cultural Perspectives on Human-Animal Intimacies*. Oxford and New York: Berg, pp. 191–210.

Pearce, F. 1991. *Green Warriors: The People and the Politics behind the Environmental Revolution*. London: The Bodley Head.

Pedersen, P. 1995. 'Nature, Religion and Cultural Identity: The Religious Environmentalist Paradigm', in O. Bruun and A. Kalland (eds), *Asian Perception of Nature: A Critical Approach*. London: Curzon Press, pp. 258–76.

Pepper, D. 1993. *Eco-Socialism: From Deep Ecology to Social Justice*. New York: Routledge.

Perry, C., E. Clark and C. von Post. 2001. 'Swimming Against the Tide: Environmental Threats to the World's Whales and Dolphins'. London: Environmental Investigation Agency.

Perthen, A. 1991. ' Sickest Dinner Ever Served. JAPS FEAST ON WHALE. VIPs Tuck Into Its Raw Flesh', *Daily Star*, 11 May, pp.1, 4–5.

Petersen, R. 1985. 'The Use of Certain Symbols in Connection with Greenlanders' Identity', in J. Brøsted et al. (eds), *Native Power*. Oslo: Universitetsforlaget, pp. 294–300.

Poirier, S. 1996. 'Inuit Perceptions of Contaminants, Environmental Knowledge and Land Use in Nunavik: The Case of Salluit'. Paper presented at the 10th Inuit Study Conference, St. John's, Newfoundland, 15–18 August.

Poole, P. 1989. *Developing a Partnership of Indigenous Peoples, Conservationists, and Land Use Planners in Latin America*. Washington, D.C.: World Bank.

Prescott, J.H. 1981. 'Clever Hans: Training the Trainers. On the Potential for Misinterpreting the Result of Dolphin Research', in T.A. Sebeok and R. Rosenthal (eds), *The Clever Hans Phenomenon: Communication with Horses, Whales, Apes and People*. New York: Annals of the New York Academy of Science, pp. 130–36.

Princen, T. 1994. 'NGOs: Creating a Niche in Environmental Diplomacy', in T. Princen and M. Finger (eds), *Environmental NGOs in World Politics: Linking the Local and the Global*. London and New York: Routledge, pp. 29–47.

Pryor, K. 1981. 'Why Porpoise Trainers are not Dolphin Lovers: Real and False Communication in the Operant Setting', in T.A. Sebeok and R. Rosenthal (eds), *The Clever Hans Phenomenon: Communication with Horses, Whales, Apes and People*. New York: Annals of the New York Academy of Science, pp.137–43.

RCSS (Royal Commission on Seals and the Sealing Industry in Canada). 1986. *Seals and Sealing in Canada: Report of the Royal Commission*. Ottawa: Ministry of Supply and Services Canada.

Redford, K.H. 1991. 'The Ecologically Noble Savage', *Cultural Survival Quarterly* 15(1): 46–48.

Regan, T. 1984. *The Case of Animal Rights*. London: Routledge and Kegan Paul.

———. 1992. 'Animal Rights: What's in a Name?' in R.D. Ryder (ed.), *Animal Welfare and the Environment*. London: Duckworth, pp. 49–61.

Revill, J. and H. Smith. 1992. 'The Whales Facing a New Threat from the Harpoon. Do We Really Want to Go Back to This?' *The Mail on Sunday*, 21 June, pp. 8–9.

Richling, B. 1989. 'Recent Trends in the Northern Labrador Seal Hunt', *Etudes/Inuit/Studies* 13(1): 61–74.

Richter, C.F., S.M. Dawson, and E. Slooten. 2003. *Sperm Whale Watching off Kaikoura, New Zealand: Effects of Current Activities on Surfacing and Vocalisation Patterns*, Science for Conservation Report No. 219. Wellington: Department for Conservation.

Ricoeur, P. 1981. *Hermeneutics and the Human Sciences: Essays on Language, Action and Interpretation*. Cambridge: Cambridge University Press.

Ris, M. 1993. 'Conflicting Cultural Values: Whale Tourism in Northern Norway', *Arctic* 46(2): 156–63.

Ritchie, E. 1989. The Dolphin's Arc: Poems on Endangered Creatures of the Sea. College Park, MD: SCOP Publications.

Ritvo, H. 1987. *The Animal Estate: The English and Other Creatures in the Victorian Age*. Cambridge, MA: Harvard University Press.

Roepstorff, A. 1997. 'Den symbolske betydning af Kalaalimernit'. Report from the seminar *Den sociokulturelle og sundhedsmæssige betydning af kalaalimernit*, Nuuk, 6–7 May, pp. 97–105.

Roman, J. 2006. *Whale*. London: Reaktion Books.

Rose, N. 2003. 'Swim-with-Whales. Request for Information', posted on marman@uvvm. uvic.ca, 18 April 2003.

Rose, N., R. Farinato and S. Sherwin. 2006. 'The Case Against Marine Mammals in Captivity'. Washington, D.C. and London: HSUS and WSPA.

Rose, T. 1989. *Freeing the Whales: How the Media Created the World's Greatest Non-Event*. New York: Birch Lane Press Book.

Ross, H.M. and B. Wilson. 1996. 'Violent Interactions between Bottlenose Dolphins and Harbour Porpoises', *Proceedings of the Royal Society* (London) B 263: 283–86.

Rothenberg, D. 1995. 'Have a Friend for Lunch: Norwegian Radical Ecology Versus Tradition', in B.R. Taylor (ed.), *Ecological Resistance Movements: The Global Emergence of Radical and Popular Environmentalism*. Albany: State University of New York Press, pp. 201–18.

Russian Federation. 1994. 'Basis for Appeal by the Russian Federation to the International Whaling Commission for Quota on Gray Whales for the Needs of the Chukotka Autonomous Okrug Aboriginal Population', 46th Annual Meeting of the IWC, Puerto Vallarta, Mexico 23–27 May (IWC/46/32).

Ryder, R.D. 1992. 'Introduction', in R.D. Ryder (ed.), *Animal Welfare and the Environment*. London: Duckworth, pp. 1–8.

Sahlins, M. 1972. *Stone Age Economics*. Chicago: Aldine.

Salt, H. 1980 [1892]: *Animals' Rights : Considered in Relation to Social Progress*. Clarks Summit, PA. : Society for Animal Rights.

Samuels, A. and L. Bejder. 2004. 'Chronic Interaction between Humans and Free-Ranging Bottlenose Dolphins near Panama City Beach, Florida, USA', *Journal of Cetacean Research and Management* 6(1): 69–77.

Sanderson, K. 1990. 'Grindadráp: The Discourse of Drama', *North Atlantic Studies* 2(1–2): 196–204.

———. 1991. *Whales and Whaling in the Faroe Islands*. Tórshavn: The Department of Fisheries.

———. 1992. 'Grind: Næringstof til eftertanke', *Norðurlandhusið í Føroyum—Árbók 1991–92*. Tórshavn: Norðurlandhusið, pp. 48–52.

———. 1994. 'NAMMCO—North Atlantic Marine Mammal Commission', in N.D. Christoffersen and C. Lippai (eds), *Responsible Wildlife Resource Management: Balancing Biological, Economic, Cultural and Moral Considerations*. Brussels: European Bureau for Conservation and Development, pp. 129–37.

Sandøe, P. 1993a. 'Jeg vil hellere være hval end høne eller gris', *Dyrevennen* (5): 8–11.

———. 1993b. 'Do Whales Have Rights?' in G. Blichfeldt (ed.), *11 Essays on Whales and Man*. Reine, Norway: High North Alliance, pp. 16–20.

———. 1993c. 'Etikk og hvalfangst', in N.C. Stenseth, A.H. Hoel, and I.B. Lid (eds), *Vågehvalen: Valgets kval*. Oslo: ad Notam-Gyldendal, pp. 151–66.

Satterfield, T. 2003. *Anatomy of a Conflict: Identity, Knowledge and Emotion in Old-Growth Forests*. Vancouver: University of British Columbia Press.

Savage, M. et al. 1992. *Property, Bureaucracy and Culture*. London: Routledge.

Scarce, R. 1990. *Eco-Warriors: Understanding the Radical Environmental Movement*. Chicago: The Noble Press, Inc.

Scheffer, V. 1991. 'Why Should We Care About Whales?' in N. Davies et al. (eds), *Why Whales?* Bath: WDCS, pp. 17–19.

Schwarz, U. 1991. 'Geldmaschine Greenpeace', *Der Spiegel* 45 (38, 16 September): 84–105.

Schweder, T. 1992. 'Intransigence, Incompetence or Political Expediency? Dutch Scientists in the International Whaling Commission in the 1950s: Injection of Uncertainty'. Cambridge: IWC/SC/44/O 13.

———. 2001. 'Protecting Whales by Distorting Uncertainty: Non-precautionary Management?' *Fisheries Research* 52(3): 217–25.

Scovazzi, T. 2006. 'The Concept of Common Heritage of Mankind and the Resources of the Seabed Beyond the Limits of National Jurisdiction', (mimeo), retrieved 27 April 2008 from http://www.iadb.org/intal/aplicaciones/uploads/ponencias/Seminario_AUS-PINTAL_2006_04_Scovazzi.pdf).

Sea Shepherd. (n.d.). 'Sea Shepherd', Pamphlet published by Sea Shepherd Conservation Society.

Sejersen, F. 1998. 'Strategies for Sustainability and Management of People: An Analysis of Hunting and Environmental Perceptions in Greenland with a Special Focus on Sisimuit', Ph.D. dissertation. Copenhagen: University of Copenhagen.

————. 2000. 'Myten om de bæredyktige inuit', *Naturens Verden* (May): 2–15.

————. 2001. 'Hunting and Management of Beluga Whales *Delphinapterus leucas* in Greenland: Changing Strategies to Cope with New National and Local Interests', *Arctic* 54(4): 431–43.

————. 2003. *Grønlands naturforvaltning: Ressources og fangstrettigheder*. Copenhagen: Akademisk Forlag.

Selle, P. and K. Strømsnes. 1996. 'Norske miljøvernorganisasjoner: En demokratisk folkebevegelse?' in K. Strømsnes and P. Selle (eds), *Miljøvernpolitikk og miljøvernorganisering mot år 2000*. Oslo: Tano Aschehoug, pp. 261–91.

Servais, V. 2005. 'Enchanting Dolphins: An Analysis of Human-Dolphin Encounters', in J. Knight (ed.), *Animals in Person: Cultural Perspectives on Human-Animal Intimacies*. Oxford and New York: Berg, pp. 211–29.

Shelden, K.E.W., D. DeMaster, D. Rugh and A. Olson 2001. 'Developing Classification Criteria under the U.S. Endangered Species Act: Bowhead Whales as a Case Study', *Conservation Biology* 15(5): 1300–1307.

————. 2003. 'Evaluation of the Bowhead Whale Status: Reply to Taylor', *Conservation Biology* 17(3): 918–20.

Shields, L. 1992. 'Be Careful What You Wish For', *Whales Alive!* 1 (2 May), p.2.

Siegel, A.J. 1985. 'The Japan-USA Accord: The Result of the Discretionary Loophole in the Packwood-Magnusson Amendment', *The George Washington Journal of International Law and Economics* 19(2): 577–615.

Sigurjónsson, J. 1982. 'Icelandic Minke Whaling 1914–1980', *Report of the International Whaling Commission* 32: 287–95.

————. 1990. 'Whale Stocks off Iceland', *North Atlantic Studies* 2(1–2): 64–76.

Similä, T. and F. Ugarte. 1991. 'Fjord Feud for Fish', *Sonar* 5 (Spring): 16–18.

Simpson, K. 1999. 'The 51st Annual Meeting of the International Whaling Commission: One Minute Before Midnight?' *Journal of International Wildlife Law and Policy* 2(3): 338–52.

Singer, P. 1978. 'Why the Whale Should Live', *Habitat* 6(3): 8–9.

————. 1990. *Animal Liberation*, revised edition. New York: Avon Books.

Slater, C. 1994. *Dance of the Dolphin: Transformation and Disenchantment of the Amazonian Imagination*. Chicago and London: The University of Chicago Press.

————. 1995. 'Amazonia as Edenic Narrative', in W. Cronon (ed.), *Uncommon Ground: Toward Reinventing Nature*. New York and London: W.W.Norton and Co., pp. 114–31.

Smith, B. 1987. 'Dolphins Plus and Autistic Children', *Psychological Perspectives* 18(2): 386–97.

Smith, E.A. and M. Wishnie. 2000. 'Conservation and Subsistence in Small-Scale Societies', *Current Anthropology* 29: 493–524.

Snyder, G. 1980. *The Real Work: Interviews and Talks: 1964–1979*. New York: New Directions.

Solesbury, W. 1976. 'The Environmental Agenda: An Illustration of How Situations May Become Political Issues and Issues May Demand Responses from Government, or How They May Not', *Public Administration* 54: 379–97.

Société des Nations.1927. *Comité d'experts pour la codification progressive du droit international, Rapport au Conseil de la Société des Nations*, Genève: Société des Nations.

Spang, M.G. 1992. 'Følelsesterror', *Verdens Gang (VG)* (28 November): 2.

Spencer, L., J. Bollwerk, and R.C. Morais. 1991. 'The Not So Peaceful World of Greenpeace', *Forbes Magazine* (11 November): 174–80.

Spencer, R.F. 1959. *The North Alaskan Eskimo: A Study in Ecology and Society*. Washington, D.C.: Smithsonian Institution, Bureau of American Ethnology.

Spong, P. 1992. 'Why We Love to Watch Whales', *Sonar* 7 (spring): 24–25.

Stefánsson, H. (n.d.). 'Nordic Whaling: Whales in the Social History and the Culture of Food in Iceland', report to Aji-no-moto.

Stenuit, R. 1968. *The Dolphin, Cousin to Man*. London: J.M. Dent & Sons.

Stevenson, M.G., A. Madsen and E. Maloney (eds). 1997. *The Anthropology of Community-Based Whaling in Greenland: A Collection of Papers Submitted to the International Whaling Commission*. Edmonton: Canadian Circumpolar Institute Press.

Stoett, P.J. 1997. *The International Politics of Whaling*. Vancouver: UBC Press.

Stoker, S.W. and I.I. Krupnik. 1993. 'Subsistence Whaling', in J.J. Burns, J.J. Montague and C.L. Cowles (eds), *The Bowhead Whale*. Lawrence, KS: Allen Press, pp. 579–629.

Stone, C.D. 2001. 'Summing Up: Whaling and its Critics', in R.L. Friedheim (ed.), *Towards a Sustainable Whaling Regime*. Edmonton: Canadian Circumpolar Institute Press, pp. 269–91.

Sumi, K. 1989. 'The "Whale War" Between Japan and the United States: Problems and Prospects', *Denver Journal of International Law and Policy* 17(2): 317–72.

Sutton, M. 1992. *Report on the 44th Annual Meeting of the International Whaling Commission*. Gland, Switzerland: WWF.

Swain, Gill. 1992. 'Having a Whale of a Time . . But Hope is Running Out for the Minkes', *Daily Mirror*, 25 June, p. 30

Sørensen, H. 1993. 'The Environmental Movement and Minke Whaling', in G. Blichfeldt (ed.), *11 Essays on Whales and Man*. Reine, Norway: High North Alliance, pp. 27–30.

Takahashi, J. 1987. 'Hogei no machi no chōmin aidenteitii to shimboru no shiyō ni tsuite', *Minzokugaku kenkyū* 52(2): 158–67.

———. 1988. *Women's Tales of Whaling: Life Stories of 11 Japanese Women who Lived with Whaling*. Tokyo: Japan Whaling Association.

———. 1998. 'English Dominance in Whaling Debates: A Critical Analysis of Discourse at the International Whaling Commission', in *Japan Review* 10: 237–253.

Tan, J.M.L. 1997. *A Field Guide to Whales and Dolphins in the Philippines*. Makati City, Philippines: Bookmark Inc.

Tapper, R. 1988. 'Animality, Humanity, Morality, Society', in T. Ingold (ed.), *What is an Animal?* London: Unwin Hyman, pp. 47–62.

Taylor, B. 1991. 'The Religion and Politics of Earth First!' *The Ecologist* 21(6): 258–66.

Taylor, E.1997: *The Far Islands and Other Cold Places. Travel Essays of a Victorian Lady*, ed. James Taylor Dunn. Lakeville, MN: Pogo Press.

Taylor, J.G. 1985. 'The Arctic Whale Cult in Labrador', *Etudes/Inuit/Studies* 9(2): 121–32.

Taylor, M. 2003. 'Why the Bering-Chukchi-Beaufort Seas Bowhead Whale is Endangered: Responses to Shelden et al.', *Conservation Biology* 17(3): 915–17.

Tester, K. 1991. *Animals and Society: The Humanity of Animal Rights*. London: Routledge.

Thomas, K. 1983. *Man and the Natural World: Changing Attitudes in England 1500–1800*. London: Penguin Books.

Thompson, M., R. Ellis and A. Wildavsky. 1990. *Cultural Theory*. Boulder, CO: Westview Press.

Thomsen, M.L. 1993. *Local Knowledge and the Distribution, Biology, and Hunting of Beluga and Narwhal: A Survey among Hunters in West and North Greenland*. Nuuk: Inuit Circumpolar Conference.

Tokar, B. 1988. 'Exploring the New Ecologies: Social Ecology, Deep Ecology and the Future of Green Political Thought', *Alternatives* 15(4): 30–43.

Turner, E. 1990. 'The Whale Decides: Eskimos' and Ethnographer's Shared Consciousness on the Ice', *Etudes/Inuit/Studies* 14(1–2): 39–52.

―――. 1993. 'American Eskimos Celebrate the Whale: Structural Dichotomies and Spirit Identities among the Inupiat of Alaska', *The Drama Review* 37(1): 98–114.

Twiss, R.J., jr. 1992. Letter to the Honorably John A. Knauss, PhD. From U.S. Marine Mammal Commission, 9 June.

Tønnessen, J.N. 1969. *Den moderne hvalfangsts historie: Den pelagiske fangst 1924–1937*. Sandefjord: Norges Hvalfangstforbund.

Tønnessen, J.N. and A.O. Johnsen. 1982. *The History of Modern Whaling*. Berkeley: University of California Press.

Uhrskov, T. and H. Færch. 1993. 'Mennesket delfinens kusine', *Berlingske Tidende* 5 September, 3rd Section, p.6.

UNCED (United Nations Conference on Environment and Development). 1992. *Agenda 21*. Geneva: UNCED.

United Kingdom. 1999. 'Opening Statement', 51st Annual Meeting of the IWC, Grenada 24–28 May (IWC/51/OS UK).

USA. 1994. 'Report of Possible Infraction', 46th Annual Meeting of the IWC, Puerto Vallarta, Mexico 23–27 May (IWC/46/Inf.1).

Usher, P. 1981. 'Sustenance or Recreation? The Future of Native Wildlife Harvesting in Northern Canada', in M.M.R. Freeman (ed.), *Renewable Resources and the Economy of the North*. Ottawa: CARC, pp. 56–71.

Vialles, N. 1994. *Animal to Edible*. Cambridge: Cambridge University Press.

Vilstrup, J. 1991. 'Greenpeace muger ud i egne rækker', *Politiken*, 4 December, p. 8.

Wallace, R.K. 2000. *Frank Stella's Moby Dick: Words and Shapes*. Ann Arbor, MI: University of Michigan Press.

Walley, C. J. 2004. *Rough Water: Nature and Development in an East African Marine Park*. Princeton, NJ: Princeton University Press.

Wapner, P. 1996. *Environmental Activism and World Civic Politics*. Albany: State University of New York Press.

Ward, E. 1993. *Indigenous Peoples between Human Rights and Environmental Protection: Based on an Empirical Study of Greenland*. Copenhagen: The Danish Centre for Human Rights.

Watson, L. 1985. *Whales of the World: A Complete Guide to the World's Living Whales, Dolphins and Porpoises*. London: Hutchinson.

Watson, P. 1993. 'An Open Letter to Norwegians', *Nordlys* 8 January.

WCED (World Commission on Environment and Development). 1987. *Our Common Future*. Oxford: Oxford University Press.

WDCS (Whale and Dolphin Conservation Society). 1992. 'Whale & Dolphin Watch', Programme of whale and dolphin watching holidays for 1992. Bath: WDCS.

Wenzel, G.W. 1991. *Animal Rights, Human Rights: Ecology, Economy and Ideology in the Canadian Arctic*. Toronto: University of Toronto Press.

―――. 1995. 'Ningiqtuq: Resource Sharing and Generalized Reciprocity in Clyde River, Nunavut', *Arctic Anthropology* 32(2): 43–60.

West, P.C. and S.R. Brechin (eds). 1991. *Resident Peoples and National Parks: Social Dilemmas and Strategies in International Conservation.* Tucson: The University of Arizona Press.

Whitaker, I. 1986. 'North Atlantic Sea-Creatures in the *King's Mirror* (Konungs Skuggsjá)', *Polar Record* 23(142): 3–13.

White, L., Jr. 1967. 'The Historical Roots of Our Ecological Crisis', *Science* 155(3767): 1203–1207.

Whyte, Sean. 1994. 'Halt the Mindless Slaughter of the Pilot Whales. Join Our campaign to Stop the *Butchers* of the Faroe Islands', Fundraising letter. Bath: WDCS.

Wilkinson, D.M. 1989. 'The Use of Domestic Measures to Enforce International Whaling Agreements: A Critical Perspective', *Denver Journal of International Law and Policy* 17(2): 271–91.

Williams, H. 1988. *Whale Nation.* New York: Harmony Books.

Williams, V. 2001. 'Captive Orcas: "Dying to Entertain You"'. Bath: WDCS.

Willis, R.G. 1990. 'Introduction', in R.G. Willis (ed.), *Signifying Animals: Human Meaning in the Natural World.* London: Unwin Hyman, pp. 1–24.

Wills, D.K. 1992. *An Ethical Examination of the Killing of Whales.* Washington, D.C.: HSUS.

Wilson, E.O. 1984. *Biophilia.* Cambridge, Mass.: Harvard University Press.

Wilson, S.C. and W.J. Jordan. (n.d.). *Whaling? An Ethical Approach.* Rusper, West Sussex: Care for the Wild.

Wintour, P. and J. Calvert. 1996. 'Labour's Million Pound Donor', *The Observer*, 1 September.

Winton, T. 1992. 'Dolphin Mania', *The Independent Monthly* (September): 14–19.

Wright, G. 1984. *Sons and Seals: A Voyage to the Ice.* St. John's: Memorial University of Newfoundland, Institute of Social and Economic Research.

WSPA (World Society for the Protection of Animals). 1988. 'Circular No. 881406'.

WWF (World Wildlife Fund). 1986. *The Assisi Declarations: Messages on Man and Nature from Buddhism, Christianity, Hinduism, Islam and Judaism.* Gland, Switzerland: WWF.

WWF (World Wide Fund for Nature). 1992. *WWF Position Statement on Whaling and the IWC.* Gland, Switzerland: WWF.

———. 2004. *Cetacean Bycatch and the IWC.* Brochure. WWF: Gland, Switzerland: WWF.

———. 2007. *WWF Annual Review 2006.* Gland, Switzerland: WWF.

WWF-Denmark. 1990. 'Letter to Danish Business Leaders', dated 19 June. Copenhagen: WWF-Denmark.

———. 1992. Letter to WWF-International, dated 21 January. Copenhagen: WWF-Denmark.

Wyland and M. Doyle. 1995. *Celebrating 50 Wyland Whaling Walls.* Laguna Beach, CA: Wyland Studios, Inc.

Wylie, J. and D. Margolin. 1981. *The Ring of Dancers: Images of Faroes Culture.* Philadelphia: University of Pennsylvania Press.

Wyllie, T. 1984. *Dolphins, ETs and Angels: Adventures with Spiritual Intelligence.* Santa Fe, NM: Bear & Company.

Yamamoto, S. 1986. 'Whaling Row Rooted in Anti-Japanese Emotion', in Japan Whaling Association (ed.), *Whaling: The Other Side of the Coin.* Tokyo: Japan Whaling Association, pp. 6–7.

Yearley, S. 1991. The Green Case: A Sociology of Environmental Issues, Arguments and Politics. London: Harper Collins Academic.

Øen, E.O. 1993. 'Hunting Methods for Minke Whales in Norway: Report from the 1992 Scientific Catch', IWC/HK/1 available to the IWC Scientific Committee, April 1993.

Øen, E.O. and L. Walløe. 1996. 'Norwegian Minke Whaling 1995', Report to the IWC: IWC/48/WK3.

Index